MEDIEVAL LEICESTERSHIRE

Recent research on the medieval archaeology of Leicestershire

Collected papers from a conference organised by Leicestershire Fieldworkers

Foreword by Michael Wood

Editing and layout by Kathleen Elkin

on behalf of Leicestershire Fieldworkers

Monograph No 3

2015

ISBN 978-0-9548200-2-2

Published by Leicestershire Fieldworkers, Leicester 2015

To cite references in this volume please reference the individual author and then the volume title as for a journal

The Illustration

The interpretive illustration on the cover and the title page is of 'The Hunter' a 14th century bench end carving in Croxton Kerrial church, east Leicestershire, by Maureen Hallahan. It is believed to represent Nicholas de Criol, Lord of the Manor. In 1246 an agreement was made in the courts of King Henry III between Nicholas de Criol and Geoffrey, abbot of the Premonstratensian order of Croxton Abbey concerning the customs and services which the said Nicholas required of the said abbot for his lands held by him in Croxton (John Nichols, 1795). The bench ends from the abbey were removed to the church at the dissolution of the monasteries.

Cover Design - Dan Haas, Media 4D, Leicester

Printing by 4Word, Bristol

Contents

Acknowledgements

Leicestershire Fieldworkers is an active county archaeology society that helps individuals and local groups investigate the remains of past human activity by practical investigation, research and small-scale excavation. It provides a forum for interested individuals to come together to hear the results of latest research both locally and nationally and provides assistance to professional archaeologists both in the field and by reporting fieldwork results to the county Heritage and Environment Record (HER). Every so often the Fieldworkers hold a conference in order to give members a roundup of research in the county and the papers in this volume are the result of a conference on medieval Leicestershire.

I am grateful to all contributors to this volume, for their patience and good humour during the editing and design process and their speedy return of amendments and search for illustrations. The Fieldworkers are also particularly grateful to Michael Wood for writing a Foreword and to Emeritus Professor Chris Dyer of Leicester University for providing the keynote speech at the conference and the lead paper in this book.

In practical terms many thanks go to Maureen Hallahan and Ken Chatterton, illustrators and designers, for Adobe software support, the illustrations and maps for several papers, and to Maureen particularly for her beautiful interpretive illustration of 'The Hunter' bench end used on the cover design and the frontispiece. We are grateful also to designer Dan Haas of Media 4D Ltd for his book cover design and his design concepts for all Fieldworker publicity. Thanks also go to John Roost and team from printers 4Word of Bristol, who have provided professional advice and assistance. Finally we would like to thank all those members of the Leicestershire Fieldworkers who have waiting patiently for this volume – we hope you will enjoy with them the results from 'doing archaeology' in Leicestershire.

Kathleen Elkin
Leicestershire Fieldworkers
January 2015

www.Leicsfieldworkers.co.uk

Chris Dyer giving the keynote lecture at the Leicestershire Fieldworkers
conference on medieval Leicestershire, held at County Hall by kind permission
of Leicestershire County Council

Contributor List

Michael Wood is a film maker, broadcaster and historian who has a special interest in the reign of Aethelstan and the Anglo-Saxon period. He is Professor of Public History at the University of Manchester. He has written numerous books to accompany his television series including 'The Story of England' which used the village of Kibworth in Leicestershire as an example of an English community that intertwined national and local history in one place.

Chris Dyer is Emeritus Professor of History in the School of History at the University of Leicester. His research in local and medieval history includes the economic and social history of medieval England, the management of landed estates, agrarian history, standards of living (including diet and housing), relations between town and country, the role of towns, landscape history, rural depopulation, and money and commerce. His current project is 'Peasant farming 1200-1540' funded by the Leverhulme Trust.

Dr Graham Jones is interested in interdisciplinary approaches to landscape history. He gained his PhD at the University of Leicester Centre for English Local History where he was Lecturer in English Topography and now an Honorary Visiting Fellow. He is based at St John's College, Oxford, working on the forests and chases of England and Wales as a Senior Research Associate in the University School of Geography. He is also a Senior Research Associate of the Catalan Institute of Classical Archaeology, University of Tarragona, and teaches at the University of Wurzburg as well as at Leicester. In 2014 he was elected FSA. His monograph Saints in the Landscape, published in 2007 by Tempus, is the first comprehensive overview of religious dedications and their cultural geography and history.

John Thomas has been a professional archaeologist since 1986, and has wide ranging fieldwork experience from across the Midlands. He began working for Warwickshire Museum Service and for the past 20 years has worked for ULAS where he currently has the role of Project Officer. He has a degree in Archaeology and an MA in Landscape Studies, both awarded from the University of Leicester. Contact: jst6@leicester.ac.uk

Wendy Scott, MA, is Finds Liaison Officer for the county of Leicestershire, based at the County Council. She is an Honorary Fellow at Leicester University and is an Associate of the Museums Association. She provides regular assistance in identification of objects to members of Leicestershire Fieldworkers and metal detector groups. Her interests lie in early medieval metalwork, particularly Viking age material and coins.

Nick Hill lives in east Leicestershire and has been recording and researching buildings in Leicestershire and Rutland for over 25 years. He is a member of the Vernacular Architecture Group, with an interest in domestic buildings of all periods and is also a member of the Leicestershire Fieldworkers. He works as a Project Manager with English Heritage, coordinating repair projects on historic buildings. He is a member of the Leicestershire Fieldworkers.

Peter Liddle has been actively involved with Leicestershire Archaeology since 1970 and is the founder of the Leicestershire Fieldworkers. He excavated with the Leicestershire Archaeological Unit and was appointed Archaeological Survey Officer for Leicestershire Museums Service in 1976 before becoming Keeper of Archaeology and managing the County's archaeological team. His final role was as Community Archaeologist. He now lectures, researches and writes on Leicestershire archaeology, fieldwalking and community archaeology. He continues his role in community archaeology as a committee member of the Leicestershire Fieldworkers.

Dr Matthew Godfrey is the Historic Church Buildings Support Officer for the Diocese of Lincoln. He is a published buildings archaeologist and has worked on projects in the UK, Greece and the Middle East. His PhD research was focused on the early medieval churches of Norfolk.

Dr Mike Hawkes is a self-employed archaeologist and illustrator. He studied archaeology at Leicester gaining his degree, MA and PhD there. He has a special interest in the churches of Leicestershire and is Archaeological Adviser to the Diocese of Leicester and the Diocese of Southwell and Nottingham. He is a member of the Leicestershire Fieldworkers and represents the local group of the Council for British Archaeology Young Archaeologists Club on the committee.

Bob Trubshaw graduated as an industrial designer. However his interests in photography, landscape, geology and archaeology led to him starting Heart of Albion Press in 1989 to publish research into aspects of Leicestershire and Rutland local history such as holy wells, standing stones, ancient crosses and medieval church carvings. This led to publishing books and booklets for other authors and became his fulltime activity in 2000. In 2009 he helped set up Project Gargoyle and is the Volunteer Co-ordinator for the project. He has been a member of Leicester Fieldworkers since 1986.

Richard Knox is currently 1485 Project Officer for Leicestershire Museums Service. He was previously Keeper of Donington Le Heath medieval manor house museum and as Heritage Development Manager played a large part in the project to discover the actual site of the Bosworth battlefield. He has worked in field archaeology since graduating from university and specialises in object identification.

Tony Brown was Staff Tutor in Archaeology in the Department of Adult Education of the University of Leicester. He has written widely on field archaeological topics in the Midlands and elsewhere.

Anthony Squires is the author or co-author of books on various aspects of local landscapes, including woodlands, parks and gardens. In November 2014 he published a study of the Royal Forest of Leighfield in Rutland (Rutland Record 34) and, with Robert Hartley, on the ancient earthworks of Bradgate Park (TLAHS 88). He is a longstanding member of the Leicestershire Fieldworkers and served on its committee for many years. He is currently researching the history of the landscape of Market Bosworth, village and parish.

Robert F. Hartley studied at Leicester University and from 1975 to 1995 was Assistant Archaeological Survey Officer for Leicestershire Museums, concentrating on earthwork surveys and aerial archaeology. He then became Keeper of Harborough Museum and in 1997 Keeper of Collections for the County Museums Service, until 2012. Five volumes of his surveys of medieval earthworks in Leicestershire and Rutland have so far been published with a further three volumes due out in late 2015. He also has a special interest in the early history of coal mining in Leicestershire.

Dr Richard Buckley is the project manager and lead archaeologist for the Greyfriars Project that found the bones of Richard III. He is co-director of University of Leicester Archaeological Services (ULAS). He has previously worked on the investigation of Leicester Castle, Leicester Abbey and numerous sites in central Leicester, including Highcross Leicester and Causeway Lane excavations. He specialises in urban archaeology and historic buildings. He was appointed an OBE for services to archaeology in the New Year Honours 2014.

Harriet Anne Jacklin, BA, MA, was the Project Osteologist for the Highcross excavations on behalf of University of Leicester Archaeological Services. Harriet currently works as a Human Osteo-Archaeologist and Archaeological Illustrator.

Angela Monckton lives in Birstall and was employed by Leicestershire Archaeological Unit and then by the University of Leicester Archaeological Services. She has worked on the environmental archaeology of Leicestershire and the Midlands for over 25 years recording plant remains in samples from sites of all periods including Causeway Lane and the recent Highcross excavations, as well as compiling some local and regional reviews. She has been the secretary of the Friends of Jewry Wall Museum for the last ten years and is a member of the Leicestershire Fieldworkers.

Kathleen Elkin started digging at Elstow Abbey in Bedfordshire when she was 16. Following several seasons digging in Bedfordshire and elsewhere and a course with the late Dr James Dyer she finally gave in and went to Leicestershire University to study archaeology. Following this, however, she made a career in manufacturing I.T., training, and sales and marketing systems consultancy, eventually ending with the dream job of project managing I.T. for Leicestershire County Council's libraries, museums and community services Department. Now retired she is a committee member of the Leicestershire Fieldworkers.

Foreword

Michael Wood

Leicestershire has a fascinating history: its pre-Roman past, which was electrifyingly illuminated recently by the sensational Hallaton hoard; the fascinating Roman remains still to be seen in the townscape and the museums of Leicester; the rich medieval architectural legacy across the county, and a small but remarkable collection of medieval buildings in the historic centre of Leicester itself. The county's position in the centre of the country makes it both the heart of England, and also, in different periods, a liminal zone where influences flowed east and west and north and south. Even its distinctive shape as a shire tells its own story: created formally in the Viking age, determined to the south-west by the man-made line of Watling Street, the border of the Danelaw, elsewhere defined by natural features around the basin of the Soar and its tributaries; the Welland to the south; and to the north and east natural features bordering a region which, as the reader will learn in these pages, may go back to very ancient tribal groupings. Even the name of the city and the shire goes back to prehistory, to the British river name Leir, the original name of the Soar at the time when the late Iron Age oppidum Ratae 'the ramparts' was already a centre of local society and economy.

The medieval shire which emerges after the age of the Anglo-Saxon migrations, in the Early Medieval period, already had deep social roots, and perhaps even a territorial identity; as might be suggested by its status in the 7-8th century when it was the homeland of a powerful but little understood grouping called the Middle Angles who had their own ealdorman, and earlier perhaps (though this is conjectural) their own kings drawn from the royal or noble lineage to which the Mercian saint Guthlac belonged

So a very interesting history. The county has also been especially lucky in its historians. Local history is at the root of historical studies, and Leicester it is often said is the home of local history. Almost at the start of British writing on local history came William Burton's Description of Leicestershire in 1622. Later, as local studies burgeoned, the London printer John Nichols compiled perhaps the greatest local history ever written, The History and Antiquities of the County of Leicester whose anniversary we celebrate this year and which is also referenced throughout this book. Sprawling, enormous in length, Nichols is still a gold mine for the local historian: indispensable for his insights into material culture as well as manorial and parish history; recording early excavations, transcribing lost Hundred Rolls, and even carefully illustrating finds of Roman mosaics and Anglo-Saxon pagan graves. That impetus continued through the 19th century with the founding of the Leicestershire Archaeological and Historical Society; then, in the mid-20th century after Fred Attenborough brought the Devonian William Hoskins to Leicester, with the Local Studies Department at the College (later the University) inaugurating the greatest phase in English local history scholarship and teaching. In archaeology particularly, the Leicestershire Fieldworkers, whose members celebrate 40 years of amateur archaeological fieldwork in 2016, and who organised the conference on which this book is based, continue to contribute through local fieldwork and research to our knowledge of the previous inhabitants of Leicestershire.

This collection then builds on a great tradition of local studies going back almost 400 years, and takes its place in a much older continuity of writing about Leicestershire and east Midlands history, and its relation to the national story. Here the reader will find these themes brought together using all the latest tools of modern scholarship, textual, archaeological, landscape and science, to bring us a very stimulating and up to date view of the state of the game .

One important new source of knowledge these last few years has been the material found by metal detectorists, and among the many artefacts discussed in this book, one of the most intriguing is the stunning Scalford bracteate, found only in 2010 by a metal detectorist at Scalford near Melton Mowbray. This 5th or 6th century pendant is a splendid piece of pagan gold depicting a head adorned with an elaborate diadem and holding a drinking vessel. It has been identified as Odin king of the gods quaffing his elixir in Valhalla. But who owned it? And what is its connection with this place? Now on show in Melton Carnegie Museum this artefact is of national significance and perhaps takes us back to the earliest migration of Anglian-led warbands in the Wreake valley in the early 500s.

Next comes the history of the Viking Age, to which Leicestershire is such important witness. This is the period out of which the historic shire emerges, starting in 874 at Repton when the 'Great Heathen Army' as the Anglo-Saxon Chronicle called it, 'shared out the land and began to plough....to make a living'. Thus began the transformation of society in the east Midlands which is revealed in the place names, dialect and custom of the later shire. This thinly documented process is becoming understood through place names, research on which has been freshly illuminated in the last few years by Barrie Cox's volumes on the place names of Leicestershire in one of most valuable contributions to the history of the county. It is now believed that the hybrid names - Grimston, Illston, Blaston, Slawston for example - which combine the English suffix 'tun' with a Viking personal name like Grim, represent the first wave settlements and preserve the names of the new Viking lords, the chief men in the army who carved the land up in 874. The 'by' names are then the second wave settlements, often outside English villages, for example like Westerby next to Smeeton and Kibworth. The thorps, on the other hand appear to be the poor fringe land left to third wave immigrants who arrived later on the coat tails of the armies, or who came over subsequently from Scandinavia, leaving their Viking field names, siks, carrs, and holms, all over the Leicestershire landscape as they still are today. This is the very stuff of local history - and shows how the intensely local can illuminate the big picture. This period forms the background to a number of the chapters.

These papers offer many fascinating insights into a formative period for the shire and city, the Anglo-Saxon age when Christianity, the Church, rulership, trade, nucleated villages and open field systems take shape. Here this collection immeasurably expands our knowledge. Leicester of course was later part of the kingdom of the Mercians, literally the 'border people' (most likely referring to the frontier with the Welsh), but in the mysterious document known as the Tribal Hidage the 'original Mercia' seems to have been in the Trent valley and the Tame in Staffordshire around Tamworth. Intriguingly, Leicester and its region were not part of this grouping (defined as the North and South Mercians by Bede) but formed a separate provincia of Middle Angles which had its own stirps regia, and later its own ealdormen, and was evidently a defined regional identity, a land situated between the Mercians and the East Angles, perhaps including the smaller tribal groups of the Fens, the lower Nene and Welland. Later written tradition of an early Anglian migration across from Norfolk and the Fens to the Trent valley is textually problematical, but may be corroborated by ongoing DNA studies, and might suggest that what became the shire was a very old entity by the time it came into the pages of Bede, conceivably a successor polity to the Corieltavi?

Bede also suggests this region was important in the missionary enterprise of St Wilfrid, and the history of Christianity is the background to the paper in this collection concerning the Church and ecclesiastical territorial organisation. Place names and church dedications, as Graham Jones shows, are a very important tool for the historian. Do 'worth' place names, for example, signify high status settlements here during the supremacy of the Mercians under Aethelbald and Offa in the eighth century - Lutterworth, Bosworth, and even Kibworth - as apparently they do too in Tamworth and to the south at Brixworth? The role in the 8th century Mercian supremacy of royal sites like Leicester, Gumley, and Glen also suggests the importance of this region to the Mercian royal family.

There are fascinating and seminal papers about the origin of villages between 8th and 11th century; on deserted medieval villages and their origins; on village morphology with new data from local digs; and on ridge and furrow systems illustrated by a brilliant series of maps made possible by surveys by Vaughan College adult education students. These chapters offer fascinating insights into little known but crucial processes in our social history - for example the links between 6th century settlements and later 10th century nucleated villages - in a way that would have been impossible using the documents alone. The origin of open field systems is also still a matter of great debate; do they arise in the later Mercian period through royal impetus, or are they part of the extension of West Saxon lordship in the 10th century? Are they the product of central planning, or the piecemeal and gradual extension of local power? This study of the open fields and their ridge and furrow systems can be expanded by grass roots community projects, such as a recent publication by the heritage and archaeology group at Great Bowden who have made a translation of the extraordinarily detailed 14th century survey of their open fields: a terrific example of local research and knowledge giving us the detail right down to individual field strips.

The post-Norman Conquest period is also strongly represented in these pages: the development of Leicester; the spread of monasteries and priories; the expansion of villages and the building of fortifications. A paper on castles in Leicestershire for example gives us a roundup of a very disparate and problematic body of material: some motte and baileys for example may now be connected with Domesday evidence for 'Frenchmen' living among the population in places like Groby, Hallaton and Kibworth.

On the history of the medieval village in general Chris Dyer, in his keynote paper, offers a magisterial survey of social life and the state of peasantry in the 12th-15th century; with fascinating evidence drawn from documents - court cases and even a Latin poem - which enables us to actually hear the voice of the people of medieval Leicestershire.

Due to the loss of its pre-Conquest archives the interpretation of the county's medieval history is unusually dependent on the imaginative sensitivity of historians and archaeologists to the surviving material clues, and many of these papers are pieces of detective work, taking archaeological, topographical, and landscape approaches to social history. They present a huge amount of new information, changing the picture out of all recognition from earlier accounts. Some papers touch on big themes of process and change in English and East Midlands society as a whole; some are close-up studies, on food and diet, disease and death. On coal mining, for example, fascinating documents from the 13th century open up the long history of industry in the county. One chapter discusses the story of the religious houses; there is also a fascinating study of the fabric of medieval churches, some of which (like St Nicholas in Leicester) are of national significance linked to which the 'gargoyles' church carvings project

is also breaking new ground with the help of photographers from the community. There is a paper on domestic architecture; not the grand houses, but the hitherto unsuspected riches of manor and smaller peasant houses still surviving in the county, with vivid insights into the materiality of the lives lived in them. Looking at Leicester Forest, the 'Army Forest' of the Viking age, another chapter reconstructs the historical geography of this crucially important feature of medieval society and economy in the county. Here the reader will also find the latest on the medieval history of Leicester itself: one of Britain's most interesting historic cities, but because of its lack of documents pre-1066, one whose early history is still little known, though that situation is fast changing now with new finds from rescue digs.

So these are just a few of the areas opened up by this fascinating collection of papers. Because of the diffuse nature of the sources, modern writing on the medieval county has perforce taken the form of many discrete contributions, scattered often through academic periodicals. Now this book brings together in one collection a vast amount of up-to-date material, much of it the product of long reflection on historical process in east Midlands society. It will be of enormous value to professional scholars and the local amateur archaeological community, and to anyone interested in the mediaeval history of the east Midlands and of England as a whole. In my experience a huge and enthusiastic number of people want to know more about their local history. This collection, with its informative illustrations, maps, plans and photos, will be a most important signpost.

Finally and above all, what comes out in these papers is the excitement of history; it shows us how the frontiers of knowledge can be expanded not only by the experts, but by collaboration between communities, local groups, and professionals. The recent galvanising experience of community archaeology digs, such as the Big Dig at Kibworth which set the ball rolling on our Story of England project for TV, shows the creative possibilities of local history everywhere; how rewarding, empowering, and illuminating it can be to explore and record the stories of our communities. The one thing for sure is that there is much more to come out: and as it does, this book will continue to be a mine of fascinating information, ideas, maps and images, and a very thoughtful and illuminating guide.

New thinking about medieval settlement, and its relevance for Leicestershire

Christopher Dyer

Introduction

Sixty-six years ago (on 18 June 1948) a landmark event in medieval settlement studies took place in Leicestershire. A group of academics attending a seminar in Cambridge drove to Leicester where W. G. Hoskins showed them the deserted village sites of Hamilton, Ingarsby and Knaptoft. M. W. Beresford, who had found similar sites in Warwickshire, participated. Other historians were present, including the formidable M. M. Postan who organised the seminar. The archaeologists who joined the expedition included Grahame Clark and Axel Steensberg from Denmark (Beresford 1986–7; Dyer and Jones 2010). This meeting gave the local discoveries of deserted villages recognition by scholars of international significance.

The visitors to the deserted village sites interpreted them in different ways. For Postan they fitted into an episode of reduced agricultural production in the fourteenth and fifteenth centuries as part of a long-term cycle of expansion and depression. Hoskins emphasised the fall in population after the Black Death, enclosure of fields, and the switch from arable to pasture in the sixteenth and seventeenth centuries. For Beresford they represented the advance of greedy commercialism, especially in the late fifteenth century, as villages practising traditional husbandry were converted into profitable sheep pastures. Axel Steensberg and the archaeologists would have been excited by the opportunity that the village sites offered for research. Earthworks of former settlement preserved in permanent pasture, were easily visible. At first the 'humps and bumps' were not understood, but later these were recognised as holloways of the village streets and lanes, banks and ditches marking the boundaries between house plots, and mounds, platforms and terraces where the houses had once stood. These distinctive traces were associated with moats, fish ponds, dovecots and other features of the same period. Excavation of sites unencumbered with modern occupation could reveal the material culture of the villagers, and the form and development of the settlements. This archaeological perspective was that adopted in the subsequent research, with the result that interest shifted from the desertion of villages to wider considerations, such as village origins and planning.

This paper will trace developments in rural settlement studies in the last sixty-six years, and will outline some current preoccupations. Throughout, the wider picture will be presented, but whenever possible I will show the relevance of the more general themes to the settlements of Leicestershire.

Sixty-six years of research

The first phase of research was co-ordinated by the Deserted Medieval Village Research Group in the 1950s and 1960s, and its great achievement was to compile in 1968 a national gazetteer and map of deserted medieval villages. Standard definitions were applied, so that merely shrunken villages, and settlements too small to be called villages were not counted. The national total came to 2,263 and they were mainly located in a string of counties which began in Northumberland in the north-east, and ran down the eastern side of the country into the midlands and then through Berkshire, Oxfordshire and Gloucestershire to include much of central southern England (Beresford and Hurst 1971, 66). Leicester's total of 67 put it in the category of counties with a high number of desertions. It was fifth in the league table, and if the county had been divided into different regions, east Leicestershire, together with Rutland where 13 sites were listed, would have scored one of the highest densities of sites in England. The national gazetteer gave no more than a map reference for each village, but Hoskins (1945) had already published an article about Leicestershire desertions, which provided much more information about individual settlements, and he followed this with plans of seven sites, surveyed by the Ordnance Survey, published with a commentary (Hoskins 1956). A detailed tabulation of data about each village in the county appeared a few years later (Deserted Medieval Village Research Group 1963–4).

Desertion and shrinkage

Subsequent work on deserted sites has not greatly changed the picture, but if the shrunken sites are included, we can appreciate that the complete desertions form part of a much larger tendency for houses to be abandoned. In 1995 in Leicestershire and Rutland a total of 149 sites showed evidence of shrinkage in the form usually of vacant plots along village streets, with the distinctive earthworks of holloways, toft boundaries and house platforms (Lewis et al 2000, 125, 128). Most manorial documents of the period 1400–1530 mention the tofts where houses once stood, or record the amalgamation of two or three once separate holdings into a single large tenement, for example at Kibworth Harcourt and Thurmaston (Howell 1983, 59–60; Hilton 1947, 103–4). Quite large parts of villages, according to test pitting at Kibworth and field walking at Loddington, were left uninhabited by the fifteenth century (Lewis 2011; Liddle 2013). Much of this desertion and shrinkage was going on between the late fourteenth and seventeenth centuries, not as a simple and direct result of the Black Death of 1349, but in a long period of low population and agrarian change. Contraction began before the Black Death, according to excavations at Anstey which showed that a house was abandoned in the first half of the fourteenth century (Browning and Higgins 2003). The desertion of villages was often only completed in the sixteenth and seveteeth centuries, as Hoskins showed in his research into places such as Great Stretton. Subsequent research has revealed other examples of villages which disappeared when their arable fields were turned into pasture closes such as Whittington in Ratby (Ball and Harwood 2010).

Village origins and planning

In the 1950s and 1960s while the identification and listing of deserted villages was continuing, a series of excavations were starting on sites all over the country, from Cornwall to Norfolk. Martinsthorpe in Rutland featured in this first wave of digging. These early interventions had no well-defined research design – they were motivated by curiosity about what lay beneath the earthworks. The questions that they addressed were 'are these mounds and depressions really village sites?', or it was expected that new light would be thrown on peasant houses and the villagers' way of life. The excavations quickly showed that settlement remains lay below the surface, and that house plans could be recovered. A puzzling feature was the absence of a great deal of evidence for earlier activity beneath the late medieval buildings and occupation. At Martinsthorpe, which was not untypical, the first phase appeared to belong to the twelfth century (Wacher 1963–4). Subsequently in other villages earlier phases of occupation have been identified, notably at Eye Kettleby where buildings have been dated to the fifth to seventh centuries, but here the early settlement evidence was adjacent to the village, not under it, and there may have been a gap in occupation until the tenth century (Finn 1997). In a number of cases the settlement evidence of 450–850 has been located outside the later village, for example at Scraptoft and Loddington, suggesting that the nucleated village began at a later date (Fisher and Upson-Smith 2011; Liddle 2013). Clearly there was no justification for the idea of Hoskins and his contemporaries that villages were commonly founded as large settlements as early as the fifth and sixth centuries. Settlement sites had changed, and large villages may have formed in the later centuries of the 'Anglo-Saxon' period, perhaps around 800–1100.

In the 1970s and 1980s the study of village morphology revived. This had been the preserve of German historical geographers, but their ideas could be applied to the analysis of village plans in this country. The deserted villages often fossilized in the turf the plan of settlements as they had been in the fifteenth, sixteenth or seventeenth century when the sites were abandoned. They clearly had forms similar to the villages which still survived, so modern maps could be used to classify and analyse the layout of streets, boundaries and plots in settlements which are still inhabited. These often had their origin in the twelfth century or even earlier, and boundary lines laid out then influenced the existing settlement. Regular row villages had clearly been carefully planned, while those where streets and houses formed a cluster seemed less deliberate. The polyfocal villages, which lay in three or more distinct nuclei, seemed to preserve a phase when settlements were growing together, but had stopped short of complete unity.

This approach to the study of existing villages has been applied to Leicestershire, which showed that clusters were more numerous than rows, especially on the high ground of the wolds in the east of the county. Rows are most frequently encountered in river valleys, such as those of the Wreake and the Soar (Lewis et al 2000, 60–2). Not just the row villages bear marks of some planning in their layout, and some interpretations have seen evidence for 'a great replanning', which in Northamptonshire was linked with the Danish conquest and subsequent reclamation of English rule in the period 850–950. Work on the Langtons in Leicestershire detects a correlation between the structure of tenures in the villages and the imposition of tax assessments which might take us back to the government of the Mercian state before 850 (Bowman 1996). Sceptics remain to be convinced that villages were planned in a coordinated campaign by those in authority, whether by lords or agents of the state. The varied form of settlements suggests that they grew in a piecemeal fashion and this involved some negotiation between the inhabitants and their superiors.

Two recently researched examples have shown that village plans could change, which reduces our confidence in believing that the layout of the modern settlement reflects decisions made a thousand years ago. At a site in Great Bowden the boundaries between plots seem to have been replanned twice, around 1200 and again in about 1450. An even more radical change at Coston led to a relocation of the settlement from the eastern side of the river Eye to its western bank around the thirteenth century. Excavators are prone to explain such topographical shifts in terms of direction from above, by the lords of the manor. Decision making in complex communities is unlikely to have been so simple (Brown 2010; Wessex Archaeology 2011; 2012).

A landscape approach

Much of the early work was focused on a single site. Plans of excavations or of earthworks tended to stop at the edge of the village site. The growth of landscape history encouraged researchers to extend their vision to include the fields, grassland, woods and other resources on which the village depended. The earthworks in Leicestershire and Rutland surveyed by Hartley include the field systems belonging to both abandoned and existing settlements (Hartley 1987; 2008). The landscape approach lends itself to a multi-period perspective, which takes into account the use of land and the

location of settlements preceding the medieval period. In Leicestershire this has been made possible at sites such as Medbourne through the plotting of pre-Conquest, Romano-British and prehistoric activity from field walking (Liddle 1994), and from historical analysis of boundaries and land units. Phythian Adams (1978) was able to suggest the survival into the early middle ages of a territory based on the Romano-British centre of High Cross. Although we suspect that only a minority of villages stood on the sites of Roman settlements, clearly the medieval inhabitants in many parts of the county inherited from their prehistoric and Romano-British predecessors cultivated fields and an already productive countryside, and of course the population may well have been made up of the descendants of the indigenous British with an unknown proportion, one suspects quite small, of Germanic incomers. The extent of continuity in social organisation or the location of settlements remains uncertain.

Historians and geographers have aided understanding of the early medieval landscape by developing the ideas of the 'multiple estate' and the minster parish. These suggest that the countryside before c.850 was dominated by important centres, such as royal vills and large minster churches, to each of which was attached a large territory. To some extent these places of authority continued to exercise a strong influence as manors with large estates, market towns or large and wealthy churches even into modern times, but the original great estates fragmented after 850 to form the parishes, manors and townships within which were established the villages, field systems, manor houses and parish churches which survive or are recorded from the eleventh century onwards. Leicestershire has its candidates for the centres of multiple estates, such as Rothley, and some minster churches, notably at Breedon can be readily identified. Detective work has suggested other candidates, and more are surely yet to be discovered (Parsons 1996).

The 1968 map of deserted villages in England showed a patchy and very often thin distribution of sites in both western England, from Lancashire to Cornwall, and in the south-east and East Anglia. This reflected the scarcity of nucleated villages in those regions where dispersed settlements predominated. In a land of scattered hamlets and farmsteads there were few villages to be deserted. Settlements were abandoned in the woodlands and uplands, and although no comprehensive list has been attempted, many hundreds of deserted farmsteads and hamlets have been identified in some regions. Rarely has a whole parish been emptied, as could happen in village-dominated regions such as east Leicestershire. One explanation is that a more pastoral agricultural economy, and the absence of the great expanses of open fields, helped to insulate the inhabitants from the sort of catastrophe which hit the village dwellers who depended on grain cultivation in much of the Midlands, or in east Yorkshire. Recognising that the great majority of medieval rural settlements can be categorised as dispersed rather than nucleated, much research has been expended on them, especially in western counties such as Cornwall, Devon, Somerset and Worcestershire. We can easily identify the areas of scattered and polyfocal settlements in north-west Leicestershire, in the parishes of Coleorton and Markfield for example, and they await more detailed investigation (Lewis 2006) Even in the parts of the county dominated by villages a few isolated sites can be observed, such as the grange site in the southwest corner of Illston-on-the-Hill. Of course, if we go back into the first millennium, we can see embedded in a large medieval village evidence for a 'pre-village nucleus', like the early Anglo-Saxon pottery found in a test pit near the church at Great Easton, and a growing number of similar observations at places such as Kibworth Harcourt, Bisbrooke (in Rutland) and Coston, as if there had once, perhaps in the seventh century, been a small hamlet from which the village grew (Cooper and Score 2006; Lewis 2011; Glover and Peachey 2011, 253; Wessex Archaeology 2011 and 2012). There is good evidence for this based on intensive research in Northamptonshire and Buckinghamshire (Jones and Page 2006).

The difference between villages and hamlets poses a problem of interpretation and explanation. We can observe, using the Leicestershire example, that the wooded, pastoral and hilly environment of Charnwood contains hamlets and farms (associated with some nucleated villages), and that east Leicestershire was dominated by nucleated villages which cultivated open fields on the clays of the vales and wolds. But before the ninth century hamlets and farmsteads were widespread in the east, and we do not know why their inhabitants were propelled into nucleation, while in the west small settlements resisted the urge to form clusters, and new settlements in the twelfth and thirteenth centuries took the traditional form of isolated farmsteads or small hamlets. The dynamics of changes in settlements and agriculture on the higher ground of east Leicestershire, the Leicestershire wolds, were analysed by Fox. He believed that this land, woody in the seventh and eighth centuries, was used by settlements on lower ground as summer pasture, giving rise to place names such as Somerby. Eventually permanent setttlements were established, and much, though not all, of the pasture and wood was cultivated (Fox 1989). In Northamptonshire also, the settlements in the period 500–700 were located in the river and stream valleys, and the cold upper slopes were not occupied until later (Williamson et al 2013, 54–9). Villages seem to have developed and multiplied in the context of an expansion of settlement and a growth in large open arable fields from the eighth or ninth centuries. This was the time when the settlements called thorps appeared. A total of 81 are known from Leicestershire and Rutland, and they have been characterised as small nucleated villages, often associated with larger settlements, which emerged as places dedicated to corn growing when that was the coming trend (Cullen et al 2011).

New preoccupations

Studies of medieval settlement in recent years have been influenced by new ideas in cultural history and the more theoretical tendencies in archaeology. Here some of the new thinking will be summarised and applied to Leicestershire and Rutland.

Previously we have been obsessed by dramatic changes such as village desertion and settlement formation. The historical and archaeological agenda was being driven by such questions as 'why were villages deserted?' or 'when and why were villages founded and planned?' These questions raised fundamental problems, and of course could be connected with wider issues such as the transition to a feudal society, and from feudalism to capitalism (to refer to an old fashioned historical agenda). In archaeological thinking village formation and dissolution could be connected to a growing stability and complexity in society, new farming methods, and a new emphasis on exchange (Hamerow 2012).

Now we are also concerned with understanding and explaining medieval settlements in the long period between their beginnings and their ends – and of course most villages and hamlets were not abandoned, and are still with us. The houses in the village constantly decayed and were replaced. We are given a rather pessimistic view of eleven villages in north Leicestershire in 1427 on the estate of Elizabeth Beaumont. Of 160 tenant holdings, 63 (39 per cent) were described as 'ruinous messuages', and 6 (4 per cent) as tofts (Dyer 2012). Tofts, plots where houses had once stood, seem to represent long-term or permanent losses, but ruinous messuages could be repaired or rebuilt, and there is evidence of the renewal process in the form of a significant number of houses standing at the present day, most of them built with crucks, the earliest dating from 1380 and mostly from the fifteenth century. A remarkable number (given the odds against survival in the last five centuries) of buildings of this period still form part of the village fabric, including ten houses at Rothley and ten buildings (seven houses and three barns) at Diseworth (Alcock and Miles 2013, 148–51).

The peasant perspective

The new thinking encourages us to see the medieval world from the perspective of the peasants themselves. How did they behave and what use did they make of their settlements? How did they occupy the spaces that they helped to create? How did the settlements work? Fieldwork and map analysis throws light on the state of the villages in their prime. For example, the south-west Leicestershire villages such as Sibson and Upton, or Frisby on the Wreake in the north-east show ridge and furrow covering virtually the whole of the village's territory, suggesting that a very high proportion of the land was used as arable when agriculture was presumably at the peak of its development in c1300, with little room for woodland and pasture (Hartley 1987, 2008). This pressure on resources, which would have been a common feature throughout the county, must have meant that the villagers devised a very strict discipline in order to keep some animals in a landscape with so much cultivation. Everyone would have been aware of the necessity of following the rules which prevented, for example, careless individuals from neglecting to mend the temporary fences

around the open fields, or which stopped selfish villagers pasturing more animals on the stubbles and fallows than the land could support. The pressures can be deduced from the material evidence on the ground, but are also reflected in the documents which record bylaws, or the stints which set limits to the numbers of animals that could be kept on the commons (Hilton 1954, 164–5). In the same way villages had to deal with their neighbours, to ensure fair shares when assets were intermingled, like the pasture rights and meadows at East, West and Thorpe Langton (Bowman 2004). Village boundaries had to be defended against the animals that might stray across them from a neighbouring settlement. The compilation of an atlas of villages and fields in Northamptonshire has revealed a larger area of pasture than was previously recognised, especially strips of grassland along the parish boundaries, but these are not so readily apparent in Leicestershire (Williamson et al 2013, 109–11).

Analysis of social space seeks to understand how a family, perhaps with two or three children and a servant or two, occupied a typical three-bay peasant house (about 5m wide by 15m long). One of c1400 excavated at Hambleton in Rutland with three rooms could have been divided into a kitchen, hall and chamber (Clough 2007, 426). Such a house might be shared, however, and flexibility in the occupation of rooms emerges from an agreement of 1454 at Diseworth, when a new tenant, William Blakewell, took over a holding, but expected that part of the house would be used by the previous tenants, Reignold and Margaret Bromelaye. Blakewell reserved for himself the chamber and parlour, with 'housing' at the upper end of hall and a hay house and hovel. The retired couple were given access to the kitchen, bakehouse and brewhouse, and could keep an agreed number of animals and poultry (Alcock and Miles 2013, 149).

Within villages the private plots and enclosures around the houses were divided from the public areas of the streets, the church yard, and greens. Villagers must have been very conscious that some areas only were accessible to everyone, in settlements that combined communal and individual dimensions in a complicated balance. One method of analysis seeks to identify spaces used by women, and as fetching water was a traditional female role one thinks of the well in Great

Dalby as a focus for congregations of women; a similar gendered space might have been near mills, where women queued with sacks of grain waiting for their turn.

Perceptions of space changed over time, and a likely part of the process of the formation of a village (some time between 700 and 1100) was in addition to the acceptance by the inhabitants of the former scattered farms of a more communal life in the village, the absorption of previously separate and enclosed plots of land into the common fields, where agreed cropping patterns and common grazing after the harvest were compulsory. We have a record of this process at Swannington, though at a later date, where a fenced assart (cleared woodland) was subdivided and transformed into a common field in the thirteenth century (Thirsk 1964). As we have seen, in the villages' heyday there was a constant tension between private interests and the common good. The profit seeking of individuals began to prevail at the end of the middle ages, leaving its trace on the site of North Marefield, where a group of large buildings and closes came to dominate the village plan in its later phases, no doubt as some wealthy yeoman or farmer ceased to regard himself as part of the peasant community and took over his neighbours' holdings (Everson 1994).

The peasant-centred approach to rural society means that researchers are conscious of the perspective of ordinary villagers, and do not give special privileges in their analysis to those in authority. It should not be assumed automatically that villages were founded by lords, that churches were built and rebuilt by lords, or that lords removed the villagers when desertion occurred. Rural settlements did not exist mainly for the lords' benefit, and the village should be allowed to have had some autonomy. The peasants had influence and could even make decisions. This is more easily argued in Leicestershire because the lords of the county were not especially powerful. There was no large Benedictine monastery like Peterborough or Crowland making heavy demands on tenants though a few manors belonged to large church estates, like Great Easton in Leicestershire and Lyddington in Rutland. Manors tended to be held by laymen, many of them relatively minor gentry with little independent power or political influence. Rents and services were quite light – for example very few tenants were expected to do labour for the lord each week (Hilton 1954, 173). Many villages were divided between a number of manors, which prevented the lords from exercising a complete control over them, and encouraged the villagers to hold their own village meetings, of which a particularly decisive example was that held to reorganise the fields at Wymeswold in 1425 (Ault 1972, 75–6).

Peasants' sense of identity was presumably focused on their village or parish, and was reinforced by attendance at church services, village meetings and to a lesser extent manorial court sessions. To modern observers, aware of the relative uniform plan and structure of housing, the lack of much industry or alternatives to agriculture, and the frequency with which peasants lived on standard units of land holding, the yardland or half yardland, villages seem to resemble one another. Those living at the time would have been aware of differences. Place-names which developed through everyday speech from the seventh century to the eleventh record the inhabitants' awareness of variations in topography or the local crops, like Langley ('the long clearing in woodland'), Appleby ('the settlement where apple trees grow'), or Stoney Stanton ('the settlement with stony soil'). Medieval people were conscious of previous sites, and recalled them as landmarks in place names such as Stretton (near a Roman road) or Burrough on the Hill, referring to the nearby Iron Age hill fort (Cox 2005).

Peasants were aware of their inferior status, especially those who in the thirteenth and fourteenth centuries were classified as unfree villeins. They were capable of organising themselves to resist what they saw as unjust treatment, to demand their freedom and to achieve better conditions as tenants. At Peatling Magna in 1265 they took sides in a national political conflict, and expressed support for the baronial reformers led by Simon de Montfort by quarrelling with royalists returning from the battle of Evesham (Carpenter 1992, 3–4). In 1276 the community of Stoughton claimed their freedom in the royal courts in opposition to their lords, Leicester Abbey, and provoked a canon to compose a Latin poem gloating over the eventual triumph of the monastic house (Hilton 1985). In Kibworth Harcourt in the early fifteenth century, when peasants everywhere were in a stronger bargaining position because of their scarcity after the 1349 epidemics, the tenants mounted a rent strike and forced their lord, Merton College, Oxford, to reduce the level of payments (Howell 1983, 50–3). These coherent episodes of resistance and agitation happen to have been recorded and have attracted the attention of historians. Small scale and sporadic defiance of those In authority would have been commonplace in villages throughout the county.

These historical insights should encourage those researching the material culture of rural settlements to look for reflections of a sense of local identity. The distinctive vernacular architecture of parts of the county suggested by the relatively numerous buildings with mud walls (or with traces of mud walls now replaced by other materials) is just one example (Finn 2009). Perhaps different styles of timber framing might have distinguished one village and another. Local distinctiveness might also be reflected in village plans and the architecture of parish churches.

Rural settlements in context: castles, churches, towns and gardens

Medieval rural settlements were for a long time studied in isolation. There was a good reason for this as it was a new subject, struggling for recognition in a field previously dominated by those who gave attention to church architecture, monasteries and castles. Now that the subject is fully established, and enjoys a high status within medieval archaeology, the time has come to include every type of settlement, because the goal should be to study whole landscapes, and the full range of society, and to see how the various elements interacted. If we are considering how people at the time perceived their world, they were not confined to their village, and they were aware beyond its boundaries of a wide range of people and places.

The castle, for example, was once seen as an alien imposition, with military functions, occupying a different world from the village with its indigenous population and agricultural preoccupations. Now the castle can be seen as part of the landscape, not always founded on a new site and drawing a settlement around it, as probably happened at Mountsorrel. Instead, castles like those at Earl Shilton and Shawell were inserted into existing villages (Creighton 1997).

The newcomers from across the Channel after 1066 often took over estates from the pre-Conquest aristocracy, and built their residences with a new style of fortification on sites which had previously been aristocratic centres, as probably happened at Groby. The new aristocracy were signalling the continuity of their rule, and associating themselves with the authority of their predecessors, anxious as they were to establish a working relationship with the majority population. Aristocratic parks can also be analysed in landscape terms, and their location primarily in the west of the county shows that lords were taking advantage of the existing pastures and woodlands rather than disrupting the open fields of the rest of the county (Squires 2004,149). The ability to make a park implied that the owners enjoyed wealth and status, and their creators were anxious to make the local population look up to them and be conscious of their superiority.

Churches were closely connected with rural settlements. Country people before 850 looked to a relatively few minsters like Breedon, and some large churches like Melton Mowbray were also closely connected to centres of local administration. The siting of the later generation of parish churches next to the manor house (often now marked by a moated site) as at Newton Harcourt and many other places, indicates that they were founded by lords. In the later middle ages, however, the ordinary parishioners played a larger role in managing, repairing and building their church through the activities of churchwardens. Those peasants who contributed so much of their modest resources to the costs of the church would have been motivated by their faith, no doubt, but also by their loyalty to the church as a community asset. Presumably the high proportion of Leicestershire churches with fabric of the fourteenth century but relatively few built or extensively rebuilt in the fifteenth, tells us, not about a decline in community spirit after 1400, but about prosperity in the countryside which was not sustained. In other regions there was more wealth to add to the fabric and ornamentation of the church in the fifteenth century.

Towns had special characteristics because of their role as centres for markets, manufacture, government and religion. But they were not cut off from rural settlements. They stood at the top of the settlement hierarchy, above the villages and the hamlets, and closely connected with the rural people in their hinterlands. By c1300 the dominant centre of Leicester itself was surrounded by a ring of well-established market towns at Market Harborough, Lutterworth, Hinckley, Market Bosworth, Ashby de la Zouch, Loughborough, Melton Mowbray and Oakham (Laughton et al 2001). Castle Donington, Hallaton, Mountsorrel and Uppingham are debatable cases which may not quite match up to the urban characteristic that a majority of the population should have been employed in a variety of non-agrarian occupations. In addition some villages had a commercial life, such as Waltham on the Wolds, where a market which was held weekly attracted traders, and a few retailers and craftsmen who were permanently resident.

Most country dwellers, more than 80 per cent of Leicestershire and Rutland's population, gained their living from agriculture, and lived within easy reach of a market town. Finds from excavations and fieldwalking reveal manufactured goods, such as pottery, metalwork, whetstones and handmills, presumably bought from towns by peasants. Pottery made at Lyveden and Stanion in Northamptonshire, Bourne in Lincolnshire, Nottingham and Chilvers Coton (Warwickshire) is found on Rutland rural sites, perhaps having reached the villages via middlemen keeping stalls in Oakham market (Clough 2007, 434–8).

Written sources tell us that country people sold livestock, wool and other produce in urban markets, such as that at Melton Mowbray in the fifteenth century (Laughton and Dyer 2002). Perhaps they distrusted the urban traders who bought cheap and sold dear, but they responded to the demands of the market by intensifying production of grain in the thirteenth century, and shifting to meat and wool as demand for cereals fell in the century and a half after the Black Death. Their visits to the town put them into contact with a busy and varied community, where they would encounter entertainments, news and impressive religious ceremonies. Some regard for urban styles is apparent from building with jettied upper storeys, a feature of houses in towns, which was adopted for rural houses, for example at Cossington and Husbands Bosworth.

Finally we must mention the relationship between village sites and modern country houses. Survey of earthworks has become more sophisticated, with the result not just that village plans and remains of houses can be identified with more confidence, but also the whole development of the site over a long period can be traced. This leads to the recognition of phases in the afterlife of village sites, which could have been remodelled into gardens linked to the large mansion that succeeded the medieval manor house or grange. Re-examination of the sites visited by the 1948 seminar showed that all of them included large areas of garden earthworks, and in the case of Knaptoft the earthworks previously identified as the site of the village mark the remains of a garden, and the village occupied a separate site some distance from the church and the manor house (Everson and Brown 2010).

Conclusion

Leicestershire's medieval rural settlement to an outside observer might seem to present a relatively simple pattern of nucleated villages spread over much of the county. The reality is a picture of great complexity of which we have at present only glimpsed the uncertainties.

Our ideas about the early stages of village development depend on a small sample of evidence, and we need more fieldwalking outside the existing settlements and the test pitting of village cores. Historians need to more systematically address the problems of early estates and minster parishes, and to investigate the tenurial complexities of sokes and manors in the later middle ages. Much more remains to be discovered about the management of fields in the villages, about occupations, and the changes in peasant society culminating in the late medieval crisis.

In the archaeological sphere, much valuable information can be gleaned from the relatively small excavations carried out under the planning process, and we hope to learn yet more about plot layouts, building types, pottery and environmental material. To take one example, the distribution of pottery from Leicestershire's own rural production centre at Potters' Marston, and the wares from kilns outside the county, can provide insights into the marketing and distribution network in which one suspects that market towns played a major part.

Marketing zones, together with such factors as village morphology and rural social structure, can help us to better understand the regional varieties of the county – not just the rather clumsy distinction between the northwest and the area dominated by the nucleated village which has been used above, but the more subtle characteristics of the wolds, the Leake valley, the Welland valley and the other subsections of the county.

We know enough about medieval rural settlement in Leicestershire to be conscious of how much more we need to learn.

Bibliography

Alcock, N. and Miles, D., 2013. *The medieval peasant house in midland England.* Oxford: Oxbow.

Ault, W. O,. 1972. *Open-field farming in medieval England.* London: George Allen and Unwin.

Ball, M. and Harwood, G., 2010. 'History of the deserted village of Whittington, Ratby.' *Transactions of the Leicestershire Archaeological and Historical Society* 84, 189–212.

Beresford, M. W., 1986–7. 'Forty years in the field: an exaugural lecture.' *The University of Leeds Review*, 29, 27–46.

Beresford, M. W. and Hurst, J. G., ed. 1971. *Deserted medieval villages.* Guildford: Lutterworth Press.

Bowman, P., 1996. 'Contrasting *pays*: Anglo-Saxon settlement in Langton hundred.' In: J. Bourne ed. *Anglo-Saxon landscapes in the East Midlands.* Leicester: Leicestershire Museums Arts and Records Service, 121–46.

Bowman, P., 2004. 'Villages and their territories: Part I and Part II.' In: P. Bowman and P. Liddle ed. *Leicestershire Landscapes.* Leicester: Leicestershire Museums Archaeological Fieldwork Group monograph no. 1, 105–36.

Brown, J., 2010. 'Medieval plots along Sutton Road, Great Bowden, Leicestershire.' *Transactions of the Leicestershire Archaeological and Historical Society* 84, 95–116.

Browning, J., and Higgins, T., 2003. 'Excavations of a medieval toft and croft at Cropston Road, Anstey, Leicestershire.' *Transactions of the Leicestershire Archaeological and Historical Society* 77, 65–81.

Carpenter, D., 1992. 'English peasants in politics 1258–1267.' *Past and Present* 136, 3–42.

Clough, T., 2007. 'Medieval settlements at Nether Hambleton and Whitwell.' In: Ovens and Sleath ed. *The heritage of Rutland Water.* Rutland Historical and Record Society: Rutland Record Series 5, 421–43

Cooper, N. J., and Score, V., 2006. 'Investigating the origins of Great Easton, Leicestershire: community archaeology meets the 'Big Dig'.' *Transactions of the Leicestershire Archaeological and Historical Society* 80, 209–14.

Cox, B., 2005. *A dictionary of Leicestershire and Rutland place-names.* Nottingham: English Place-Name Society.

Creighton, O., 1997. 'Early Leicestershire castles: archaeology and landscape history.' *Transactions of the Leicestershire Archaeological and Historical Society* 71, 21–36.

Cullen, P., Jones, R. and Parsons, D. N., 2011. *Thorps in a changing landscape.* Hatfield: University of Hertfordshire Press.

Deserted Medieval Village Research Group, 1963–4. 'A provisional list of deserted medieval villages in Leicestershire.' *Transactions of the Leicestershire Archaeological and Historical Society* 39, 24–33.

Dyer, C., 2012. The value of the inquisitions post mortem for economic and social history. In: M. Hicks, ed. *The fifteenth century inquisitions post mortem. A companion.* Woodbridge: Boydell, 97–115.

Dyer, C. and Jones, R., 2010. *Deserted villages revisited*. Hatfield: University of Hertfordshire Press.

Everson, P., 1994. 'The deserted village remains of North Marefield, Leicestershire.' *Medieval Settlement Research Group Annual Report* 9, 22–7.

Everson, P. and Brown, G., 2010. 'Dr Hoskins I presume! Field visits in the footsteps of a pioneer.' In: C. Dyer, and R. Jones, *Deserted villages revisited*. Hatfield: University of Hertfordshire Press.

Finn, N., 1997. 'Eye Kettleby, Leicester Road, Melton Mowbray.' *Transactions of the Leicestershire Archaeological and Historical Society* 71, 88–9

Finn, N., 2009. 'Mud and frame construction in South Leicestershire.' *Vernacular Architecture* 40, 63–74.

Fisher, I., and Upson-Smith, T., 2011. 'Scraptoft, Station Road.' T*ransactions of the Leicestershire Archaeological and Historical Society* 85, 243.

Fox, H., 1989. 'The people of the wolds in English settlement history.' In: M. Aston, D. Austin, and C. Dyer, ed, *The rural settlements of medieval England*. Oxford: Blackwell, 77–101.

Glover, G. and Peachey, M., 2011. 'Bisbrooke, Village Farm, Main Street', *Transactions of the Leicestershire Archaeological and Historical Society* 85, 253.

Hamerow, H., 2012. *Rural settlements and society in Anglo-Saxon England*. Oxford: Oxford University Press.

Hartley, R. F., 1987. *The medieval earthworks of north-east Leicestershire.* Leicester: Leicestershire Museums, Arts and Records Service.

Hartley, R. F., 2008. *The medieval earthworks of south-west Leicestershire. Hinckley and Bosworth.* Leicester: Leicestershire Museums Archaeological Fieldwork Group monograph no 2.

Hilton, R. H., 1947. *The economic development of some Leicestershire estates in the 14th and 15th centuries.* Oxford: Oxford University Press.

Hilton, R. H., 1954. 'Medieval agrarian history.' In: *Victoria County History of Leicestershire* vol 2. London: Oxford University Press, 145–98.

Hilton, R. H., 1985. 'A thirteenth-century poem on disputed villein services.' In: R. Hilton, ed. *Class conflict and the crisis of feudalism, essays in medieval social history.* London: Hambledon Press. 108–13.

Hoskins, W. G., 1945. 'The deserted villages of Leicestershire.' *Transactions of the Leicestershire Archaeological and Historical Society* 22, 241–64.

Hoskins, W. G., 1956. 'Seven deserted village sites in Leicestershire.' *Transactions of the Leicestershire Archaeological and Historical Society* 32, 36–51.

Howell, C., 1983. *Land, family and inheritance in transition*. Cambridge: Cambridge University Press.

Jones, R. and Page, M., 2006. *Medieval villages in an English landscape. Beginnings and ends.* Macclesfield: Windgather Press.

Laughton, J., Jones, E. and Dyer, C., 2001. 'The urban hierarchy in the later middle ages: a study of the east midlands.' *Urban History* 28, 331–57.

Laughton, J, and Dyer, C., 2002. 'Seasonal patterns of trade in the later middle ages: buying and selling at Melton Mowbray, Leicestershire, 1400–1520.' *Nottingham Medieval Studies* 46, 162–84.

Lewis, C., 2006. 'The medieval period (850–1500).' In: Cooper, N, ed. *The archaeology of the East Midlands*. Leicester Archaeology Monographs 13.

Lewis, C. 2011. 'Kibworth Harcourt, Kibworth Beauchamp and Smeeton Westerby.' *Transactions of the Leicestershire Archaeological and Historical Society* 85, 228–30.

Lewis, C., Mitchell-Fox, P. and Dyer, C., 2000. *Village, hamlet and field. Changing medieval settlements in central England.* Macclesfield: Windgather.

Liddle, P., 2013. 'Loddington parish survey.' *Transactions of the Leicestershire Archaeological and Historical Society* 87, 256–7.

Liddle, P., 1994. 'The Medbourne area survey.' In: M. Parker Pearson and R. T. Schadla-Hall, ed. *Looking at the land. Archaeological landscapes in eastern England.* Leicester: Leicestershire Museums, Arts and Records Services.

Parsons, D., 1996. 'Before the parish: the church in Anglo-Saxon Leicestershire.' In: J. Bourne ed, 1996. *Anglo-Saxon landscapes in the East Midlands.* Leicester: Leicestershire Museums, Arts and Records Service, 11–35.

Phythian Adams, C., 1978. *Continuity, fields and fission. The making of a midland parish.* Leicester: University of Leicester Department of English Local History Occasional Paper 3rd ser. 4.

Squires, A., 2004. 'Parks and woodland in medieval Leicestershire 1086–1530.' In: P. Bowman and P. Liddle ed. *Leicestershire Landscapes.* Leicester: Leicestershire Archaeological Fieldwork Group, Monograph No. 1, 141–53.

Thirsk, J., 1964. 'The common fields.' *Past and Present* 29, 3–25.

Wacher, J. S., 1963–4. 'Excavations at Martinsthorpe, Rutland, 1960.' *Transactions of the Leicestershire Archaeological and Historical Society* 39, 1–19.

Wessex Archaeology 2011 and 2012. 'Coston near Melton Mowbray.' *Transactions of the Leicestershire Archaeological and Historical Society* 85, 220–1; 86, 218.

Williamson, T., Liddiard, R., and Partida. T., 2013. *Champion. The making and unmaking of the medieval English midland landscape.* Liverpool: Liverpool University Press.

The origins of Leicestershire: churches, territories, and landscape

Graham Jones

Introduction

In the decades since our introduction to Glanville Jones's 'multiple estate' (Jones 1961) and John Blair's minster parish (Blair 1988),[1] attempts to identify Leicestershire's earliest churches and pre-hundredal structures have mainly concentrated on area studies.[2] Blair himself notes how some 'relatively settled' areas such as Leicestershire 'still seem very thin' in their number of minsters, asking 'whether the contrast is simply in the surviving sources' (Blair 2005, 152, 315-6). While the national and regional pictures remain incomplete,[3] uncertainty clings to the shape of religious provision before and after the Augustinian mission, the process of Christianisation, the extent of Danish colonisation, the impact of reforms, and the emergence of the parochial network. This ramifies back and forth with secular matters: cultural identity, nucleation, manorialisation, and here the existence of Leicestershire itself.

Locating pre-Conquest churches is not the issue. By the eleventh century few places were more than a reasonable if lengthy walk from a church (Parsons 1996, 11-35). The number looks similar to that of 'small hundreds' and *villae integrae* (taxation units) two centuries later. One persistent explanation for the deeper problem is that Danish incomers so disrupted and reorganised the territorial landscape that earlier arrangements are impossible to recover. Archaeology is now challenging this.

Neat parcelling-out of the landscape need not be Danish. Like the open fields, it may be older.[4]

Rather than 'Where are the minsters?' better to ask 'What territories were served by minsters?' Can they be identified and their extents estimated?[5] Can they be categorised? Sub-kingdoms, provinces, folk territories, and *regiones* (Bassett 1993; Hooke 1998) are not easily distinguished from each other and from hundreds and wapentakes. Moreover, a network of minsters, monastic or secular, with neatly dovetailing *parochiæ*, will not alone reveal the ancient devotional landscape. Places of religious or ritual resort came in many guises. What became Leicestershire had a richly varied religious geography as this study shows, but we should expect it from continental evidence. In southern Germany, for example, churches were first built at fords or crossroads, hilltops, burial barrows, or springs for baptism, 'perhaps the pre-Christian centres of *gaue* or hundreds' (Wood 2005, 79-80).

Furthermore, the idea that lords' churches, *eigenkirchen*, emerged in England only in the century or so before the Norman Conquest looks increasingly vunerable. Numerous places in Leicestershire appear likely to have been furnished much earlier with churches, oratories or chapels supplementary to episcopal and 'proto-parochial', minster provision. Again, continental evidence supports this. Wilfrid, bishop in Leicester *circa* 692-706, spent time in Francia like many other English clerics, exposed to a pattern of church provision already two centuries in the making.

1 Jones 1961, 'Settlement Patterns in Anglo-Saxon England', was reassessed by Barnwell and Roberts 2011, alongside some of his seminal texts. See also Barrow's 'small shires' (Barrow 1973). Blair 1988 (ed), Minsters and Parish Churches: The Local Church in Transition, 950-1200, was reviewed by Cambridge and Rollason 1995, 87–104. For additional reading see Blair 2005.
2 Roffe 1996, 107-20; Foss 1996, 83-105; Phythian-Adams 1978 [on Claybrooke and district]; Bowman 2004, 105-36 [on south-east Leicestershire].
3 Comparative studies include Foard 1985, 185-222; Everitt 1986; Croom 1988; Hase 1988; Blair 1991; Pitt 1999; Hall 2000; Hadley 2000; Winchester 2008, 14-21.

4 See for example Oosthuizen 2006 and 2013, and her contribution and others' in Higham and Ryan 2010.
5 Bassett who discusses this issue (2007a, 115-42) has reconstructed early Midland *parochiæ* elsewhere, arguing for Romano-British diocesan origins in some cases. See also Bassett 1989, 225-56; 1991, 1-23; 1992a, 14-15; 1992b,13-40; 2000, 1-27. My matching conclusion about Worcester is in Jones 1996. Bassett's westernmost *parochiæ* can be fitted into a series of large early units along, and mostly spanning the Severn from Bristol to north-east Wales.

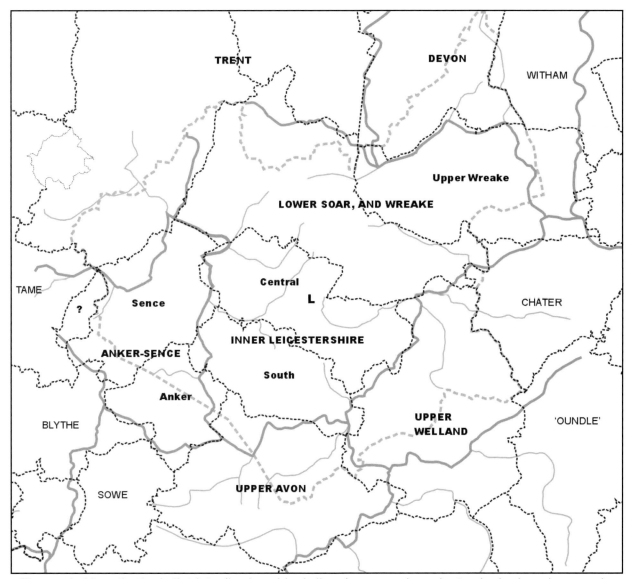

Figure 1: Hypothetical districts (broken black lines) mapped against principal and secondary watersheds south of the Trent (dark tint) and Leicestershire's county boundary (lighter, broken tint). L = Leicester.

As Susan Wood describes, in Frankish cities (generally places with a Roman past, like Leicester) baptisms took place in the cathedral or an attendant baptistery; further basilicas, closely tied to the cathedral, housed honoured relics; others marked burial places – often of a revered bishop – outside the walls (Wood, *op. cit.*). In the country, the parish church serving a large area was normally in a *vicus*, a substantial rural settlement, often a pre-Christian cult centre; it had probably been built by order of the bishop or count (the English ealdorman's counterpart), and was staffed and maintained by the bishop. An increasing phenomenon was the private oratory, built by a landlord on his villa, probably for his own and his household's convenience rather than for his tenants. The household had to attend the cathedral or parish church for the great feasts and almost certainly for baptism.

The word *parochia* still meant primarily the bishop's territory, or a large, loosely defined region within it served by what was almost a subsidiary cathedral. However the Council of Orleans in 541 spoke of 'parishes constituted in the houses of powerful men' and of 'anyone having or asking to have a parish (*diocesim*) in his land'. Similarly, when Wilfrid visited Rome, he would have passed through a countryside where the beginnings of a 'growing swarm of small private churches' was adding to Italy's network of important baptismal churches (*plebes*, vernacular *pievi*) under episcopal control, with their own dependent oratories (Wood 2005, 66-67, 86). In Switzerland and Bavaria, 100 churches have been discovered to have origins *circa* 600-750. Local nobility were 'busy studding the landscape with proprietary churches in which they could receive lavish burial' (Burnell and Jones 1999, 83-106 at 88).

Recovering Leicestershire's pastoral centres and related territories is hampered by a county boundary which everywhere looks artificial, permeable, the result of arbitrary expansions or contractions. Though the geography of the Midland shires is thought likely to perpetuate aspects of 'military territories which surrounded the fortified settlements of the kingdom of Mercia' (Bassett 2007b, 53-85, fn 78), Leicestershire 'probably evolved in the tenth century', no earlier than Edward the Elder's conquest of the Danelaw *circa* 920, and with the use of Watling Street to divide English from Danish Mercia dated to 886-913 'in the course of unchronicled struggles and negotiation' (Stafford 1985, 137). Significantly, then, parish or township boundaries transgress both Watling Street (itself diverting from a natural feature, the Severn-Trent watershed)[6] and the Welland, and the shire boundary along the Soar arguably truncates a *regio*. The Eye Brook gives way to a 'weak' boundary across headwaters of the Chater. Neither Sewstern Lane nor the watershed of the Witham is respected. The boundary with Nottinghamshire intrudes into the Vale of Belvoir. Townships were shared with Derbyshire, and so on.

Paradoxically this strange boundary is a help, because it frees the observer to allow for earlier land-units – with central places served by major churches – which ignore it. Clues to such units include clustered place-names suggesting function, specialism or location, like Charlton, Hardwick, Norton.[7] Peter Sawyer argued that *tūn* names were intrinsically subsidiary by the mid-Anglo-Saxon period, *circa* 650-850 (Sawyer 1979), the 'long eighth century' which Stephen Rippon associates with large-scale investment in landscape management (Rippon 2010, 39-64). Place-names alluding to churches, e.g. Kirkby and Misterton, may occupy the same category, though they may pinpoint provisioning rather than church locations. Paul Cullen, Richard Jones and David Parsons have recently concluded that *bý* names represent pastoral colonisation and *thorps* arable (Cullen *et al*,

2011, 110-11, 127-32). Peripheries may be indicated by names in -*worth*, 'small, single homesteads, often in remote situations' (Smith 1970, 274; Hooke 1996, 85-87), though circumstance could promote their status, as at Market Bosworth and Tamworth.

Fragmented mother parishes are evidenced by former chapelries (Phillimore 1912; VCH 1905-64; Nichols 1795-1811; Humphery-Smith 1984), payments in lieu of lost income, and two-and three-fold geographical separation[8] of central-place or proto-urban functions: court, church, and market. The latter often evolved from king's *tūns*, collection centres for food rents or renders, often the reeve's vill rather than the king's (Sawyer 1983, 273-99). Sunday markets, originally in the churchyard and archaic in the twelfth century, may be diagnostic. Parishes spanning rivers where this is not the norm may survive from trans-riverine units. Boundaries can be eloquent (Winchester 2000; Richardson 1996): whether weak and meandering, strongly fixed, e.g. on watercourses and ridges, or suggestive of partition – zig-zagging as through open-field furlongs, coming close to the church, panhandled, etc.[9] In areas of gentle topography, curvilinear churchyards seem diagnostic of older managed landscapes than the rectilinearly planned, nucleated villages of Midland England. Hilltop, spring-head, riverside and isolated churches also speak differently to those slotted into planned villages. Those with floors level with, or raised above, their yards may have different origins (on man-made mounds, for example?) from those which are sunken.

Hundreds and wapentakes may preserve ancient entities, but their quartering of Leicestershire looks like a consequence of shiring. Wariness is also needed when using Domesday (Morris 1976-79). Cadastral architecture – the mathematical relationship

6 Examples of such boundary transgressions are reviewed by Williamson 2012, 94-97.

7 Place-name interpretations rely on Cox, 1998-2009, The Place-Names of Leicestershire, English Place-Names Survey 75, 78, 81, 84, and Cox 2005, A Dictionary of Leicestershire and Rutland Place-Names; also on Ekwall 1960; Watts 2004. On relational names, Finberg 1964, 144-50.

8 The late Mick Aston's term was 'dispersal' (Aston 1985).

9 For a map view of this see Roger Kain and Richard Oliver (2001), 'Historic Parishes of England and Wales: an Electronic Map of Boundaries before 1850 with a Gazetteer and Metadata', held online at the UK Data Archive http://discover.ukdataservice.ac.uk/ - access at subscribing institutions or registration required for use. Large-scale nineteenth-century Ordnance Survey mapping is on-line at the University of Edinburgh Edina archive and can be accessed at subscribing institutions via http://edina.ac.uk/.

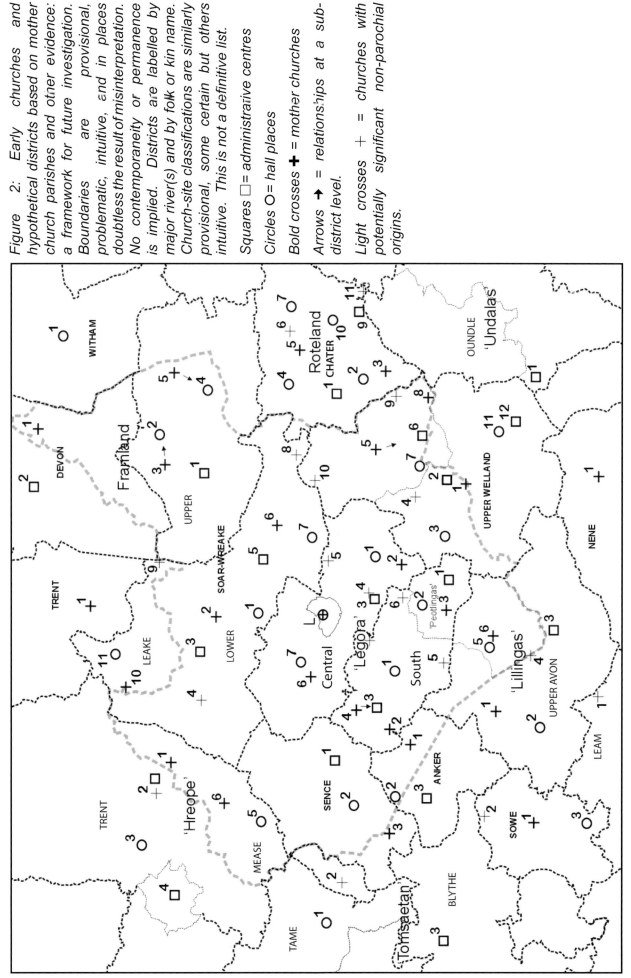

Figure 2: Early churches and hypothetical districts based on mother church parishes and other evidence: a framework for future investigation. Boundaries are provisional, problematic, intuitive, and in places doubtless the result of misinterpretation. No contemporaneity or permanence is implied. Districts are labelled by major river(s) and by folk or kin name. Church-site classifications are similarly provisional, some certain but others intuitive. This is not a definitive list.

Squares □ = administrative centres

Circles O = hall places

Bold crosses ✚ = mother churches

Arrows ← = relationships at a sub-district level.

Light crosses + = churches with potentially significant non-parochial origins.

Inner Leicestershire
'Legora'
South

1 Croft O
2 Barwell +
3 Earl Shilton □
4 Kirkby Mallory +
5 Leire +
6 Foston +

Lower Sence/
'Peotlingas'

1 Knaptoft □
2 Peatling Magna O
3 Peatling Parva +

Central Sector

1 Great Glen O
2 Wistow +
3 Wigston Magna (All Saints) □
4 Wigston Magna (St Wigstan) +
5 Thurnby +
6 Ratby +
7 Groby O

Leicester (L)

'St Nicholas'
St Mary in Castro
St Margaret

Northern
Leicestershire
Upper Wreake (Eye)/
Framland

1 Melton Mowbray □
2 Waltham-on-the-Wolds O
3 Scalford +
4 Wymondham O
5 Buckminster +

Devon

1 Bottesford +
2 Orston □

Lower Soar and lower
Wreake

1 Rothley O
2 Barrow-upon-Soar +
3 Loughborough □
4 Shepshed +
5 Queniborough +
6 South Croxton +
7 Keyham +
8 Owston +
9 Willoughby-on-the-Wolds (Vernemeton) +
10 Ratcliffe-on-Soar +
11 Gotham O

Trent

1 Flawforth +

Upper Avon/'Lillingas'

1 Monks Kirby +
2 Newnham O
3 Lilbourne □
4 Holywell (Caves Inn, Tripontium) +
5 Lutterworth O
6 Misterton +

Upper Welland

1 Market Harborough (St Mary in Arden) +
2 Great Bowden □
3 Gumley O
4 Church Langton +
5 Hallaton +
6 Medbourne □
7 Welham O
8 Bringhurst +
9 Holyoaks (Mirabel) +
10 Tilton +
11 Desborough O
12 Rothwell □

External Ring of
Primary Churches
Tame/
Blythe/'Tomsaetan'

1 Tamworth O
2 Polesworth +
3 Coleshill □
Not shown: Lichfield +

Coventry/'Sowe'

1 Coventry +
2 Exhall +
3 Stoneleigh O

Leam

1 Offcurch +

Nene

1 Brixworth +
Not shown: Daventry +

Oundle/'Undalas'

1 Kettering □
Not shown: Oundle +

Peterborough

Not shown: Peterborough +

Chater/'Roteland'

1 Ridlington □
2 Uppingham O
3 Lyddington +
4 Oakham O
5 Hambleton +
6 Whitwell +
7 Empingham O
8 Stamford □
9 Barrowden □
10 North Luffenham O
11 Tixover +

Witham

1 Grantham O

Outer Leicestershire
Trent Valley/'Hreope'

1 Breedon +
2 Melbourne +□
3 Repton O
4 Burton on Trent □
5 Measham O
6 Ashby-de-la-Zouch +
Not shown: Southwell +

Sence

1 Market Bosworth □
2 Sibson O
3 Mancetter +

Anker

1 Hinckley +
2 Higham-on-the-Hill O
3 Nuneaton □

of fiscal obligations to tenurial and other land-units - is another useful technique (Hart 1992; 1968, 55-66; 1970; 1974). It nevertheless carries a caveat about mistaking eleventh-century conditions for something older. Large districts, multiple estates, and landed units approximating to minster parishes share similarities which make them difficult to differentiate: heavily exploited cores and a generally upland, pastoral periphery. Often high-status functions survived around the estate caput; and sometimes archaic tenures involving renders and obligations to kings or earls (the latter succeeding sub-kings in the west Midlands and wielding regal power in palatine counties). Smaller sub-hundredal groupings of vills included land booked out to ministers and clerics, while on smaller estates everywhere upland and lowland settlements were linked by common lordship. In the background are Romano-British estates, corresponding with the Merovingian 'villa-region' in which the *mansus* was the basic unit of settlement (Halsall 2007, 221). Conflating evidence is a continual risk, but only by bringing data together can threads be disentangled.

Scientific study of church and other religious dedications shows that they carried specific associations (Jones 2007)[10] and that superior centres generally adopted superior cults: Peter and Paul, representing *Romanitas*, civic (royal) authority; Michael, captain of heavenly hosts (hilltops), angel of death (cemeteries) and baptism/healing (riversides, pools); Andrew, mission and baptism (revered by Augustine's master, Gregory the Great, and by Wilfrid); John the Baptist, baptism, wood-pasture; and Mary at the earliest periods, associated with arable and harvest (Assumption, August 15, and Nativity, September 9) as well as the motherhood of Christ. Especially significant are the apostle Bartholomew, legendary appropriator of temples for Christian worship, and Helen, mother of Constantine. She represents ideal monarchy (her portrait was imitated on coins for Offa's consort Cynethryth, unique in Anglo-Saxon England) and perhaps pastoral wealth. St Helen's-Day-in-the-Spring, May 3, began annual Pennine migration with cattle to high summer pastures, and followed

10 For the dedications cited in this study see the on-line datasets of TASC, the project for a Transnational Database and Atlas of Saints' Cults, at Leicester University: http://www.le.ac.uk/users/grj1/tasc.html; and the UK Data Service, deposit 4975.

Beltaine – May Day in Celtic-speaking lands, when pre-Norman cattle renders, 'Beltancu' in Lancashire, *treth calan mai* in Wales, and elsewhere 'cornage' or 'noutgeld', were due to the king's reeves.

Territorial boundaries often shadowed watersheds and Figure 1 shows hypothetical districts mapped against principal and secondary watersheds. Pre-industrial communities were self-resourcing, accessing river-meadows and high pastures and benefiting from secure, shared river routes with optimally organised market hinterlands. They are primary building blocks for the cultural provinces or regional societies argued by Charles Phythian-Adams (1993, 2007). This survey is therefore organised around drainages. Figure 2 locates churches within these drainages and should be referred to for locations in the survey that follows.

After detailing the ring of primary churches outside the county, the survey first examines 'Outer Leicestershire': the Trent drainage (including Breedon and Ashby-de-la-Zouch districts), the Market Bosworth and Hinckley/Nuneaton districts in the Anker and Sence drainage, the Lutterworth district on the upper Avon, and Market Harborough's on the upper Welland. It then addresses those areas drained by the Soar and Wreake: 'Northern Leicestershire' on the Wreake and lower Soar (plus Bottesford and other vills in the Vale of Belvoir), and finally 'Inner Leicestershire' on the upper Soar and including Leicester itself.

The author regrets that space necessarily allows few citations of sources and published work, and no detailed maps. The compressed text is intended to raise questions, stimulate discussion and encourage further work.

The external ring of 'primary' churches

Tame-Blythe/'Tomsaetan'

Beyond Leicestershire lay a ring of large pre-Conquest units served by major churches (for overview see Parsons 2001, 50ff). **Lichfield**, where St Michael's pre-dated Chad's cathedral of *circa* 670 (Mary, then Peter) (Bassett 1992b), had Tamworth as its corresponding royal vill with a secondary minster, originally St Edith's nunnery, at **Polesworth** (see also Anker-Sence drainage below). Facing across the

Tame-Blythe confluence are **Coleshill** (Peter and Paul), centre of a royal estate and large parish with a Sunday market, and Curdworth to the north (not shown on map), whose name echoes that of Penda's grandfather Creoda.

Sowe

Coventry's minster was perhaps of eighth/ninth-century date (*op. cit.*), though Exhall, on its *parochia*'s northern edge, 'angle of land pertaining to an *ecclesia*', looks older. Stoneleigh, to the south of Coventry, is the matching royal estate. Lichfield and Coventry were country places in landscapes with ritual potential: 'open field/veldt in a grey forest' (Letocetum, modern Wall on Watling Street), and Cofa's tree, both on hills with adjacent pools and Michael churches.

Leam

Offa's name marks **Offchurch**, overlooking the Fosse west of Southam. St Gregory's was linked to the cult of Offa's supposed son Fremund. Dunchurch (Peter) on Dunsmore, just south of Rugby, is the other place in the Leam valley defined by religious activity.

Nene

On the Nene side of its watershed with the Leam is **Daventry**. Holy Cross stood in a strikingly curvilinear yard off the main thoroughfare, west of a large Iron-Age enclosure overlooking Romano-British Bannaventa on Watling Street. However, Fawley was the hundredal mother church and Weedon, *wēoh dūn* (Peter and Paul), the royal vill – given to Penda's granddaughter St Wærburh, with her disciple Alnoth enshrined at adjacent Stowe.

Chapelries, place-names, and boundary patterns suggest **Brixworth**'s *parochia* marched on the east with that of **Kettering** (Peter and Paul). Northampton itself might once have been served from Brixworth, with St Peter's as a royal chapel. Visible for miles, Brixworth church sits on a ridge above a pool. Its patronal cult, All Saints, was promoted at Rome *circa* 800. Had it once honoured Michael?

Oundle ('Undalas')/Peterborough

Oundle (Peter and Paul), with a Sunday market and eight hundreds, doubtless the *provincia* reported by Bede, was one of Wilfrid's federated monasteries. Across the Nene was a Romano-British settlement.

Peterborough minster (Peter and Paul, probably Andrew earlier) was founded at Medehamstede by king Peada in 655. Nearby on the Welland is Flag Fen, a prehistoric ritual complex. Peterborough, a soke centre, lay downstream from Romano-British **Castor**, Cyneburh's monastery.

Roteland/Chater

Rutland is divided by a major watershed. Its northern streams feed the Wreake, so Alstoe hundred is considered with Leicestershire. In the south, *Roteland*, dowry of English queen-consorts (Phythian-Adams, 1977, 63-84), the Chater and tributaries converge with the Welland. Uppingham, '*hām* of the upland dwellers' (Peter and Paul) with 'Thor's *leāh*' to the west, had pilgrimages to St Mary's spring and a church image of Michael. It formed a church-manor pair with its chapelry, Queen Edith's soke-centre of Ridlington (Andrew). However, adjacent Preston's name suggests an early church-place also, and immediately south of Uppingham is the Bishop of Lincoln's manor of Lyddington (Andrew) (see also Upper Welland).

Edith's manors of Oakham and Hambleton look like poles of a Vale of Catmose estate divided off from a larger territory dependent on the king's manor of Empingham, pivotal to *Roteland* and where St Peter's churchyard lies on the south of a playing-card shaped settlement core, with 'Old Prebendal House' sandwiched between the church and a chapel of St Botolph. Oakham had fairs of John the Baptist and the Invention of the Holy Cross ('St Helen's-in-the-Spring'. Helen was patron of a pilgrimage chapel at nearby Langham). Oakham and Hambleton's churches were Domesday possessions of a King's Clerk, Albert of Lorraine. This marks minster status for one of them, probably **Hambleton** (Andrew), mother church of the royal chapel of St Peter at Stamford and probably also once of Whitwell, named after the spring which flowed under its hilltop church of Michael.

Parochial topography around **Stamford** clearly predates its attachment to Lincolnshire. The boundaries of St Michael's, one of fourteen medieval parishes, make sense in relation to those of the Castertons (Peter and Paul at Great Casterton, a Romano-British walled settlement) and Ryhall, with its local saint Tybba. St Michael's also spans the Welland, extending into, and thus again predating the soke of Peterborough, as far as Wittering, named from the Witheringas, a people of the Tribal Hidage.

A further folk-name, the Hwicce, was preserved in Witchley Hundred, chiefly along the Welland between Stamford and the Eye Brook. **Barrowden** ('tumuli *dūn*') (Peter) was the Domesday royal soke centre. North Luffenham (John Baptist) belonged to the Queen. Here the advowson went with Oakham Castle, while a churchyard-chapel of Mary had its own burial ground. Tixover's isolated church beside the Welland – a chapel of Ketton, first-named royal Domesday manor of Northamptonshire and Rutland – has an extremely rare patron, St Faith.

East and north of Rutland, extensive districts were served by the churches of **Bourne** (Peter and Paul), supposedly patrimony of Hereward the Wake, and **Grantham**, another possession of Queen Edith. Its enshrined patron Wulfram arrived in the tenth century: the church had a rare chantry of Peter, and another of John the Baptist (see Bottesford, below). A number of seventh-century *parochiæ* along the Trent complete the circle, beginning with the minster parish of **Southwell** (Mary), supposedly founded by Paulinus, *circa* 627. The others follow.

1. 'Outer Leicestershire'
Trent Valley/'Hreope'
Leicestershire's best-known early church, **Breedon**'s hilltop minster founded in an Iron-Age fort by the *princeps* Frithuric *circa* 700 (Stenton 1970, 158; Foot 2006, 275), associates more easily with Derbyshire. A strong boundary divided its medieval parish from those of the lower Soar, and significantly coincides with the watershed which also encloses its western, Derbyshire neighbour Melbourne (Michael). A royal demesne manor in 1066, Melbourne had extensive berewicks on the opposite side of the Trent which interlocked with outlying portions of **Derby**'s parishes of Michael and Peter (two of six churches there in 1086). Derby's earlier name, Northworthy, locates it more easily within the Melbourne estate than in relation to Tamworth, a presumption based on Breedon's foundation by a prince of the Tomsaetan, 'dwellers on the Tame'.

Westward there is no clear demarcation between Melbourne's estate and the large area linked manorially and ecclesiastically to **Repton** (Wi[g]stan), five miles away. (Was Leicestershire's boundary drawn to separate

Breedon's 20 hides, previously joined to Repton's 30?) Repton's minster was operating by *circa* 600 (according to tradition), or *circa* 700 from a further land-grant by Frithuric, and became a royal mausoleum (Biddle 1992) – Wigstan was enshrined there. Its assets included lead mines in the Peak, and its *parochia* appears to have included another minster at **Burton-on-Trent** (Tringham 2003, 3-5, 48-53). Here too the Trent is spanned, and Burton's ancient parish, pushing into Needwood, comes tantalisingly close to that of **Hanbury**. The latter, on a major Trent tributary, the Derwent, was Wærburh's first burial-place. Together with nearby Tetbury it is best seen in the context of a Mercian royal territory.

Burton, like neighbouring Newton, Barton, Walton, Stretton, and Stanton, has a name indicating subsidiarity; a reeve's *tūn*, perhaps? Repton's name hints at territorial identity: 'hill of the people called Hreope or Hrype'. How they related to the 'dwellers on the Tame' is difficult to assess. Their name is Germanic, while '*saetan*' peoples have been characterised as occupying land where British populations remained an important part of the social mix.

Breedon's patrons are Mary and a prince Hardwulf, one of four saints venerated there. The others were Fretheric (Frithuric), Cotta, and Benna. Beonna (another form of the shortened name), ruler of East Anglia *circa* 758, may be Beornred, briefly ruler of Mercia in 757 after the murder at Seckington of king Æthelbald (Archibald, Fenwick and Cowell 1996, 1-19). However, Breedon's original patron was probably Andrew, as at Burton and also Peterborough, whose monks established the minster (one of Breedon's townships was Andreskirk). A shared association with 'Celtic' saints is striking: David at Repton, Modwen at Burton, Brigid at Stanton on a principal approach to Breedon (whose name is a British-Anglian hybrid). Margery Tranter has pointed out the place-names Walton, Bretby and Ingleby (Tranter 2003). An intriguing Welsh tradition described Guthlac, *alumnus* of Repton and son of Penwalh ('chief of the British speakers'), sojourning at Llangollen in Powys, perhaps in exile (Jones 2015).

Mease valley
Repton's *parochia* included places in the catchment of the Mease, which flows into the Trent less than a mile downstream from the confluence with the Tame. Here are the

Seals (Netherseal, Overseal), townships complicatedly divided between Derbyshire and Leicestershire and interdigitating with the large parish of **Ashby de la Zouch** (Helen). Together they make a compact unit, a further such unit including Measham in Derbyshire, a royal Domesday manor, and bordering Ashby's southern neighbour Packington in Leicestershire (Helen also). The 'ash-tree place' had a St Anne's well and the local place-name Prestop, (?)'priest's valley'. Were Ashby and Measham a church-manor pair?

Anker-Sence drainage
Sence

The southernmost vills of the Mease group link more easily with a royal estate dominating the basin of the Sence, chief tributary of the Anker, itself a tributary of the Tame. (Appleby, problematically, divides between this group and Measham's.) The administrative centre, **Market Bosworth**, 'of the Queen's Holding' in 1086, was surrounded by clustered chapelries and relational and specialist vills. They include Congerstone ('king's *tūn*'), Carlton, Barton, Shenton, '*tūn* on the Sence', and the 'new hall', Newbold Verdon. (Angus Winchester has linked *boðl* names to bode-service - watching duty (Winchester 2008, 18-19). Newbold is on a three-way watershed at the district's edge.) Bosworth church (Peter and Paul) had long-surviving collegiality (a priest and deacon in 1086), a curvilinear yard, and a nearby spring. Sibson, 'Sigeberht's *dūn*' (Botolph), on the Sence looks a likely secular counterpart, with adjacent Wellsborough, 'the wheel hill', as a hypothetical place of assembly and ritual – around a henge? Sibson's parish reached **Mancetter** (Manduesseum) on Watling Street, where the walled settlement has produced a mid-fifth century coin, while St Peter's and the manor house stand within a related fort. Sheepy parish, from which Sibson may have separated, spanned the road, the Anker, and the shire boundary, pre-dating it therefore. Mancetter and its chapelries Atherstone (Æthelred's *tūn*) and Oldbury (named from a hillfort), all in Warwickshire, complete a coherent territory and offer a plausible narrative: a Romano-British Christian presence relocated to Mancetter's fort but eclipsed as secular power moved to Atherstone and then Bosworth. If Æthelred is the Mercian ruler who agreed a boundary with the Danes and married Alfred's daughter Æthelflæd, both

Atherstone's preservation within English Mercia and Bosworth's membership of the Queen's Holding make sense. Eight miles up Watling Street at the Anker's confluence with the Tame is Tamworth, the Mercian royal vill to which Bosworth/Mancetter may ultimately have looked. Edith, sainted princess-abbess of Polesworth upstream from Tamworth, is the noteworthy patron of Orton-on-the-Hill, another major early parish. Possibly Polesworth should be considered part of the Bosworth/Mancetter entity.

Anker

A second group of parishes occupies the Anker's headwater basin, flanked by the *parochiæ* of Coventry, Monks Kirby, and Barwell. Like Sheepy, Hinckley parish (Mary) overlapped Watling Street. Hinckley's chapelries interlocked with those of Higham on the Hill (Peter and Paul), making a religious/lay pair. Higham's boundaries in turn continue those of Nuneaton (earlier Eaton, 'river *tūn*') in Warwickshire, which with Hinckley belonged in 1066 to Harding, Butler to Queen Emma in 1062 and son of another royal minister, Eadnoth the Staller. Nuneaton's dedication (Nicholas) looks late; its twelfth-century fair, on Holy Cross day, May 3, suggests Helen, but the nunnery commemorated Mary. Boundary evidence supports the further inclusion in this territory of Bulkington and Wolvey in Warwickshire, plus in Leicestershire another church/manor pair, Burbage ('ridgetop *burh*', a Domesday manor of Coventry Abbey, probably given by Earl Leofric or Godiva) and Aston Flamville.

Half-way between Mancetter and Venonae (High Cross), Watling Street is crossed by the Harrow stream. The *hærg* or 'shrine', a tribal meeting place, probably lay near one of the head-springs west of Hinckley, perhaps at Hollycroft or Wyken. The latter, like Higham, stands on the spur dividing the Bosworth and Hinckley districts. Possibly these were two parts of a single territory, served by churches of Peter and Paul, and Mary respectively.

Upper Avon/'Lillingas'

Misterton is on everyone's list of minster candidates. Testing its claims necessitates a preliminary look at a minster in Warwickshire. They lay in adjoining compartments of the complex topography of the upper Avon, which was overridden by two large estates and their suspected *parochiæ*. These in turn ignored and therefore probably predate the shire boundaries. On the Avon itself was Newnham, one of the 'new-steads' assigned to the villa-replacement phase of English settlement. Its religious pair was the minster at **Monks Kirby**, earlier Kirkbury (Mary), rebuilt in 1077 with two priests, and Giles added to its dedication. Chapelries known or inferred included Smite, named after the Avon tributary which Kirkbury overlooked. Smite, in turn, had its own chapelry – Brinklow, its church on the hill whose summit, a suitable pre-Christian devotional focus, provided a sight-line for the Fosse. The interlinked estate and parish probably extended ten miles north to south, reaching to the Dunsmore ridge and the outskirts of Rugby. At the northern end the ancient parish took in some – probably once all – of the vills around Claybrooke on the Leicestershire side of the Avon/Soar watershed, the hypothesised *territorium* of Venonae where the Fosse crosses Watling Street (Phythian-Adams 1978). Northernmost was Sharnford. Here royal lordship survived in 1086 as king's alms-land enjoyed by Aelfric the Priest, with another manor in the hands of the bishop. Newnham's owners on the eve of the Conquest were likely relatives of Earl Leofric, their lands delimited in the east by an Avon tributary, the Swift. Lutterworth lies on its upper reaches, but the Leofricings' lands ended at Watling Street.

Misterton's name, *tūn* with, or provisioning a minster, is much discussed, but rarely in its local context. Lutterworth, facing Misterton across the valley, looks like the central place of a district whose antiquity it evidenced by place-names like Walton and Walcote, *tūn* and *cot* of British-speakers (the latter three-quarters of a mile from Misterton), Wakeley, 'watchers' burial-mound', and Misterton itself.

Misterton church is small but its medieval patron was Andrew. Some curvature in the churchyard perimeter could be residual in a replanned landscape. Misterton Hall's lake draws attention to the volume of water entering the Swift here; Andrew's baptismal association could be relevant. A similar point may be made about John the Baptist's patronage of the riverside hospital below Lutterworth which had springs within its curtilege – the spot where, at the end of the Middle Ages, John Wyclif's bones were cast into the river (Walsham 2010).

Six of the diocesan bishop's 14 Domesday lands in Leicestershire were in Misterton parish (at Poultney, Cotes de Val, and Misterton itself) or adjoining it (Walcote, Kimcote, and Swinford), 27.25 carucates in all (half, 13.5 carucates, at Kimcote) – the endowment of a decayed minster? A round 30 carucates is achieved by adding in the two-and-a-half carucates of king's alms-land which Arnbern the Priest held at Swinford. The Misterton lands were all held by a Godric, otherwise unknown in Leicestershire. If he and Arnbern held former collegiate land, this might explain the two medieval rectories at Misterton, a feature shared with Hallaton and Sheepy.

Misterton lacks Lutterworth's imposing site just across the valley, its church (Mary) opening onto a large yard. Maybe that was the minster, provisioned by Misterton. The jury is out, especially now Google Earth shows cropmarks on the hill between Misterton and Walcote. Also Lutterworth's 13 carucates, with two each at Misterton and Catthorpe, were held by Earl Ralph, perhaps by gift of his uncle King Edward or by right of his wife Gytha. Another secular-ecclesiastical pairing seems more plausible, serving a block of interlocked vills from Lutterworth to the Avon and from Watling Street to the Swift/Soar watershed.

Much commends a larger territory occupying the whole upper Avon drainage as far as Crick, Naseby, and Husbands Bosworth, where a neolithic causewayed enclosure points to the antiquity of the watershed as a boundary. The rising lands south of the Avon could be characterised as the pastoral counterpart of more arable country around Lutterworth. Crossing points at Stanford and Swinford (the latter indicating stock movements) strengthen the idea. Just south of the Avon is Lilbourne, which together with land on the west of Watling Street was held after 1066 by Earl Aubrey, perhaps the vestige of a royal manor. Lilbourne had a castle and a Sunday market, and was one of the few places where foreign merchants could buy wool through the Leicester market. The sheep probably grazed the slopes below Crick, whose simplex name (Old Welsh *creic*) describes the hill crowned by its church (and largely curvilinear yard) of Margaret, the shepherdess saint. Lilbourne looks plausible as such a territory's administrative centre, forming a lordship/church pair with Crick but with another devotional *locus* closer to hand. This is Holywell within the defences of

Romano-British Tripontium. Holywell chapel, fronting Watling Street, vanished before the Reformation, the site occupied by Caves Inn, now Coton Farm.

A possible pre-Conquest religious presence at Tripontium, suggested to me by Peter Liddle, prompts comparisons with Mancetter. Like Mancetter and the Sence, Tripontium ('Three Bridges') seems the natural fulcrum for an upper Avon entity which included the town's *territorium*. Lilbourne's name shares its first element with 'Lilling', known from the Claybrooke estate. Perhaps the 'Lillingas' – ancestors of Leofric's cousins at Newnham, even – acquired a post-Roman lordship spanning Watling Street as well as the Avon.

A further scenario sees the Kirkbury *parochia* taking in the vills around Venonæ as a result of the Leofric family's ancestors pushing their power northwards at the expense of the lords of Croft (see under 'Inner Leicestershire'). Leofric's father was Earl of the Hwicce, the Severn/Avon people whose bishop-seat was Worcester. Lichfield diocese's medieval salient across north-eastern Warwickshire has a strange shape, with the rest of the county in the Worcester diocese. Leofric is chiefly associated with Coventry, but his home ground may have lain more centrally within the Avon's catchment area. The northern boundary of the Hwicce's British predecessors, the Dobunni, may have lain further north than conventionally understood, making them neighbours of the Corieltauvi.

Upper Welland

Parishes and lordships spanning the Welland suggest a further territory predating the shire (Roffe 1996, 107-20). Neighbouring Theddingworth and Lubenham, Leicestershire, had daughter settlements in Northamptonshire (Hothorpe and Thorpe Lubenham). Lubenham's looks like a detachment from East Farndon. That in turn has wider implications for lordship since Lubenham's boundary with Great Bowden on the Leicestershire bank carries across the Welland as Thorpe Lubenham's boundary with Little Bowden. Little Bowden's scarp-slope chapelry of Little Oxendon (Helen) fits between Farndon and Great Oxendon, the latter's eastern boundary continuing that of Little Bowden. A relationship between Lubenham and Bowden is significant because Great Bowden (Peter and Paul) was

a royal vill in 1086 and head of a soke, while Lubenham's topographically linked northern neighbours included Gumley, a Mercian council meeting place in the reign of Offa.

Godmund's *lēah* (Helen) would fit a hunting lodge, with the royal residence within easy reach – at Lubba's *hoh* perhaps, or even what became Market Harborough. **St Mary in Arden**, Harborough's now redundant mother church, belonged *circa* 1200 to the rector of Great Bowden (Peter and Paul), within which Harborough lay. Though clerks were uncertain whether it was *capella* or *ecclesia*, it was actually the Pentecostal pilgrimage church for communities as far away as Kibworth in the thirteenth century ('as is the custom of the country') and as late as the fifteenth it was regarded as Kibworth's 'mother church'.[11] Much points to a minster on a pre-Christian sacred site. Its large, curvilinear yard overlooks the Welland which divided Great from Little Bowden. Eighteenth-century excavation for a family grave within the outline of the vanished medieval church nave unearthed quantities of cremation material, Romano-British or prehistoric. A short distance north, many Roman coins (but very little building material) have been found in gardens along The Ridgeway, leading to the hilltop overlooking Harborough, an area dotted with springs. The coins may mark a Romano-British religious site, possibly later occupied by a periodic rural fair, given finds of Anglo-Saxon metalwork. 'Arden' is from a British/Gaulish word meaning 'high' (*cf.* the Ardennes and Arden forest), suggesting Ardwinna as the deity venerated. Harborough's medieval street fairs were notable. Harborough's patron, Denis, is a fair saint from his cult at Paris. However, Denis was martyred on Montmartre and it is conceivable that Harborough's foundation brought a hilltop fair down to the Welland crossing.

The extent of Bowden soke's 300 hides, largely corresponding to Gartree Hundred, is closely matched south of the Welland by three hundreds of Northamptonshire. One was attached to **Rothwell** (Holy Trinity) – named from a (?red) spring and like Harborough an important fair place. It was the soke centre to Desborough's royal hall. Rothwell hundred occupied much of the long, thin, east-west upper drainage of the Ise, a tributary of the

11 Michael Wood kindly alerted me to this from his research for his television series 'Story of England'.

Nene which separates the Welland valley from the fan-shaped basin surrounding Brixworth. Overlooking the Ise from the south are the intriguingly named Maidwell and Lamport ('long market').

Several other churches in Gartree Hundred had dependent chapels. Notwithstanding Kibworth Harcourt's relationship to Mary in Arden, its dedication (Wilfrid) hints at landholding by bishops of Leicester attending the king at Gumley and Great Glen (see under 'Inner Leicestershire'). Conceivably Kibworth was exchanged for Knighton (see below). Church Langton (Peter), hilltop mother church of the Langton settlements, is highly visible, close to a prehistoric circle (if that explains Whirlygig field) and a St Anne's well, and a mile from the transitional villa/early-Anglian site on the Langton Brook. Billesdon's curvilinear yard, its parish's position abutting the ridgeway (marked by Coplow), and its midsummer dedication (John the Baptist) hint likewise at an older ritual *locus*. Billesdon's name links it to a lost Bilton in Hallaton (see below) and suits seasonal stock movement.

Towards the eastern end of Gartree hundred, Medbourne's curvilinear yard stands at a convergence of routeways, including a side-road from Port Hill on the Gartree Road where an Anglian cemetery in 'The Old Churchyard' followed a Romano-British settlement. Weston and Sutton, south of the Welland, may have names relating to Medbourne. The king kept Medbourne's advowson, having granted the manor away, but the church lacked the status of St Michael's, **Hallaton**. The parishes intermixed in a probable lay-clerical pair. Hallaton had two rectories, high-status burials (a pre-Conquest grave slab is in the north aisle), and a local saint Morrell whose hilltop chapel and cemetery site overlooking his spring is the starting point of the annual bottle-kicking and hare-pie scramble. It overlay a rectilinear feature reminiscent of a small rural Romano-British shrine. It is also close to an Iron Age temple site where ritual feasting and deposition of coins and fine metalwork was practised (even then a long-standing custom, judging by a broken Bronze Age rapier found nearby) (Jones 2007, 63, 129-31). Hallaton's likely minster status is underlined by tenurial links to the north and the Bilton-Billesdon connection. Also within Hallaton's putative

orbit was Welham on the Welland (Andrew), together with its chapels. Its name may contain the term *wēoh*, or shrine, and *hām* suggests this was the hall site for a territorial unit bounded by the Welland and the Langton and Eye Brooks, administered from Medbourne.

Alternatively, this unit should be associated with Rutland. The queen's hilltop manor of Whatborough, just east of Tilton and at the source of the Chater, hints at this. One of the Eye Brook's sources is a spring just south of St Peter's, Tilton, where the Humber/ Wash watershed is crossed by a ridgeway. Hallaton looks like the mother church for the district – except that in the south-east angle is **Bringhurst**, whose hilltop church has a curvilinear yard around which the village's houses are grouped. Peter Liddle may be right in suggesting it represents an early monastic site. Its dedicatee by 1754, Nicholas, hardly supports that – unless he replaced a more important patron. Bringhurst's chapelry of Easton Magna has Andrew, and that aligns Bringhurst (and Welham) with the Andrew dedications in Rutland. They begin immediately on the other side of the Eye Brook with the episcopal palace church of Lyddington and its probable former chapelry Stoke Dry (east bank) and Stoke's west bank hamlet Holyoaks. These are among a string of religiously significant places along the Eye valley. Others are Prestley Hill, Prestgrave, Priest Hill, *Thor's leāh* below Uppingham, and Bradley Priory Holy Well. Two hoards of Late Roman coins are recorded in Holyoaks Wood, adjoining Mirabel hermitage. Re-use of a shrine-site might be suspected.

2. Northern Leicestershire
Upper Wreake (Eye)/Framland

Melton Mowbray (Mary) had several large chapelries and probably others which had gained parochial status by the thirteenth century. The parish overlapped substantially with a multiple estate acquired by Geoffrey de la Guerche from his Leofricing father-in-law (see Newnham, above). The 'middle *tūn*' indicates a central place, effectively the equivalent of a 'king's *tūn*', an administrative and market centre. Melton may have attracted a pre-Conquest mint. It had a Burton (Lazars) and a church *tūn*, Kirby Bellars, whose name, location at a Romano-British settlement site, and dedication, Peter and Paul, point to some significant status within the estate.

Another candidate religious centre to partner Melton's secular *caput* interposes between Melton and its detached members Eastwell and Goadby Marwood. This is **Scalford**, which on one interpretation of a tenth-century list of pilgrimage places had its own saint, Egelwin. A copious spring, a source of the Wreake, flowed from just below the churchyard (?at the 'shallow ford') – a potential focus of devotion and/or baptism. Martin was patron saint by 1754, and there was a Michaelmas fair, but there was also a medieval devotional image of Peter and Paul. One of William I's servants had a small manor here, a likely last vestige of royal lordship; most of the parish had been Earl Waltheof's.

A royal hall site offers itself at Waltham-on the-Wolds. Barry Cox interprets '*wald hām*' as a hunting lodge (Cox 2001), and between it and Scalford are Chadwell and Wycomb, Domesday members of the king's Rothley manor. Wycomb is one of several places named '*wīc* (?for *vicus*) *hām*' associated with Romano-British administrative units and adjoins Goadby Marwood, a small Romano-British town. The vills of the Upper Wreak divide neatly east and west, with Melton and Waltham in the western half. Maybe Waltham was the summer hall and the permanent hall should be sought elsewhere, say Wymondham, which lies centrally in the eastern half.

The drainage of the Wreake (known as the Eye above Melton) extends east to Market Overton/Thistleton, thus including northernmost Rutland. Overton's church lies within the Romano-British enceinte associated with a temple of Veteris (?The Old One) at a source of the Witham, and its locational name best relates to Wymondham. Both had Peter and Paul as patrons. (Elsewhere in Wymondham was Burrowchurch chapel, perhaps identical with St Peter's chapel at 'Burgh'.) Wymondham with Stapleford constituted a substantial, 48-carucate estate of Henry of Ferrers in 1086. Its major northern neighbour is **Buckminster** (John Baptist), probably its ecclesiastical pair, a Domesday possession of the Bishop of Lincoln. Bucca's church is built into a westward slope with a modern east-end crypt extension which just might have developed an existing burial place. Like the other east Framland parishes, Buckminster's boundary runs along the Witham side of the watershed, following Sewstern Lane.

The point where the watershed turns to divide the Wreake from the Devon is linked to the lane at Wyville, '*wēoh* stream', by King Lud's Entrenchments. The boundary line is then followed eastward across the Witham valley north of Skillington, so that it is tempting to see Buckminster as the one-time mother church of an area split later between Leicestershire and Lincolnshire.

Upper Devon and related drainages

Northernmost Framland sits oddly on the headwaters of the south-flowing Devon. **Bottesford** (Mary), the 'palace ford', sits between two major Domesday manors: Orston, a royal soke centre a mile or so east of Romano-British Margidunum near the Trent, with a boundary linked to Bottesford's, and Grantham, centre of an estate of Queen Edith (see 'External Ring' above). Bottesford and its dependencies form the northern end of a string of parishes carved from an existing arable landscape, judging by their boundaries. On one side the scarp of the Wolds, ending at Belvoir, cuts them off from the rest of Leicestershire; on the other they face a similar block in Nottinghamshire, grouped around Orston. Despite Orston's two Domesday priests, the more impressive church is Bottesford's, in a curvilinear yard half-enclosed by the Devon, its west door beside the 'palace ford' and its rectory in similarly large grounds on the other bank.

The regularity of these parishes and townships – possibly a result of Danish re-planning, ends where Long Clawson meets the upper Smite. From there the wedge of townships northwards as far as the Cropwells, and west to the Fosse, has an integrity. One of the Cropwell manors was a Domesday possession of the Archbishop of York (representing the canons of Southwell minster), with detached wold-land at Hickling. Old Dalby may not fit this block easily, but its church of John the Baptist attracts notice for its curvilinear yard, and as the nearest to the summit where the wold scarp meets the watersheds of the Smite, Fairham and Leake. The site of Vernemeton is close by (see below).

Lower Wreake and lower Soar

A striking feature of the medieval geography of the district along the lower Soar and lower Wreake, extending into High Leicestershire as far as the Humber/Wash watershed, was the complex interlinking of places subject manorially or ecclesiastically to Barrow, Rothley, and Loughborough. Several were shared between Barrow and Rothley or between Barrow and Loughborough, sometimes with third-party tenants. A handful of Rothley chapelries beyond the watershed may have resulted from land acquisitions, but in general it is hard to avoid the conclusion that behind this network lies a single territorial entity with the three neighbouring *capite* at its core (cf. Loughborough's economic hinterland 1397-1431, Postles 2015, 190, fig 8).

All enjoyed high-status in 1086: Rothley was a royal manor, Barrow-on-Soar had been assigned to Earl Hugh of Chester as successor to 'Earl' Harold, and the manor of Loughborough was also in Hugh's possession, having previously been shared by 'five thegns' (conceivably servants of Edward the Confessor). As well as their widespread sokes and chapelries to the east, both Rothley and Barrow had home parishes which extended into Charnwood. Since Harold was in fact king (though never recognised as such by William) it is not unreasonable to see Barrow and Rothley as two components of a royal estate, the first hived off to create a stopping place for Hugh en route to and from his palatine shire of Chester via his castle at Tutbury. Rothley is reminiscent of Gumley, well-placed to have been a royal hunting lodge on the edge of Charnwood. Barrow, 'at the glade', on its hill overlooking the Soar, is an intuitive focus for ritual, perhaps associated with a royal hall. Its titular cult, Holy Trinity, possibly represents a development of, or parallel to Christ Church, a frequent naming in the Conversion period. However, by 1086 **Rothley** (Mary) appears the more important ecclesiastical centre, with its Anglian churchyard cross and a chapel of the murdered Mercian prince Wigstan ('the churchyard of St Wystane in the temple of Rothley', Lloyd 1973, 41). Loughborough, 'Luhheda's *burh*', destined to become the district's market town, had the smallest soke of the three, but like the others it spanned the Soar. Its *burh* ('defended enclosure') is perhaps to be associated with the church's large curvilinear yard, not impossibly enclosing an early monastery. The local name Prestwold may point in the same direction. Nevertheless, with its patron saints Peter and Paul, Loughborough looks equally suitable as the reeve's vill and trading-place relative to a king's hall at Barrow and its attendant minster

at Rothley. Boundaries support a further or alternative relationship with **Shepshed**, royally owned and still hidated in 1086, whose church (Botolph) occupies a spur site on the eastern parish margin approached by Butthole Lane. Shepshed's boundaries are continued by those of Belton (John Baptist), whose rectilinear yard faces a large marketplace. At nearby Hathern, Harrow (*hærg*?) Lane leads off towards the 'Sheep's Head'. Christianisation of a sacred place makes better topographical sense of Shepshed than 'sheep's headland'.

The sokes of Loughborough, Barrow, and Rothley, like that of Gartree, may have brought together more than one earlier entity, but their components fit together too neatly to ignore the existence of an underlying territory. For example, the townships east of the Soar and south of the Wreake fall into two blocks, divided by Ridgemere Lane (mere = boundary) from the Wreake to Billesdon Coplow on the Soar/Welland watershed. At the Wreake end of the northern block is Queniborough (Mary), 'the queen's *burh*', with its probable manor/church partner, **South Croxton**, where the Bishop of Lincoln held one of the two manors. Croxton's hilltop church (John Baptist) contains a possible fragment of Anglo-Saxon sculptured stone. Other probable early churches are Gaddesby (Michael) and Owston (Andrew). On the upland margin is Burrough hillfort, locale of the Whitsun festivities recorded by Leland *circa* 1540 and difficult to contextualise without a religious element. Like Halstead ('holding place'), it was a natural corralling point for cattle driven from lowland vills to summer pastures. Immediately east of Burrough-on-the-Hill is Somerby. Harold Fox saw this as a natural transhumance landscape.

Tucked beside Queniborough but divided from it by the Ridgemere is Syston (Peter and Paul), which with its probable dependencies occupies the lower end of the southern block. The upper-end is taken up by Keyham, High Leicestershire's only *hām*; Beeby (Guthlac), 'bee-keepers' *bȳ*; Leofric's manor of Scraptoft and its ancient mother church Humberstone, 'Hunbeorht's stone' (Peter and Paul); and, surrounding Keyham on three sides, Hungarton (Botolph) with its chapelries Ingarsby and Quenby, 'the queen's or women's *bȳ*'. Keyham, sole member of Barrow and Rothley in the southern block, shared parochial rights with Hungarton in Baggrave – significant because

Baggrave is on the far side of Ridgemere, apparently carved out of Croxton.

In summary, this block looks like a bipartite estate of the Queen (reflecting that of the king across the Soar), with halls at Queniborough and Keyham, a church centre at Croxton, and the reeve at Syston. Belgrave's relationship with the estate is discussed under Inner Leicestershire.

Lower Soar, Leake drainage

It is probable that the hypothesised Lower Soar territory spanned and therefore predated the shire boundary along the river. Harold held manors on both banks. Approaching the Trent, the Soar's left bank is occupied by townships and manors associated with Shepshed and Loughborough while on the right bank sit *Kings*ton-on-Soar (Wilfrid), its mother church Ratcliffe (Holy Trinity), and its 'Sutton'. The natural extent of the *regio* would take in the vills along the Leake, which joins the Trent at Kingston. These, including Leake itself, West (Helen) and East (Mary), interpose between the Soar (and almost immediately the Trent) and a group of vills at the valley's upper end which comprised the detached wold division of Nottinghamshire's Broxstowe hundred. They also face Leicestershire lands across the Fosse. The rest of the upper Leake valley is occupied by the large parish of Wymeswold (church, Mary; fair, Peter and Paul), which looks like a continuation of the Loughborough-related townships of Prestwold and Hoton.

A plausible hall-place for the Ratcliffe and Leake group is neighbouring Gotham (Lawrence), to which Barton and Clifton on the Trent seem related. These occupy the angle between the Leake watershed, the Trent and the Flawforth Brook. On the other bank of the stream is its eponymous, isolated and ruined church (Peter) at the junction of three parishes. Coming this close to Nottingham confronts the investigator with an inescapable challenge. Turning the map on its head, how far south would one construe a pre-shiring territory based on Nottingham?

The Lower Soar *regio*'s outer bounds must remain a matter for future research, but its possible post-Roman origins are clear. A Romano-British settlement developed at Quorn, on the opposite bank of the Soar from Barrow but in its parish, and Stanford-on-

Soar's church was built over a villa, respecting its layout. Moreover, where the young Leake stream crosses the line of the Fosse (in the Nottinghamshire parish of Willoughby-on-the-Wolds which fills the narrow gap between the Fosse and Wymeswold parish) lay Vernemeton, 'the great grove', with its attendant settlement on the road itself.

St Bartholomew's, Quorndon, recalls a characteristic of English dedications honouring the temple-appropriating apostle: their statistically positive, geographical correlation with places whose names are indicative of non or pre-Christian ritual or worship. The *bēaru* of Barrow, Quorndon's mother church, might have functioned as a sacred grove overlooking the Soar. Further off, in Wymeswold parish, Barry Cox has identified two 'Harrow', *hærg* names, and two from *alh*, also meaning 'shrine' or 'temple' (Cox 2004). The *Alhfleot*, 'temple stream', must be the one which rises at Six Hills and forms Wymeswold's eastern boundary before passing Wysall, the *hōh* or 'spur' of the *wēoh* (*wīh* or *wīg*), yet another Old English term for a temple. At a stretch, all these names might have related to Vernemeton, whose site was indeed appropriated for Christian use, Bartholomew-fashion. After burials there with Germanic-style grave-goods came a chapel, on a hilltop known as The Wells, and annual games (Camden 1722, 531, 541, 575). Peter Liddle tells me the site has yielded Anglo-Saxon metalwork of a type associated with clerical vestments. Moreover, land at Willoughby-on-the-Wolds was held in 1066 by Ernwy, probably the king's clerk of the same name who held decayed minsters elsewhere in England. This hints at a valuable chapel endowment – if not also an income from pilgrims – which survived into the eleventh century. One possible factor for the continuity of Vernemeton as a devotional place is the longevity in this district of communities whose Romano-British identity was recognised by landlords describing themselves as Anglian. They include Walton-on-the-Wolds, *Cumberdale* in Wymeswold, *Cumberlea* in Seagrave, and *Tralleswellehul* in Burton-on-the-Wolds.

Vernemeton stands at a transitional point on the Fosse, a meeting point for those among the Corieltauvi, 'peoples of the rivers', who inhabited the Trent and Soar valleys. A trading place is also plausible. Venonae and the temple at Market Overton would fit the same model – as might some as yet undetected pre-Christian structure beneath the church at Breedon.

3. Inner Leicestershire/'Legora' South

Another issue dogging any presumption of a territory centred on Barrow, Rothley and Loughborough is its relationship with early medieval Leicester, whose post-Roman desertion is under re-examination – and the same applies south of Leicester, too. Here the starting place for reconstructing the territorial geography is **Croft**, probably the Mercian council assembly place in 836. Archangel Michael's church sits not on the summit of Croft's strikingly high and isolated hill, but by its stream.[12] Stephen Mitchell suggests the *cræft* ('machine') was a mill powered by a Roman lock feeding Leicester's aqueduct, the Raw Dyke (Mitchell 2009). Whatever royal estate supported the assembly's needs had been fragmented by 1066. Eleven carucates at Croft itself were almost equally divided between the antecessor of William I's castellan and sheriff, Hugh de Grandmesnil (possibly Earl Waltheof or his shire reeve), and the royal servant Harding, succeeded here as at Hinckley by Earl Aubrey of Northumbria. Detached parts of Harding's holding, associated in the 13th century by the advowson of St Michael's, lay in Broughton Astley at Sutton-in-the-Elms (the 'south *tūn*'). This transgresses the arbitrary boundary along the Fosse which divides parishes and townships from Monks Kirby to Narborough.

Other cross-Fosse, and more importantly, cross-Soar tenures linked Stoney Stanton and Leire, and Sapcote and Frolesworth, while parts of Croft's near-neighbour Huncote lay in Cosby – presumably the areas later known as detached parts of **Narborough** parish. In a further example of separated lay and religious functions, Narborough was a manorial constituent of Huncote while Huncote was a chapelry of Narborough (All Saints, but with a midsummer fair of John the Baptist). The 'northern enclosure' seems relative to Croft. Its inclusion with Huncote and Cosby in an earlier estate of Croft would also make sense of the otherwise odd egg-timer shape of Croft (with Broughton) and Thurlaston with Normanton,

medieval parishes which paid their tithes to Croft. Since Thurlaston and Normanton reached, as Huncote and Narborough did, into the heart of Leicester's royal forest, it is easy to see Croft as a base for hunting like Rothley and Gumley (see below). Cosby's ancient patron Helen was the model of queenship (the church was part of the endowment of St Augustine's, Leicester, below), and on the Fosse where Cosby's parish meets Croft was the dynastically and supernaturally significant Guthlac stone where the men of Guthlaxton wapentake assembled. Bearing in mind the seemingly humble status of Huna's *cot* and the modest size of St Michael's, it is worth considering whether Narborough's *burh* might have surrounded an early monastic site, as suggested for Loughborough. The Bishop of Lincoln's Domesday manor at Leire also has interest because its name points to a spring, a source of the *Legra*, the river (otherwise the Soar) which gave its name to Leicester. Conceivably the spring had been sacred to the river-deity. However, the bishop's successors did not enjoy the advowson of the church, whose siting within the settlement looks conventional.

Fragmentation may have been accompanied by settlement shifts. A lost Domesday manor, Legham (presumably sharing the first element of its name with Leire), and a farm-name Langham, in Cosby, hint at earlier arrangements. Some slight survivals of royal rights persisted in Croft's neighbourhood. On its south-western flank is Stoney Stanton and the latter's probable daughter settlement, Sapcote; immediately west of Croft is Potters Marston, whose common boundary with Stoney Stanton is interdigitated. Potters and stone-cutters would be natural specialist communities on an important royal estate. Stoney Stanton and its outliers at Primethorpe and Sutton were held in 1086 by William I's Steward or Bursar, Robert Dispensator. The clincher was also at Sutton: land of the king's alms.

Further signs of fragmentation are the two oddly-shaped, dovetailing groups of settlements further west which coalesce around Barwell and Kirkby. Despite its proximity to Croft, Potters Marston, together with its western neighbour Elmesthorpe formed a long salient of the parish of **Barwell** (Mary), three-and-a-half miles to the west, of which they were both chapelries. However, Elmesthorpe's

---

12 Lloyd 1973 listed Croft's patron as Peter, which would suit the royal hall, but did not specify his source.

name and the shape and character of its northern boundary make it clear that it was a daughter settlement of Earl Shilton. Barwell's six miles wide parish surrounded Earl Shilton on three sides, but the latter was a chapelry of Barwell's northern neighbour **Kirkby Mallory**. The obvious conclusion is that Barwell and Kirkby, whose medieval parish was similar in extent, were two parts of an larger, earlier entity, whose coherent shape is demonstrated with the addition of Barwell's further chapelry of Stapleton and Peckleton, another chapelry of Kirkby.

This does not look like a straight-forward secular-religious pairing, however. Certainly Barwell, by its name and its gift to the canons of Coventry, appeals to an intuitive guess that it occupies an ancient site of worship or ritual. Kirkby, 'the church bȳ', looks more like a church's endowment than a secular *caput* or a church site in its own right. Neither its Anglo-Scandinavian name nor its location gives any obvious sign of antiquity as the present All Saints was built in 1220 on the lord's demesne (Dugdale 1693, 832). It is possible that it was chosen as the religious centre for a secular lordship based at Earl Shilton (Peter) at a time when that lordship obtained parochial rights independent of some previous ecclesiastical dependency on Barwell.

In 1174 Kirkby's demesne lord was constable of Leicester castle – possibly hereditary service tenure, since the Conqueror's castellan, Hugh de Grandmesnil, held the bulk of Kirkby, and also Shilton – which had its own castle. Shilton, whose church occupies a site consistent with the castle's bailey, is later found attached to Leicester castle and including a tenement tied to finding a keeper of the king's court there. Peckleton was associated with custody of part of Leicester Forest, so Kirkby parish as a whole related to royal administration.

Barwell and Kirkby look like two early parochial centres in a large but fragmenting 'multiple' estate, serving royal and reeve's *tūn* centres at Croft and Shilton respectively. Counter-intuitively, both are peripheral to their medieval parishes. Kirkby church looks like a component of a regular manorial village complex. Possibly an earlier (?pre-nucleation) church/chapel lay close to the Roman road linking Leicester and Mancetter. An appropriated roadside shrine site is conceivable – neighbouring Stapleton's name may refer

to a *stapol* or post, sculpted to represent a cult figure, and intriguingly its patron is the shrine-destroying Martin. Barwell stands on the edge of an area once intercommoned with Hinckley, Burbage and Earl Shilton's daughter settlement, Elmsthorpe. Paul Bowman has suggested a pre-Conquest estate comprising three 'primary vills', Burbage, Barwell and Hinckley (Bowman 2004, 109-11). However, this could only be part of a much larger territory, one that by 1066 was dominated by three large landholdings: those of Coventry Abbey and previously Earl Leofric (Barwell, Burbage, Potters Marston, part of Kirkby Mallory); Harding (Croft, Hinckley, Nuneaton, Sapcote); and predecessors of Hugh de Grandmesnil (Shilton, Peckleton, and the rest of Kirkby).

Another explanation for Barwell's peripheral location is possible. An odd tongue of Hinckley, almost cut off from the rest of the parish, stretches to within 100 yards of Barwell church and is difficult to explain unless it relates to the geography of the intercommoned area. If so, Barwell church and the manorial core sat on the edge of, if not within, the intercommoned and conceivably once disputed area. They are isolated from a further settlement core further north where several roads and pathways meet at Goose Green. Barwell gives no evidence of being a major focal settlement, so there must have been good cause for the church's siting. It stands prominently atop a steep slope which is part of the Soar/Anker watershed. Just to the east is a chalybeate spring – the 'Boars Well' which gave Barwell its name? The partly-curved churchyard is offset from the rectilinear manorial precinct. A cremation urn was dug up in the close immediately to the north, and Romano-British roof tiles in the large rectory garden on the west, from a building which need not have been domestic. St Mary's potentially occupies an isolated ritual site of great antiquity, suitable for a tribal boundary meeting place like the Harrow brook *hærg* or 'shrine' only two miles away at Hinckley.

Lower Sence/'Pēotlingas'

Another cross-Soar parish linked Enderby with its chapelry Whetstone. On the west bank of the river at Aldeby stood St John-by-the-Water (so called in 1528), unusually a chapel with burial rights and not far from a Romano-British cemetery. Eindrithi's *bȳ* (Margaret) looks like the grazing hamlet of Narborough, while Whetstone's boundary zig-zags as if through Cosby's fields. Should Blaby and its daughter-settlement Countesthorpe join this group? Blaby could be Whetstone's *bý*, but they also make a coherent block with Foston, whose hilltop church overlooks them, with a chalybeate spring close by. Bartholomew, dedicatee by 1754, would suit an ancient ritual site, and Nichols reported a statue of the apostle on the west wall of the tower, but two wills of 1527 call it St Edmund's.

The question is important because it is unclear how the suggested territorial unit around Croft related to the group of similarly sized, interlocking settlements on the headwaters of the Whetstone and Countesthorpe brooks, immediately south of Blaby-Countesthorpe-Foston. The group is bounded by a major tributary of the Soar, the Sence (or Glen), the estates or sokes centred on Great Glen and Great Bowden, and the Soar-Avon watershed. The focal settlements, the **Peatlings**, Magna and Parva, appear to preserve the name of a kin-group, the Pēotlingas. St Andrew's, Peatling Parva is set in a small, raised, hemispherical yard with its rectory in an adjoining rectilinear plot. Reorganisation is suggested not only by the townships' similar size and polygonal shapes, but also by boundaries which zig-zag as if through the strips of open fields, as between Peatling Magna and Arnesby. That the relatively late founding of daughter settlements was a cause is strongly hinted by the names Arnesby, Shearsby, Willoughby, Ashby, and Bruntingthorpe. A clue to underlying land-use is the series of roughly parallel routeways fossilised in lanes, boundaries and property lines linking the southern outskirts of Leicestershire and the higher ground along the Soar-Avon watershed. Seasonal stock movements, even transhumance come to mind, mirroring those suggested across High Leicestershire. A plausible solution is that this coherent group of settlements represents an area of intensive grazing on both high ground and meadows – the 'water leys' evidenced in the name Willoughby Waterlees – related to the Croft landed-unit.

There are traces of remaining royal lordship in this district in the form of 'king's alms land' at Peatling Magna (tenanted in 1086 by a royal clerk, Godwin) and at Shearsby. The latter was a probable chapelry of **Knaptoft**, whose name,

prominent spur site and chapelries suggest a substantial residence. Bruntingthorpe, a likely daughter settlement of either Knaptoft or Peatling Parva, 'belonged to Leicester' in 1086 'with its customary dues' and had land archaically measured in hides. This pre-Danish survival, sometimes with carucates added to hides, is arguably an echo of royal or comital organisation on a large scale. Bruntingthorpe also had four socmen in Smeeton, a probable early chapelry of Saddington later taken into Kibworth parish, which paid Saddington a pension in consequence. Saddington belonged to the Queen's Fee, which is intriguing since the holder of Knaptoft and most of its chapelry at Shearsby was Harding, Queen Emma's Butler. Saddington's patron is Helen. Knaptoft's dedication (the church has long been ruined) may have been Peter, if not Peter and Paul, since Peter is patron of its pensionary daughter church at Arnesby, where his figure stands on the eastern gable.

An anomaly in Knaptoft's ecclesiastical geography is that its parish included part or all of its south-western neighbour Walton, which by the late middle ages was pastorally served by Kimcote in return for an annual payment from Knaptoft's rector. That gave rise to the combined civil parish of Kimcote and Walton, with 24 of its 84 yardlands attributed to the ecclesiastical parish of Knaptoft. Thus Knaptoft extended beyond the watershed into the area which otherwise neatly fits into the drainage of the Swift with Lutterworth and Misterton. A further anomaly is the inclusion in Kimcote parish of a detached portion, Cotes de Val (Domesday *Toniston*), in the far north-west corner of its western neighbour Gilmorton. The straightish line which shadows the Soar/Avon watershed and defines the southern edges of Bruntingthorpe, Peatling Parva, Ashby Magna, and Dunton Bassett, may not be the territorial boundary that at first sight it seems. It is more plausibly explained as the relict line of a road linking the Romano-British settlement on the Gartree Road at Port Hill, Medbourne, with Venonæ on Watling Street. If Kimcote and Gilmorton are added to the Peatling group of settlements, whose aggregated Domesday assessment was 108 carucates and 5 bovates, that total rises to 141 carucates and 5 bovates, close to Bowman's ideal 144. However, this transgresses the suggested integrity of the settlements around Lutterworth and Misterton, and threatens to mix the putative lands of the Peatlingas and Lillingas. What is certain is that Walton's name establishes a time horizon consonant with British speech, perhaps in the late sixth, early seventh century.[13]

Central sector

There is a splendid symmetry to the tenurial and parochial geography of **Leicester** and its neighbourhood. Its longitudinal axis is the Soar, with the Roman and medieval walled town tilted to the diagonal in the river's meander. A lateral axis runs outwards from the town's north and south sides. Occupying the innermost segments of the respective quadrants were Leicester's East Field (in St Margaret's parish) and South Field (in St Mary de Castro) east of the river, and west of the river a part of St Mary's which included the lost Bromkinsthorpe plus friths and commons plausibly associated with Aylestone and Braunstone, and finally the area which included Beaumont Leys and the abbey of St Mary-in-the-Meadows, a Beaumont foundation. Moving outwards along the Soar, on its eastern bank north of Leicester lay the Beaumont manor of Belgrave; to the south Aylestone. Both parishes had chapelries on either bank. Extending the envelope west to the Rothley Brook, the south-west quadrant was completed by Glenfield parish, the north-west by Thurcaston. Across the brook, this entire sector faced the parish of Ratby and coterminous lordship of Groby – what Tom Cain (1990) has argued was the core of a royal estate. East of Leicester, the lateral axis follows the Roman Gartree Road, apparently slicing through another, equally large royal estate, probably the place of the Mercian council assembly 'at Glen' in 849. It included a retainers' *tūn*, Knighton, a probable reeve's vill at Wigston, and beyond them in the upper basin of the Sence the probable royal centre, Great Glen. The whole district is 17 miles across and eight miles wide.

The area's medieval dedications reveal striking symmetries, too: Belgrave's Peter and Paul (icons of *Romanitas*) and Aylestone's Andrew (Peter's brother); Ratby's ancient patron Gregory (apostle and first patron of the English, representative of the Roman church, died 604) and Great Glen's Cuthbert

13 Cf. Margaret Gelling's comments about Hints, on Watling Street near Lichfield (Gelling 1988, 101).

(abbot of Lindisfarne, patron of Northumbria, representative of the 'Celtic' church, died 687). Gregory and Cuthbert are mirrored in the dedications of the lost church immediately east of St Nicholas, 'under two roofs conjoined by medial columns': its patronal saint Augustine, disciple of Gregory (also died 604) – both often associated with royal churches – and the titular of the other half of the church, best interpreted as an aisle, Columba, teacher of Cuthbert (died 597).

The congruity of Leicester's outer suburbs comes into sharp focus as their topography and lordships are explored. Leicester's eastern suburb and East Field constituted the inner half of the Bishop of Lincoln's Domesday holdings, the so-called Bishop's Fee, the parish of St Margaret's. The outer half was St Margaret's chapelry, Knighton. Problematically, these lay like diagonally related squares on a chessboard, meeting only at their common corner. If the Bishop's Fee is treated as a detachment from the parish and lordship of Belgrave, as the symmetrical geography suggests, this allows Knighton to be associated with the neatly contiguous South Field, in St Mary's parish, and in the other direction with the equally neatly placed (and tenurially linked) Wigston Magna and Oadby. Possibly Knighton was received in exchange for Kibworth (see above). The bishop is an unlikely original holder of the *cnicht's tūn*, which provided the board of the junior household retainers of a royal or comital lord. The South Field, while including the burgesses' common (an echo of the retainers?), was part of the endowment of the Newarke College, presumably by Henry, Earl of Lancaster, and plausibly in descent from Robert Beaumont as Count of Meulan (holder of Aylestone) rather than as Earl of Leicester, supplanter of Hugh de Grandmesnil's son Ivo (holder of Belgrave). Interestingly, therefore, Knighton's boundary with Aylestone apparently zigs-zags through (?common) open fields.

St Cuthbert's, **Great Glen**, has an Anglo-Saxon sculptural fragment and was mother church of Great Stretton and probably the other relationally-named vills, Little Stretton, King's Norton, Burton Overy, and Carlton Curlieu, plus Gaulby and Illston. However, the advowson, as Jill Bourne has pointed out, lay in the twelfth century with the lordship of Wistow (Bourne 1996, 147-64). The 'holy place of Wigstan', reputed stream-side place of the king's assassination on June 1, 849 (quite possibly during the assembly at Glen), later had chapelries at Kilby, Fleckney, and Newton Harcourt, but may not then have had a church. **Wigston Magna**, on the other hand, had two Domesday churches, one of them doubtless St Wigstan's on the hill, potentially a pre-Christian *locus*, a likely resting-place for the royal corpse on its way to Repton for burial, and still a pilgrimage centre in the sixteenth century. Wigston, demesne caput of Hugh de Grandmesnil as successor to the Confessor's nephew, Earl Ralph, was still then archaically assessed in hides. Though its daughter settlement Oadby was divided from Great Glen by the Old Mere, that may be a Romano-British relict, since it runs at right-angles from the Gartree Road. North of the road, Houghton-on-the-Hill, Evington, and Stoughton-Thurnby (another secular-religious pair) probably belonged to Glen: Evington is separated from Leicester's East Field by Spinney Lane ridgeway. Thurnby's hilltop church was anciently Holy Innocents, an exceptionally rare medieval example of this dedication. Some vaguely remembered multiple devotion, even martyrial or pre-Christian, is not impossible.

Wigston's boundary with **Aylestone** and its chapel Glen Parva also zig-zags as through furlongs, as it does with Newton Harcourt on the east. Was 'Ægel's *tūn*' also in the Glen estate? Glen Parva's name suggests so. In 1066 Aylestone was divided between Ælfgifu, widow of Ælfgar, Earl of Mercia after his father Leofric (her chief demesne in 1086) one Leofwin, and Saxi, a royal thegn, tenant-in-chief of Narborough/Huncote. His manor here became the *caput* demesne of Robert Beaumont, whose men obtained Leofwin's land, plus holdings in Blaby and Whetstone. St Andrew's beside the Soar occupies an appropriate site for communal baptism – its yard a quarter of the village core – and had a further chapelry at Lubbesthorpe. If Aylestone was part of Glen, the same must apply to the large parish of Glenfield ('clean, cleared', a different etymology), which included Braunstone, and with which Aylestone's lands interlocked.

Glenfield may once have been superior to Groby, which it faced across the Rothley Brook, and was part of the same estate in

Cain's view (Cain 1990). Kirby Muxloe, a Glenfield chapelry, now notable for an Iron Age hilltop enclosure with (?ritual) cauldrons and Bronze Age rapier, faced Ratby. Jurisdictional and other links bound Ratby/Groby to these and other vills from Desford to Glen Parva. Nevertheless, **Ratby**'s antiquity cannot be doubted and Peter Liddle has raised the possibility of an early church at **Groby**. Bury Camp is a probable Iron Age enclosure, and rights in Ratby of Bromkinsthorpe in the parish of St Mary's, Leicester, have been taken by Cain as evidence that Ratby was a royal estate centre (Cain *op. cit.*). St Bartholomew, Kirby, recalls the Christianising role of Gregory, whose church at Ratby stands in one corner of a large enclosure. Ratby's probable extent to the Soar/Anker watershed and the highest point of Charnwood is revealed by a pensionary payment from Markfield ('boundary veldt'), names, and topography.

Rather than two royal estates, the evidence demonstrates one. Glen's arable pole in the east complemented a pastoral pole reflected in the *bý* names Ratby, Groby, Kirby. Between the Soar and Rothley Brook was interposed *Herewode*, the 'army-' or 'people's-wood' which became Leicester Forest and in which the burgesses had timber and grazing rights. Eight townships met where the Roman road to Mancetter crossed high ground – known later as Kingstanding, where royal parties shot at game. Ratby/Groby's shared interests in Charnwood may indicate a relationship with the Barrow-Rothley-Loughborough entity, but nearer at hand is its relationship with **Belgrave**, earlier Merdegrave, 'wood with martens', suggesting a hunting lodge. Belgrave's parish (Peter and Paul) was extensive, including South Thurmaston and Birstall. The 'burh place' overlooked the Soar – a desirable elite location. St James', anciently St John's, stands on an east-facing slope with evidence of an east-end crypt adduced by Steve Mitchell (Mitchell 2012, 11-14).

Belgrave's tenant in 1086 was Hugh de Grandmesnil, possibly in succession to Waltheof. Ulf, Edwardian holder of Ratby and Groby, may have been Waltheof's tenant; these lands too went to Hugh. An important anomaly in the geographical coherence of the Queniborough-Syston block of vills, discussed earlier, is its incompleteness without Belgrave. The latter's parish seems to have been carved out of an existing landscape sometime after 920, since it took in southern Thurmaston, a *tūn* acquired by someone with a Danish name. However, Leicester's East Field, also associated with Belgrave, may have been laid out at the time of the town's repopulation. The Humber Stone may give a clue, if it preserves the name of the east Midlands ealdorman Hunbeorht documented in 832 and 852. Humberstone shares Belgrave's dedication, Peter and Paul. A further possibility is that Belgrave's parochial boundary adopted the surviving outline of one of Roman Leicester's fields, overriden by the settlement which became Thurmaston and where a large 'Anglo-Saxon' cemetery was established.

Leicester

All the foregoing suggests the booking out to regional ealdormen of royal land around Leicester, outlying Glen and other seminal vills – and the city itself – remaining in the hands of the king. The mother church of this large area is almost certain to have been in **Leicester**. Its *parochia* and assets were probably used to endow St Mary de Castro, whose name indicates association with the castle, like St Peter's, Stamford, and countless other castle chapels across Europe. St Mary's was perhaps built after the reconquest of the Danelaw. Soon after 1066 it became a secular college and subsequently its assets were transferred to the new abbey.

The early mother church's identity has puzzled scholars. There can be no doubt that Roman Ratae had a bishop, probably operating from a private house before Constantine made Christianity the state religion. Thereafter church building took place in the empire's cities alongside the transformation of temples, Bartholomew-style. In Leicester a colonnade found north of the tower of St Martin's has been architecturally assigned to that period and might be part of a basilican appropriation of a temple, since a pit filled with animal bones was found under the floor of the tower. St Martin's respects the Roman street alignment, not that of Guildhall Lane. Though St Michael's origins are obscure, burials in its probable cemetery respected a rectangular Romano-British building near which was found a curse plaque invoking a deity Maglus. St Margaret's appears to stand in an extra-mural Romano-British cemetery, conceivably over a Christian grave chapel. Why was this place chosen for the later (?post-Danish) suffragan cathedral (to which Pentecostal processions were directed from the intramural churches) and the East Field for the Bishop's Fee? Allen Chinnery has supported the suggestion that the bishop was awarded part of the land of the Danish borough (Chinery 1986, 43-48) – land in Belgrave in fact.

What happened to the Mercian cathedral? Its continuing importance is confirmed by the line of Leicester's main medieval east-west street, direct from the East Gate to St Nicholas. Construction over, and in alignment with the entrance and exercise hall of the baths, and incorporation into its westwork (and property) of the baths' ceremonial and ritual entrance, the Jewry Wall, indicates foundation by high authority. Richard Morris' suggested baptistery in the baths (Morris 1991, 20, fn. 32) would have allowed it to function as an episcopal church, candidates gathering as was usual in a western narthex, processing to their baptism, and returning for the eucharist through an arch appropriately once embellished with a sculpture of Janus – 'dead in Christ, in Christ made alive'.

East of the baths stood the Forum and, directly east of this church, the Basilica. Later burials occurred near the basilica's western end, where St Augustine's must have stood – again with high authority. Were basilican walls appropriated? Did it form an axial pair with the episcopal church, like St Paul's and St Augustine's in London? In his 1098 account of its blind anchorite, Goscelin described St Augustine's, Leicester, as 'notable' and parochial (serving St Nicholas' parish?) (Goscelin 1688, 429-30, I, *cap* 8.53). In Alan Thacker's view, promotion of Augustine's cult began in the 730s, with the Council of Clovesho (very likely Brixworth) honouring him with Gregory and ordering observance of his feast (Thacker 1999, 383-84). Augustine was later revered by Edward the Elder's son Æthelstan (died 939) and Cnut. Columba's presence could have commemorated Wilfrid's Northern origins, Offa's bid for an archbishopric at Lichfield (founded by the Northerner Chad), peace between English and Danish Mercia, the Northerner Waltheof's earldom – or something else.

After Leicester's bishop decamped to Dorchester rather than submit to Danish authority, existing churches inevitably suffered neglect. The building of Mary de Castro and the gift of Cosby's church to St Augustine's may both have been part of ecclesiastical restoration. As manorialisation hastened the break-up of minster *parochiæ*, new parishes across the Glen estate reduced Leicester's *parochia*, arguably that of 'St Nicholas' (known as such only since 1220), to a rump. Even within Leicester's walls, there were four privately-owned churches in 1086. In 1107 'St Nicholas' was assigned to St Mary de Castro, which could have acquired its extra-mural parish much earlier as part of its own endowment, perhaps by episcopal agreement in return for the site of St Margaret's and the Bishop's Fee.

Conclusion

Leicestershire's territorial building blocks, like tectonic plates, constantly shifted, overrode, fused and fractured. Nevertheless, helped by the resilience of ecclesiastical boundaries and sites, they resolve into a few essential groupings, variably influenced by landform and land-uses. The density of primary churches mirrors settlement. Thirty-one within Leicestershire lie east of the Fosse, where better soils are found, only 17 to the west. If we apply Roberts and Wrathmell's zone of heavy nucleation, which includes the south-west, (Roberts and Wrathmell 2000) the split becomes 39/9.

Leicester reveals itself as the hub of a large, coherent territorial unit. A royal villa estate balanced an arable, hidated economy in the east with extensive wood-pasture in the west. To the south was well-watered dairy land perhaps with seasonal herding. Its mixed-farming potential probably contributed to the complex breaking-up of one or possibly two underlying royal estates, followed by Danish reorganisation.

This is the land of the Legora, the people on the river which gave its name to Leire. The Leicester-folk sound British, like the Weogoran of Worcester. 'Inner' Leicestershire might preserve something of Ratae's *territorium* as Worcester's extramural parish of St Helen's appears to preserve that of Vertis. Barry Cox suggests that downstream from Leicester the Legor/Leire became the Soar – reinforced by the Lear legend recorded by Geoffrey of Monmouth. Again, the constituent units are coherent: arable lands along the Soar and

Wreake, rising to the Wolds, wood-pasture in Charnwood, and grazing with strong likelihood of transhumance along the ridges and valleys of High Leicestershire. Frequently in this study, the model of two *hāms* in a landed unit, suggested to me by Charles Phythian-Adams, has looked promising – reminiscent of summer and winter residences, the Welsh *hendref* ('old steading') and *hafod* ('summer place'). At the local level, application of Cullen, Jones and Parsons' (2011) interpretation of *b̄ys* as polyfocal, pastoral, and I would add daughter settlements, resolves numerous issues of how individual villages relate to their neighbours.

In summary, Leicestershire is essentially the valleys of the Soar and Wreake plus such large peripheral parts of other regions that one guesses at fossilised results of divide-and-rule. This would explain why its boundary slices through Belvoir Vale, and follows Watling Street, dividing Hinckley from Nuneaton and Lutterworth from Rugby. Fortunes of war played their part. That 'all the army that belonged to Northampton northward to the Welland' surrendered to Edward the Elder in 921 implies that north of the Welland there was part which did not. Playing off Danish and English Mercians may explain why still in the mid-eleventh century so much of Leicestershire was in the hands either of the Northumbrian earl, or of the Leofricings, descended from ealdormen of the Hwicce in the southwest Midlands.

From a century before the Danes' arrival, Offa's hand may well be visible in the parcelling out of the arable over large areas of Leicestershire, imposed on an essentially Iron Age landscape.[14] Furthermore, hints in roads, pre-enclosure lanes, boundaries, and property lines along the Fosse, the Gartree Road, and other Romano-British routes leave one curious if Offa's predecessors inherited an imperial estate extending over parts of the later county and beyond it. Was it obtained from a king who was minting coins at Leicester – see the moulds found in Bath Lane – and meeting his peers at the shrine of the Hallaton hoard? Perhaps it passed into the fisc without conquest, bequeathed to Rome or the emperor by a client who knew them well. We may even know his name (or that of a close relative), and have part of his ceremonial uniform, thanks to

14 As Oosthuizen (2006) is showing in Cambridgeshire. See also Tony Brown, this volume, and Roberts 2008 on the tide of nucleation.

the coins from Hallaton and the parade-ground helmet ritually buried with them.

Strong regal interests could explain why Leicester, Croft, Glen and Gumley constitute a unique cluster of Mercian council meeting places, why Peter (with or without Paul) and Helen were significantly more frequent here as dedicatees, why both *bý* and Domesday royal holdings east of the Soar are so dense (Roberts 2008, Figs 10.3, 10.4), why William I's sheriff Hugh de Grandmesnil acted without an earl, and why holdings of, and place-name references to the queen and queens' courtiers are a running theme. Marc Anthony Meyer, discounting the concept of a 'queen's demesne', nevertheless noted certain estates 'held by successive [Anglo-Saxon] queens', and this of course includes Rutland (Meyer 1993, 75-113, at 104).

Royal assemblies required the presence and provisioning of the royal retinue and those of the earls, bishops and abbots who counselled the king and ratified decisions. This is one possible reason for Leicestershire's rich ecclesiastical geography. Early churches include basilicas, minsters (whose collegial or monastic organisation is largely lost to view), chapels and oratories – estate centre churches like Great Glen and Croft probably originated as chapels attached to notables' halls. Another pointer is that though vunerable to founders' fortunes, early churches often occupied sites of enduring emotional significance. This may partly explain the distance of so many parochial churches from the optimally-sited manorial and administrative centres – religious-secular pairings are a notable feature of this survey. Supernatural power routinely trumps its mortal counterpart, through fear but also attachment to family graves and memories of life-changing encounters. Some central places had large *parochiæ* but it is peripheral places, often suiting ritual, which equally arrest the eye. They include Barwell, Leire, Peatling Parva, Knaptoft, Thurnby, Billesdon, Tilton, Scalford, Buckminster, and former temple sites at Market Overton/Thistleton and Willoughby-on-the-Wolds – perhaps also Breedon and Burrough Hill. Isolated churches, those on river islands and promontaries, beside rivers, in enclosures, and at places with names redolent of pre-Christian religion, these too require further investigation. Re-use or development of religious *loci* at Romano-British settlement sites – Mancetter, Tripontium, Market Harborough, and Leicester – also demand attention. Are we to assume that the sixth-century inhabitants of the Waltons, Bretbys and Walcots were not at least nominally Christian, looking for episcopal baptism and pastoral care? The emerging picture is of a transformative society in which priests, kings and people were setting out the territorial and spiritual bounds and needs of their local worlds.

Bibliography

Archibald, M. M., Fenwick, V. H. and Cowell, M. R., 1996. A sceat of Ethelbert I of East Anglia and recent finds of coins of Beonna. *British Numismatic Journal* 65.

Aston, M., 1985. *Interpreting the Landscape. Landscape: History and Local Archaeology.* London: Routledge.

Barnwell, P. and Roberts, B., (eds) 2011. *Britons, Saxons and Scandinavians: The historical geography of Glanville R J Jones.* Turnhout: Brepols.

Barrow, G., 1973 (2nd edn 2003). *The Kingdom of the Scots: Government, church and society.* Edinburgh: Edinburgh University Press.

Bassett, S., 1989. Churches in Worcester before and after the Conversion of the Anglo-Saxons. *Antiquaries Journal* 69.

Bassett, S., 1991. Anglo-Saxon Shrewsbury and its churches. *Midland History* 16.

Bassett, S., 1992a. Medieval ecclesiastical organisation in the vicinity of Wroxeter and its British antecedents. *Journal of the British Archaeological Association* 145.

Bassett, S., 1992b. Church and diocese in the West Midlands: The transition from British to Anglo-Saxon control, in, J. Blair and R. Sharpe (eds), *Pastoral Care Before the Parish.* Leicester: Leicester University Press.

Bassett, S., 1993. *The Origins of Anglo-Saxon Kingdoms*. Leicester: Leicester University Press.

Bassett, S., 2000. Anglo-Saxon Birmingham, *Midland History* 25.

Bassett, S., 2007a. Boundaries of knowledge: mapping the land-units of late Anglo-Saxon and Norman England. In: W. Davies, G Halsall and A. Reynolds, (eds), *People and Space in the Middle Ages, 300-1300*. Turnhout: Brepols.

Bassett, S., 2007b. Divide and rule? The military infrastructure of eighth- and ninth-century Mercia. *Early Medieval Europe* 15.

Biddle, M. and Kjølbye-Biddle, B., 1992. Repton and the Vikings, *Antiquity* 66, 36-51.

Blair, J., (ed), 1988. *Minsters and Parish Churches: The Local Church in Transition, 950-1200*. Oxford, Oxford University Committee for Archaeology, Monograph 17.

Blair, J., 1991. *Early Medieval Surrey: Landholding, Church and Settlement Before 1300*. Stroud: Sutton.

Blair, J., 2005. *The Church in Anglo-Saxon Society*. Oxford: Oxford University Press.

Bourne, J., 1996. 'An Anglo-Saxon royal estate *Aet Glynne* and the murder of St Wigstan'. In: J. Bourne, *Anglo-Saxon Landscapes in the East Midlands*. Leicester: Leicestershire Museums, Arts & Records Service.

Bowman, P., 2004. Villages and their territories. In: P. Bowman and P. Liddle, (eds), *Leicestershire Landscapes*. Leicester: Leicestershire Museums Archaeological Fieldwork Group.

Burnell, S. and Jones, E., 1999. The archaeology of conversion on the Continent in the sixth and seventh centuries. In: R. Gameson, (ed.), *St Augustine and the Conversion of England*. Stroud: Sutton Publishing.

Cain, T., 1990. Introduction. In: A. Williams and R. W. H. Erskine, *The Leicestershire Domesday*. London: Alecto Historical Editions.

Cambridge, E. and Rollason, D., 1995. Debate: The pastoral organisation of the Anglo Saxon Church: a review of the 'minster hypothesis'. *Early Medieval Europe*, 4: 1.

Camden, W., 1722. *Britannia: or a Chorographical Description of Great Britain and Ireland*, 2nd edn, rev. E. Gibson. London: Awnsham Churchill.

Chinnery, A., 1986. Leicester at Domesday. In: C. Pythian-Adams, ed. *The Norman Conquest of Leicestershire and Rutland: A regional introduction to Domesday Book*. Leicestershire Museums Publication 48. Leicester: Leicestershire Museums, Art Galleries and Records Service.

Cox, B., 1998, 2001, 2004, 2009. *The Place-Names of Leicestershire*. Nottingham: English Place-Name Society, volumes 75, 78, 81, 84.

Cox, B., 2005. A Dictionary of Leicestershire and Rutland Place-Names. Nottingham: English Place-Name Society

Croom, J., 1988. The fragmentation of the minster *parochiæ* of south-east Shropshire. In: J. Blair, (ed) *Minsters and Parish Churches: The Local Church in Transition, 950-1200*. Oxford, Oxford University Committee for Archaeology, Monograph 17.

Cullen, P., Jones, R. and Parsons, D., 2011. *Thorps in a Changing Landscape*, Explorations in Local and Regional History 4. Hatfield: University of Hertfordshire.

Dugdale, W., Bt., 1693. *Monasticon Anglicanum*, 2. London. Online digital edition available at https://archive.org/details/monasticonanglic00dugd

Ekwall, E., 1960. *The Concise Oxford Dictionary of English Place-Names*, 4th edn. Oxford: Oxford University Press.

Everitt, A., 1986. *Continuity and Colonization: The Evolution of Kentish Settlement.* Leicester: Leicester University Press.

Finberg, H. P. R., 1964. Charltons and Carltons. In: *Lucerna. Studies of some problems in the early history of England.* London: Macmillan.

Foard, G., 1985. The administrative organisation of Northamptonshire in the Saxon period. *Anglo-Saxon Studies in Archaeology and History* 4.

Foot, S., 2006. *Monastic Life in Anglo-Saxon England, c.600-900.* Cambridge: Cambridge University Press.

Foss, P., 1996. Market Bosworth and its region – Clues to its early status and connections. In: Bourne, J., (ed), *Anglo-Saxon Landscapes in the East Midlands.* Leicester: Leicestershire Museums, Arts & Records Service.

Gelling, M., 1988. *Signposts to the Past*, 2nd edn. Chichester: Phillimore.

Goscelin, 1688. '*Historia Translationis Sancti Augustini*'. In: *Acta Sanctorum,* May VI, ed by G. Henchenius, and D. Papebroch, Brussels.

Hadley, D., 2000. *The Northern Danelaw: Its Social Structure, c.800-1100* (Studies in the Early History of Britain). London and New York: Leicester University Press.

Hall, T., 2000. *Minster Churches in the Dorset Landscape.* Oxford: British Archaeological Reports, British Series 304.

Halsall, G., 2007. Villas, territories and communities. In: W. Davies,G. Halsall and A. Reynolds, (eds), *People and Space in the Middle Ages, 300-1300.* Turnhout: Brepols.

Hart, C., 1968. The Hidation of Huntingdonshire, *Proceedings of the Cambridge Antiquarian Society* 61.

Hart, C., 1970. *The Hidation of Northamptonshire.* Department of English Local History Occasional Papers. Leicester: Leicester University Press.

Hart, C., 1974. *The Hidation of Cambridgeshire.* Department of English Local History Occasional Papers. Leicester: Leicester University Press.

Hart, C., 1992. *The Danelaw.* London and Rio Grande, Ohio: Hambledon Press.

Hase, P., 1988. The mother churches of Hampshire. In: J. Blair, (ed), *Minsters and Parish Churches: The Local Church in Transition, 950-1200.* Oxford: Oxford University Committee for Archaeology, Monograph 17.

Higham, N. and Ryan, M., ed, 2010. *The Landscape Archaeology of Anglo-Saxon England.* Woodbridge: Boydell & Brewer.

Hooke, D., 1998. *The Anglo-Saxon Landscape. The Kingdom of the Hwicce.* Manchester: Manchester University Press.

Hooke, D., 1996. Changing settlement patterns and land-use in midland and southern England in the early medieval and medieval period. *Ruralia* I, Supplement 5 (Prague).

Humphery-Smith, C. R. (ed.), 1984. *The Phillimore Atlas and Index of Parish Registers.* Chichester: Phillimore.

Jones, Glanville, 1961. Settlement patterns in Anglo-Saxon England. *Antiquity* 35

Jones, Graham, 1996. *Church dedications and landed units of lordship and administration in the pre-Reformation diocese of Worcester.* Unpub. PhD thesis, Leicester University.

Jones, Graham, 2007. *Saints in the Landscape.* Stroud: Tempus.

Jones, Graham, 2015 forthcoming. 'A gazetteer of dedications honouring, and places otherwise associated with St Guthlac, with commentary'. In: A. Thacker and B. Yorke, (eds), *Proceedings of 'Guthlac of Crowland: Celebrating 1300 Years' conference 2014.* London: University of London, Institute of English Studies.

Kain, R. and Oliver, R., 2001. *Historic Parishes of England and Wales: an Electronic Map of Boundaries before 1850 with a Gazetteer and Metadata*. UK Data Archive, Colchester, Essex.

Lloyd, P., 1973. *A study of the dedications given to religious buildings in Leicestershire before the Reformation*. Unpub. MA thesis, University of Leicester.

Meyer, M. A., 1993. The Queen's 'demesne' in later Anglo-Saxon England. In: M. A. Meyer, (ed.) *The Culture of Christendom: essays in medieval history in memory of Denis L. Bethell*. London: Hambledon Press.

Mitchell, S., 2009. The Raw Dykes. Paper presented to the Leicestershire Archaeological and Historical Society, March, 2009.

Mitchell, S., 2012. Subterranean Church Structures in Leicestershire. *Leicestershire Historian*, 48. Leicester: Leicestershire Archaeological and Historical Society.

Morris, J., (gen. ed.) 1976-79. *Domesday Book*. 1977, 21, *Northamptonshire*, ed. F. Thorn and C. Thorn; 1979, 22, *Leicestershire*, ed. P. Morgan; 1976, 23, *Warwickshire*, ed. J. Morris and J. Plaister; 1978, 27, *Derbyshire*, ed. P. Morgan; 1977, 28, *Nottinghamshire*, ed. J. Morris. Chichester: Phillimore.

Morris, R., 1991. Baptismal places: 600-800. In: I. Wood and N. Lund, (eds), *People and Places in Northern Europe 500-1600. Essays in honour of Peter Hayes Sawyer*. London: Boydell & Brewer.

Nichols, J., 1795-1811. *The History and Antiquities of the County of Leicester*. In five volumes. London: John Nichols. Repub. 1971, Leicestershire Library Service with S. R. Publishers.

Oosthuizen, S., 2006. *Landscapes Decoded: The Origins and Development of Cambridgeshire's Medieval Fields*. Hatfield: University of Hertfordshire Press.

Oosthuizen, S., 2013. *Tradition and Transformation in Anglo-Saxon England: Archaeology, Common Rights and Landscape*. London: Bloomsbury.

Parsons, D., 1996. Before the parish: The church in Anglo-Saxon Leicestershire. In: J. Bourne, *Anglo-Saxon Landscapes in the East Midlands*. Leicester: Leicestershire Museums, Arts & Records Service.

Parsons, D., 2001. The Mercian Church: archaeology and topography. In: M. P. Brown and C. A. Farr (eds), *Mercia: An Anglo-Saxon Kingdom in Europe*. Leicester: Leicester University Press.

Phillimore, W. P. W., (ed.) 1912. *Rotuli Hugonis de Welles Episcopi Lincolniensis AD MCCIX –MCCXXXV*. Lincoln.

Pitt, J.,1999. *Wiltshire minster parochiæ and west Saxon ecclesiastical organisation*. Unpub. PhD thesis, Southampton University.

Phythian-Adams, C., 1977. Rutland reconsidered. In: A. Dornier (ed.), *Mercian Studies*. Leicester: Leicester University Press.

Phythian-Adams, C., 1978. *Continuity, Fields, and Fission: The Making of a Midland Parish*. Department of English Local History Occasional Papers, Third Series 4. Leicester: Leicester University Press.

Phythian-Adams, C., 1993. Introduction: An agenda for English local history. In: C. Phythian-Adams, (ed.), *Societies, Cultures and Kinship, Cultural Provinces and English Local History*. Leicester: Leicester University Press.

Phythian-Adams, C., 2007. Differentiating provincial societies in English history: spatial contexts and cultural processes. In: B. Lancaster, D. Newton and N. Vall, (eds), *An Agenda for Regional History*, pp. 3–22. Newcastle Upon Tyne: Northumbria University Press.

Postles, D., 2015. *A Town in its Parish: Loughborough, Origins to c.1640*. Loughborough: Dave Postles.

Richardson, M., 1996. *Parish boundaries, minster* parochiæ *and parish fragmentation in Leicestershire: New methods of boundary analysis.* Unpub. MA dissertation, University of Leicester.

Rippon, S., 2010. In: N. Higham, and M. Ryan, (ed.), *The Landscape Archaeology of Anglo-Saxon England.* Woodbridge: Boydell & Brewer.

Roberts, B. and Wrathmell, S., 2000. *Atlas of Rural Settlement in England.* London: English Heritage.

Roberts, B. K., 2008. *Landscapes, Documents and Maps: Villages in Northern England and Beyond AD 900-1250.* Oxford: Oxbow.

Roffe, D., 1996. Great Bowden and its Soke. In: J. Bourne, *Anglo-Saxon Landscapes in the East Midlands.* Leicester: Leicestershire Museums, Arts & Records Service.

Sawyer, P., 1979. *Names, words and graves: early medieval settlement.* Leeds: University of Leeds.

Sawyer, P., 1983. The royal *tun* in pre-Conquest England. In: P. Wormald, D. Bullough and R. Collins, (eds.), *Ideal and Reality in Frankish and Anglo-Saxon Society. Studies presented to J. M. Wallace-Hadrill.* Oxford: B. Blackwell.

Smith, A. H., 1970. *The Place-Name Elements*, 2. Nottingham: English Place Name Society 26.

Stafford, P., 1985. *The East Midlands in the Early Middle Ages.* Leicester: Leicester University Press.

Stenton, F. M., 1970. Medeshamstede and its Colonies. In: D. M. Stenton, (ed.), *Preparatory to Anglo-Saxon England, Being the Collected Papers of Frank Merry Stenton.* Oxford: Oxford University Press.

Thacker, A., 1999. In Gregory's shadow? The pre-Conquest cult of St Augustine. In: R. Gameson, 1999, (ed). *St Augustine and the Conversion of England.* Stroud: Sutton Publishing.

Tranter, M., 2003. Name, Race, Terrain: The Making of a Leicestershire Boundary. In: D. Hooke, and D. Postles, (eds), *Names, Time and Place: Essays in Memory of Richard McKinley.* London: Leopard's Head Press.

Tringham, N., 2003. *A History of the County of Stafford: Burton-upon-Trent.* Victoria County History, 9. Woodbridge: Boydell and Brewer.

Walsham, A., 2011. *The Reformation of the Landscape: Religion, Identity, and Memory in Early Modern Britain and Ireland.* Oxford: Oxford University Press.

Watts, V., 2004. *The Cambridge Dictionary of English Place-Names.* Cambridge: Cambridge University Press.

Williamson, T., 2012. *Environment, Society and Landscape in Early Medieval England: Time and Topography.* Woodbridge: Boydell.

Winchester, A., 2000. *Discovering Parish Boundaries.* 2nd edn, Oxford: Shire Publications.

Winchester, A., 2008. Early estate organisation in Cumbria and Lancashire. *Medieval Settlement Research* 23.

Wood, S., 2005. *The Proprietary Church in the Medieval West.* Oxford: Oxford University Press.

Victoria County History of Leicestershire, 1905 – 1964, Vols 1 – 5. London: University of London.

Infilling the blanks: modern development and the archaeology of currently occupied medieval rural settlement in Leicestershire and Rutland

John Thomas

Introduction

Leicestershire and Rutland are particularly well blessed with earthwork remains of the medieval landscape (Hartley 1983, 1984, 1987, 1989, 2008) (fig 1). In particular the remains of 'lost villages' in the two counties played an important part in the development of rural settlement studies in England, with the pioneering work of W. G. Hoskins (Hoskins 1937, 1945, 1955), and Maurice Beresford and John Hurst (Beresford & Hurst, 1972).

The attraction of mysterious earthwork sites has continued to appeal to archaeologists, resulting in a bias of attention towards deserted villages rather than Currently Occupied Rural Settlements – hereafter given the acronym CORS (Lewis, 2007). Until relatively recently for example much of the main research-led work in Leicestershire and Rutland has been undertaken at deserted settlement sites (for example at Martinsthorpe – Wacher 1964; South Croxton – Pearce and Mellor 1986, Brooksby – Christie 2002 and Nether Hambleton and Whitwell – Clough 2007). In purely practical terms the difficulties involved in accessing suitable sites within CORS, in comparison to the choice on offer at a deserted site has also contributed to this imbalance.

Following the introduction of PPG16 in 1990 however, archaeological work in response to 'village infill' development within CORS has increased, helping to redress this imbalance (fig 2). In Leicestershire and Rutland for example over fifty sites of varying scale have revealed archaeological evidence for the origins and development of rural villages that survived the main phases of desertion, contributing important new information to the history and nature of settlement in the medieval countryside.

Admittedly the information gathered from CORS is not without problems: the location of each site and the level of recording undertaken are entirely dependent on the scale and nature of each new development. Nevertheless, the results of these projects have highlighted the extent to which medieval remains can survive in such contexts and their research potential has rightly been highlighted (Dyer 1997, Lewis 2006, 212; and 2007). Additionally recent projects involving test-pitting within CORS have indicated the significant contribution to knowledge that research in such locations can offer (Aston and Gerrard 1999, Lewis 2006 (and regular updates on the Higher Education Field Academy CORS project in the Medieval Settlement Research Group annual report), Cooper and Priest 2003, Cooper and Score 2006, Jones and Page 2006).

However, although there has been a significant increase in projects within CORS, a key problem has been the general lack of publication of individual sites or synthesised results for wider areas. Unfortunately the small-scale and piecemeal nature of much of this work has not lent itself easily to meaningful publication. Inevitably much information lies unpublished in 'grey literature' reports and is not readily available to researchers or, crucially, to contract archaeologists working in unfamiliar areas. This is not just a problem for medieval studies, but for all periods, given the increase in data resulting from the rise of contract archaeology in recent years (Bradley 2006). The great potential for this new information to add to our understanding of the past has recently been illustrated for prehistoric Britain and Ireland (Bradley 2007), but for other periods remains a largely untapped resource.

The Leicestershire and Rutland CORS project

The broad aim of the Leicestershire and Rutland CORS project has been to create a synthesis of the archaeological evidence from the various projects to provide both an accessible 'overview' and also a usable framework for analysis, interpretation and comparison. Of the fifty or so sites that have produced evidence, approximately fifteen can be given 'case study' status, based on their size, the archaeological information they have produced and their potential for future

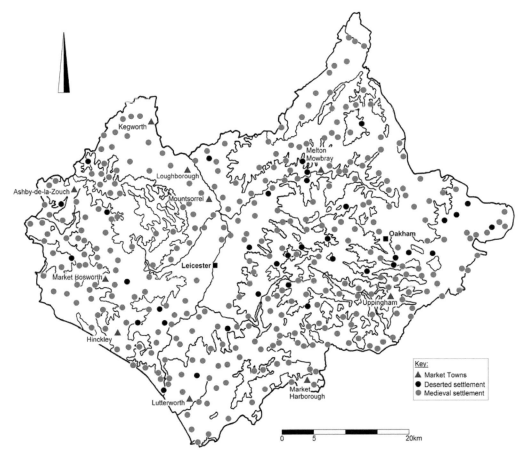

Figure 1: Distribution of medieval settlement in Leicestershire and Rutland

exploration. The results of these sites will form the basis of the study, supplemented by information from smaller projects. The key questions we can raise are 1) How can such reviews help identify pre-village activity? 2) What can be understood about village origins and development over time? 3) What can be understood about village life from the material culture?

The project timeline

The chronologies used in this review are based on the regional ceramic sequence for Leicestershire and Rutland and are intended to reflect the wares and date ranges associated with the sites that are under consideration (Table 1 opposite). Pottery is often the only source of dating for such sites and given the relatively imprecise nature of this method the date-ranges are necessarily broad.

Results of the project

Pre-village settlement

As well as providing information about medieval origins and development, many of the study sites have revealed evidence for longer histories of settlement, perhaps in part highlighting the suitability of particular

parts of the landscape for occupation. A small excavation in Kirby Bellars churchyard in 1960 highlighted the potential for such sites to contain long sequences of occupation, with deposits indicating activity between the 2nd to the 14th centuries (Grimbley 1966, Liddle 1982). As a result of the increasing amount of excavation in CORS further examples of 'pre-village' occupation have been revealed adding to our understanding of the historic depth of medieval settlement sites.

An extreme example was unearthed at Glaston, where evidence for a *c.*30,000 year old Palaeolithic hunters camp and hyena den was revealed during excavations which initially focused on medieval village remains (Cooper 2001, Thomas and Jacobi 2001). Additionally, a flint scatter and a discrete pit containing pottery also reflected activity in the Mesolithic and Bronze Age (Cooper and Thomas 2001), whilst earlier excavations in an adjacent field had recovered Bronze Age cremations and Anglo Saxon burials (Powell 1950, Leeds and Barber 1950). Glaston provides a good example of the kind of palimpsest of archaeological activity that can be encountered in a village context although it is not unique. At Saxby,

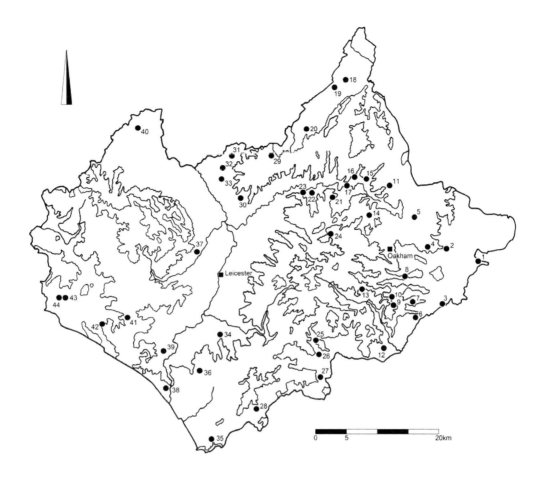

Figure 2: List of CORS where PPG16-related work has been undertaken:

1) Tinwell 2) Empingham 3) Barrowden 4) Whitwell 5) Cottesmore 6) Seaton 7) Glaston 8) Manton 9) Uppingham 10) Ayston 11) Wymondham 12) Great Easton 13) Loddington 14) Whissendine 15) Saxby 16) Freeby 17) Wyfordby 18) Barkstone-le-Vale 19) Plungar 20) Long Clawson 21) Burton Lazars 22) Eye Kettleby 23) Kirby Bellars 24) Burrough-on-the-Hill 25) Stonton Wyville 26) Thorpe Langton 27) Great Bowden 28) Husbands Bosworth 29) Old Dalby 30) Seagrave 31) Wymeswold 32) Burton-on-the-Wolds 33) Walton-on-the-Wolds 34) Countesthorpe 35) Swinford 36) Dunton Bassett 37) Anstey 38) Claybrooke Parva 39) Sapcote 40) Hemington 41) Stapleton 42) Stoke Golding 43) Sheepy Parva 44) Sheepy Magna.

Ceramic Phase	Pottery Types	Approximate Date Range
Early Anglo-Saxon	Hand-made/local manufacture	*c.* 450-650
Middle Anglo-Saxon	Predominantly hand-made. Small quantities of imported Ipswich and Maxey ware	*c.* 650-850
Saxo-Norman	Coarse Stamford ware, St Neots ware, Lincoln shelly ware	*c.* 850-1100
Earlier Medieval	Fine Stamford ware, Potters Marston ware, Stanion-Lyveden ware	*c.*1250-1400
Medieval	Very Fine Stamford Ware, Chilvers Coton ware, Nottingham ware	*c.*1250-1400
Later Medieval	Bourne Ware	c.1400-1500

Table 1: Pottery types and associated ceramic phases

for example, prehistoric evidence included an *in-situ* Neolithic flint knapping scatter as well as Bronze Age and Iron Age features, all preserved beneath medieval remains (Thomas 2001). A long-lived boundary ditch in the centre of Cottesmore had Iron Age origins but was a feature continually into the early Roman period (Thomas 1999a); further Roman remains to the east suggest a persistent focus of settlement (Trimble 2008). More extensive areas of Iron Age settlement have also recently been revealed beneath medieval remains at Walton on the Wolds (Chapman *et al* 2005) and Whissendine (Browning 2004), both previously unknown sites.

It would be unwise to stretch ideas of continuity of occupation to the above examples but they do serve as a reminder that by the time people began to live together in villages, the landscape had already been settled, worked and re-worked by many generations and elements such as ploughland, boundaries and ponds will have been often re-used and adapted.

Village origins and development

There is general agreement that the origins of medieval villages are linked to the laying out of the open fields in the period between *c.*800– 1200 (Oosthuizen 2006), but the precise mechanisms by which they were formed remain much debated. The relatively imprecise nature of available dates from pottery found at relevant sites in fact allows scope for a number of alternative interpretations of the evidence. However, the arguments fall into two broad camps: on the one hand, the apparently sweeping changes in the countryside leading to the formation of villages has convinced some that this was the result of a centrally based 'great replanning' of the landscape (Brown and Foard 1998). On the other hand a more evolutionary scenario for the village is proposed, whereby smaller settlements gradually expanded or came together to form larger groups in a piecemeal fashion (Lewis *et al* 2001, 238). This latter proposal also found support in evidence from the Whittlewood Project, where the main settlements apparently grew outwards from a series of small pre-village nuclei (Jones and Page 2006, Jones *et al* 2006).

Results from extensive fieldwalking programmes in Leicestershire and Rutland have shown that a dispersed pattern of Early Anglo-Saxon farmsteads and hamlets lay behind the village landscape (Liddle 1994; Bowman 1996). The Medbourne area survey for example (Liddle 1994), revealed a pattern that suggests the earliest Stamford ware pottery (*c.*850 1150) does not appear on Early Anglo-Saxon sites unless they subsequently become medieval villages. This phenomenon appears to reflect a reorganisation of the rural settlement pattern during the Middle Anglo-Saxon period, resulting in either abandonment of sites, relocation, or a transformation into nucleated villages around which the open field systems developed. It is possible, therefore, that the general lack of recognisably Middle Anglo-Saxon settlement sites in the two counties is due to the fact that they lie beneath CORS. Recent discoveries of Middle Anglo-Saxon pottery from Uppingham (Armour-Chelu 1999) and Wymondham (Pickstone and Connor 2008) indicate that such material was reaching the area, albeit in limited quantities, but the fragmentary nature of the associated archaeology at both sites hinders further interpretation of their context.

The relationship between prior Anglo-Saxon settlements and the eventual village sites is compelling but not entirely clear. Where excavation has occurred it is evident that the fieldwalking scatters of Early Anglo-Saxon pottery do provide a good indication of settlement, as at Eye Kettleby (Finn 1997, 1998) and the recent Time Team project at Knave Hill, Stonton Wyville (Wessex Archaeology 2008). At Eye Kettleby the juxtaposition of a 6th century Anglo-Saxon hamlet adjacent to deserted village earthwork remains presents an interesting situation where it could be assumed on face value that one transformed into the other over time (fig 3). Limited excavation work at the DMV however, suggests a 10th or 11th century origin for its establishment (Finn 1999a/b, 2000) indicating that the links between the two settlements are far from clear cut. A comparable example can also be seen in Rutland where a substantial scatter of Early Anglo-Saxon pottery lies centrally between the deserted village of Martinsthorpe to the west, and Manton to the east (fig 4). Again this juxtaposition of settlements may seem to suggest some sort of continuity but, as at Eye Kettleby, it is difficult to prove direct links. The earliest dated pottery recovered from Martinsthorpe indicated 12th to 13th century

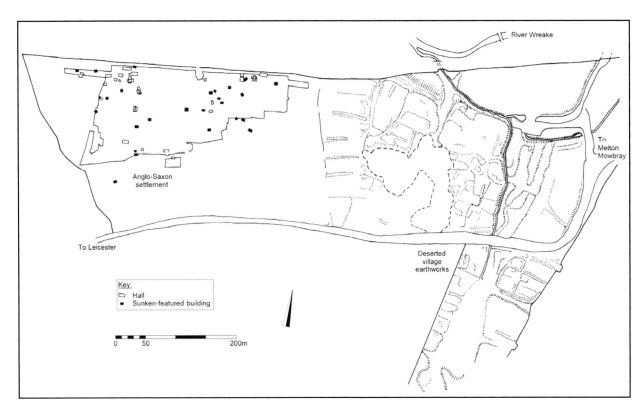

Figure 3: The close spatial relationship of 6th century Anglo-Saxon settlement and 10th-11th century village remains at Eye Kettleby, Leicestershire

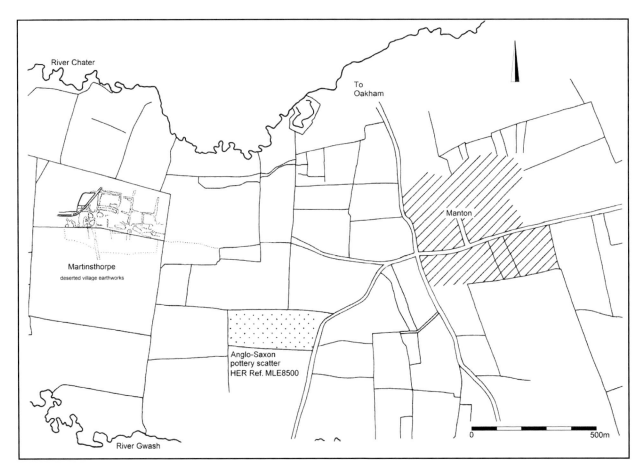

Figure 4: Juxtaposition of an Early Anglo-Saxon pottery scatter, deserted village remains at Martinsthorpe and the Currently Occupied Rural Settlement of Manton, Rutland.

occupation (Wacher 1964), while the earliest plot boundaries at Manton were dated to the 10th or 11th century (Tate 2007).

The Anglo-Saxon evidence

A number of sites have produced small quantities of residual Anglo-Saxon pottery in later features, suggesting they were earlier foci of activity. This may also be inferred from the small group of Anglo-Saxon cemeteries that have been identified adjacent to and within CORS (for example at Glaston in Leeds and Barber 1950, Seaton in Pollard 1997, 1999 and Stoke Golding in Coutts *et al* 2007). Several other sites have produced slightly more tangible evidence for Anglo-Saxon activity: two separate, but neighbouring projects in Whissendine have revealed a pair of Early Anglo-Saxon boundary ditches on a similar alignment and apparently part of the same system of land division (Browning 2007; Hyam 2006); a shallow pit adjacent to one of the ditches contained pottery, animal bone and charcoal suggesting nearby occupation (Hyam 2006, 4). At Loddington a trial trench evaluation has also revealed evidence of occupation, characterised by deposits containing pottery, burnt stone and iron slag indicating an area of

Early Anglo-Saxon metalworking (Hunt 2008). While both of these sites offer tantalising evidence for Early Anglo-Saxon occupation in close association with later village remains, the fragmentary nature of these deposits makes it difficult to understand fully their nature and the detail of their relationship to later developments.

In neighbouring counties excavations have suggested that where Anglo-Saxon occupation and later villages coincide the nature of settlement changes considerably over time. At Raunds Furnells, Northamptonshire, for example, an Early to Middle Anglo-Saxon settlement preceded village formation on the same spot but was noticeably different in character to the later remains (Audouy and Chapman 2009). Further work on the Leicestershire and Rutland sites is needed before any firm conclusions can be drawn; however it is possible that a similar pattern of development occurred on at least some of the sites that became nucleated villages.

Early signs of nucleation: village activity during the late 9th to 11th centuries

The earliest evidence for the formation of villages from the two counties suggests a

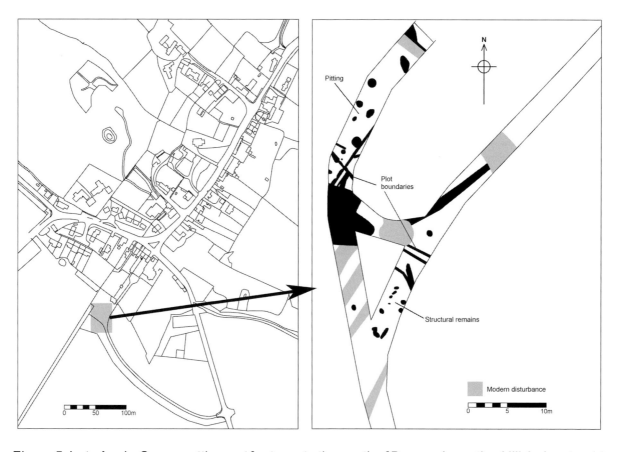

Figure 5: Late Anglo-Saxon settlement features to the south of Burrough-on-the-Hill, Leicestershire

period of activity during the 10th and 11th centuries, dated broadly by the presence of early Stamford wares, pottery from St. Neots and Lincolnshire shelly wares. Interestingly, however, a number of sites have revealed evidence for slightly earlier origins, suggesting that village development may, in places, have been an occasional and scattered process, perhaps relating to particular local circumstances.

Occupation in the 9th-10th century is evident in the centre of Cottesmore where a pit containing domestic debris including pottery, animal bone and broken quernstones was found in association with a nearby gully and ditch (Thomas 1998a). Although the associated finds from these features is suggestive of nearby occupation little more can be said about the exact nature of the site. Interestingly however, the linear features adopted a very different orientation to later plot boundaries that were established in the 11th-12th centuries, indicating re-planning of the settlement at some point. In contrast, the orientation of a substantial Late Anglo-Saxon boundary ditch at Claybrook Parva was mirrored by 10th-11th century developments of the boundary system some twenty metres away, reflecting continuity of the originally established line (Jarvis 2001).

A fuller picture of Late Anglo-Saxon settlement emerges on the southern fringes of Burrough-on-the-Hill where a dense area of apparent plot boundaries, pits and structural remains was uncovered during a watching brief (Thomas 2000 and see fig 5). The limitations of the work offered only a window onto these remains, but it was clear that several phases of activity were represented, indicative of fairly intensive activity at this time. The proximity of this area to the main historic core of the village is interesting, but based on present evidence it is difficult to judge if this represents early development of Burrough or a discrete focus of occupation pre-dating the formation of the village.

Development of the village plan in the 10th and 11th centuries

The main evidence for village formation is represented by 10th-11th century activity characterised by the laying out of property boundaries demarcating rectangular farmyards (tofts) and associated gardens or orchards (crofts) which often ran away from the main

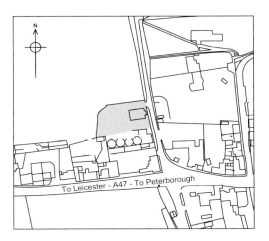

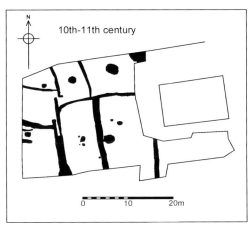

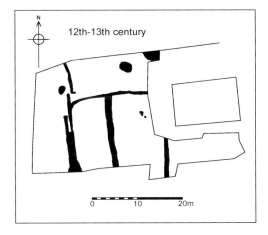

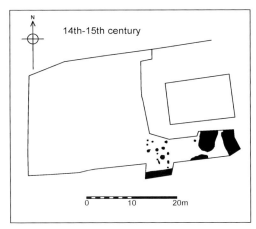

Figure 6: Development and decline of toft and croft features at Glaston, Rutland

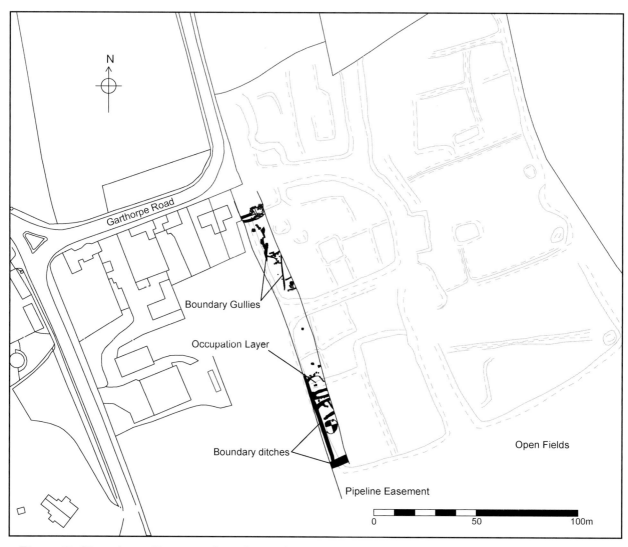

Figure 7: Shrunken village earthworks and archaeological remains at Saxby, Leicestershire

thoroughfares in regular strips. Evidence for this phenomenon comes from excavations at various sites across the two counties. A particularly complete example at Glaston consisted of the rear end of a toft approximately 20m wide, defined by ditches (Cooper and Thomas 2001: fig 6). A central ditch dissected the enclosed area and was apparently broadly contemporary with the main setting out of the toft, perhaps defining two distinct activity areas; the toft appeared to run away from the main street frontage where, presumably, the associated dwelling was located. A series of small paddocks or enclosures attached to the rear of the toft may have represented the croft, although, apart from several quarry pits, there was little other evidence within these areas. Low level activities within the toft were represented by a scatter of post holes and several pits associated with a thin spread of finds.

Similar evidence characterised Earlier Medieval development at Saxby, where a pipeline through village earthworks on the edge of the modern settlement enabled partial examination of two distinct plots (Thomas 2001a and 2001b: fig 7). The southernmost plot appeared defined by ditches which formed the boundary with the open fields. Space within the plot was organised around a system of gullies that effectively sub-divided the area, perhaps for different uses. The southern part of this plot was relatively empty, with the exception of a possible square enclosure, but in the northern half a distinct occupation layer of finds-rich soil was associated with pitting and a small post-built structure. The structure was perhaps too small to have been a dwelling, although the large amounts of pottery, butchered animal bone and burning that were associated certainly signify nearby domestic activities. Space in the northern plot was also carefully defined by gullies which delimited at least two rectangular plots; scattered post holes hinted at associated structural activity, while an area of pitting to the north of the plots suggested a designated area for refuse disposal. Interestingly the plots in the northern area lay on a different orientation to those in the south, evidently a result of reorganisation at some point.

Some of the larger excavations hint at a fairly regular format to the early village plot layout, potentially allowing patterns to be extrapolated from more limited views. Thus trial trench evaluations at Empingham (Thomas 1997), Thorpe Langton (Cope-Faulkner 2002) and Burton Lazars (Burrows 2005), have all revealed evidence for carefully arranged networks of boundary gullies indicative of early toft and croft establishment. It is difficult to determine, from such small areas, how much we are seeing evidence for settlement 'planning'. There is

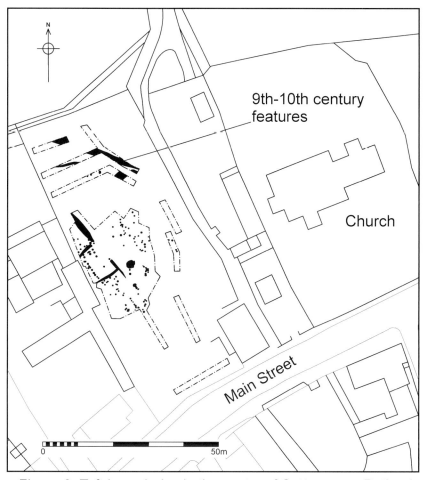

Figure 8: Toft boundaries in the centre of Cottesmore, Rutland

reasonable evidence, from continuity of form between some early village plots, to suggest it does. However, other sites illustrate the variety of boundary definition that existed between and potentially within settlements.

At Manton early boundary activity consisted of a loose arrangement of gullies, probably forming part of a rectangular toft on a north-south alignment. The rear of the plot was not so clearly defined, although its orientation appeared to be respected by a linear arrangement of pitting that followed the line established by the gullies (Tate 2007). A similar boundary system at Cottesmore was represented by both gullies and rows of post holes on similar alignments (Thomas 1999a) (fig 8). This may be a product of two clear phases of boundary definition as at least some of the post holes were stratigraphically later than the gullies. The relatively shallow and impermanent nature of the gullies, however, might also indicate their role as markers for the post-built boundaries. In contrast to these apparently flimsy boundaries, a toft on the edge of Freeby was defined by a long-lived sequence of substantial ditches (Thomas

1999b), clearly setting the plot apart from the adjacent street. A stream on the eastern side of the toft may also have served as a natural boundary in conjunction with the ditches. A cobbled surface in association with a drainage channel and scatter of post holes probably related to structural activity in the north-western corner of the toft, closest to the street. Limited excavations at Stoke Golding show that individual tofts were separated by a long lived system of gullies projecting away from the street line, but in turn the general toft area was distinguished from the frontage by a substantial ditch (Coutts *et al* 2007).

In contrast to the fairly regular nature of toft and croft plans reflected in many examples, evidence from Whissendine indicates an alternative arrangement (Browning 2007). Here 10th-11th century activity was characterised by a scatter of enclosures defined by a combination of gullies and post-built fences. A spread of post holes and occasional pits hinted at occupation, although there were few associated finds, perhaps suggesting the enclosures related to stock control and lay away from the main living areas.

49

Village continuity and change – developments in the 12th and 13th centuries

A second clear phase of village activity in the study area is indicated at a number of sites that underwent significant phases of development during the 12th and 13th centuries. The evidence suggests that some villages were at the formative stages of nucleation at this time, although continued activity is also evident at settlements with earlier origins.

At Glaston, the toft boundaries were maintained and occupation continued along broadly similar lines to those established in the Saxo-Norman period, as was the case at Saxby where the early tofts and crofts showed evidence of continued activity into the 12th-13th centuries. In contrast other sites with earlier origins show evidence of considerable reorganisation in this period. A re-orientation of the overall village alignment at Manton is evident in the creation of a new toft boundary overlying its predecessor. At Whissendine a more extensive and regularly arranged pattern of boundaries was established in the 12th-13th centuries, apparently reflecting a more formalised system of tofts and replacing the earlier set of smaller enclosures that had previously been in use. New phases of development at other villages also indicate a slightly later move towards nucleation,

although in most cases residual pottery and stray features indicate this was taking place on sites of earlier occupation.

The most complete plan of a toft and its overall organisation comes from Anstey, where evidence for 12th and 13th century occupation has been unearthed as a result of two excavation phases (Browning and Higgins 2003; fig 9). The focus of occupation was a raised toft area defined on at least one side by a boundary ditch, and separated from the open fields by a hollow way to the rear. Space within the toft appears to have been segregated by a series of inter-related smaller boundaries that were generally aligned with the hollow way. Fragmentary remains of cobbled surfaces throughout the area probably related to yards or pathways associated with buildings. Varied evidence for buildings consisted of compacted gravel foundations to support sill-beams and probable post-built structures. A conspicuous rectangular gap within a yard surface at the rear of the toft may also have been the site of a building adjacent to the hollow way. None of the buildings produced direct evidence of domestic use, although environmental information suggests a bias towards domestic waste from features on the western side of the toft. It seems likely that the main dwelling lay outside the excavated area, closer to the street frontage.

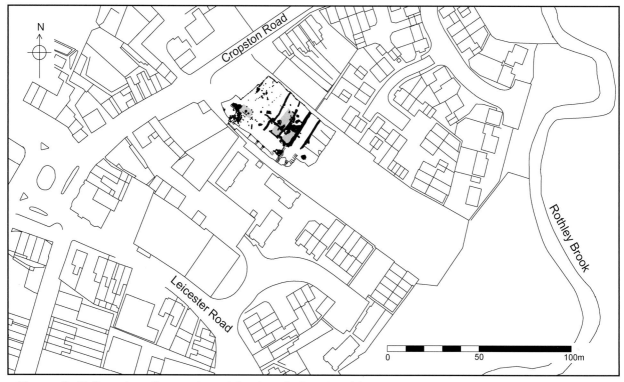

Figure 9: Toft and croft remains at Anstey, Leicestershire

While the Anstey toft appears to represent a relatively new development, it is in fact clear from a fairly large assemblage of residual pottery that earlier activity occurred on or near the site in the 10th and 11th centuries. Quite what form this early occupation took is difficult to determine as no features could be directly associated with this phase, which was most likely buried beneath the raised platform.

Excavations at the closely related villages of Sheepy Parva and Sheepy Magna in west Leicestershire, have revealed strikingly similar evidence indicative of intensive 12th to 14th century settlement on the main street frontage, although residual earlier material also provides persuasive evidence of previous phases of occupation at both sites (Sturgess 1999; Jarvis 2004). Indeed, the nature of the archaeology at both sites reflects busy settlement areas that were prone to frequent change. At Sheepy Parva, a complicated pattern of ditches and gullies provided a partial view of two tofts lying adjacent to the street frontage and defined by a long-lived system of boundary ditches. Space within each toft was divided by smaller gullies and fences that may have defined small enclosures. A probable timber building was located in the eastern toft lying adjacent to the road; its full plan slightly obscured by later pitting. The character of remains and the broad range of pottery associated with this site suggest a long-lived settlement with several phases of development but it has proved difficult to clearly distinguish individual phases. A similar pattern of roadside development emerged only *c*.400m to the north-west in Sheepy Magna. Although more fragmentary than on the neighbouring site, a series of ditches and gullies, cobbled surfaces, pitting and structural remains all related to occupation within a toft that was predominantly active in the mid-13th century.

In contrast to the roadside location of the Sheepy sites, evidence from elsewhere has shown that complex evidence of occupation need not always be located close to the street frontage. Remains at Old Dalby reflected ground plans of two partially revealed tofts that were occupied mainly in the late 12th to early 14th centuries (Hyam 2008). The tofts were divided by a long-lived boundary ditch projecting away from the main street frontage and connected to a network of smaller ditches and gullies lying at right angles to the main boundary. Pottery and animal bone assemblages from the boundaries and associated pits reflected the site's close proximity to domestic activity, although the area seems likely to have been some distance from the main area of habitation that may have been closer to the street.

The bewildering tangle of boundaries that are often encountered on village core sites highlights the fluid and dynamic nature of developing village plans as different parts of the settlement might be given over to different uses at particular times. Clearly village plans were rarely static and were often reorganised, resulting in complex ground plans of overlapping phases. Depending on the scale of project and subsequent level of archaeological investigation it can be extremely difficult to understand the sequence of development.

The changing nature of plots within CORS is well illustrated by excavation work at Great Bowden where complex settlement remains had accumulated over several phases of occupation (Brown 2007). Early origins for occupation of the site are hinted at by a small scatter of 10th-11th century pottery associated with several shallow features. The main phase of activity on the site occurred in the 12th century when at least two tofts were established. The domestic nature of the related finds indicates these were probably the rear ends of properties fronting onto the medieval street. Activity diminished in the late 12th-13th century when the disused plot boundaries were filled in and the site apparently became part of a single large area, defined at the rear by a boundary ditch. Low numbers of finds from this period imply partial site abandonment as supported by the fact that the area became covered by a spread of silty clay likely to have accumulated as a result of standing water. Redevelopment in the 13th century saw the establishment of three new boundaries set *c*.7m apart, creating three separate E-W aligned plots. Irregular pits in two of the plots suggest deliberate tree or shrub planting, hinting that they may have been used as orchards. Finally, after these plots had gone out of use, a new arrangement of boundary ditches was

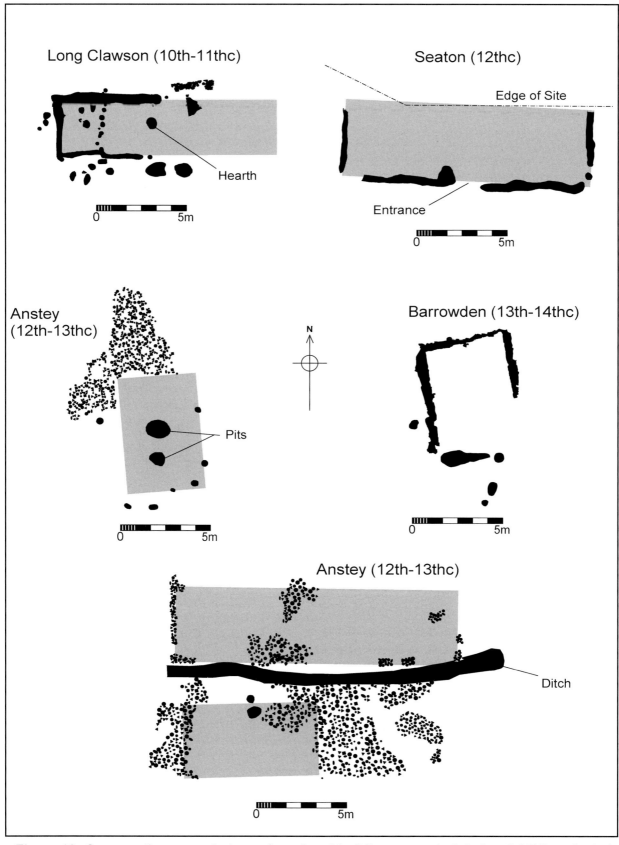

Figure 10: Comparative ground-plans of medieval buildings revealed during CORS projects in Leicestershire and Rutland

established in the 14th century which formed a more substantially defined series of tofts.

Buildings

In contrast to the relatively abundant information relating to early tofts, there has been little corresponding evidence revealed for associated dwellings. In part this must be a result of the locations of individual episodes of work, which often focus on areas away from the main street frontage. Equally, however, the relatively insubstantial nature of buildings from this period might leave little archaeological trace, or could be prone to removal during episodes of rebuilding or reorganisation on the same spot.

Fragmentary evidence for Saxo-Norman timber buildings has been recovered from excavations at Saxby (Thomas 2001a), Eye Kettleby (Finn 1999b) and Wyfordby (Jarvis 2002), but the most complete building of this period was discovered on the eastern side of Long Clawson (Hunt and Coward 2006) (fig 10). This building was associated with a centrally placed hearth, suggesting domestic use. The structural remains related to a building measuring c.4.3m wide by at least 7m long, although the eastern extent was not clearly defined and the overall length could feasibly be doubled. The building was defined by a series of shallow slots containing regularly spaced post settings, commonly referred to as post-in-trench construction. A possible internal partition was marked by a line of smaller post holes towards the western end of the building and substantial pairs of post holes to the east suggested a cross-passage.

A similar building dating to the c.12th century has been excavated at Seaton (Richards 2005). This was also constructed using the post-in-trench method and had a centrally located entrance in the southern long side. The northern side of the building was not observed; but its estimated dimensions of c.13.5m x 4.5m suggest it was similar in size to the Long Clawson example. A number of buildings were excavated at Anstey, although alternative construction techniques appear to have been involved. Here, rectangular gaps in cobbled yard surfaces probably represented the sites of timber or mud-built structures, most likely agricultural buildings due to their lack of hearths or other domestic indicators. Another building was partially supported by linear spreads of cobbling, probably supporting sill-beams, while others appear to have been partly constructed of earth-fast posts (Browning and Higgins 2003).

There has been little evidence for buildings with stone foundations, although fragmentary remains of such structures at Barkstone-le-Vale (Richards and Challis 2002) and Empingham (Thomson 2002), were both associated with pottery from the 12th century onwards; the incomplete nature of these buildings may reflect episodes of stone robbing for re-use elsewhere. At Barrowden, limestone wall footings have been identified during trial trenching (Kipling 2003) and excavation at another nearby site in the village has provided evidence of a more fully preserved limestone building datable to the later medieval period (Meek 2000). One end of this building had been built into a terrace, helping its survival. A width of c.4.4m could be ascertained although the original length is likely to have been more than the c.6m that remained. Charred plant remains and burnt bone from possible floor layers within the walls hint at a domestic role for the building.

Village life: the material culture of medieval rural settlements

Pottery, animal bone and charred plant remains are regularly recovered in variable quantities from excavations within CORS. These assemblages all offer valuable information towards understanding the lives of the village inhabitants and activities carried out in the tofts and crofts. Generally, however, the finds groups associated with these sites are small, perhaps not surprising considering that the majority of the refuse would likely have been incorporated into middens and ultimately spread on the fields. This problem is further exacerbated when the find groups are broken down between the site phases, making it very difficult to see patterns emerging over time. Organic finds, particularly animal bone, are also subject to differential survival depending on taphonomic histories (the study of decaying organisms over time) and the level of acidity characterising local geologies. Personal items have occasionally been found, but are few and far between, often giving the impression that these sites were fairly impoverished. Such items will have been highly valued and looked after and loss may have been infrequent, or, alternatively, once broken they may have been recycled.

Pottery

Pottery assemblages are undoubtedly subject to a number of biases; however the characteristics of these groups can give a broad indication of the chronology and nature of the occupation on a particular site within a settlement. A range of pottery forms is generally found; typically jars, bowls, pitchers and jugs, representing the essentially domestic and agricultural nature of these settlements, bearing in mind that many pottery vessels were multi-functional. Not only is pottery a valuable (often the only) source of dating for particular deposits, but the assemblages can also inform on local patterns of trade and exchange and the nature of activities on particular sites.

For much of Leicestershire and Rutland a particular range of pottery fabrics is closely associated with the growth and development of medieval villages, providing a reflection of the network of trade and exchange. Not surprisingly, in the Saxo-Norman period much of the pottery supplied to these eastern rural communities was traded from Stamford, an important pottery production centre at this time whose products were widely distributed throughout the two counties and much of the rest of England and sometimes beyond. Thus Stamford ware is predominant on most of the study sites with Saxo-Norman origins, particularly in the villages of Glaston, Cottesmore and Whissendine in Rutland. Pottery from Lincoln, and the St. Neots and Torksey/Thetford wares or type wares originating in the south midlands and East Anglia, was also present, but in more limited quantities.

The influence of the Stamford pottery industry during this period is equally evident at more westerly sites such as Anstey in Leicestershire, where a sizeable assemblage of Stamford ware was found despite the village lying more than 50km to the west of the town. Over time the dominance of Stamford wares was replaced by a wider range of pottery types as new industries were established in the 12th and 13th centuries. Despite this increase in available wares the distribution of these new types appears to have been largely influenced by the proximity of settlements to particular production centres.

Much of the pottery found in the villages of Rutland and eastern Leicestershire in the Earlier Medieval period was either shelly ware or Potters Marston ware. Whilst the latter is from a known production centre south-west of Leicester and is tempered with a coarse grained igneous rock, easily identifiable by eye, the origins of the shelly wares are less clear. Some of this material can be related by vessel types and decoration to the kilns at Stanion and Lyveden in north-east Northamptonshire, but much of the shelly ware probably originates from other, as yet unknown, production centres in Northamptonshire. Similarly, sources further north for some of the shelly wares, perhaps in southern Lincolnshire, cannot be discounted. Unlike the wide-ranging distribution patterns of traded Stamford ware, the study sites suggest that the easterly trade in Potters Marston was much more limited. Less than a dozen sherds of Potters Marston was found at Whissendine, for example, and none at Glaston further to the east, whilst shelly wares, including those from Stanion and Lyveden, and Bourne wares or type wares from South Lincolnshire characterised the earlier medieval assemblages in both villages. A comparable site may be Freeby, where alongside some Potters Marston products, shelly wares were clearly the preferred choice, accounting for 97% of the assemblage.

Sites further west had access to a slightly different range of pottery. At Anstey, Potters Marston wares dominate, doubtless due to the village's close proximity to the production centre, only 13km to the south. A significant proportion of the pottery, however, was traded from Nottingham during the 13th and 14th centuries and, by the later medieval period, the source of most of the pottery was a major production centre based on Chilvers Coton in Nuneaton, Warwickshire, approximately 26km to the south-west. Similar patterns were evident at Sheepy Magna and Sheepy Parva, close to the Warwickshire border, where limited quantities of pottery from Coventry were also found.

Animal bone

Animals were clearly important to the inhabitants of medieval villages, serving as sources of food such as meat, milk, cheese and eggs, but also providing hides, skins and wool. Larger animals such as cattle and horses would also have been used for traction, particularly ploughing and the processing of crops.

Bone assemblages are regularly recovered from village core excavations, generally consisting of the main domesticated species such as cattle, sheep and pigs, and to a lesser extent, horses, domestic fowl, dogs and cats. In contrast remains of wild species are rarely recovered, with deer and fox occasionally represented. Almost all of the study sites have produced animal bones but individual assemblages are generally small and fragmentary, making both intra and inter site comparison difficult. The largest group (c.767 bones) was recovered from Whissendine but when this was broken down the total for each phase was reduced, hindering recognition of any overall trends. Whilst such problems are exacerbated by biases in survival, differential recovery rates must also be taken into account when assessing the bone groups from these sites. The poor size of some assemblages might also reflect the peripheral position of a site in relation to the main area of occupation.

Individual features have sometimes produced interesting groups which stand out from the overall site assemblage. A well at Manton for example produced an assemblage that included both butchery and domestic waste, presumably reflecting disposal of remains from separate activity areas. Goose remains dominated an assemblage from a pit at Saxby, while two features at Wymondham produced bone groups consisting entirely of small mammal and bird remains. These included domestic species such as fowl, bantam, goose and duck and wild taxa such as rabbit, partridge, pigeon and lapwing. The unusual nature of this assemblage is particularly interesting given the manorial context of the Wymondham site, possibly providing an insight into differences in resources at sites of contrasting status.

Plant remains
Evidence for the pastoral and cultivated environment and for diet has been systematically gathered as a result of environmental sampling during excavation within CORS, with some sites producing surprising amounts of material representative of agricultural and domestic activities.

Assemblages thought to represent domestic waste, typically characterised by a low density of remains consisting of mainly cereal grains and weed seeds, have been found from a few sites including those at Anstey, Freeby,

Barrowden, Claybrook Magna, Long Clawson and Stapleton (Monckton 2004a). Perhaps not surprisingly some of these have been found in close association with apparently domestic buildings as at Anstey (where the assemblage was related to a distinct house platform), and at both Barrowden and Long Clawson (where charred plant remains were recovered from probable floor layers within buildings). Other similar samples are not so obviously linked to buildings but can reasonably be assumed to indicate nearby domestic activities. Alongside cereal remains, occasional fruit seeds and stones indicate that wild foods were gathered, and the likely cultivation of fruit trees within crofts. A scatter of irregular pits at the back of a plot at Langton Road, Great Bowden may have represented deliberate planting of shrubs or trees, suggesting that this part of the property served as an orchard (Brown 2007, 7).

The Anstey plant remains are particularly important as two distinct assemblages appear to represent refuse resulting from both domestic and agricultural activities. Charred refuse from a western boundary ditch probably represented waste from agricultural processing while a scatter of features to the east probably resulted from domestic food preparation (Monckton 2004b, 162). Both groups provided information on the crops and diet of the site inhabitants. Cultivated food remains included bread wheat, edible legumes and some rye, oats and barley, whilst hazelnuts indicated that parts of the diet were gathered. The legumes were small, perhaps suggesting they were grown following a fodder crop, or possibly fallow in a crop rotation system. Weeds, including stinking mayweed, indicated cultivation of the heavy clay soils, while others such as corn cockle and cleavers, were typically associated with autumn sown crops such as wheat and rye. The distribution of these remains within the toft suggests that separate activities were carried out in particular areas.

Plant remains relating to the working life of villagers have a very different character to domestic ones, often rich in chaff and weed seeds, indicating agricultural processing of cereals. At Wyfordby, for example, evidence for cereal storage and processing included remains of bread wheat, glume wheat, barley and possibly oats (Jarvis 2002). Similar evidence was recovered at Old Dalby (Monckton 2008), although here the chaff was sparse and there was more abundant evidence for weeds suggesting localised cultivation. Plant remains from Old Dalby also included rivet wheat as well as bread wheat which is more commonly found on village sites. Both types of wheat are known from medieval contexts in Leicester where it was consumed but not grown; however until recently evidence for its cultivation was scarce. The site at Old Dalby is the latest addition to a small, but growing number of village sites, including Saxby and Whissendine, where rivet wheat has been found and apparently cultivated alongside bread wheat as a mixed crop.

Crafts

Limited evidence for small-scale craft and industrial activities has been revealed on a number of sites across the two counties either directly or indirectly as inferred from associated finds. Much of the evidence relates to domestic level metalworking, remains of which have been associated with a range of periods. The earliest evidence indicates 5th-6th century Early Anglo-Saxon ironworking at Loddington where an area of tap slag and burnt ironstone was revealed (Hunt 2008, 9). At Lilac Farm, Mill Lane, Cottesmore, a concentration of layers and pits dating to the 12th-13th centuries produced large quantities of iron tap slag, partially burnt iron ore and hearth/furnace lining indicative of iron smelting in the near vicinity (Clarke 2002, Trimble 2008) perhaps relating to commercial output. Small quantities of iron slag were also present in 10th/11th century features at Claybrooke Parva (Jarvis 2001), Great Bowden (Brown 2007), and 14th/15th century deposits at Stoke Golding (Coutts et al 2007). At Anstey larger pieces of iron slag had been used as packing in post holes (Browning and Higgins 2003, 70).

Evidence for weaving has been found in 9th-10th century deposits at Burrough on the Hill village (Thomas 2000) and in Burton Lazars (Burrows 2005) where a clay loom-weight and bone pin beater have been found respectively. A group of quernstones from a similarly dated pit at Cottesmore provides evidence of nearby domestic crop processing (Thomas 1999a).

At Seaton, industrial activity was indicated by a closely related group of five elongated clay-lined pits dating to the 10th/11th centuries (Richards 2005). The pits lay in a linear formation and had been deliberately arranged to follow the grounds natural slope. The pits were deeper and more steeply cut on their upslope sides, in contrast to the opposite ends which were shallower. The exact purpose of the pits is unclear, although their form and positioning might indicate some form of water management system, perhaps related to either tanning or dyeing. Two other features at Seaton were characterised by in-situ burning in small pits and associated with burnt clay and stones. Their nature suggests a role in industrial processes, perhaps as short-use hearths, but unfortunately there was little evidence to say exactly what this was.

A similar feature at Old Dalby consisted of a stone-lined, horseshoe shaped pit containing charcoal and burnt organic material (Hyam 2008). The organic remains consisted of species consistent with field margin clearance and had perhaps been used as kindling to provide a source of heat for an unspecified industrial function. Another enigmatic stone-lined feature at Freeby dated to the 13th or 14th century although there was very little associated evidence to understand its original function (Thomas 1999b).

Conclusion

This study has sought to review the considerable amount and value of new archaeological information that has been generated as a result of developer-funded projects within CORS in Leicestershire and Rutland. Despite the variable size of individual projects, each positive result contributes information towards our understanding of the origins, functions and growth of rural settlement in the region. Furthermore, each site offers information on settlements that survived, at a time when others were going into terminal decline, and are therefore representative of the successful majority. The results of these projects highlight the extent to which undisturbed archaeological remains can survive within CORS, and provide comparable evidence to that previously recovered from excavations on deserted sites, on buildings, plans, plots, economies and material culture.

As relatively new areas for research, the land covered by CORS represents comparatively 'blank' areas on the archaeological map for all periods (although map and plan analysis can provide outline models of growth). An important point to come out of this research is the frequency at which remains of pre-village occupation have been recovered. Not only does this remind us that medieval villages are just a chapter in the continuing cycle of settlement of the landscape, but it also raises questions about the degree of settlement continuity at certain places. To what extent do these palimpsests of archaeological activity reflect real continuity or evidence of preferred locations for dwelling?

One key question has been the degree of continuity between the dispersed Anglo-Saxon settlement pattern and the early formation of villages. In Leicestershire and Rutland, many sites have yielded small scatters of residual Anglo-Saxon pottery sherds, while others have nearby associated cemeteries hinting at possible settlement continuity; however, even at such sites where Anglo-Saxon and medieval settlements are spatially close, such as Eye Kettleby, the relationships are far from clear, with a gap of many centuries distinguishing the end of the old settlement and the start of the new. Settlement may have developed along similar lines to those in Northamptonshire, where a dispersed pattern of small, frequently moving settlements became abandoned by the 9th century in favour of larger, nucleated villages (Brown and Foard 1998). Alternatively, some villages may have developed from existing foci of occupation; a pattern identified at some settlements included in the Whittlewood project (Jones and Page 2006).

This study has offered some tantalising examples where remains of Anglo-Saxon and early medieval occupation overlap, although the scale of intervention on each site does not currently enable clear conclusions to be drawn. Inevitably, where there is such a relationship, the earliest remains are at risk of fragmentation or complete removal by the later activities. There is a marked absence of recognisably Middle Anglo-Saxon pottery from many of the study sites, although clearly wares of this period were arriving at some settlements in eastern parts of the region. It is possible that other parts of the region were aceramic during this period, or that pottery was in more limited supply and therefore under-represented and difficult to recognise during excavation.

There is considerably more evidence for the early stages of nucleation from the study sites, as represented by a recurring pattern of plot arrangements adjacent to the main village streets. The development of the nucleated village plan is apparently characterised by a distinct chronological divide between the east and west of the study area, with the earliest developments occurring in Rutland and High Leicestershire during the 10th and 11th centuries. Admittedly there are many potential biasing factors that could be responsible for this apparent phenomenon, both archaeologically and as a result of individual site circumstances. It is interesting to note that many Warwickshire villages (immediately south-west of the study area) do not display signs of full nucleation before the 11th-13th centuries (Dyer 1996, 118). Evidently occupation on 10th-11th century pre-village sites in the county had different characteristics as seen on recent excavations such as at Coton, near Rugby (Palmer 2003) showing that the nucleated form was adopted by different areas at different times in reaction to local circumstances.

Although early village plans were composed of broadly similar elements, the study has highlighted the variety in which individual plots were defined, whether by large, imposing ditches or relatively insubstantial lines of posts. Once defined, the tofts and crofts were often sub-divided and became the setting for a range of activities including temporary containment of livestock, craft areas, orchards and small cottage gardens. By the many pits and quarries often found, it is clear that the toft was also a source of raw materials – notably clay and gravel that could be used to build and maintain dwellings and agricultural structures. In contrast to the evidence for plots and the activities therein, evidence for associated buildings has been relatively slight and with the exception of Anstey, evidence for both on the same site has not been achieved. The lack of building evidence from these sites may in part be a result of the locations of excavated areas, often set back from the main street frontages, although the setting of the Long Clawson building suggests that dwellings were not always situated in prominent positions. What the evidence does suggest is that early village buildings were predominantly constructed of timber, mud-walling or a combination of the two. Remains of such buildings may be very slight and difficult to recover under unfavourable archaeological conditions. Nevertheless it is clear from this study that a variety of new medieval buildings have been revealed as a result of recent projects which can inform

57

construction techniques and the lives of those who used and dwelt in them.

Finds groups are often limited in comparison to larger contemporary assemblages from urban sites, however, the artefacts provide further information on the lives and activities of the village inhabitants. Pottery not only reveals patterns of trade but sheds light on the growing consumerism of the peasantry – particularly in the later medieval period. Evidence of farming practices and diet can be found in plant remains and animal bones left behind after processing or consumption.

It is clear from the data that once established the village plan did not stand still, but could be highly dynamic, with frequent alterations and reorganisation over time. This phenomenon can be seen in the variability in which individual plots changed or became abandoned, but by extension must reflect the changeable nature of the wider village, as settlement reshaped and attention was focussed elsewhere at particular times in response to phases of growth or decline. Indeed this process is still an integral part of village development, which is why archaeologists are currently able to excavate within them as new homes are built, and effectively dispels the traditional view of the village as timeless and unchanging.

In conclusion, it is clear from this review that important and well-preserved archaeological remains frequently survive within CORS.

It is also evident that this information has considerable potential to contribute towards our understanding of medieval rural settlement, both to develop and refine current theories on their origins and subsequent evolution. CORS offer one of the few resources of evidence for rural medieval communities and the archaeological remains within them are therefore crucial to our understanding of the lives of 'ordinary' people and places. However, these remains exist in a vulnerable state due to increased 'village infill' development, and as such are a threatened resource. Given the relative imbalance of 'case study' sites in this review, compared to the overall number of interventions, it is clear that the quality of information recovered is directly related to the methodology applied. High quality information has been recovered as a result of controlled excavation under strict archaeological conditions. In contrast the value of information recovered from projects with less rigorous conditions attached, such as 'watching briefs', is diminished even though the resource may be of comparable quality. The changing character of rural settlement will inevitably involve further redevelopment of areas containing these important remains. It is therefore vital that future strategies for managing developments within CORS ensure the maximum retrieval of archaeological information if we are to piece these lost histories back together.

Acknowledgements

This study has been developed from an original idea, involving James Meek, for a more limited project focusing on villages in Rutland. The level of work in recent years across the two counties made it necessary to widen the scope of the project to include sites in Leicestershire. Thanks are due to my colleagues (and ULAS directors) Richard Buckley and Patrick Clay for providing research funds to bring the project to fruition and for commenting on an earlier version of the resulting article. Illustrations are by the author and Michael Hawkes and part-funded through a research grant made available through the Medieval Settlement Research Group. I am very grateful to the long list of site directors (both ULAS colleagues and beyond) who provided information on their sites and the Leicestershire Archaeological Fieldwork Group for inviting me to speak at their 'Archaeology of Medieval Leicestershire' conference and giving me the impetus to bring the research to a conclusion. Additionally I would like to thank Jennifer Browning, Angela Monckton and Deborah Sawday for providing information on the relevant archaeozoological, environmental and ceramic evidence respectively. Finally I would like to express my gratitude to Neil Christie, the late Paul Courtney, Chris Dyer, and Carenza Lewis for their interest in the project and for providing thought provoking comments and advice on earlier drafts. Any mistakes that remain are entirely my responsibility.

Bibliography

Armour-Chelu, R., 1999. *London Road, Uppingham, Rutland: Archaeological Evaluation.* Unpublished Lindsey Archaeological Services Report No. 378.

Astill, G., 1988. 'Rural Settlement: the Toft and Croft.' In: G. Astill and A. Grant, eds, *The Countryside of Medieval England.* Oxford: Blackwell, 36–61.

Audouy, M. and Chapman, A., 2009. *Raunds: The Origin and Growth of a Midland Village AD 450–1500.* Oxford: Oxbow Books.

Beresford, M. and Hurst, J. G., 1972. *Deserted Medieval Villages: Studies.* Guildford and London: Lutterworth Press.

Bowman, P., 1996. 'Contrasting *pays*: Anglo-Saxon Settlement and Landscape in Langton Hundred.' In: J. Bourne (ed.) *Anglo Saxon Landscapes in the East Midlands.* Leicester: Leicestershire Museums, Arts and Records Service, 121–146.

Bradley, R., 2006. 'Bridging the two cultures: Commercial archaeology and the study of prehistoric Britain.' In: *Antiquaries Journal* 86, 1–13.

Bradley, R., 2007. *The Prehistory of Britain and Ireland.* Cambridge: Cambridge University Press.

Brown, J., 2007. *Archaeological Excavations at 24–26 Langton Road, Great Bowden, Leicestershire.* Unpublished Northamptonshire Archaeology Report.

Brown, T. and Foard, G., 1998. 'The Saxon Landscape: A Regional Perspective.' In P. L. Everson and T. Williamson (eds.) *The Archaeology of Landscape: Studies Presented to Christopher Taylor.* Manchester: Manchester University Press, 67–94.

Browning, J., 2004. 'Whissendine, Stapleford Road.' *Transactions of the Leicestershire Archaeological and Historical Society* 78, 176.

Browning, J., 2007. *Archaeological Excavations on land off Stapleford Road, Whissendine, Rutland.* Unpublished ULAS Report No. 2007–066.

Browning, J. and Higgins, T., 2003. 'Excavations of a Medieval Toft and Croft at Cropston Road, Anstey, Leicestershire.' *Transactions of the Leicestershire Archaeological and Historical Society* 77, 65–81.

Burrows, A., 2005. *An Archaeological Evaluation at Melton Road, Burton Lazars, Leicestershire.* Unpublished Northamptonshire Archaeology (NA) Report No. 05/106.

Chapman, P., Fisher, I. and Maull, A., 2005. *Late Iron Age and Roman Occupation and Medieval Field Boundaries at Melton Road, Burton on the Wolds, Leicestershire.* Unpublished Northamptonshire Archaeological Unit (NAU) Report.

Christie, N., 2002. 'Brooksby. From Village to Hall to College: Survey and Excavations at Brooksby 1999–2001.' *Transactions of the Leicestershire Archaeological and Historical Society* 76, 100–104.

Clarke, S., 2002. *An Archaeological Evaluation of Land at Lilac Farm, Mill Lane, Cottesmore, Rutland.* Unpublished ULAS Report No. 2002–160.

Clough, T., 2007. 'Medieval Settlements at Nether Hambleton and Whitwell.' In R. Ovens and S. Sleath, ed. *The Heritage of Rutland Water.* Rutland Local History and Record Society, Rutland Records Series No. 5.

Cooper, L., 2001. 'The Glaston Glutton and Other Strange Beasts.' *Rescue News* 83, 1–3.

Cooper, L. and Thomas, J., 2001. 'Glaston, Grange Farm.' *Transactions of the Leicestershire Archaeological and Historical Society* 75, 158–9.

Cooper, N. J. and Priest, V., 2003. 'Sampling a Medieval Village in a Day: The 'Big Dig' Investigation at Great Easton, Leicestershire.' *Medieval Settlement Research Group Annual Report* 18, 53–6.

Cooper, N. J. and Score, V., 2006. 'Investigating The Origins of Great Easton, Leicestershire: Community Archaeology Meets The 'Big Dig'. *Transactions of the Leicestershire Archaeological and Historical Society* 80, 209–14.

Cope-Faulkner, P., 2002. *An Archaeological Watching Brief on Bowden Road, Thorpe Langton, Leicestershire.* Unpublished Archaeological Project Services (APS) Report no. 61/02.

Coutts, C., Gethin, B. and Jones, C., 2007. *Archaeological Recording west of Park House, 4 Main Street, Stoke Golding, Leicestershire.* Unpublished Warwickshire Museum Field Services Report No. 0655.

Dyer, C., 1996. 'Rural settlements in medieval Warwickshire.' *Transactions of the Birmingham and Warwickshire Archaeological Society* 100, 117–32.

Dyer, C., 1997. 'Recent Developments and Future Prospects in Research into English Medieval Rural Settlements.' In: G. de Boe and F. Verhaeghe, (eds.) *Rural Settlement in Medieval Europe.* Papers of the 'Medieval Europe Brugge 1997' Conference – Volume 6, 55–61.

Finn, N., 1997. 'Eye Kettleby, Leicester Road, Melton Mowbray.' *Transactions of the Leicestershire Archaeological and Historical Society* 71, 88–91.

Finn, N., 1998. 'Melton Mowbray, Eye Kettleby, Leicester Road.' *Transactions of the Leicestershire Archaeological and Historical Society* 72, 178.

Finn, N., 1999a. 'Melton Mowbray, Eye Kettleby, Leicester Road.' *Transactions of the Leicestershire Archaeological and Historical Society* 73, 108.

Finn, N., 1999b. *Eye Kettleby Leicestershire: Revised Assessment and Updated Project Design.* Unpublished ULAS Report No. 1999–35.

Finn, N., 2000. 'Melton Mowbray, Eye Kettleby, Leicester Road' *Transactions of the Leicestershire Archaeological and Historical Society* 74, 250.

Grimbley, A. E., 1966. 'Kirby Bellars.' *Transactions of the Leicestershire Archaeological and Historical Society* 41, 69.

Hartley, R. F., 1983. *The Medieval Earthworks of Rutland.* Leicester: Leicestershire Museums, Arts and Records Service.

Hartley, R. F., 1984. *The Medieval Earthworks of North-West Leicestershire.* Leicester: Leicestershire Museums, Arts and Records Service.

Hartley, R. F., 1987. *The Medieval Earthworks of North-East Leicestershire.* Leicester: Leicestershire Museums, Arts and Records Service.

Hartley, R. F., 1989. *The Medieval Earthworks of Central Leicestershire.* Leicester: Leicestershire Museums, Arts and Records Service.

Hartley, R. F., 2004. 'Mapping the Medieval Landscape.' In: P. Bowman and P. Liddle, (eds). *Leicestershire Landscapes.* Leicestershire Museums Archaeological Fieldwork Group Monograph No. 1, 137–40.

Hartley, R. F., 2008. *The Medieval Earthworks of South-West Leicestershire: Hinckley and Bosworth.* Leicester: Leicestershire Museums Archaeological Fieldwork Group Monograph No. 2.

Hoskins, W. G., 1937. 'The fields of Wigston Magna.' *Transactions of the Leicestershire Archaeological and Historical Society* 19, 163–198.

Hoskins, W. G., 1945. 'The Deserted Villages of Leicestershire.' *Transactions of the Leicestershire Archaeological and Historical Society* 22, 242–264.

Hoskins, W. G., 1955. *The Making of the English Landscape.* London: Hodder and Stoughton.

Hunt, L., 2008. *An Archaeological Field Evaluation on land at Loddington Hall, Main Street, Loddington.* Unpublished ULAS Report No. 2008–059.

Hunt, L. and Coward, J., 2006. *An Archaeological Excavation at Croft House, 32 East End, Long Clawson, Leicestershire.* Unpublished ULAS Report No. 2006–002.

Hyam, A., 2006. *An Archaeological Evaluation on land to the rear of 5, Melton Road, Whissendine, Rutland.* Unpublished ULAS Report No. 2006–116.

Hyam, A., 2008. *An Archaeological Excavation and Watching Brief at 16–30 Main Road, Old Dalby, Leicestershire.* Unpublished ULAS Report No. 2008–056.

Jarvis, W., 2001. *An Archaeological Watching Brief on land adjacent to Claybrook Hall, Claybrook Parva, Leicestershire.* Unpublished ULAS Report No. 2001–102.

Jarvis, W., 2004. 'Sheepy, Sheepy Magna, Trout Ponds Farm.' *Transactions of the Leicestershire Archaeological and Historical Society* 78, 171.

Jarvis, W., and Derrick, M., 2002. 'Wyfordby.' *Transactions of the Leicestershire Archaeological and Historical Society* 76, 125.

Jones, R., Dyer, C. and Page, M., 2006. 'Changing Settlements and Landscapes: Medieval Whittlewood, Its Predecessors and Successors.' *Internet Archaeology* 19. http://intarch.ac.uk/journal/issue19/

Jones, R. and Page, M., 2006. *Medieval Villages in an English Landscape. Beginings and Ends.* Bollington: Windgather Press.

Kipling, R., 2003. *An Archaeological Evaluation at Durant Farm, Main Street, Barrowden, Rutland.* Unpublished University of Leicester Archaeological Services Report No. 2003–157.

Leeds, E. T. and Barber, J. L., 1950. 'An Anglian Cemetery at Glaston, Rutland.' *Antiquaries Journal* 30, 185–9.

Lewis, C., 2006. 'The Medieval Period.' In: N. J. Cooper, (ed.) *The Archaeology of the East Midlands. An Archaeological Resource Assessment and Research Agenda.* Leicester: Leicester Archaeology Monograph 13, 185–216.

Lewis, C., 2007. 'New Avenues for the Investigation of Currently Occupied Medieval Rural Settlement: Preliminary Observations from the Higher Education Field Academy.' In *Medieval Archaeology* 51, 133–163.

Lewis, C., Mitchell-Fox, P. and Dyer, C., 2001. *Village, Hamlet and Field.* Bollington: Windgather Press.

Liddle, P., 1982. *Leicestershire Archaeology – The Present State of Knowledge Volume 2. Anglo-Saxon and Medieval Periods.* Leicester: Leicestershire Museums, Arts and Records Service: Archaeological Report No. 5.

Liddle, P., 1994. 'The Medbourne Area Survey.' In M. Parker Pearson and R.T. Schadla-Hall, (eds.) *Looking at the Land. Archaeological Landscapes in Eastern England.* Leicester: Leicestershire Museums, Arts and Records Service, 34–6.

Meek, J., 2000. 'An Archaeological Excavation of a Medieval Building at Main Street Farm, Barrowden, Rutland.' *Rutland Record* 20, 425–9.

Monckton, A., 2004. 'Investigating Past Environments, Farming and Food in Leicester, Leicestershire and Rutland: The Evidence From Plant and Animal Remains.' In P. Liddle and P. Bowman eds. *Leicestershire Landscapes.* Leicester: Leicestershire Museums Archaeological Fieldwork Group Monograph No. 1, 154–171.

Monckton, A., 2004a. Appendix 5: Charred Plant Remains in A. Hyam, *An Archaeological Excavation on land at 16 Main Street, Stapleton, Leicestershire.* Unpublished ULAS Report No. 2004–104.

Monckton, A., 2004b. 'Investigating Past Environments, Farming and Food in Leicester, Leicestershire and Rutland: The Evidence From Plant and Animal Remains.' In: P. Liddle and P. Bowman (eds.) *Leicestershire Landscapes.* Leicester: Leicestershire Museums Archaeological Fieldwork Group Monograph No. 1, 154–171.

Monckton, A., 2008. 'Charred Plant Remains'. In: A. Hyam, *An Archaeological Excavation and Watching Brief at 16–30 Main Road, Old Dalby, Leicestershire.* Unpublished ULAS Report No. 2008–056.

Oosthuizen, S., 2006. *Landscapes Decoded: The History of Cambridgeshire's medieval fields.* Hatfield: University of Leicester Department of English Local History and University of Hertfordshire Press.

Palmer, N., 2003. 'Warwickshire (and Solihull) – The Medieval Period.' http://www. iaa.bham.ac.uk/research/fieldwork_ research_themes/projects/wmrrfa/ sem5.htm

Pearce, T. and Mellor, J. E., 1986. *Excavations at North Manor Farm, South Croxton, Leicestershire.* Leicestershire Museums, Arts and Records Service: Archaeological Report No. 11.

Pickstone, A. and Connor, A., 2008. 'Wymondham, Main Street.' *Transactions of the Leicestershire Archaeological and Historical Society* 82, 290–1.

Pollard, R., 1997. 'Seaton, Thompsons Lane.' *Transactions of the Leicestershire Archaeological and Historical Society* 71, 98–9.

Pollard, R., 1999. 'Seaton.' *Transactions of the Leicestershire Archaeological and Historical Society* 73, 118.

Powell, T. G. E., 1950. 'Notes on the Bronze Age in the East Midlands.' *Proceedings of the Prehistoric Society* 16, 65–80.

Richards, G., 2005. *Archaeological Excavations Undertaken at West Farm, Seaton, Rutland.* Unpublished ULAS Report No. 2005–158.

Richards, G. and Challis, K., 2002. *An Archaeological Watching Brief at Middle Street, Barkstone-le-Vale, Leicestershire.* Unpublished Trent and Peak Archaeological Unit Report.

Roberts, B. K. and Wrathmell, S., 2002. *Region and Place. A Study of English Rural Settlement.* London: English Heritage.

Sturgess, J., 1999. *An Archaeological Watching Brief, Salvage Recording and Photographic Survey at Mill Lane, Sheepy Parva, Leicestershire.* Unpublished ULAS Report No. 1999–67.

Tate, J., 2007. *An Archaeological Excavation and Watching Brief on land at Dairy Farm, Lyndon Road, Manton, Rutland.* Unpublished ULAS Report No. 2007–101.

Thomas, J., 1997. *An Archaeological Evaluation on land at Main Street, Empingham, Rutland.* Unpublished ULAS Report No. 1997–41.

Thomas, J., 1999a. 'Cottesmore, Main Street.' *Transactions of the Leicestershire Archaeological and Historical Society* 73, 118.

Thomas, J., 1999b. 'Freeby.' *Transactions of the Leicestershire Archaeological and Historical Society* 73, 98.

Thomas, J., 2000. *An Archaeological Watching Brief during Construction of a New Driveway to the Rear of Burrough House, 16, Main Street, Burrough-on-the-Hill, Somerby, Leicestershire.* Unpublished ULAS Report No. 2000–154.

Thomas, J., 2001a. 'Saxby, Saxby Village Drain.' *Transactions of the Leicestershire Archaeological and Historical Society* 75, 152–3.

Thomas, J., 2001b. *An Archaeological Watching Brief and Salvage Recording during Construction of Saxby Village Drain, Saxby, Leicestershire.* Unpublished ULAS Report No. 2001–27.

Thomas, J. and Jacobi, R., 2001. 'Glaston.' *Current Archaeology* 173, 180–4.

Thomson, S., 2002. *Archaeological Investigations on land at Loves Lane, Empingham, Rutland.* Unpublished Archaeological Project Services Report No. 196/02.

Wacher, J., 1964. 'Excavations at Martinsthorpe, Rutland, 1960.' *Transactions of the Leicestershire Archaeological and Historical Society* 39, 1–19.

Trimble, R., 2008. *Archaeological Excavation, Evaluation and Watching Brief on land at Lilac Farm, 19 Mill Lane, Cottesmore (COML08).* Unpublished Archaeological Project Services (APS) Report No. 112.08.

Wessex Archaeology 2008. *Knave Hill, Stonton Wyville, Leicestershire. Archaeological Evaluation and Assessment of Results.* Unpublished Report Ref. No. 65309.01.

Further reading

Medieval Villages in an English Landscape: Beginnings and Ends. Richard Jones and Mark Page. Windgather Press, 2006.

Village, Hamlet and Field: Changing Medieval Settlements in Central England. Carenza Lewis, Paul Mitchell-Fox and Chris Dyer. Windgather Press, 2001.

The Countryside of Medieval England. Grenville Astill and Annie Grant (eds.) Blackwell, 1988.

An Atlas of Rural Settlement in England. Stuart Wrathmell and Brian Roberts. English Heritage, 2000.

Region and Place: A Study of Rural Settlement. Stuart Wrathmell and Brian Roberts. English Heritage, 2002.

The Annual Report of the Medieval Settlement Research Group (MSRG) also has yearly updates on medieval rural settlement studies. For membership details go to: http://www.britarch.ac.uk/msrg/

An important early medieval gold bracteate pendant from Scalford, Leicestershire

Wendy Scott
Finds Liaison Officer for Leicestershire and Rutland

Introduction

A stunning late fifth or early sixth century gold pendant called a 'bracteate' was found by Mr. Chris Bursnall in Scalford parish, Melton Mowbray, whilst metal-detecting on 14 July 2010 (fig 1). The object was speedily reported by the finder and after initial investigation was taken down to the British Museum for expert analysis (Treasure case 2010 T414). With only a handful of these items known in the area, it was immediately apparent that this was a rare and special find. The most notable other example is also gold and is from Market Overton (now in the British Museum). It also shares with the Scalford pendant the accolade of 'unique' imagery. Both of these finds have added very useful information to the study of English bracteates, in particular their development and adaptation from the original Scandinavian examples. In addition the new find from Scalford can claim a first in early Anglo-Saxon imagery; one which wonderfully illustrates the traditions of the Germanic homelands, where these objects originate.

What is a Bracteate?

The term bracteate comes from the Latin *'bractea'* – leaf or thin piece of metal. This name refers to their thin bodies (they are also known as foils because of this). The thin sheet of metal is transformed into a bracteate by being placed over a metal matrix (a negative, concave image) and being hammered from behind, forming a crisp positive single-sided image. Other early Medieval circular pendants are also sometimes referred to as bracteates, although those not made with an embossed foil are not technically the same. In high medieval Germany the term was also applied to silver coinage and has also been used in prehistory for gold discs sewn onto clothes.

Bracteates appear to have developed from pendants made out of late Roman gold medallions in Scandinavia in the 5th century. Fine examples of these pendants were still made in the 6th and 7th centuries by the Anglo-Saxons featuring gold coins as centre pieces. Some have elaborate cloisonné

Figure 1:
The Scalford
Bracteate

garnet borders such as one from Forsbrook, Staffordshire (British Museum).

Bracteates developed from these pendants and featured stylized images based on coins. It is thought that they represented a form of status symbol, with imagery based on Roman emperors thus conveying the prestige of their wearers. The imagery gradually shifted from Imperial motifs to those illustrating Germanic religion/myth, but when this shift occurred is hard to establish. Many Scandinavian examples feature very stylized animal motifs with ribbon-shaped bodies which echo interlace, they may represent something figurative which is now lost to modern eyes.

The different classes of Bracteates are defined by Gaimster as follows;

- A-bracteates: showing the face of a human in profile, modelled on late Roman imperial medallions, sometimes accompanied by one or more animals, additional signs and inscriptions

- B-bracteates: one to three human figures in standing, sitting or kneeling positions, often accompanied by animals, signs and inscriptions

- C-bracteates: showing a male's head above a quadruped, often interpreted as the Germanic god Odin/Woden, frequently accompanied by one or more further animals, signs and inscriptions

- D-bracteates: showing one or more highly stylized animals, rarely accompanied by signs and never by an inscription

- E-bracteates: showing an animal triskele under a circular feature

- F-bracteates: as a subgroup of the D-bracteates, showing an imaginary animal sometimes accompanied by another animal, signs or inscriptions

(Gaimster 1992)

Bracteate Distribution

Around 1000 examples of 5th and 6th century gold bracteates are known across Early Medieval Europe, the majority coming from Scandinavia, where they may have emerged as a new form of votive item around AD 450. It is believed that the Bracteate and other objects such as gold foils, began to appear as replacement objects for use in ritual deposits. Weapon hoards were previously

used in Iron Age Scandinavia. In the central area of distribution the bracteates appear as single votive deposits or as part of small precious metal hoards. Some of these are buried close to 'central places' and this could reflect a significant change in ritual practice at this time characterised by a change from large communal sacrifices in sites that were used over long periods of time, like weapon deposition, to smaller depositions closer to settlements and thus possibly under the control of the 'king' (or leader) of these newly emerging central places.

There are various theories explaining the iconography of bracteates. Lotte Hedeager suggested that the imagery on bracteates, particularly types A, B and C, depicts Odin's journey to the underworld, where it was believed he could contact the ancestors. The Bracteate may have been believed to be an instrument for communicating with another world (Hall 2009 and see also L. Hedeager, paper in Anglo-Saxon Studies in Archaeology and History 10, 1999 for further discussion).

The pattern of distribution suggests that they have at least a dual meaning, being used for both their religious/mythical properties and as items used in prestige display. Bracteates found in the north of their distribution area (southern Scandinavia and northern Germany) are confined to hoards, confirming their function as votive offerings. However, those found in the Southern area (northern France, Poland, Frisia , England, central and southern Germany) appear only in graves, suggesting a different emphasis on their ritual meaning. Perhaps the objects were also used in gift exchange and thus have some bearing on a persons social status.

To complicate this pattern, those found in Western Norway and Gotland, on the Western and eastern edges of their distribution area, are found in both contexts (Gaimster, 1999). It has also been suggested that some of the English examples could be votive deposits, as some are found as single finds. Perhaps the truth of their status is a mixture of both ideas. The objects may have had dual value to an individual, both as an object of precious metal, thus conveying wealth, and also an object of amuletic protection. The meaning may be amplified simply by communal deposition in a hoard. Or it may be the 'leader' is showing his status and power by providing all the significant material to make up a votive hoard. The difference in deposition therefore may simply reflect regional practice.

The Scalford Bracteate
(Figs 1 and 2)

Below is an excerpt from the Treasure report, written by Dr Charlotte Behr of Roehampton University, which describes the object and discusses its significance.

Description: The pendant is made of a disc of gold sheet that is scratched, torn and bent in several places. A simple gold strip serves as loop. The centre is decorated with the design of a male head with bust. In the tradition of the image of the emperor on late Roman coins and medallions that served as model the head is shown in profile. The hairstyle is decorated with a diadem ending in a framed triangle of three dots with a spiral in front above the forehead and in cross-shaped double lines behind the head. The coat is lined by two dotted borders and consists of four parts with stylized folds, the upper two ending in two mirror-image spirals. The three lines ending in open semi-circles on the back of the coat reflect the three pendilia, pendants ending in a precious stone or pearl, hanging off the imperial brooch (Sebesta & Bonfante 2001, 244). The bent feature in front of the coat may be discussed hypothetically as an arm with a hand holding a conical drinking vessel decorated with three bands at its upper end in front of the mouth. In front and behind the head are several symbols and imitations of Latin letters. Along the edge of the flan are incisions imitating a beaded framing wire.

Discussion: The find is only the sixth known A-bracteate (defined as a pendant with an anthropomorphic head in profile) from early Anglo-Saxon England (Behr 2010; Behr & Marzinzik 2011). Whereas the find and its iconography have close links with Scandinavian bracteates, it was most probably made in England as it is possible to tell from some technical idiosyncrasies, like the absence of a framing wire and the undecorated loop. If the identification of the drinking vessel is correct, this would be a unique element within bracteate iconography.'

Figure 2: Scalford bracteate; Illustration by Jane Sandoe, clearly showing the drinking vessel and pendilia.

Dr Behr has also noted that the Scalford Bracteate has an unusually large depiction of the pendilia. This is part of an item which illustrated imperial status and is often seen on late Roman imagery, for example, the mosaics from Ravenna. It is probable that this is done to emphasise the status of the wearer. This could point to some knowledge of Christianity or the power of the cross as a symbol. However on Scandinavian examples the cross is a commonly used sign on bracteates so it may be simply an example of a motif being copied.

English bracteates

In England 54 are known – 44 are gold, 8 are silver and two are bronze. The majority, 34, are D bracteates showing stylized animals. Most come from the south east, although their distribution runs up to the Humber. Eastern Kent has the highest density with 29 examples so far (all but one are a D bracteates). Twenty-two whole and fragmentary examples have been recorded by the Portable Antiquities Scheme (PAS) (all areTreasure cases – see www.finds.org.uk).

There is much debate about where and when the English bracteates were made. It is believed that some of them were imports, particularly the A type which are thought to be the earliest. However there is an argument that those found in Kentish cemeteries, all close to 'royal' centres and all D bracteates, form a coherent group produced in that area. The proximity to royal estates may show an attempt to identify the Kentish Kings with descent from Jutland and therefore, from the god Woden. It has been suggested that the Anglian type of bracteate (ie those not belonging to the Kentish group) were probably produced here, but show some parallels with the Gotland bracteates suggesting a link with the two regions some generations before the emergence of the rich boat burials in both places in the seventh century.

The PAS has also recorded two rare bracteate dies, which would have been used as patterns for the bracteates. One comes from Essex, PAS Ref ESS-13B5E6 and a stunning later example comes from Norfolk, PAS Ref NMS-808582. These dies are important evidence for their manufacture in England and treble the number of known dies, as only one example, from Postgården in Jutland, was known prior to 1999.

A unique depiction

The main addition that makes the Scalford example special is the drinking vessel. Although there is Scandinavian imagery portraying drinking scenes, there is so far no other depiction of drinking on early Anglo Saxon material. Margrethe Watt (in Behr, 2010) has suggested that those objects which do illustrate drinking can tell us much about its ritualistic aspect in Germanic society and the role of the sexes within this. Drinking was an important social act, it features heavily in literature such as Beowulf and was used to swear oaths, illustrate status etc. She has noted that the women that appear on these objects, largely gold foils, are shown with drinking horns, this perhaps emphasizes their role as cup fillers, whilst males are shown with smaller vessels from which they drink. It is also possible that the women are indeed images of Valkyries, who are often portrayed offering a drinking horn to those lucky enough to be welcomed into Valhalla. In the Scalford Bracteate the combination of Roman imperial and Germanic ritual imagery shows a point of transition in early Medieval England.

This Bracteate belongs to an exclusive set of 'unique' bracteates from England. The Market Overton example (fig 3) which was found in a grave context during excavation, is also a unique 'F' Bracteate. It is the only example which depicts a bird above the quadruped, where there should be a male head. Perhaps

Figure 3: F Bracteate from Market Overton

the bird is one of Odin's Ravens? If the suggestion is correct that the human figure is indeed this god, then this would make sense to the fifth or sixth century viewer.

The existence of several unique motifs confirms the insular development of Bracteates. These new images could represent one-off commissions or are new ideas being tried out. We do not yet know whether they were trial pieces or were copied on other Bracteates yet to be discovered. Despite this uncertainty, the discovery of this item has added a significant new example to the corpus of English Bracteates. The bracteate has been acquired by Leicestershire County Museums Service. It is displayed and interpreted in Melton Carnegie Museum in Melton Mowbray for all to enjoy.

Acknowledgements

I would like to thank Dr Charlotte Behr for her very generous sharing of knowledge and advice. I have borrowed very heavily from her work. We would both like to express our thanks to the Leicestershire Archaeological and Historical Society for generously providing funding for the object's illustration, undertaken by Jane Sandoe. Last but not least, thanks to Chris Bursnall for reporting his find immediately, and to the landowner for allowing him to search his land. Without them the object may never have been rediscovered and our knowledge would be the poorer for it.

Bibliography

From the Treasure report,

Behr, C., 2010. 'New Bracteate Finds from early Anglo-Saxon England', *Medieval Archaeology* 54.

Behr, C. and Marzinzik, S., 2011. '*Near Holt, Norfolk: Anglo-Saxon gold bracteate* (2009T657)', TAR 2009.

Behr, C., 2011. The A-Bracteate from Scalford, Leicestershire', *Transactions of the Leicestershire Archaeological and Historical Society*, 85, p 97–105.

Sebesta, J. L. and Bonfante, L. 2001. *The world of Roman costume.* University of Wisconsin Press.

General

Behr, C., 2011. 'An unusual new gold A-bracteate find from Scalford, Leicestershire'. In: Reynolds, A. , Brookes, S., Harrington S, *Studies in Anglo-Saxon Art And Archaeology, papers in honour of Martin G Welch*, BAR 527, Oxford: Archaeopress (Oxbow)

Behr, C., 2010, 'New Bracteate Finds from early Anglo-Saxon England'. *Medieval Archaeology* 54.

Gaimster, M., 1992. 'Scandinavian gold Bracteates in Britain. Money and media in the dark ages'. *Medieval Archaeology* 36 1992. (ads.ahds.ac.uk/catalogue/adsdata/arch-769-/.../36_001_028)

Hall, R., 2009 *Exploring the world of the Vikings.* New York: Thames and Hudson,.

Hedeager, L,. 1999. 'Split Bodies in the Late Iron Age/Viking Age of Scandinavia'. In: Dickinson T. M. and Griffiths, D., eds *Anglo-Saxon Studies in Archaeology and History* 10,

On-line

British Museum database, www.britishmuseum.org/research/search_the_collection_database.aspx

The Portable Antiquities Scheme database Finds.org.uk Go to advanced search and enter Bracteate in the description contains field. This will show you all the examples and the dies.

Medieval houses of south-east Leicestershire and Rutland: recent research

Nick Hill

Introduction

This paper considers the medieval domestic dwellings of south-east Leicestershire and Rutland, focusing on the evidence of standing buildings rather than below-ground archaeology. Although many areas of the country have seen extensive work on standing medieval houses in recent decades, very little systematic research has been carried out on the subject in Leicestershire or Rutland, and even less has been published. What follows can therefore only be a preliminary exploration of the topic for one part of the county, based mainly on the author's own research over the last decade. An overall synthesis will need to await the completion of more extensive research, though some emerging characteristics of considerable interest can already be highlighted.

The 'medieval' period covered here runs from the earliest surviving houses of the late 12th century up to the mid-16th century, when that defining characteristic of the English medieval house, the open hall, gave way to buildings with a full first floor and enclosed fireplaces. The area of study is largely defined by the 'stone belt', the great Jurassic formation which runs north-eastwards across England from Dorset to Yorkshire, crossing Rutland and the eastern part of Leicestershire (fig 1). This underlying geology naturally dictates much of the character of local buildings, which are sharply differentiated from the buildings of the rest of Leicestershire.

To set the context, it must be immediately admitted that, compared to the richer south-eastern counties of England, medieval houses are quite rare in the study area. Taking the

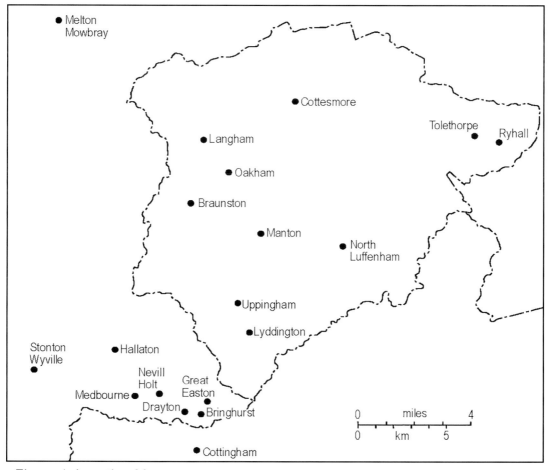

Figure 1: Location Map

county of Rutland, about 25 surviving medieval houses have so far been identified (though many of these await detailed examination, and no doubt others remain to be discovered). In the Rutland Military Survey of 1522, the number of persons assessed for the value of their property was 1,424, which may (very roughly) equate to the number of households (Cornwall 1963, 11). A total of 25 houses would thus represent a survival rate of only 1.8%. A major study of the medieval houses of Kent concluded, by contrast, that around 14% of the mid 16th-century houses survived (Pearson 1994, 146). However, although the overall rate of survival is very low, the study area has been found to contain a fine set of pre-1400 houses, with seven in Rutland and five in nearby East Leicestershire, forming one of the best clusters of early houses in the country.

Late 12th and earlier 13th century: aisled halls

Most of the earliest English houses which still survive are aisled halls, having a large open hall whose wide-spanning roof is supported by aisle posts. The hall at Oakham Castle (Fig 2) has long been recognised as 'one of the most remarkable as well as most ancient examples of Domestic Architecture in England' (Dollman & Jobbins 1861, B). From the similarity of its finely sculptured capitals to those at Canterbury Cathedral, it has been dated to c.1180–90. Although it has lost its original roof structure, the 4-bay hall survives in an extraordinarily complete state.

Very finely crafted, and with an arcade built of stone, Oakham is an exceptional building. More typically, aisled halls were of timber, with examples dating from the mid 12th to the late 13th century scattered widely across the country (Sandall 1986; Walker 1999). Within Leicestershire the best known example, though much altered, is the Hall at Leicester Castle with stone walls but timber arcade posts, dating from c.1150. Within the study area, evidence has been discovered in recent years for two examples of aisled halls. At the Manor House, Medbourne, the upper part of an aisled structure survives (Fig 3), which has been tree-ring dated to 1237 (Hill 2001). It has passing braces and notch-lap jointing of early type, though the asymmetrical pattern of bracing is unusual. Of at least three bays in length, it had timber aisle posts, though these are now missing. Currently the earliest known standing manor house in Leicestershire, it was built for William de Chaworth, documented as holding the manor in 1235–6. The second example is at nearby Nevill Holt Hall, where excavation in 2000 discovered a large post hole in the hall, on the line of a later base cruck truss of c.1288, presumably for an aisle post (Priest 2000).

A small building of this early period which has not been investigated recently is Priory Cottage at Manton. It is of two storeys with thick stone walls, and has a small round-arched window, apparently of pre-1200 date, to the first floor. It was probably part of the adjoining priory. There are a number of examples of such two-storey, stone buildings across the country, dating from the late 12th or 13th centuries. Once identified as 'first floor halls', these are now generally thought to be chamber blocks, with a principal chamber on the upper floor. The notable example in Leicestershire is the Manor House at Donington le Heath, of late 13th century date.

Figure 2: Oakham Castle (Parker & Turner, 1877, frontispiece)

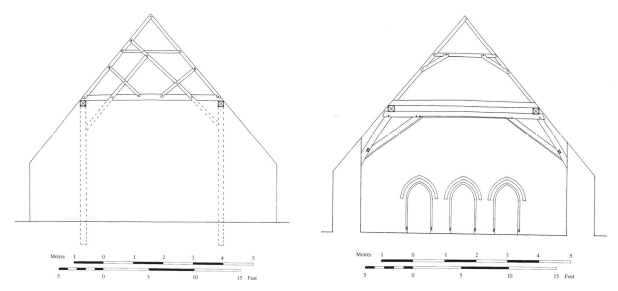

Figures 3 and 4: The Manor House, Medbourne: left – reconstruction of aisled truss, dated to 1237. Only the upper part of the truss survives, but the passing braces originally ran on down to the aisle posts, which may have been earth-fast; right – reconstruction of the 'short principal' truss dated to 1287 at the centre of the hall, with aisles and service doorways.

Later 13th century and 14th century: base crucks and stone walls

From the late 13th century, across the country, aisled trusses at the centre of open halls were superseded by a variety of forms which sought to eliminate the aisle posts, which must have caused an obstruction within the open space of the hall. The most widely used structure to achieve this was the base cruck, with large curving timbers rising from near ground level to support a collar beam and the arcade plates. A variation on this, found in association with stone walls, is the 'short principal' roof, where the bases of the principal timbers are carried on the stone wall, rather than extending down to the ground. Examples of base cruck or 'short principal' roofs of late 13th and 14th century date are widely spread across the country, with 171 examples plotted on a recent distribution map (Alcock 2002). A detailed study in Kent concluded that base cruck halls were typically built by a more geographically mobile, newer gentry class, rather than old-established families (Pearson 1994, 56).

At Medbourne Manor House, tree-ring dating has produced an important and unusually precise set of dates to indicate the change from aisled construction to the base cruck type (Hill 2001). As noted above, the partially surviving roof structure of the aisled hall has been dated to 1237. Fifty years later, in 1287, the hall was rebuilt with a 'short principal' roof, eliminating the aisle posts, though retaining various

parts of the earlier roof structure (fig 4). The building of 1287 also had walls built of stone, as can be seen in the splendid surviving set of three service doorways in the cross-passage. Besides indicating the transition from aisled to base cruck type structure, this house might therefore mark the move from timber-framed to masonry construction for gentry houses of the area. Evidence can also be pieced together to show that the house had a fully developed plan form, with a three-bay hall containing a cross-passage, and a projecting cross-wing at the lower end, housing service rooms on the ground floor and a fine first floor chamber, or solar above (fig 5 overleaf). Around the country, other examples of early cross-wings often also had the main solar over the service end, rather than in the normal later medieval location, at the 'high' end of the hall, beyond the dais with the lord's table.

Another base cruck type roof survives at nearby Nevill Holt Hall (fig 6 overleaf), again replacing an aisled structure (Hill 1999). Documents record that oak timber was supplied for building work in 1288, and tree-ring dating has confirmed this, with a date range of 1275–99 (Vernacular Architecture 39, 2008, 108). Evidence survives to show that the build of 1288 once again had walls of stone. Like Medbourne, the hall was of three bays, containing a cross-passage. The rest of the 1288 plan form has been subsumed within later developments, but it seems that the service end here was in-line, rather than

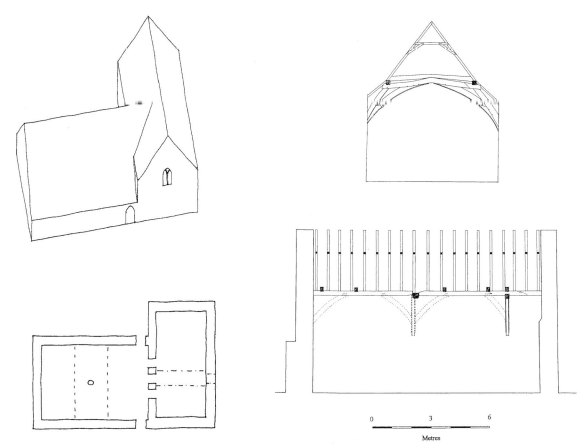

Figure 5: The Manor House, Medbourne: reconstruction of c.1287. The low-end crosswing housed services, with a solar above.

Figure 6: Nevill Holt Hall:base cruck type roof of c.1288. The half-bay now houses a cross passage, but the original hall may have extended for a full three bays. Cross and long section.

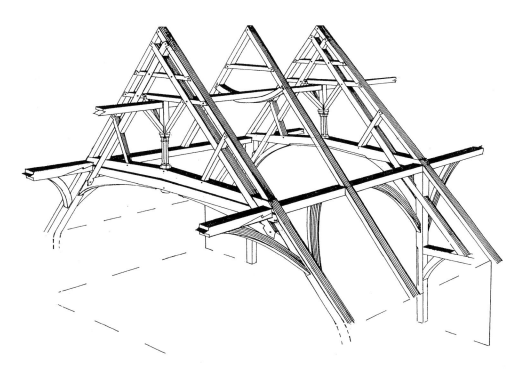

Figure 7: Quaintree House, Braunston: base cruck roof of c1307 (Cecil Hewett).

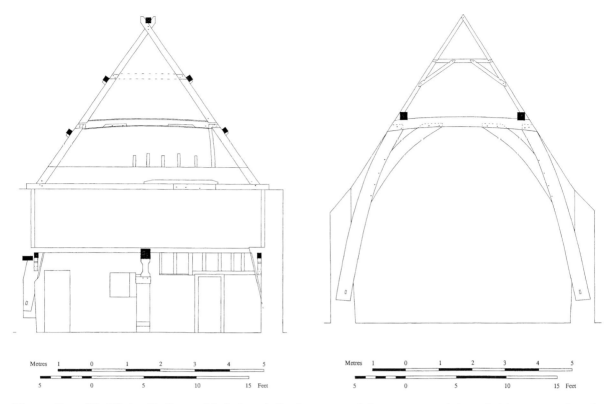

Figure 8 and 9: Glebe Cottage, Hallaton: left – base cruck truss as surviving; right – reconstruction. There may well have been a double collar, but any evidence for this has been lost.

formed as a cross-wing, with a cross-wing containing an undercroft and solar at the 'high' end of the hall.

Quaintree House at Braunston, Rutland (fig. 7) has a base cruck roof which was recorded by Hewett and Gibson in 1981 and subsequently tree-ring dated to *c.*1307 (Vernacular Architecture 22 (1991), 45). The hall is of two bays with a base cruck truss, and a spere truss with aisle posts defines the cross-passage. There is a very fine upper roof structure, with double collars, a crown post and additional 'passing braces', parallel to the principal rafters. Hewett and Gibson suggested that the existing stone walls are a replacement for original timber-framed walls, though further investigation might indicate otherwise.

There is a more fragmentary survival at Glebe Cottage, Hallaton (figs 8, 9), which was formerly the northern of two village rectories (Hill 2006). The massive blades of a base cruck truss, cut off at first floor level, survive in the ground floor walls. Further investigation revealed the cut-down collar of the base cruck truss and an early rafter in the rebuilt later structure. The rear wall was found to contain evidence of a tall hall window and, a rare

survival, the arched head of a laver, a niche containing a basin for washing hands, similar to a church piscina (fig 10). It seems this was another hall of the late 13th or early 14th centuries, with a central base cruck truss and walls built of stone.

The last two examples of base crucks are in town houses, at Melton Mowbray (outside the main study area) and Oakham. Only parts of the open truss survive at 5 King St,

Base cruck

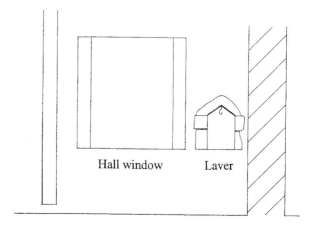

Figure 10: Glebe Cottage Hallaton: reconstruction of rear wall, with hall window and laver.

Melton Mowbray, but enough remains to allow a reasonably complete reconstruction (fig 11). This structure has been tree-ring dated to 1330 (Vernacular Architecture 39, 2008, 108). Some developing sophistication is visible here, as the roof has a finely moulded, diminutive crown post and a moulded cornice over the arcade plate, though there is still a double collar. Joints are now of mortice and tenon type, with none of the earlier lap joints.

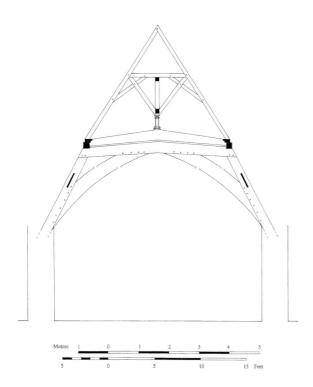

Figure 11: 5 King St, Melton Mowbray: reconstruction of base cruck/short principal

Evidence for the walling material is unclear, but it seems more likely to have been of stone than timber. This was probably a three-bay hall, with evidence for a former further in-line section at the 'high' end of the hall, probably containing a solar. During the early 14th century, Melton was an important centre of the English wool trade, and this was no doubt the home of one its rich wool merchants.

Flore's House, in Oakham, has been well-known as a medieval building for many years, but the main hall range has now been tree-ring dated to 1378 (Vernacular Architecture, 41, 2010, 94), making it much the latest base cruck in the area (figs 12–13). It has a very finely carpentered roof structure, with a crown post roof to the upper part. Although the crown post is plain, the quality of the timber and jointing is excellent throughout,

and the wallplate, acting also as a cornice, is finely moulded. This is the only base cruck identified in the area where each blade must have been erected separately, with the arcade plate placed in position before the collar was added. In all the other examples, the blades and collar could have been assembled on the ground and 'raised' as a single unit, with the arcade plate placed on top, usually followed by a second collar. The design of the timber structure at Flore's House is also very well integrated with the stone walls, the cruck blades fitting into wall slots, with the front face neatly flush. The stonemasonry has high quality features, with a deeply moulded arched front doorway and an ornately carved stone laver in the cross-passage. The hall is of three bays, incorporating a cross-passage, without any spere posts. Beyond the south gable wall of the passage, a cross-wing was built in 1407–10 (Vernacular Architecture, 41, 2010, 94), with a stone-built ground floor and two upper floors of timber-framing, jettied to the east front. This cross-wing may have replaced an earlier in-line service end. At the north end, the original roof structure continued for at least another bay, presumably housing an in-line solar at the 'high' end of the hall, though this was later replaced with a cross-wing. With the recent study and tree-ring dating,

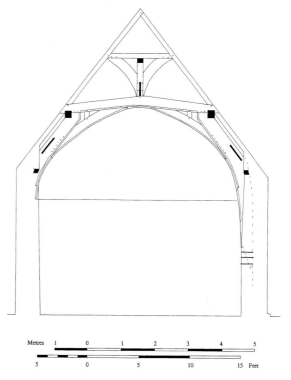

Figure 12: Flore's House, Oakham: base cruck truss as existing, with single collar and crown post, dated to 1378.

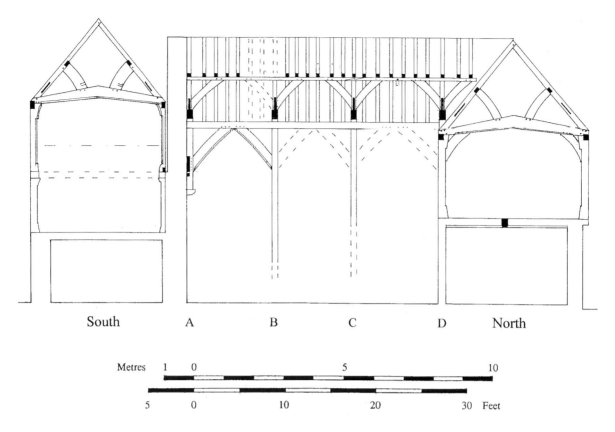

| South | A | B | C | D | North |

Metres 1 0   5   10

5   0   10   20   30   Feet

Figure 13: Flore's House, Oakham: long section with 3-bay hall of 1378 and service crosswing of 1407–10 (to the left). The former in-line high end has been replaced by a later cross-wing.

Flore's House can now be recognised as one of the best early surviving town houses in the country. The tree-ring dating confirms that it was built by William Flore, Oakham's major wool merchant and controller of the works at Oakham Castle in 1373–80. The south crosswing must have been built by his son Roger, an important figure, who served several times as Speaker to the House of Commons.

These six base cruck halls, ranging in date from 1287 to 1378, form a coherent cluster of important early buildings. As noted in my paper of 2001 on Medbourne Manor House, 'there is a strongly defined regional type here, not fully recognised previously, with stone walls and a base cruck/short principal roof structure to the hall', with several more examples in the adjoining stone-belt area of Northamptonshire (Hill 2001, 58). The stone walls contrast with the timber-framed walls found in base cruck halls to central and west Leicestershire, as found at Leicester Guildhall, the demolished 19, Thorpeacre, Loughborough (Alcock and Barley 1972) and Aylestone Hall, Leicester (which probably had a base cruck spanning the open hall; Finn 2007).

Apart from these base cruck halls, a number of other houses of this early period have been identified in the study area, all of them stone-built. The most complete is College House, Oakham (figs 14–17 overleaf), which was a prebendal house of Westminster Abbey, so a rather special-purpose building, not an ordinary house. Its structure is certainly unusual in the area, with the only roof identified which is of full crown post type, rather than the type with an upper crown post set over a base cruck , as noted above. The main block is a stone-built range which has a single large chamber on the first floor, with a three-bay open roof of crown post type, tree-ring dated to 1319–39 (Vernacular Architecture 30, 1999, 90). The tall, chamfered crown posts are set on slightly cambered tie beams, with four-way straight braces up to the collar purlin and rafters. Parallel rafters are set inside the main principal rafters, forming a scissor pattern and fixed mainly with lap joints. The gable ends are built of stone, with trusses set against them. This fine chamber, 9.7m by 4.3m, must have been heated by a lateral stack; the roof timbers are clean, with no sooting from an open hearth. Indeed, the trimmer for this stack still survives,

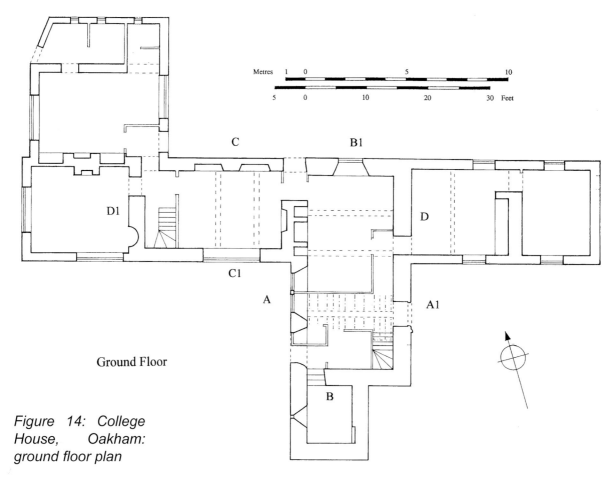

Metres 1 0 5 10

5 0 10 20 30 Feet

C

B1

D1

D

C1

A

A1

Ground Floor

B

Figure 14: College House, Oakham: ground floor plan

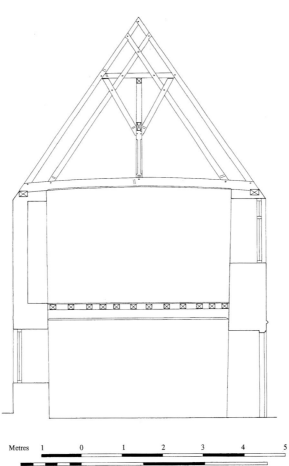

Figure 15: College House, Oakham:crown post roof at A-A1 with parallel 'scissor' rafters, dated to 1319–39.

Metres 1 0 1 2 3 4 5

5 0 5 10 15 Feet

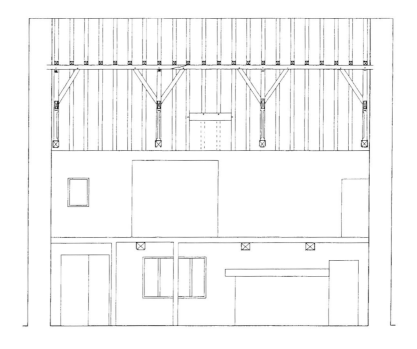

Section B-B1

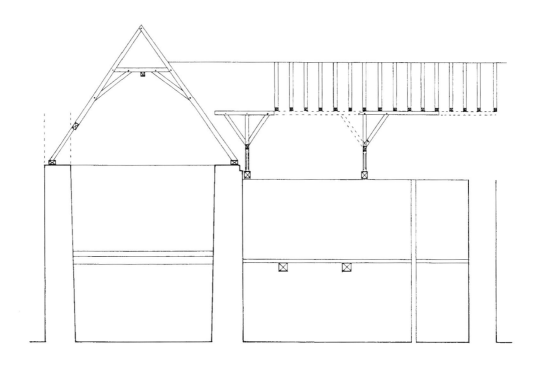

Section D-D1

Figures 16 and 17: College House, Oakham: top- long section of crown post roof at B-B1, with original trimmer between rafters for first floor fireplace: bottom -section of main range and cross wing at D-D1

between two of the rafters (fig 16). Entry to the ground floor is by a fine moulded doorway with a shallow pointed arch, though the access route up to the first floor is unclear. A smaller stone block is attached to the south gable, perhaps for service use, or a large garderobe to serve the main chamber. Abutting the north end of the main range on the west is another range at right angles which contains a further crown post roof of at least two bays, though this block has been much altered later. No doubt there were other buildings which formed this prebendal complex, probably including a ground floor open hall, with the surviving building acting as a chamber block.

Much less complete is the Green Dragon, Ryhall, where a vaulted cellar of 13th century date survives (fig 18). It has two bays of quadripartite vaulting, with plain chamfered ribs springing from shaped corbels. It is quite small, only 3.4m wide by 4.9m long, but is complete, with an original segmental-arched doorway in the east gable and two small windows in the north wall. The cellar is set about 1.7m below ground and has lost the building over it, though other fragmentary evidence survives for a larger complex, including a tall arched doorway set at a raised level to the west. This was clearly the site of the original manor of Ryhall, and the fine vaulted cellar indicates a building of some ambition. However, it is of unusual and puzzling character, much smaller than the undercrofts which accompany chamber blocks of this period elsewhere, and set well below ground level. The space above it may have been a chapel, with a window in the east gable. The adjoining tall doorway presumably gave access to a larger chamber or hall, but the relationship of this to the cellar is unclear.

There is another fragmentary survival at the Manor House, Stonton Wyville, where two service doorways remain to mark an early cross-passage. The doors are of plain, two-centred arch type, similar to those at Medbourne Manor. This was probably another stone-built house of late 13th or early 14th century date, with a base cruck hall and service end cross-wing, with solar over. The cross-wing was later reconstructed, probably around 1500 by Sir Robert Brudenell, with a low-pitched roof covered in lead. Further additions and alterations were made in the 17th and 18th centuries, with the loss of the original main hall.

One of the most impressive buildings of the 14th century in the area was the Bishop's Palace at Lyddington, where the Woodfields excavated evidence for a very large hall of c.1320–40, to which the surviving building acted as a chamber block (C. and P. Woodfield 1981–2). Only a few features of this date remain, the rest having been largely swept away in the major rebuilding during the 15th century. Another intriguing fragment is at Tolethorpe Hall, where building work led to the discovery of an early cross wall with a pointed arched doorway of 13th-14th century date. The doorway was later blocked and a wallpainting scheme of linked doorways was applied to the cross-wall. The hall was approached through a gatehouse which has an arched entrance, perhaps of 14th century date. At Melton Mowbray, Anne of Cleves House has thick stone walls probably dating from the foundation of a house for priests in 1384, and a surviving doorway with pointed arch.

The above account completes the tally of all the standing

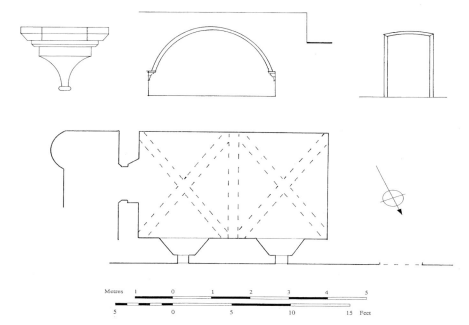

Figure 18: The Green Dragon, Ryhall: vaulted cellar of 13th century.

domestic buildings so far identified in the study area which date before 1400 – a total of 14 houses.

15th and 16th century: crucks

All the pre-1400 buildings discussed so far are of quite high status, belonging to the lord of the manor or people of higher rank, the owners often being documented and identifiable. As we come into the 15th century, houses of the ordinary farming population start to survive, which are very different from the high status buildings examined above. The standard local type of construction uses crucks, a pair of large curving timbers which reach from near ground level up to the apex of the roof. Crucks have been found very widely across the country except in the south-east and eastern England, with over 4,000 examples now recorded (Alcock, personal communication), mostly dating from the later 14th to the 16th centuries. Crucks were very popular because they provided an economical and straightforward

system to construct the standard type of late medieval house, with a hall at its centre, open right up to the ridge of the roof.

Crucks of 15th and 16th century date survive quite widely in the area (figs 19–20). In Rutland, seven examples have been found so far, with a further two demolished. Several of these have been identified only through the listed building descriptions, and no doubt much more evidence remains to be discovered. More intensive research has been done in some villages of south-east Leicestershire. A fairly comprehensive study of Great Easton by the author over many years, including access during building works, has brought the total of known crucks for this one village up to ten (including one demolished). In four of these cases, only the lower part of the cruck blades remains, embedded within later stone walls and cut off at first floor level. More examples of such survivals no doubt wait to be discovered in other houses. At Bringhurst, all three of this

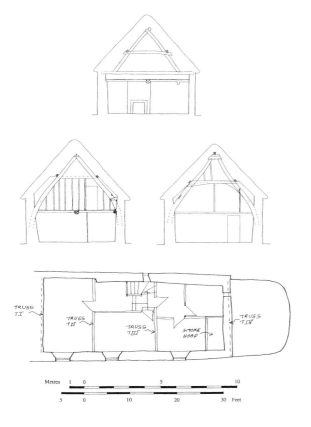

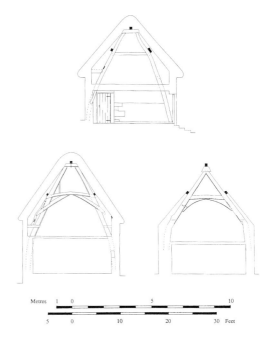

Figure 20: Crucks: from top, then left to right

34–36 Churchgate, Hallaton: irregular blades, lapped collar and long yoke to apex

4 The Cross, Hallaton: open truss to hall, with unusual lapped arch braces

4 Church Lane, Lyddington: open truss to hall, with well-shaped blades, tenoned collar and arch braces with long tenons. The unusal high quality of the carpentry is probably due to a connection with the nearby Bishop's Palace.

Figure 19: 6 Church Bank, Great Easton: the most complete cruck house in the village. Open truss at centre of the two-bay hall, with irregularly shaped blades and crude arch braces. Truss II may have had a closed partition. Truss I at the gable end, although of non-cruck type, may have been original, with crude mud infill. (1st floor, TI, TII and TIII)

small village's older houses have been found to contain crucks. One example has been found so far at Drayton, and another was lost some years ago. Investigations at Hallaton have found five cruck houses (including one demolished). The level of survival, particularly at Great Easton, demonstrates very clearly that the normal good quality peasant house of the late medieval period was built with crucks.

The surviving evidence is often rather fragmentary, but a number of the principal features of the local type can be pieced together. The typical plan of village houses is of three bays, with a 2-bay open hall and a single bay service end. Only one example of an original first floor structure to the end bay survives, at 34–36 Churchgate, Hallaton, with an axial beam supported on posts and broad, heavy joists. It may be that most houses had no such upper floor, but were single-storeyed throughout. The cruck structures themselves generally have gently curving blades, without a pronounced elbow, though some are of ogee shape (a curve shaped somewhat like an 's'). An almost universal feature is the apex construction, where the blades are tenoned into a heavy yoke, which carries a square-set ridge. Collars are mainly of simple lapped type, projecting to carry the purlins on their backs. The open truss of the 2-bay halls often has rather crude arch braces, and wind braces were also generally provided, though few survive. Rafters are now generally of ash pole type and of later date, though the original rafters may well have been similar. Clear evidence for the original external walls is usually lacking, but the indications are that walls were of mud or, at later dates, of stone. Investigation at a few houses has found that the cruck blades, which often now rise from quite high up in the walls, did reach right down to near ground level, and so are full crucks, not 'raised' crucks. The lower parts of the blades, encased in stonework during the 17th century, have often rotted out. There are a few indications that the gable ends may have had mud walls up to eaves height and rather crude non-cruck trusses above, with mud infill or cladding on timber studs.

Firm dating evidence is rare, though most of the local crucks are generally thought to date from around 1450 to 1550. The earliest dated example in the area is Bede House Farm, North Luffenham, where the cruck chamber block is dendro-dated to c.1395–1424 (Vernacular Architecture 23, 1992, 52), but this is an atypical building whose hall range has a non-cruck, arch-braced roof dated to 1433. The more typical date range is probably indicated by the 1466–91 date for 29 High Street, Hallaton (Nottingham University Tree-Ring Dating Laboratory, unpub. report, 1989). A late use of crucks is seen at Church Farm, Bringhurst, dendro-dated to c.1579–1615, which has a rather crude, hybrid cruck truss with the main blades reaching only to the upper collar, and has original walls of stone rather than mud (Hill, 2005). Even later is the narrow one-bay crosswing at 11 Hunts Lane, Hallaton, dated to c.1609–34, added to an earlier two-bay cruck range (Nottingham University Tree-Ring Dating Laboratory, unpub. report, 2001).

In the rest of Leicestershire, to the west of the stone-belt, crucks are also widespread but generally associated with timber-framed walls (Webster 1954). However, in the adjoining stone-belt area of north Northamptonshire a number of crucks of similar type to the study area were recorded around 1960, with walls probably of stone (Seaborne 1963). More recently, an exceptionally interesting cruck house was discovered at Cottingham, only half a mile from the Leicestershire border. Dendro-dated to 1262, this is currently the earliest dated cruck structure in the country. Its relationship to the later type of local crucks remains a matter of debate (Hill and Miles 2001).

15th and early 16th century: other buildings

Apart from crucks, remaining evidence for houses of 15th or earlier 16th century date in the area is quite rare. This is interesting, as it contrasts quite strongly with the pattern found nationally. Sarah Pearson (2001), using the data for 712 houses tree-ring dated from the 12th century up to 1600, showed that by far the largest number of houses date from the mid-15th century onwards.

Two large houses have major work dating from this period. At Nevill Holt, Thomas Palmer added a porch and oriel window of finely carved masonry, though the base cruck hall itself was retained largely unchanged (Hill 1999). This was followed in the mid-16th century by the addition of a very extensive western range. Built by Sir Thomas Nevill, this was, most unusually for the area, constructed in brick, copying high status houses of the period in southern England. The second major house is the Bishop's Palace at Lyddington, where the surviving stone-built chamber block range is very largely a creation of the 15th and early 16th century. Probably due to the influence of the Bishop's Palace, Lyddington has been found to contain evidence of other buildings dating from around the early 16th century. At 11 Stoke Road, parts of a smoke-blackened roof survive from an open hall, of clasped purlin type, with stone walls. There is a similar roof, though probably re-set, at 3 The Green, again of clasped purlin type, with two late medieval stone doorways, now blocked. An outbuilding at Cottesmore Hall has a Tudor doorway and window together with other fabric, but this is all re-used from the original Hall, which was rebuilt in the 18th century. Late medieval masonry features however are still in situ at Glaston Manor, including a moulded two-centred arched doorway (perhaps late 14th century) and two cavetto (a concave section shaped to a quarter circle) and roll-moulded windows (early 16th century).

In this stone-belt area, timber-framed construction was very rare outside the towns of Uppingham and Oakham, but one or two timber buildings have come to light. A very interesting recent discovery was at 50 Well Street, Langham (figs 21–22). Building work uncovered the remains of a fully timber-framed building, with a one-bay central hall, a two storey service end and a two storey cross-wing. The timber frame had full-height main posts supporting heavy tie-beams, and probably had close studding throughout, with no mid-rail. Tree-ring dating suggested a date of c.1468, with a first floor inserted in the hall in c.1540 (Nottingham University Tree-Ring Dating Laboratory, unpub. report, 2006). The whole frame was then encased in masonry, dated by the roof to c.1681. In various other parts of the country, good quality medieval timber buildings which have been later encased in stone occur quite frequently. However, this is the only example yet found on the stone belt of Leicestershire, Rutland or adjoining parts of Northamptonshire. This suggests that, apart from crucks, there was no tradition of timber-framing in the rural areas of the stone belt.

An exception to prove this rule has recently been investigated at 24 Main Street, Lyddington (fig 23 overleaf). This is a four-bay building, whose front wall had a fine set of curved braces, sadly known now only through early photographs, as the frontage was rebuilt in the early 20th century. Analysis showed that the timber-framing was confined to the front and rear upper walls, with the gable ends and ground floor of stone. On the first floor was a pair of fine two-bay chambers, each with a central display truss supporting the clasped purlin roof. The two chambers were probably heated by fireplaces in the cross wall which

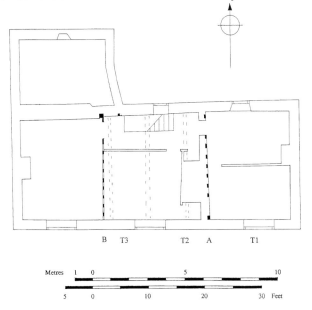
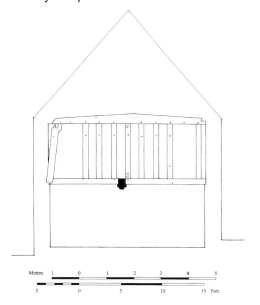

Figures 21 and 22: 50 Well Street, Langham. Left – First floor plan, with hall (originally open) to centre, crosswing to left and service end to right. Dated c1468. Right – Cross section at A, with front wall post and first floor beam to service end.

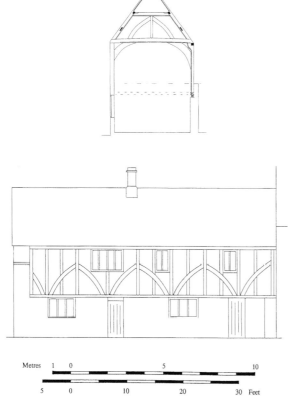

Figure 23: 24 Main Street, Lyddington: open truss to first floor chamber and reconstructed front elevation, with timber-framing over stone ground floor. Circa early 16th century.

separated them. Dating to around the early 16th century, and with no associated hall, this is a highly unusual structure. It seems likely that it was built as a pair of high class lodgings for use in association with the Bishop's Palace. This would explain the unusual use of timber-framing, the curved braces clearly being intended to express the building's status. Only one other timber-framed building has been found in rural Rutland, at North Luffenham Hall, where a barn has a close studded upper floor (vertical timbers set close together), over ground floor walls of stone (Marsden 1958).

As in other stone-built areas, timber-framing did occur in the towns, which were influenced by aspirations to a more national style, not simply the local vernacular. The only surviving example yet identified is at Flore's House, Oakham, where the two timber-framed cross-wings are both built over a masonry ground floor. However, old photographs show several further examples in both Uppingham and Oakham of timber-framed construction with jettied upper floors, now altered or demolished (see eg Metcalfe 1997).

As soon as one passes off the stone belt into the adjoining area of Leicestershire to the west, timber-framing replaces stone as the normal medieval building technique. On the edge of the stone belt, at Hallaton, is a very fine fully timber-framed building, 10–14 Churchgate (Hill 2003). Probably a manor house, this building was of six bays, with full close studding and an unusual 'stub tie-beam' roof, a very advanced roof type which created a high open arch (fig 24). Dating from *c.*1484–1509, the hall roof here is unsooted, so there must have been a chimneystack from the start.

Conclusion

As set out above, the survival rate of medieval buildings in the study area is very low (less than 2% in Rutland), so one must be very cautious about any conclusions which can be drawn. Nevertheless, some interesting patterns can be traced, and these gain further validity when set against the evidence from other parts of the country where more extensive investigation has been undertaken.

As elsewhere in the country, the evidence indicates that the earliest domestic halls were of aisled construction. However, aisled buildings seem to have been superseded during the late 13th century by base cruck or short principal roofs, eliminating the arcade posts from the hall. In some parts of the country, where the timber-framing tradition was dominant, aisled construction carries on into the 14th century (eg Stenning et al 2003). As discussed above, the base cruck/short principal structure appears to be particularly characteristic of higher status houses in this stone-belt area, as found also in adjoining Northamptonshire. A similar pattern has been found in the stone buildings of Somerset, where an extensive tree-ring dating programme has found 13 base cruck dating from 1287 to 1342, though the majority of these are two-tier base crucks, a more specific regional type (Penoyre 2005).

Although a good number of late 13th and 14th century buildings remain, it is usually only the main hall which survives, all of the other parts of the building or wider complex having disappeared. A glimpse of what has been lost is afforded by a document of 1302 which sets out the division of Nevill Holt between four sisters (Hill, 1999). Margaret received the hall, an upper room, a kitchen, a bake-house and a room above the great gate; Alice had a chapel,

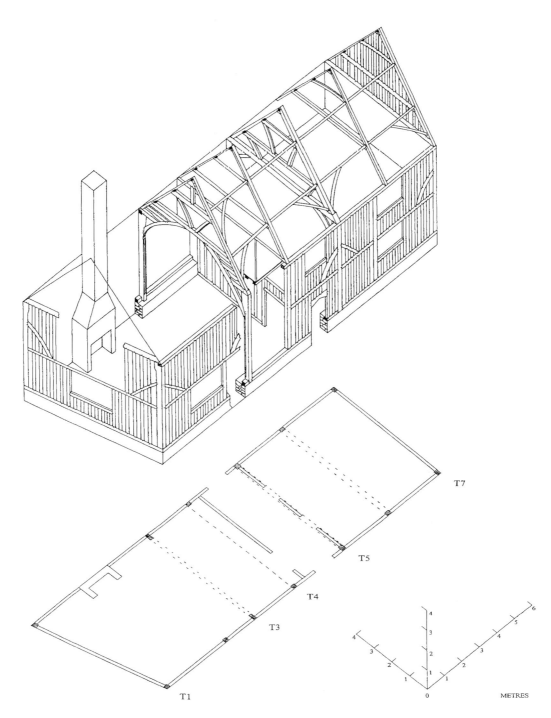

Figure 24: 10–14 Churchgate, Hallaton: reconstruction view. The open hall has a high arching roof, but was built with a chimneystack. Dated c 1484–1509.

a room beside the stable, a stable next to the gate and a granary; to Maud were assigned a long room at the end of the hall and other rooms next to the long room; while Mabel received a grange, a cart-house, a long stable and a dovecote. No doubt archaeological evidence remains to be discovered of such associated buildings, as in the excavations at the site of the medieval manor of Holyoak, to the north of Great Easton, where an extensive complex of 13-14th century date was revealed (Brown 1971–2).

The second characteristic medieval building type of the area is the cruck, surviving examples probably dating mainly from around 1450–1550, though a few of later date have also been found. The more intensive fieldwork in south-east Leicestershire has found quite extensive survival, enough to show that this was the standard construction type for the good quality peasant house of the area. Because survival is very fragmentary, the features of these houses remain rather elusive. However, it appears that the cruck frames, although built by professional carpenters, were relatively unsophisticated in comparison with some cruck areas, with lapped collars and rather crude bracing. Walls were generally of mud, occasionally perhaps of stone, but not timber-framed. Most crucks across the timber-framed areas of southern and western England, and also Wales, had much better quality carpentry, with better-shaped blades, tenoned collars, well-formed arch-braces, and decorative features such as cusping. Crucks in the stone or cob areas of the south-west were also of better quality, though in much of northern England, such as Yorkshire or Cumbria, crucks were often rather cruder.

Although the early gentry houses in the area included some good quality carpentry, the later medieval houses seem to have very little good work in timber. While the quality of local stonemasonry rose to a peak of high excellence in the course of the 17th century, these later houses also have very few carpentry or joinery features of note. As Wood-Jones (1963, 14) has said, for the similar stone-belt area around Banbury, there is 'little to suggest the existence of a preceding timber tradition of any quality …. Roofs, beams and partitions – which might be expected to reflect earlier building practices – are invariably of poor scale and craftsmanship, and entirely lack enrichment.'

The pattern of building cycles revealed in the area is perhaps the aspect of this study which is of greatest wider interest. The outburst of building activity amongst the rural gentry during the late 13th and early 14th century, both in timber and stone, has been recognised across the country in the pattern of tree-ring dated buildings (Pearson 2001). This period seems to have been a high point of the medieval economy. It is interesting to note that in Rutland, Leicestershire and Northamptonshire it is this period in which church building also reaches its fullest flowering. The building boom appears to have been followed, as Pearson says, 'by a crisis of confidence that lasted until the mid 15th century'. The Black Death of 1348–9 was a catastrophe for medieval society, leading to the death of perhaps as much as half the population of England, and bringing many other changes in its wake. Across much of England and Wales, as Pearson shows in the study of tree-ring dates, building amongst the gentry picked up again from around 1450,

with by far the greater number of surviving medieval houses dating from 1450–1550. This late medieval golden age seems, on the basis of surviving evidence, to have passed by Rutland and south-east Leicestershire. No doubt this is in considerable part due to the wave of major rebuilding which got underway from the late 16th century, but the lack of even fragmentary evidence does suggest that, for whatever reason, the rural gentry built little at this time. Much more survives from the late 13th to early 14th century than from the 15th or early 16th century. Church building work of this period is also scarce, being generally restricted to re-roofing work, often with the addition of clerestoreys. Woodfield found a similar pattern in the larger medieval houses of Northamptonshire, with 70% of houses dating before 1400, and only 30% dating 1400–1485 (Woodfield 1981). Much of the late medieval national building boom was in timber-frame construction, particularly in southern and eastern England, and this may account for a great deal of the tree-ring dating evidence. However, building activity did also continue in some stone-built areas, such as Somerset and Devon. Nor did all timber-framed areas follow the general trend; in Oxfordshire's Vale of the White Horse most medieval gentry houses pre-date 1350, with very little late medieval activity (Currie 1992).

The buildings which do survive in the area from the late medieval period are the lower status cruck-built houses, which contrast strongly with those of the late 13th and early 14th century. The overall extent of survival is not yet clearly established, but few buildings survive in anything other than a fragmentary state. The contrast with cruck-built houses of the same period in well-researched areas such as Shropshire (Mercer 2003) or Radnorshire (Suggett 2005) is dramatic. In these counties, cruck houses survive in very large numbers, with good quality features even in many of the smaller houses.

The over-riding factor which undoubtedly affects the survival of all medieval houses in Rutland and south-east Leicestershire is the great rebuilding in stone, which started at the highest level near the end of the 16th century and gradually swept all before it during the course of the 17th and 18th centuries. The new houses had no need of a medieval style open hall, but were of two storeys throughout. A strong local building tradition, with very high quality masonry features, became established over the early decades of the 17th century, though it took some time before the lower status houses succumbed to the new style. Of the earlier gentry houses, only a few of the best quality houses were able to resist the onslaught, with most previous buildings completely demolished and rebuilt, albeit on the same site. The cruck-built houses, with their low eaves and mud walls, were also largely swept away, though in some instances parts of the cruck frame survived, with the external walls rebuilt in stone. The most complete cruck survivals tend to be those where the house slipped down in social status to cottage level, where the low headroom of the first floor bedchambers was still considered tolerable. As can be seen by examining early village photographs, such buildings continued to suffer a high attrition rate into the mid 20th century.

Acknowledgements

I am very grateful to all the local owners who have kindly allowed access to their houses. Without their cooperation, none of this research would be possible. Thanks are due also to Nat Alcock, Bob Meeson and John Walker, who provided valuable comments on an earlier draft of this paper.

Bibliography

Alcock, N. W., 2002. The Distribution and Dating of Crucks and Base Crucks. *Vernacular Architecture* 33, 67–70.

Alcock, N. W. and Barley, M. W., 1972. Medieval Roofs with Base-Crucks and Short Principals. *Antiquaries Journal* 52, 132–168.

Brown, G., 1971–2. The Medieval Manor of Holyoak. *Transactions of the Leicestershire Archaeological and Historical Society* 47, 70.

Cornwall, J., 1963. *The People of Rutland in 1522*. Reprinted from *Transactions* 37 (1961–2) by Leicestershire Archaeological and Historical Society, Leicester.

Currie, C. R. J., 1992. Larger Medieval Houses in the Vale of White Horse. *Oxoniensia* 57, 81–244.

Dollman, F. T. and Jobbins, J. R., 1861. *An Analysis of Ancient Domestic Architecture, Vol I*. London: Batsford.

Finn, N., 2007. Aylestone Hall: The Biography of a Medieval Manor House. *Transactions of the Leicestershire Archaeological and Historical Society* 81, 89–126.

Hewett, C. A. and Gibson, A., 1981. *Quaintree House, Braunston, Rutland*. Typed report, copy lodged at Oakham Public Library.

Hill, N., 1999. Nevill Holt: The Development of an English Country House. *Archaeological Journal* 156, 246–293.

Hill, N., 2001. The Manor House, Medbourne: The Development of Leicestershire's Earliest Manor House. *Transactions of the Leicestershire Archaeological and Historical Society* 75, 36–61.

Hill, N., 2003. 10–14 Churchgate: Hallaton's Lost Manor House? *Transactions of the Leicestershire Archaeological and Historical Society* 77, 12–34.

Hill, N., 2005. On the Origins of Crucks: An Innocent Notion. *Vernacular Architecture* 36, 1–14.

Hill, N., 2006. *Glebe Cottage, Churchgate, Hallaton, Leics*. Historic building survey report, copy lodged at Record Office for Leicestershire, Leicester and Rutland.

Hill, N. and Miles, D., 2001. The Royal George, Cottingham, Northamptonshire: An early cruck building. *Vernacular Architecture* 32, 62–67.

Marsden, T. L., 1958. *Minor Domestic Architecture in Rutland and Vicinity*. PhD thesis, Manchester University.

Mercer, E., 2003. *English Architecture to 1900; The Shropshire Experience*. Logaston Press, Herefordshire.

Metcalfe, J. P. W., 1997. 'Cased' Houses in Uppingham: 50 and 52 High Street East. *Rutland Record* 17, 302–313.

Pearson, S., 1994. *The Medieval Houses of Kent: An Historical Analysis*. Swindon, RCHME.

Pearson, S., 2001. The Chronological Distribution of Tree-Ring Dates, 1980–2001: An Update. *Vernacular Architecture* 32, 68–69.

Penoyre, J., 2005. *Traditional Houses of Somerset*. Somerset Books.

Priest, V., 2000. *Archaeological Evaluations at Nevill Holt Hall, Nevill Holt, Leics*. University of Leicester Archaeological Services Report No 2000/157.

Sandall, K., 1986. Aisled Halls in England and Wales. *Vernacular Architecture* 17, 21–35.

Seaborne, M. V. J., 1963. Small Stone Houses in Northamptonshire. *Northants Past and Present* (1963) 141–150. Also: A Postscript on Cruck Construction. *Northants Past and Present*, 1971/2, 366–69.

Stenning, D. F. with Andrews, D. D. and Tyers, I., 2003. Small Aisled Halls in Essex. *Vernacular Architecture* 34, 1–19.

Suggett, R., 2005. *Houses and History in the March of Wales: Radnorshire 1400–1800*. RCAHMW.

Turner, T. H. and Parker, J. H., 1877 (2nd ed.). *Some Account of Domestic Architecture in England, vol. 1: From the Conquest to the End of the Thirteenth Century*. J H Parker, Oxford.

Walker, J., 1999. Late 12th and Early 13th Century Aisled Buildings: A Comparison. *Vernacular Architecture* 30, 21–53.

Webster, V. R., 1954. Cruck-framed Buildings of Leicestershire. *Transactions of the Leicestershire Archaeological and Historical Society* 30, 26–58.

Wood-Jones, R. B., 1963. *Traditional Domestic Architecture in the Banbury Region*. Repub. 1986. Banbury: Wykham Books.

Woodfield, P., 1981. The Larger Medieval Houses of Northamptonshire. *Northamptonshire Archaeology* 16, 153–195.

Woodfield, C. and Woodfield, P., 1981–2. The Palace of the Bishops of Lincoln at Lyddington. *Transactions of the Leicestershire Archaeological and Historical Society* 57, 1–16.

Dating References:

Vernacular Architecture

Vol 22, 1991, 45 (Quaintree House, Braunston, Rutland)

Vol 23, 1992, 52 (Bede Lane Farm, North Luffenham)

Vol 30, 1999, 90 (College House, Oakham)

Vol 39, 2008, 108 (5 King Street Melton Mowbray, Nevill Holt Hall)

Vol 41, 2010, 94 (Flore's House, Oakham)

Nottingham University Tree-ring dating Laboratory unpublished reports

1989 (29 High Street, Hallaton)

2001 (11 Hunts Lane, Hallaton)

2006 (50 Well Street, Langham)

Religious Houses of Leicestershire and Rutland

Peter Liddle

Introduction

The aim of this paper is to review the archaeological and landscape evidence for the religious houses of Leicestershire and Rutland. It is not intended to repeat information published previously (particularly McKinley 1954, Liddle with O'Brien 1995) but rather to summarise briefly evidence for each site and review progress, whilst extending the scope of that paper from abbeys and priories to at least a brief consideration of other classes of site.

Abbeys and Priories

In 1995 14 abbeys and priories were identified and described in the Leicestershire Archaeological and Historical Society Transactions Volume 69 (Liddle with O'Brian 1995) and are listed below.

Place	*Order*	*Founding Date*
Belvoir	Benedictine	1076
Bradley	Augustinian	-1234
Breedon	Augustinian	-1122
Brooke	Augustinian	-1153
Charley	Augustinian	-1190
Croxton Kerrial	Premon-stratensian	c.1159
Garendon	Cistercian	1133
Grace Dieu	Augustinian nuns	1235+
Kirby Bellars	Chantry Augustinian	1316
Langley	Benedictine nuns	c.1150
Launde	Augustinian	-1125
Leicester	Augustinian	1139
Owston	Augustinian	-1161
Ulverscroft	Augustinian	-1153

Spinney Nunnery

It is now possible to add a 15th site. In the Lincoln Diocesan records there is an Episcopal confirmation charter dated between 1148 and 1166 recording the creation of a nunnery called Spinney dedicated to St Mary on land in or around Melton Mowbray granted by Gundred and her son Roger de Mowbray, lord of Melton (Thompson 1991, 210, 229). The grant is for the site itself, a carucate of land in 'the lordship of Melton next to Spinney', a mill in Buceby, a meadow called Esselouenga and 10 acres around the monastery with the island next to the mill. In the very north east of Melton parish is Spinney Farm and next to the stream is an earthwork site that must represent the nunnery. This has been surveyed by Fred Hartley (Hartley 1987, 11, 37) and his plan reveals a square with raised areas around them that could be a claustral arrangement (fig 1 overleaf). The site seems never to have been referred to again and was presumably short-lived. Pottery recovered from the site suggests 12th and 13th century and later occupation and it may be that the site continued in use, perhaps as a grange of Monks Kirby Priory in North Warwickshire, west of Lutterworth, to which the site was re-granted in a charter by Roger and Nigel de Mowbray before 1177.

Spinney can be added to the distribution map of abbeys and priories (fig 2 overleaf) but does nothing to redress the strange lack of sites in the south of the county. We will return to this later in the paper. Ten sites have some surviving evidence of building plans with, in addition, Belvoir Priory represented by an 18th century plan (Nichols, 1795, 75–81). These plans range from, at the top end, Leicester and Croxton Abbeys with more or less complete plans of claustral (and some additional) buildings, to Owston Abbey where only part of the church survives, and Charley and Langley where the plan is largely inferred from the footprint of existing buildings.

Owston Abbey

Progress has been made at a number of sites. At Owston Abbey a campaign of surveying has moved on our understanding, helped by a most useful plan of 1793 by John Pridden (Nichols 1798, 760a) and a drawing by the Buck Brothers in 1730 (*ibid*, figs 3, 4, 5). This shows a large 15th century gatehouse joined corner to corner with the church. It seems likely that

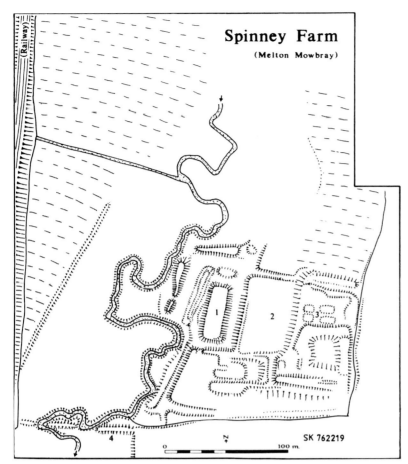

Figure 1: Spinney farm near Melton Mowbray.

Substantial moated platform (1), a terrace, perhaps for a garden or orchard (2), a group of four small rectangular "pillow mounds" (3) and on the south side an area of foundations presumably representing farm buildings. Immediately south-west of the moat was a pond of undetermined extent retained by a dam (4) across the flood plain. (© plan and text – R F Hartley 1987)

Figure 2: Location of the Abbeys and Priories of Leicestershire (from Liddle with O'Brien 1995) with addition of Spinney

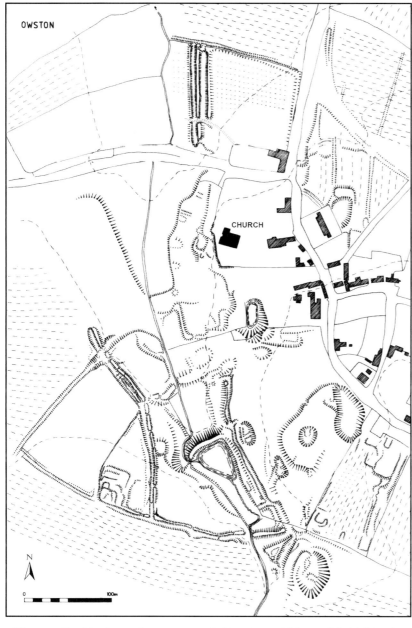

Figure 3: Earthwork survey of Owston Abbey (R F Hartley, unpublished)

an original Abbot's lodging in the west range of the claustral buildings has been extended westwards in the first floor of the gatehouse with guest accommodation, perhaps, also located here. The gatehouse is clearly visible as an earthwork (most obviously at its south-west corner). It is clear from the window arrangement in the present church that the cloister was immediately to its south and the cloister garth shows on a resistivity survey undertaken by Leicestershire Fieldworkers, which also shows indications of the south range (presumably the refectory) although most is covered by a concrete farm yard. The east range with possible other buildings to the east are visible on the printouts but are by no means clear. The church must have been at least twice as long as it is now – and perhaps more. The scale of the arcades separating the nave from the north aisle certainly suggests a much larger building. The valley to the south of the Abbey is full of earthworks representing (as well as quarrying) fishponds and possible gardens, which have been surveyed by Fred Hartley (Liddle 1982, 45).

Figure 4: Owston Abbey view of the north side (from John Nichols, 1798 Vol 2, pt2, 760a)

Figure 5: View of north side of church in 2013

91

Langley

At Langley Dr John Jolleys recorded a complete skeleton near the south –east corner of the house and noted other disarticulated human remains during the digging of a drainage trench. The present house has two parallel stone-built ranges (Douglass, 1988) and seems likely to follow the footprint of the nunnery. The position of these burials strongly suggests that the south range of the house sits on the church with the cloister on its north side as is often the case in nunneries. The north range would then represent the refectory while the present east range replaces the chapter house and sacristy with dormitory over. The missing west range would conventionally have guest accommodation and the prioress' lodging. Dr Jolleys also recorded a relatively insubstantial stone feature with an east-west face parallel to, and around 2 metres south of, the existing south wall. It partially overlay the burial. A more substantial north-south wall some 10 metres to the west suggests the possibility of a Lady Chapel, lying south of an aisleless church.

Grace Dieu

At Grace Dieu the basic claustral layout of the Augustinian nunnery is clear, but recording of the structure after ivy clearance as part of the process of consolidation and a short campaign of evaluation has moved us forward in our understanding of the site. The site was converted into a mansion of the Beaumont family at the Dissolution and was lived in until the 1690's. Parts of the site were then used as a tenant farm until after 1800. There is very well preserved below ground archaeology which was revealed in 11 test pits dug by Graham Keevil. These have shown that the church had a tower inserted in the late medieval period, have defined the west range only previously known from a Buck Brothers drawing of 1730, showing that it extended south of the presumed refectory, and suggest that the chapter house was probably never longer than it is now. The monastic kitchen appears part of an L-shaped structure, although it is not clear if some or all of this range is pre- or post-Dissolution in date (Keevil 2006).

Launde

At Launde building recording, resistivity surveying and small scale excavation (Beavitt, 1995) has allowed a hypothetical reconstruction of the priory's claustral plan (Fig 6; Liddle with O'Brien 1995, 2–3). Beyond the cloister what is plausibly the priory kitchen is visible on the geophysics outside the southwestern corner of the ha-ha. A possible gate house and some outer court buildings have also been noted. Support for this general interpretation is afforded by what appears to be a sketch of the house on the Whatborough Map of 1586 (Liddle 2003). This shows an earlier version of the mansion with 3 ranges of building around a courtyard suggesting that, at this stage the claustral buildings were being re-used. Walls have been recorded during an evaluation in the area of the ha-ha west of the present mansion (Hyam 2007). These were both north-south walls of which one was in line with the south wall of the nave and the other in line with the south wall of the present building's south wing.

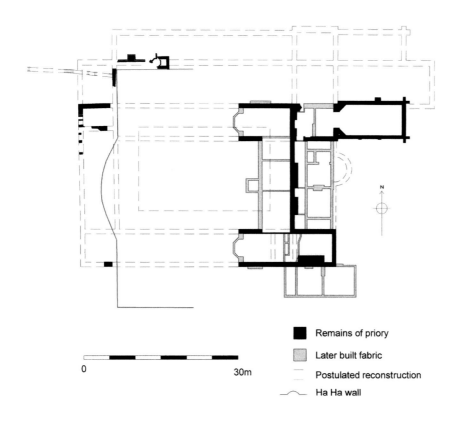

Remains of priory
Later built fabric
Postulated reconstruction
Ha Ha wall

0   30m

Figure 6: Plan of Launde Abbey (Neil Finn)

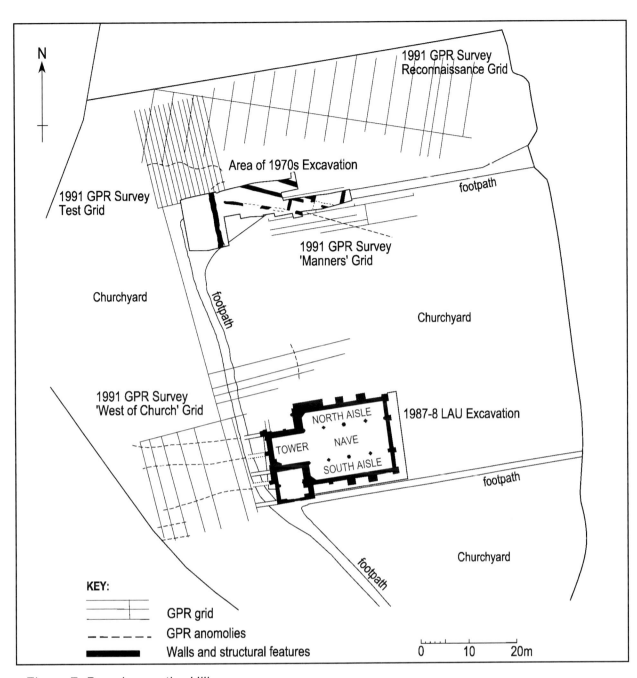

Figure 7: Breedon on the Hill

This broadly supports the hypothesis of how the claustral buildings were converted into the existing mansion, but suggests that the church and refectory were somewhat longer than previously suggested. A stone newel stair base found in the 1960s by Mr A E Grimbley suggests the possibility of a west tower.

Breedon on the Hill

Breedon is Leicestershire's only documented Saxon monastery, founded c.675 AD, and now represented by a remarkable collection of carvings. The monastery was re-founded in the 1120's as a cell of Nostell Priory. The present nave, north and south aisles and the west tower are all survivors of the medieval monastic church, the tower being Norman and the rest a 13th century rebuilding. Excavation (fig 7) has shown that the 13th century plinth of the south aisle continues south. The present porch covers most of whatever structure there was here, but the foundation diverges eastward from the porch walls suggesting that a polygonal structure was originally intended. This can hardly be an earlier porch as the surviving church represents the canons' part of the church. They would enter from the north and parishioners from the west, where the parish nave was still partly standing in Nichols' day. One possibility may be a shrine containing the relics of St Hardulph to whom the church is partly dedicated. Many Saxon saints were being translated into new shrines at this time. The cloister seems to have lain to the north of the church, with the position of a building, probably the dormitory, suggested by a roof scar on the north wall of the tower. Plans of Ann Dornier's 1975 excavations (Dornier 1976) remain elusive but a set of photographs with many points of reference has been found which has allowed the monastic kitchen to be securely located which will help in reconstructing the size of the cloister.

Ulverscroft Priory

Ulverscroft Priory is the best preserved local monastic site (figs 8 and 9). The church forms the north range and the guest hall the west range, while the outer wall of the refectory survives on the south next to the Prior's Lodging (Keay 1935; Baker 1981). Substantial survey work has been undertaken by Jonathan Clarkson and team (Clarkson 2007) in the wake of a disastrous collapse of the Prior's Lodging. While severe damage has been done to this part of the complex it has also revealed much and led to further work on the site. The Prior's Lodging may originally have been in the west range, probably on the first floor. In the 15th century the south end of the north-south dormitory block was converted with a 3rd floor added under a new east-west roof. It was refenestrated and a substantial fireplace inserted in the ground floor parlour. This room was originally linked to a warming house to the east dated 1240–50 by dendrochronology. To its east the east-west range is also now believed to be medieval and not 18th century.

The earliest dendrochronology dates yet produced on the site are early 13th century. Work on the roof of the west range, traditionally (and probably correctly) identified as the Guest Hall, suggests re-roofing in around 1533 as is implied in the documents. There is evidence of some high status post-dissolution use, probably as a hunting lodge, continuing a tradition of hunting at the priory. Resistivity survey south of the buildings has revealed a number of structures. One (fig 9) is clearly the kitchen, its site already predicted on the basis of a windowless area of wall in the surviving south wall of the refectory. South of this is a complex of other buildings. This is a conventional site for guest accommodation but could equally be the infirmary. It is particularly sad that such a fine site is in danger of further deterioration.

Leicester Abbey

At Leicester Abbey Richard Buckley of ULAS directed a series of training excavations for University of Leicester archaeology students, mostly re-examining and recording structures revealed by Waller K Bedingfield from 1929 onwards (Bedingfield 1931; Buckley 2006. See plan, Buckley this volume). This campaign tackled many of the problems in understanding the site. The inner gatehouse developed from a relatively simple rectangular structure at the end of a 'halt-way' leading from the outer gate in the precinct wall. This was developed late in the medieval period into a substantial structure with its own kitchens and with a series of polygonal towers on its south face. These are clearly shown in the Buck Brothers 1730 drawing and were found in excavation. This was probably a new Abbot's lodging built c.1500 that became the focus of the later Cavendish House mansion on the site.

Around the cloisters consolidation of the displayed foundations showed that there is surviving medieval fabric in the south wall of the church and in the cloister walls, while there is an *in situ* medieval tiled floor in the east cloister walk (Jones 2010). A robber trench of the south wall of the dormitory block was found, indicating this was much shorter than Bedingfield believed (although this may have been extended later in the medieval period).

Substantial work has been undertaken on the kitchen block south-west of the claustral complex. It was square in outside plan but octagonal internally with diagonally set ovens in each corner reminiscent of the surviving abbot's kitchen at Glastonbury. There is evidence of late rebuilding with a passage running to another structure to the west, perhaps the Kings Tower mentioned in the Dissolution survey.

In 2006 and 2007 the presumed infirmary south-east of the cloisters was examined, including a hall with some late medieval tiles surviving *in situ*. Between the infirmary and kitchen the presumed guest range was explored in 2008 and 2009 proving rather more complex than expected. An east–west range had an internal corridor on the north side and a series of cell like rooms to the south. The centre of the range could not be examined because of a path but south of this was a series of other rooms including a substantial stone floored garderobe, with a drain running

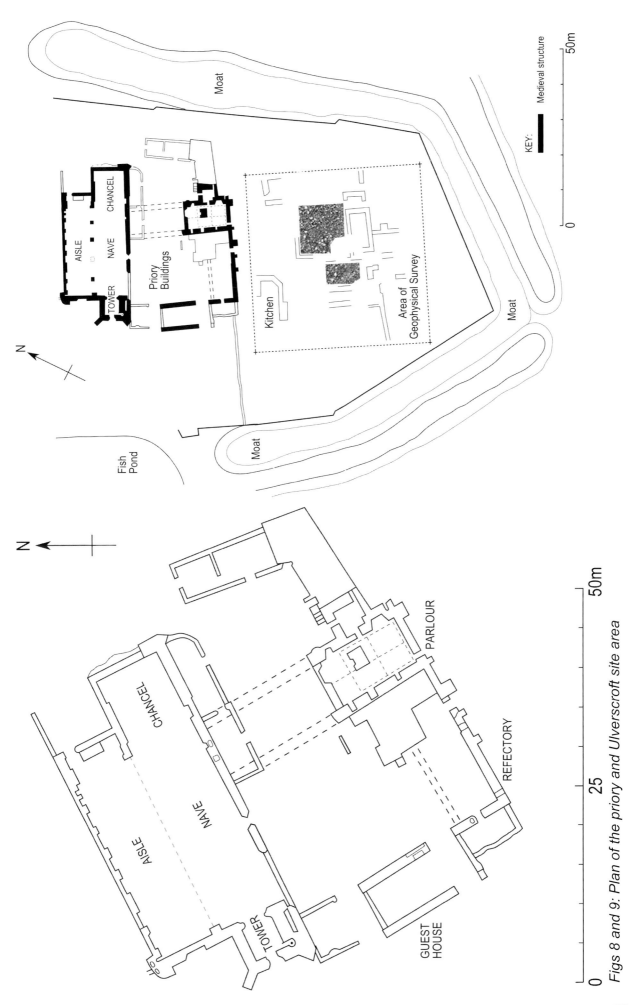

KEY:

▬ Medieval structure

Moat

Fish Pond

Moat

Moat

AISLE

NAVE

CHANCEL

TOWER

Priory Buildings

Kitchen

Area of Geophysical Survey

N

N

AISLE

NAVE

CHANCEL

TOWER

PARLOUR

REFECTORY

GUEST HOUSE

0   25   50m

0   50m

Figs 8 and 9: Plan of the priory and Ulverscroft site area

95

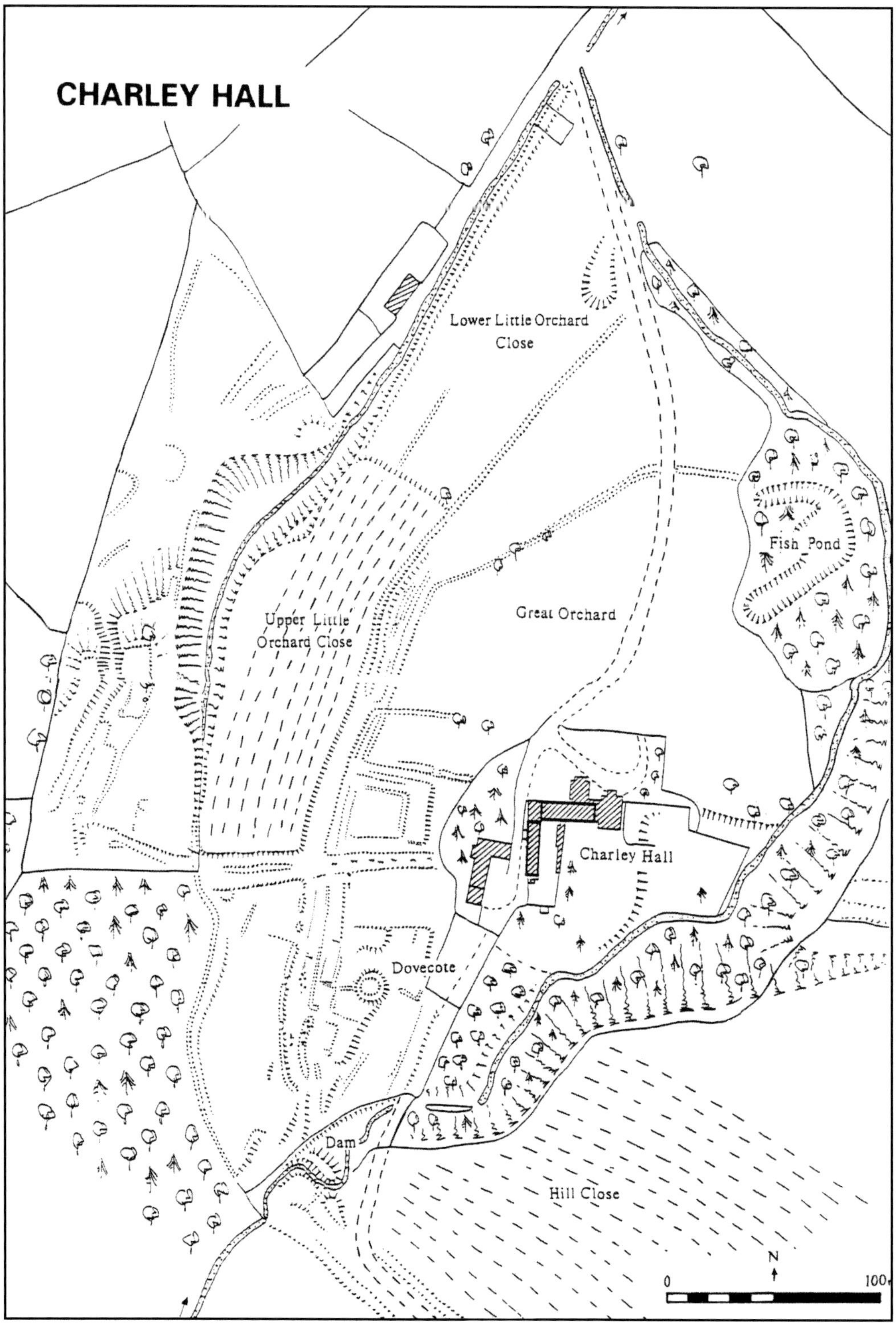

CHARLEY HALL
Lower Little Orchard Close
Fish Pond
Great Orchard
Upper Little Orchard Close
Charley Hall
Dovecote
Dam
Hill Close
N
0
100

Figure 10: Charley Priory (R F Hartley unpublished)

southwards. A bay window was attached to the north side of this range suggesting that the guest hall itself was on the first floor. Other rooms were found running north from the range defining a yard to their east and perhaps linking to structures found east of the kitchen.

Charley Priory

No substantial work has been undertaken recently at the other 7 sites. Charley Priory was merged with Ulverscroft in *c.*1465 and was long assumed to have completely disappeared. However, two stone ranges at right angles to one another within the present Charley Hall were probably the church and west range of the priory. Earthworks show the gate house, a dovecote and ancillary buildings (fig 10).

Garendon

At Garendon Brian Williams directed excavations for the Loughborough Archaeological Society in the 1960s. These revealed the east end of the abbey church and the east range, including the chapter house. The Abbey main drain was also investigated. The now demolished Garendon Hall perhaps

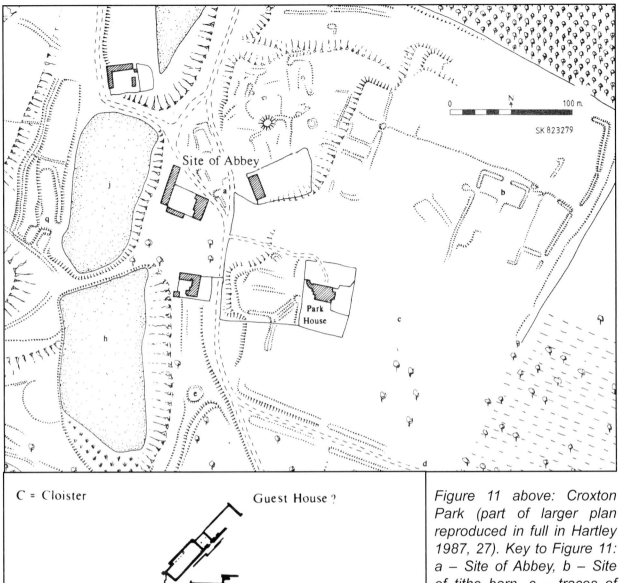

C = Cloister

Guest House ?

Infirmary

C

Church

N

0   50 m.

Figure 11 above: Croxton Park (part of larger plan reproduced in full in Hartley 1987, 27). Key to Figure 11: a – Site of Abbey, b – Site of tithe barn, c – traces of quarrying, h and j – 2 of a line of 6 or 8 ponds, q – smaller ponds opposite the Abbey.

Figure 12 left: Croxton Abbey; plan of excavated buildings 1922–1926. (R F Hartley 1987)

incorporated part of the west range of the Abbey and study of photographs taken before the demolition may help to resolve this. (Williams 1965; Williams 1969).

Croxton Abbey

At Croxton Abbey work by the 9th Duke of Rutland recovered the plan of the claustral area and associated buildings. Unfortunately the Duke never published his work and we must rely on the most useful notes and plan produced by Sir Alfred Clapham (Herbert 1945. Fig 12 after Herbert in Hartley 1987) until the extensive site

diaries and photographs preserved at Belvoir Castle can be analysed. This was one of the largest excavations undertaken on any of the local sites. It revealed a complex development of the site.

The church starts with an aisleless cruciform plan with a standard claustral plan to the north. The dormitory is in the east range with the chapterhouse projecting to the east and the reredorter (latrine block) at its north east corner, with what are presumably drains (although not distinguished as such on the plan) running to the west. The refectory is in the north range with, perhaps, the kitchen at its west end, while the west range may have been guest accommodation and the Abbot's lodging. In the 13th century the cloister was extended eastwards over the former site of the dormitory with a lavatorium (ritual washing place) projecting into the cloister garth.

The church was extended eastwards and a new huge north transept (unless this is a series of chapels) joining up to an extended chapter house was built, whilst a south aisle was added, with a chapel (perhaps a Lady Chapel), at its east end. In 1443 we know that there were 6 altars. After a disastrous fire in 1326 (caused apparently by a careless plumber) there was substantial rebuilding. At some stage more chapels were added to the south. Remains of one of these are said to have been incorporated into existing buildings. It is said that the dormitory was no longer in the east range, perhaps moving to the west range, while the kitchen seems to be relocated to the east end of the refectory and the reredorter disappears. The refectory was used as the basis for the first post Dissolution building on the site, somewhat complicating matters.

A block to the north on a north east to south west alignment, includes what appears to be a large hall, 2 square rooms with pillar bases down the middle (suggesting an upper floor) and then an additional hall. What appear to be drains run along the south wall. Clapham cautions us that this is 'only in part medieval and the piers and responds in the north-eastern part are re-used material'. It may represent new guest accommodation or an infirmary. Foundations east of the chapter house are even more difficult to interpret and seem to be part of a larger, mostly unexcavated, set of buildings.

Hartley's earthwork survey (fig 11 – central part of his plan only) puts the cloister into its context with what appears to be a farm complex to the east. Between this and the cloisters there may be another large set of buildings. West of the cloisters the valley contains a magnificent flight of fishponds, clearly of medieval origin although some were modified later (Hartley 1987, 8, 26–7).

Belvoir Priory

For Belvoir Priory, a cell of St Albans, we are reliant on even earlier sources. Nichols prints a plan of foundations visible in his day that are most odd. The church is shown with north and south aisles, a west tower, a 'chancel' and a series of chapels, several containing burials. The cloister lies to the north and in the centre of the cloister garth is an octagonal buttressed building identified as the chapter house that also contained burials. No conventional claustral buildings are noted, although some of the 'domestic buildings' of the priory were said to have been excavated early in the 20th century. Perhaps notes remain at Belvoir Castle that could throw further light on the site. Hartley's earthwork survey reveals terraces and what may be precinct banks, but it would appear that a tramway passes through the priory site disrupting any earthworks there may have been (Hartley 1987, 6, 18–9).

Bradley Priory

Bradley Priory is almost as difficult to understand. There are some earthwork remains but much of the site has been ploughed. Scatters of stone, tile and pottery mark the site and the succeeding buildings that were finally demolished, although not before they had been drawn by John Tailby for Nichols (Nichols 1798, 509–10). The large quoin stones suggest that this farmhouse was a remodelled priory building. Although what may be the main drain can be traced, no plan can yet be produced although geophysical survey would be instructive.

Brooke Priory

At Brooke Priory there are superb garden earthworks (Hartley 1983, 9–10) which are associated with the mansion which replaced the priory (a cell of Kenilworth). Nothing is known of the monastic plan.

Kirby Bellars

Kirby Bellars Priory remains the most elusive of all the sites. The village sits amongst a complex series of earthworks (Hartley 1987, 10, 32–4). The assumption that the parish church was also the priory church is wrong. The priory was founded in 1316 as a secular college, becoming a priory in 1359, and the original charter makes it clear that it is at 'no small distance from the parish church' and 'in the high road'. This makes the area around Kirby Park, adjacent to the present A607, the most likely area. Fieldwork may help to resolve the situation.

Alien cells

Recent work by Hinckley Fieldworkers at Hinckley Priory, a cell of the French Abbey of Lire, has identified plausibly medieval foundations in a small scale evaluation on the site, immediately south of the parish church. Modern buildings lie over much of the site and it is not clear if there was ever a conventional claustral plan. A review of documentary evidence has recently been published (Wallis 2012). A second alien cell, this time of St Georges de Boscherville, was at Edith Weston. Nothing is known of the site and its character, although a set of ponds north of the village has been tentatively linked to it (Hartley 1983, 14).

Friaries

In the 13th century Leicester, like most major urban centres, attracted the new orders of friars. There were 4 orders present – Dominicans (Black Friars), Franciscans (Greyfriars), Augustinians (Austins) and Friars of the Sack – but perhaps only 3 sites.

The Black Friars were in the north-west corner of the walled town and whilst the outline of the precinct is known the claustral buildings have not been found, although this is an area ear-marked for redevelopment.

The Austins probably took over the buildings of the Friars of the Sack, who had gone by 1295–6 when the Bishop of Lincoln decreed that their empty house beyond the West Bridge had to stay in religious use. The Austins first appear in documents in 1300, and extended their site in 1304. The date of 1254 given by the medieval writer, John Capgrave, seems unlikely as no local references can be found in the second half of the 13th century. A campaign of excavation in the 1970s revealed a plan that developed over many centuries (Mellor 1981). The church was at the south end with the claustral buildings to the north and a second 'little cloister' to the north again.

In 2012 a series of trenches by ULAS has revealed much of the plan of the Grey Friars cloisters. The church lay at the north end of the precinct, parallel to Peacock Lane and St Martins, while the chapter house and east cloister walk has been revealed to the south. This has hit the headlines internationally as the remains of Richard III have been discovered in the choir and the site is now part of the visitor centre.

Hospitals

The other predominantly urban religious foundation was the hospital, although relatively little recent work has been done. These typically lie on the edges of medieval towns close to the roads. These include Lutterworth, where excavation has revealed part of the hospital graveyard and a few cobble floors with evidence of more substantial buildings close by (Chapman 2002); Castle Donington, where earthworks and standing buildings in The Spital mark the site and where small scale excavation revealed walls (Hartley 1984); Oakham, where the chapel survives; five separate sites around Leicester; possibly Loughborough where there is documentary evidence; and Melton Mowbray where burials have been recovered in an area called 'The Spital'. An atypical location for a site, outside Tilton, was a leper hospital, later a grange of Burton Lazars, marked by earthworks.

The Newarke

The Newarke Hospital (fig 13) was created immediately south of Leicester Castle and partly survives (now part of De Montfort University). This was a foundation of the Earls of Lancaster and was clearly of infirmary hall type, where the beds were effectively within a chapel and the major benefit was in witnessing the Elevation of the Host (although in these secular days we may consider regular meals and clean clothing may also have helped!). This site was quickly upgraded into a secular college, although the hospital survived within the new foundation (and, indeed, survives to the present day as the Trinity Hospital building, their function as sheltered accommodation now relocated to modern buildings to the west).

The College of the Annunciation of St Mary in the Newarke was a magnificent creation. It was arranged around a courtyard. Grouped around this was the hospital building on the north side, a very smart new collegiate church on the south side (which except for a couple of arches in the Hawthorn Building of De Montfort University (DMU) does not survive) and canon's houses, although only the ground floor of one of these survives as the Chantry Building of DMU. The Wygston's Chantry house, a 16th century addition, also survives as part of Newarke Houses Museum. John Leland, the King's Antiquary, visited the site in the 1530s and describes a 'large and fair'

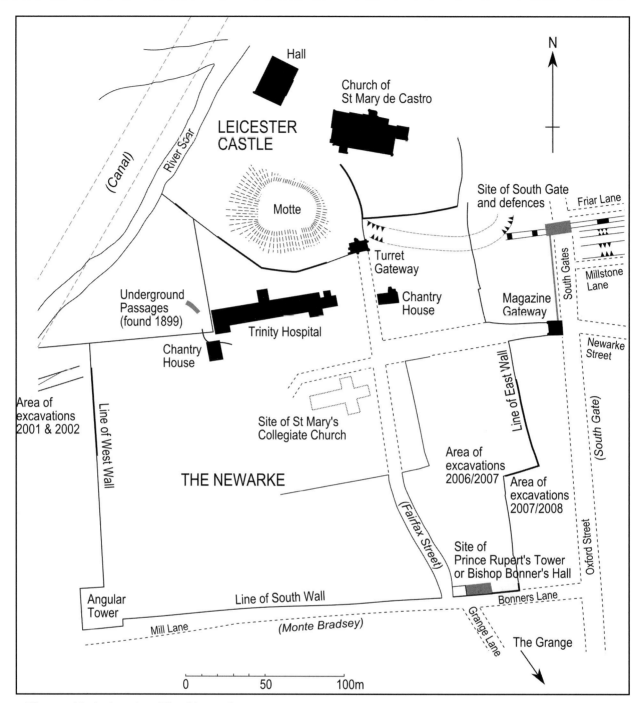

Figure 13: Leicester, The Newarke

cloister south-west of the church. The walls of the Newarke enclosure survived in reasonable state late enough to be photographed (Courtney & Courtney 1995). They survive to the north, where the Turret Gateway allowed access to the castle, but elsewhere have been cleared away except for the fine monastic-type gatehouse known as the Magazine Gateway. On the southern walls the building called Rupert's Tower (or Bishop Bonner's Hall), perhaps part of a southern gateway to the enclosure, has also gone but was recorded before demolition (Herbert 1940).

Military orders

Most local sites of the military orders, which have their origin in the Crusades, were, effectively, granges. The exception is Burton Lazars, which was the chief house of the Knights of St Lazarus, an order of leper knights. The site at Burton Lazars has some excellent earthworks (Hartley 1987, 7, 24), but it is unclear which are medieval and which go with the later mansion of the Hartopp family on the site, which may have incorporated the master's house. Medieval documents also refer to a gate house, chapel, graveyard, chapter house and courtyard. It is tempting to think that this may have had a monastic-type plan but it is impossible to be sure despite the valiant efforts of David Marcombe and the Burton Lazars Research Group. They have, however, located the remains of stonework from the chapel which was rebuilt in the 15th century as the order repositioned itself in a world where leprosy had become rare (Marcombe 2003). An area of tile floor and a nest of ovens found in 1913 by the 9th Duke of Rutland (then Marquis of Granby) and Captain Lindsay suggest well preserved archaeology on the site and this offers some hope of finally sorting this site out.

Elsewhere, the Knights Templar are represented by the chapel and hall surviving at Rothley (Fosbrooke, 1922) and the Hospitallers by earthworks at Beaumont Leys (Hartley 1989, 42), which may give an idea of what should be expected at Heather, Old Dalby and Swinford where sites have yet to be definitely located.

Landscape

It is clear that the location of the abbeys and priories is disproportionately located in areas of woodland and waste – five around Charnwood and woodland to the north, four around Leighfield Forest in the east and two in smaller areas of heath and waste. Breedon was an Anglo-Saxon foundation within a hill fort while Belvoir, Kirby Bellars and Leicester were sited in relation to their founders' main residence. Although it should be noted that Leicester Abbey was – unlike its predecessor college at St Mary de Castro (and the later Newarke College) – not sited in or near the castle itself but in the meadows north of the town adjacent to the wooded area of Beaumont Leys into which the Abbey demesnes expanded (Squires 2006).

The reason for these locations seems straightforward. This was the easiest –and cheapest – way to carve out a home farm for a new house without (at least generally) affecting existing settlements. More detailed studies of individual sites may help flesh out the details. It is easy enough – at least in some cases – to reconstruct the landscape around houses at the time of the Dissolution. At Charley, for instance, an estate map of 1702 links us through field names to the landscape of 1553, only a few years after the Dissolution. This is clearly an enclosed landscape. Understanding the landscape 400 years earlier when the house was created is more difficult. Ridge and furrow implies an open field system and this

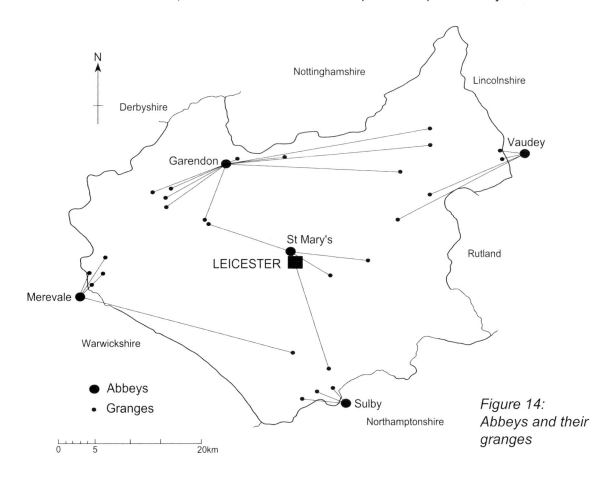

Figure 14: Abbeys and their granges

presumably relates to the settlement recorded in Domesday, which is recorded as 'waste'. This means that it was not yielding taxes rather than it was not in agricultural use. Charley, like many small settlements, is poorly documented but it seems at least possible that a hamlet co-existed with the priory for much of the period of its existence.

At nearby Ulverscroft it is clear that the Priory was dropped into pre-existing enclosures. The name – meaning 'the enclosure of Ulf' – suggests that these existed before the Norman Conquest (Ulf was named in Domesday as the pre-Conquest owner). The enclosures contain ridge and furrow indicating arable cultivation but not enough to support even a hamlet. This may have been an assart, later worked by the Priory's farm servants.

The mid-Forest location of these two houses is more obvious when looked at on the 1754 map of Charnwood Forest, particularly when the later enclosures are restored to the Forest. The liminal location of Grace Dieu and Garendon is also obvious reminding us that one function of religious houses was to give lodgings to travellers. Documentary sources show us that the Forest was important for the houses' herds and, particularly, flocks that were a major source of income.

Around Bradley Priory we can reconstruct the landscape by a combination of field walking and documentary evidence. The Priory was situated in what is now the northern part of Nevill Holt parish in an area of ancient woodland which has been divided up between the parishes of Medbourne, Blaston, Horninghold, Stockerston, Great Easton and Nevill Holt. There is existing ancient woodland in Park Wood, Bolt Wood, Holyoaks Wood and Great and Little Merrible Woods, but it is clear from field names that there were also woods called Blaston Merrible and Bradley Merrible that have long since been cleared (making it very likely that the hermitage of Merrible mentioned in the 13th century is an alternative name for Bradley). Around the woods were wood pasture areas including Blaston Moor, Medbourne Cow Pasture, and Great Easton Park and Pasture. Fieldwalking has shown that in the Late Iron Age and Early Roman periods there was settlement in this boulder clay area although this never penetrated the high ground around the Stockerston Crossroads. During the later Roman period the tide of settlement receded with no recorded Anglo-Saxon settlement and no sign of ploughing until perhaps the late 12th or 13th centuries, probably marking the foundation of the priory itself. Documents indicate a sheepcote north of the priory, presumably for running sheep on Blaston Moor, part of which had been granted to the priory.

Granges

The landscape of the county was affected by more than the creation of the houses themselves but by their extensive landholdings. Sybil Jack has estimated that the Houses had around 20% of the county's income and an interest in some 70,000 out of 500,000 acres in Leicestershire (Jack 1966). Religious houses seem to have been relatively conservative land managers with no evidence of pushing for early enclosure in the Late Medieval period. A major impact was the creation of granges (Courtney, 1981), particularly in the 12th century by the Cistercians of Garendon, Merevale, Vaudey (Lincs) and Sulby (Northants), who seem to have carved the county into areas of interest (fig 14). A Cistercian grange was in some senses a mini-monastery acting as a farm standing outside the manorial system and the open fields. It follows that these can only be created on areas not within the system (such as commons, heaths and moors) or areas removed from the system. While little work has been done on the landscape context of these early granges, it is clear that, for instance, Vaudey's Saltby Grange was carved out of Saltby Heath (Hartley, 1987, 13, 39, 63) while Hugglescote Grange was carved out of Charnwood Forest. The typical farm – exemplified beautifully by Garendon's Sysonby (ibid, 15, 37) and Blesswell Granges (ibid, 9, 23) – is a grid pattern with evidence of buildings in the centre with stock enclosures around. The best example of a surviving Cistercian grange barn is at Merevale's Newhouse Grange in Sheepy Parish, where dendrochronology dates suggest construction in the early 16th century (Fosbrooke, 1914, 85–6). Fragmentary earthworks here suggest a typical grid pattern of earthworks (Hartley 2008, 51).

The Augustinians came late to the Cistercian style grange. The word grange actually means barn and Leicester Abbey, for instance had a Master of Granges who controlled a series of barns for collecting grain from tithes and abbey lands. These were typically worked as rectorial demesnes with their holdings (a combination of demesne and glebe land) worked within the open field system. In the later 15th century Leicester Abbey – by far the biggest monastic landowner in the county – began to reorganise some of their holdings into granges. The first seems to have been Ingarsby, where in 1469 the village was deserted to create enclosed fields for cattle and sheep. Subsequently, re-organisations to create granges occurred but never at the expense of destroying a village community. The documents at Stoughton and for Horsepool Grange at Stanton under Bardon show, instead, an intricate series of land swaps with the local peasantry to consolidate abbey land to enclose it and turn it over to pasture. At Stoughton the new grange was created –probably in 1492 – in the far south –west of the parish and the open fields re-ordered to accommodate it without recourse to removing the village. Their fellow Augustinians at Owston may well have been responsible for the clearing of North Marefield, which they leased from the Hospitallers, but this did not give rise to a new grange being close enough to the Abbey to be worked from the home farm.

Conclusion

Since this subject was last reviewed in 1995 our understanding of the plans of many sites has moved forward considerably, although work remains to be done. Whilst little work has been done on the detailed landscape histories of these sites and their granges, what has been done points to the usefulness of this approach in future research.

Acknowledgements

Thanks to Mike Hawkes for additional plans and map. Fred Hartley for allowing reproduction of some or part of his plans of sites from his Medieval Earthworks series currently all out of print except for South-west Leicestershire and for unpublished plans.

Bibliography

Baker, N., 1981. The west range of Ulverscroft Priory and its roof: a survey. Transactions of the Leicestershire Archaeological and Historical Society 56, 10–17.

Beavitt P., 1995. Geophysical and Building Survey at Launde Abbey. Transactions of the Leicestershire Archaeological and Historical Society 49, 22–31.

Bedingfield, W., 1931. Presidential Address 1930–1. *Transactions of the Leicester Literary and Philosophical Society 32*, 5–24.

Buckley, R., 2006. *Leicester Abbey.* Leicester: *Leicestershire Archaeological and Historical Society.*

Chapman, S. A., 2002. Lutterworth. Mill Farm. *Transactions of the Leicestershire Archaeological and Historical Society 76*, 114–8.

Clarkson, J., 2007. *Ulverscroft Priory.* York: Field Archaeology Specialists.

Courtney, P. & Courtney, Y., 1995. In: *The Changing Face Of Leicester*, 43–68. Stroud: Alan Sutton.

Courtney, P., 1981. The monastic ganges of Leicestershire. *Transactions of the Leicestershire Archaeological and Historical Society 56*, 33–45.

Dornier, A., 1976. Breedon. *Medieval Archaeology 20*, 165.

Douglass, S.. 1988. Langley Priory. *Transactions of the Leicestershire Archaeological and Historical Society 62,* 16–30.

Fosbrooke, T., 1914. Newhouse Grange, Sheepy, Leicestershire. *Transactions of the Leicestershire Archaeological and Historical Society 11, pt 1.*

Fosbrooke, T., 1922. Rothley – the Preceptory. *Transactions of the Leicestershire Archaeological and Historical Society 12 pt 1, 1 – 34.*

Hartley., 2008. *The medieval earthworks of South-West Leicestershire.* Leicester: Leicestershire Museums Archaeological Fieldwork Group.

Hartley, R., 1989. *The medieval earthworks of Central Leicestershire.* Leicester: Leicestershire Museums Arts and Records Service.

Hartley, R., 1987. *The medieval earthworks of North-East Leicestershire.* Leicester. Leicestershire Museums Arts and Records Service

Hartley, R., 1984. *The medieval earthworks of North West Leicestershire.* Leicester: Leicestershire Museums Arts and Records Service.

Hartley, R., 1983. *The medieval earthworks of Rutland.* Leicester: Leicestershire Museums Arts and Records Service.

Herbert, A., 1945. Croxton Abbey. Leicestershire. *Transactions of the Leicestershire Archaeological and Historical Society 22*, 240–1.

Herbert, A.. 1940. Rupert's Tower, Leicester. *Transactions of the Leicestershire Archaeological and Historical Society 21*, 187–90.

Hyam, A., 2007. *An Archaeological evaluation of the Ha-ha and Stable block at Launde Abbey, Leicestershire.* Leicester: University of Leicester Archaeological Services Report 2007–60.

Jack, S., 1966. Monastic Lands in Leicestershire and their administration on the eve of the Dissolution. *Transactions of the Leicestershire Archaeological and Historical Society 41*, 4–40.

Jones, S., 2010. Leicester Abbey Grounds, Abbey Park. *Transactions of the Leicestershire Archaeological and Historical Society 84*, 341–2.

Keay, W. A., 1935. Ulverscroft Priory . In *Transactions of the Leicestershire Archaeological and Historical Society 18*, 88–92.

Keevil, G. A., 2006. *Grace Dieu Priory, Belton, North-West Leicestershire – Archaeological Evaluation Report.*

Liddle, P., 2003. Launde Abbey. *Archaeological Journal*, 268–70.

Liddle, P. with O'Brien, L., 1995. The Archaeology of the Abbeys and Priories of Leicestershire. *Transactions of the Leicestershire Archaeological and Historical Society 69*, 1–21.

Marcombe, D., 2003. *Leper Knights.* Woodbridge: The Boydell Press.

McKinley, R., 1954. Religious Houses. In W. Hoskins, *(Victoria) County History of the County of Leicester vol 2*, 1–53.

Mellor, J. A., 1981. *The Austin Friars, Leicester.* Council for British Archaeology Research Report 35.

Nichols, J., 1795. *The History and Antiquities of the County of Leicester, vol 2, part 1: Framland Hundred.* London: John Nichols.

Nichols, J., 1798. *The History and Antiquities of the County of Leicester, vol 2, part 2: Gartree Hundred.* London: John Nichols.

Squires, A., 2006. The landscape of Leicester Abbey's home demesne lands to the Dissolution. Story, J. *Leicester Abbey*, 75–94. Leicester: *Leicestershire Archaeological and Historical Society.*

Thompson, S., 1991. *Women Religious:The Founding of English Nunneries after the Conquest.* Oxford: Clarendon Press.

Wallis, A., 2012. The Medieval Priory of Hinckley. *Transactions of the Leicestershire Archaeological and Historical Society 86* , 139–147.

Williams, B., 1965. Garendon Abbey. *Bulletin of the Loughborough Archaeological Society 8*, 3–14.

Williams, B., 1969. Summary of the Excavations at Garendon Abbey 1966–7–8. *Bulletin of the Loughborough Archaeological Society*, 9–11,17,26.

The archaeology of the medieval church in Leicestershire

Dr Matthew Godfrey
(Standing Buildings Adviser to the Diocese of Leicester)
Dr Mike Hawkes
(Archaeological Adviser to the Diocese of Leicester)

Introduction

One of the most enduring features of our landscape is the parish church with its tower or spire silhouetted against the skyline which, until very recent times, was the tallest structure to be seen in the countryside (Cantor 2000, 19).

Churches and their associated churchyards are an important and unique source of information in which architecture, craftsmanship, social change, worship and settlement studies are inseparable. Until the later 20th century, churches tended to be viewed more as works of art and architecture to be studied in isolation, detached from their surroundings, but they are places in their own right and should be seen as key elements of the pattern of settlement (Morris 1989, 2). This serves to open up a whole new aspect of church study.

Our medieval parish churches are treasured buildings comprising the vast majority of listed buildings in this county; they are also working buildings that serve the community and it is unrealistic for them to be viewed as something to be left undisturbed, incapable of being changed, and consequently unable to meet the needs of their current custodians. The majority of these great buildings are also often supported and maintained on limited resources and change is not carried out lightly.

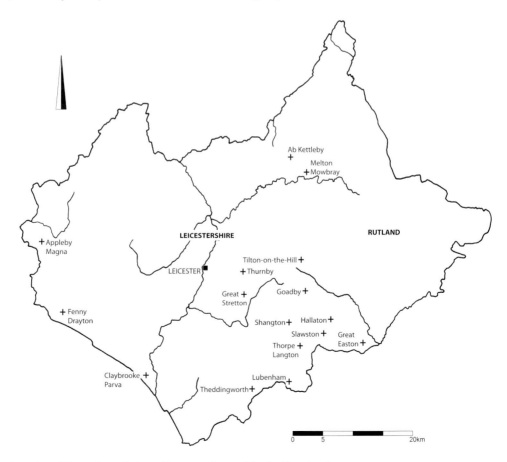

Figure 1: Leicestershire church locations referred to in the text

Archaeology is about the discovery of our past and typically is regarded as involving excavation, digging down into the ground. In order to properly understand the development of a church it is necessary not only to carry out a full-scale survey of the building above ground, but also undertake comprehensive excavation below ground both inside and outside the building. Opportunities for this level of investigation have been and still are strictly limited, being both expensive to carry out and particularly disruptive to the use of the building. In fact, perhaps surprisingly, no churches in Leicestershire have been subjected to such detailed study. Where excavation has been possible further afield, as for example in Yorkshire at Wharram Percy and in Essex at Hadstock and at Rivenhall, the evidence shows that there might be numerous phases of re-building prior to the establishment of the stone churches that now occupy these locations, as well as other buildings dating from the Roman period to as late as the 17th century (Muir 1992, 127).

Avoiding costly and disruptive works, how then can we seek to learn more about our churches and their individual development? One way is by carrying out a closer study of the structure of the church, looking at its fabric and architectural detail – buildings archaeology. Secondly we can adopt more of a 'landscape approach' to the archaeology of the church: placing the church in its setting by looking at the surrounding landscape and the nature of its archaeology. This paper will explore these two routes and draw on a variety of examples from across Leicestershire (fig 1).

Church fabric

Fortunately for church archaeology the days of demolition and comprehensive restoration so common in the Victorian period and so apparent in a high number of the county's church buildings is over. Nowadays church buildings are treated far more sensitively with the above and below ground archaeology firmly rooted in a secure archaeological framework comparable to that used on important listed and historical secular buildings (Morris 2002, 19). This change, however, is only a relatively recent one and the discipline of church archaeology is still in its infancy.

Prior to the emergence of church archaeology as a sub-discipline, many of the county's churches suffered at the hands of over zealous restorers. These works were largely confined to the 19th century, although there are examples of failure to recognise the importance of medieval fabric earlier and later than this. At St Luke, Thurnby, for instance, the medieval chancel was pulled down in its entirety under a faculty granted in 1779, although it was subsequently replaced by a Victorian one in 1870–3 (Brandwood 2002, 2 and 127). The extent of Victorian restorations varied in degree, but such schemes are typified by brick floors being replaced with colour tiles, stained glass appearing in windows, box pews being removed and ceilings often removed to leave exposed timberwork (Brandwood 1990, 73). Many of these changes were based on the notion that the architects of the 19th-century Gothic revival had a better idea of what constituted 'medieval' than the original builders. To us such work would be shocking today, but in the eyes of a Victorian this was often seen as an enhancement, given the fact that the Victorians did not place such a high value on ancient buildings as we do today (Miele 1998, 103).

Examples of this are numerous throughout the county but one example that many will be familiar with is St Mary de Castro in Leicester. Here the list of changes throughout the 1840s is extensive: nave east gable rebuilt; north side clerestory windows replaced, west end of nave rebuilt, pews and galleries taken out, and the plaster removed from the walls, giving us the naked masonry visible today (Brandwood 2002, 103–4). This clearance resulted in what was almost certainly not the general internal appearance of a medieval church but in Victorian eyes it did fit the notion of how a medieval church should look (Brandwood 1990, 74). A medieval church interior would have been plastered and covered with a variety of colourful wall paintings such as the fragments that still remain in All Saints, Lubenham.

Ironically, it is this destructive period in the 19th to early 20th century that led to the first stages of the discipline of church archaeology that we have at present. Until this period there was no recognised system of how to describe or classify church architectural style until Thomas Rickman published his 'attempt to discriminate the styles of English architecture from the conquest to the reformation' in 1817, and it is really Rickman who gives us the formalised Norman, Early English, Decorated and Perpendicular style terminology that we still use today (Meile 1998, 117; Coldstream 2002, 40; see also Morris 1989, 299–301).

St Nicholas church, Leicester, is a structure which includes many of these different styles of architecture: a Norman central tower, an Early English chancel, and a Decorated chapel on its southern side. The church overall is a very important one in the region, being a very early foundation thought to date back to at least the 10th century and perhaps even earlier (Taylor and Taylor 1980, 384–5). There are also suggestions that it was a cathedral see as early as c.680, although a see based on Leicester can only be proven to exist from 737 when Bishop Torthelm was recorded here (Pevsner, 2003, 215). Additionally, St Nicholas demonstrates just how drastically 19th century alterations can destroy early fabric: for instance, the piers of the south arcade were replaced with a large brick arch c. 1825 (Semeonoff n.d, 6); a new north aisle was constructed in 1875–6 replacing the former medieval one thought to have been demolished in the 17th century, a new north transept was built in 1888–9, and the tower was drastically restored after unsuccessful local protests against such work in 1904–5 (Brandwood, 2002, 104). Fortunately the wishes of the Rev Richard Davies and others in the late 1820s were not carried out: they had advocated complete rebuilding.

What the above examples highlight is that potentially a high proportion of medieval church fabric may have been lost, obscured or changed beyond recognition. However, with a little practice 19th century alterations are generally quite easy to identify and new work and alterations usually look crisper than the surviving medieval fabric, and in the case of St Nicholas there is the extensive use of 19th-century brickwork. Moreover, these later alterations are usually accompanied by far more documentary evidence than medieval alterations. Other useful sources may exist to guide us. The Transactions of the Leicester Archaeological and Historical Society which date back to 1855 give a number of accounts of churches in the county. For example, Poole's detailed description of the development of St Mary de Castro church (1855, 3–11) and Herbert's architectural survey of All Saints church, Theddingworth (1941, 116–124). There are also more recent publications such

as Brandwood 2002 and Parsons 1978, 1980 and 1984 which summarise the unpublished material for almost every church in the county. In contrast the work of the eminent Leicestershire historian John Nichols (1795–1811) gives views of almost every Leicestershire church prior to later Victorian restorations.

The further back one tries to trace changes within a medieval church, the less documentary evidence there is. Some churches may be mentioned in Bishops' registers from the 13th century and the occasional important early church may even be recorded in Domesday Book – for example St Mary at Melton Mowbray is recorded by implication with two priests recorded in the vill which is suggestive of its status before the Norman Conquest (Parsons 1989, 55). However, these early records almost never describe the church fabric and it is not really until the 16th century when churchwardens' accounts start to become more common that we can see what changes were being made to a specific building at a specific time. These accounts are by no means available for every church and some records may not survive until much later. It is in these instances where analysis of the development of the building fabric and of medieval architectural styles may be the only way by which the evolution of the church in the medieval period can be traced. Indeed, it is by close observation of the fabric that we can see how a church may have expanded or even been reduced in size during the Middle Ages.

Architectural styles

Four main architectural styles are identified for medieval England with labels first used by Rickman in 1817. There is much debate on the actual validity of these styles and their labels, but the general date ranges that are now accepted are (Coldstream 2002, 40):

Norman c. 1066–1170

Early English c. 1170–1250

Decorated c. 1250–1350

Perpendicular c. 1350–1550

It is important to realise that these dates are a broad guide and in some churches an earlier style of architecture may have persisted longer due to local fashion or the individual choice of the patron. Similarly the architecture just before and after the Norman Conquest in 1066 is particularly problematic as there

Figure 2: St Michael, Hallaton, The north aisle arcade looking east.

is a considerable overlap with Anglo-Saxon styles of architecture due to the fact that masons continued with the styles that they were familiar with and quite often used some Norman architectural elements in their work.

Identifying different architectural styles is often quite straightforward. For instance, St Michael's, Hallaton (fig 2), illustrates the change from the semi-circular arch typical of the Norman period to the sharply pointed arch of the subsequent 13th-century Early English period. On the north aisle arcade, the three western bays are of late Norman date with circular piers with square abacuses decorated with waterleaf or scallop mouldings (Pevsner 2003, 172). These merge into the Early English pointed arch arcade showing development in an easterly direction. A similar development is seen in a westerly direction (not visible on fig 2) with a comparable 13th century pointed arch extending towards the Early English tower and spire. This tower would have been an important landmark and shows that by the 13th century spires were becoming more common.

Figure 3: St Nicholas, Leicester, showing the western most Anglo-Saxon window opening above the later Norman north aisle arcade.

Being able to determine the style or styles of architecture used is only part of the standing building archaeology, and working out the different contexts of the architecture is often far more challenging. In below-ground archaeology new layers normally overlay older layers therefore the deeper you dig the older the context becomes. In building archaeology this is not always the case and it is quite common to encounter a newer feature such as a window or aisle arcade beneath a much older feature. Again we can return to St Nicholas, Leicester, where the original Anglo-Saxon aisleless church had aisles added in the late 11th century (Taylor and Taylor 1980, 385). The two surviving arches of the north aisle undercut two late Anglo-Saxon double splayed windows with semi-circular heads constructed of reused Roman tiles (see fig 3). This not only illustrates later contexts beneath earlier ones, but also shows the popular medieval technique of inserting new openings into an existing wall rather than taking the wall down and rebuilding it.

However, not all evidence is quite as easy to interpret and the testimony from the church at Thorpe Langton is a good example (fig 4). This is a 'classic' Leicestershire church largely dating from 1300, although the tower is a little earlier. The fabric evidence here shows a number of features. Taking the tower as the earliest feature it is possible, by looking specifically at the lower plinth and disjointed stringcourses on the west wall of the north aisle, to argue that the latter was a later addition. Also it is possible to make out the remnants of an earlier buttress adjoining the tower. This development shows that, potentially, the first church at Thorpe Langton was an aisleless structure, which developed with the addition of aisles – this expansion of the church plan being indicative of further accommodation required for an increasing population and also for additional altars.

At All Saints, Slawston a further type of expansion can be seen but this time upwards. Figure 5 illustrates a number of tell-tale features. Firstly there is a change in wall thickness above the window at the bottom of the picture. This indicates that an upper clerestory level has been added to the nave of the church. Secondly, confirmation of this can be found by looking at the remains of the earlier, sharply pitched roof slope below the east window of the tower when compared

Figure 4: St Leonard, Thorpe Langton, the dotted line indicating the possible outline of a former buttress; note also the abrupt change in plinth profile and the discontinued stringcourse on the lower section of the wall.

Figure 5: All Saints, Slawston, Note the change in wall thickness and the remains of the earlier sharply pitched roof which was removed when the clerestory was added.

109

Figure 6: All Saints, Lubbenham, showing the blocked western arch of the south aisle and later 15th century clerestory above.

to the shallower one of the later clerestory. Stylistically this later clerestory is quite an early one being of 14th-century date, although of course it is later than the tower it abuts. Clerestories are a common addition in the late 14th and 15th century when builders were aspiring to create buildings that were almost transparent and filled with light and such additions have often been viewed as corresponding with long standing prosperity of lay communities (Hayman, 2007: 63).

An alternative aspect of fabric evidence is where the church shows a change of plan not from addition as with the above examples, but from deletion and a reduction from its earlier extent. A very clear example of this is All Saints, Lubenham, (fig 6), one of the few churches in Leicestershire to have had some detailed excavation work prior to installation of replacement sections of timber floor (see Wells et al. 1990).

This church also escaped any major Victorian restoration work and is therefore a good example of a largely unrestored parish church that exhibits a number of different architectural

phases. In addition, it is blessed with some surviving medieval wall paintings (see below). This church went through a series of changes throughout the medieval period, including the addition of north and south aisles, enlargement of the chancel and additions of north and south chancel chapels, but some of these features were later removed during the 16th century (Wells et al 1990, 1). The most obvious of these can be seen in figure 6. In a classic example of building archaeology it is clear that the west end of the south aisle has been removed, as the internal 13th century arch has become part of the external wall fabric, and accordingly been blocked up; later, a window was inserted. The straight vertical joint reveals where the clerestory above this arch simply butts up against the earlier tower, thus showing this as a later 15th century addition. A church with such a complex fabric history such as this one is a good indicator of the social and economic fluctuations that have occurred in this settlement across time. Noticeably, the deletions here are useful in showing that these are much later than the Black Death, indicating no immediate demographic impact from this on the church or village.

Development of the church landscape

The medieval church was both a physical and a spiritual landmark for the parish. However it also served to reflect the prosperity and generosity of the well-to-do of that parish while being an overt symbol of the status which the local lord had achieved. The majority of our parish churches date from a period when most other building was undertaken in timber, mud and thatch – materials which do not endure – and therefore the stone-built parish church is almost always the oldest surviving building in our towns and villages. They can be regarded as indicators of established village settlement and they can reflect the fluctuating fortunes of the population – ie their congregation; as has been shown above, churches can not only grow but they can also shrink, and in extreme cases they can even vanish.

Often the attempt is made to link the establishment of villages to the creation of churches. Arguably the start of medieval village formation in England occurs during the 7th century and coincided with the re-conversion to Christianity (Muir 1992, 42), however in the early medieval period, the Church served a slightly different function for the population when compared with the accepted view of the later medieval 'parish church'.

Prior to the Conquest of 1066 churches served one of three key functions:

- Cathedrals
- Monastic and collegiate churches for monks and travelling priests
- Churches built by secular lords serving local populations

Consequently, at this time, such buildings were far less numerous and it is estimated that fewer than one in five settlements were served by a church, the majority of which would have been constructed of wood. The 11th century saw a gradual move to replace these timber churches with ones of more permanent construction and this process gathered pace, being stimulated by Norman entrepreneurship and patronage, and further enriched architecturally under this Norman influence (Blair 2005, 416).

The period that marked the development of 'parish' churches as we know them now started in the 12th century with two courses of action: the building of new churches and the enlargement of those that were already in existence. Many of these new churches were paid for by manorial lords or groups of land-holders who, in turn, claimed a large percentage of the tithes and other parish revenues, whilst also exercising the right to select the parish priest (Friar 1996, 287).

The church in the landscape

Geographically the church as a physical structure was very much at the heart of the village, which itself lay at the heart of the parish. Parish boundaries not only defined the parish, but also the extent of the associated farmland – arable, meadow, pasture and woodland (Jones 2001, 15).

The parish pattern itself has remained largely unchanged since the 13th century, although its origins can be traced back to the late Saxon period and the time of the Norman Conquest (Winchester 2000, 12). The early minster churches of the 7th or 8th centuries were royal or Episcopal foundations that were served by clergy who went out and ministered to the population of a large area, an estate or other identifiable territory. By the 9th and 10th centuries 'field churches' had become established within these territories where the worship was conducted. Initially these churches may have had a vague, ill defined territorial area however the formalisation of 'tithe' payments as the main source of income for the clergy could have contributed to the creation of parish boundaries. The relationship between estate and parish boundaries is further enhanced because such churches often owed their origins to landowners who wished to have a church to serve their estate, thus the territory of the parish would have equated to that of the founder's estate.

While the church was the central focus of the parish and was the building of the people, it was also often built close to the manor house, the centre of local power. Most of these medieval manor houses are no longer in existence, although often their sites are still discernable, for example at Appleby Magna, St Michael's Church and the moated manor site still sit in close proximity to each other (see fig 7(a), below). Elsewhere, manorial sites have become transformed and are now sometimes represented merely by a farm.

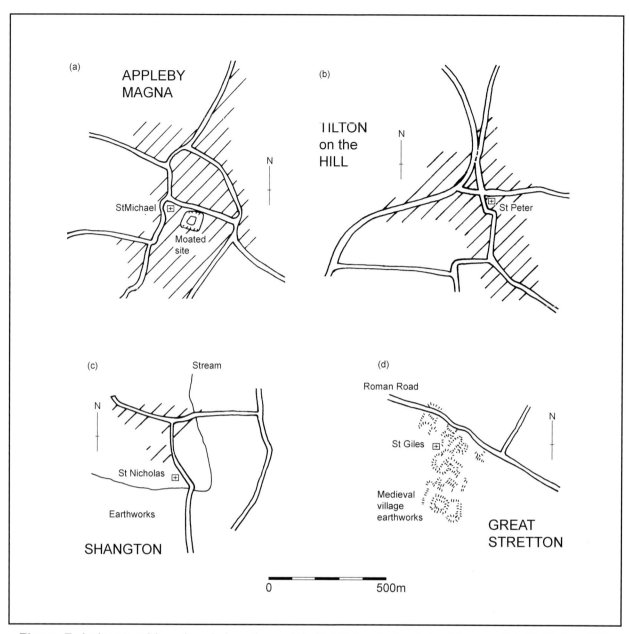

Figure 7: Leicestershire church locations: (a) St Michael, Appleby Magna, (b) St Peter, Tilton on the Hill, (c) St Nicholas, Shangton, (d) St Giles, Great Stretton (based on Ordnance Survey extracts)

Topographically, in many cases the church might still be centrally located and the village has continued to grow around it in a reasonably regular pattern as is the case with the church of St Peter at Tilton on the Hill (fig 7b). Elsewhere, a change or shift in settlement or population, or even loss of population means that the church is now more on the periphery of the settlement as at Shangton, where the church of St Nicholas now lies to the south of the present village overlooking the stream and deserted earthworks – traces of earlier settlement (fig 7c) or, like St Giles, Great Stretton, stands in total isolation amidst the earthworks of the deserted medieval village – as Pevsner puts it: 'A church without a village' (2003, 169) (fig 7d).

Archaeological excavation has revealed interesting origins to some of our churches, for example at Ab Kettleby (Allsop 1998), Fenny Drayton (Bradley-Lovekin 2006) and Great Easton (Priest & Cooper 2004). The discovery of fragments of Roman material – pot, tesserae, etc. – may be indicative of an earlier settlement presence on some church sites, although this should not necessarily suggest religious continuity. There may have been an element of opportunism in re-using Roman material in the building of churches whilst also making use of a site that, having possibly been that of a villa, might itself have been a symbolic centre of local power. This is not just a rural feature, since, as noted above, Roman material can clearly be seen incorporated into the walls of

St Nicholas Church, Leicester – exploiting, no doubt, materials from the adjoining site of the forum at the heart of the former Roman town.

The church in society

Not only was the Church physically at the heart of the community, but it also had a spiritual role to play. This was not only for 'high days and holy days' – it was central to daily life: the Church, in the form of the parish, provided the framework for everyday life. The Church recorded births and deaths, and conducted weddings and baptisms, while saint's feast days and religious festivals marked the passing of the seasons and of the years (Jones 2001, 15).

The nave, which was the responsibility of the parish (Muir 1992, 134), served as a place of worship, and was the equivalent of the modern village hall as home to a number of more earthly activities and entertainments such as 'church ales' and 'miracle plays'. In contrast to the lime-washed interiors and regimented pews that are often found in churches nowadays, the interior of the pre-Reformation church was often a light, open space brightly decorated with coloured window glass and wall paintings reflecting the theology and teaching of the medieval church (Friar 1998, 485). An example of a re-erected and refurbished medieval church with all of its warmth and colour can be seen at the National Museum of Wales, St Fagans, in the form of St Teilo's Church from Llandeilo Tal-y-bont (Nash 2009). A change in the internal appearance of churches came about quite violently at the time of the Reformation when the new emphasis on the preaching of (lengthy) sermons saw the introduction of pews (Taylor 2004, 41), while such bright decoration was deemed to be inappropriate.

The Reformation and the Commonwealth period of the 16th and 17th centuries also saw the suppression of 'frivolous and drunken entertainments' and orders were given that 'they shall take away all other monuments of feigned miracles, pilgrimages, idolatry and superstition; so that there remain no memory of the same in walls, glass-windows or elsewhere in their churches or houses' (Harries & Hicks 2001, 11). As a result of this, much decoration, including many wall paintings, was lost, although some, somewhat fortuitously, became sealed beneath layers of whitewash. A number of these paintings have been re-discovered in the course of refurbishment (Friar 1998, 487), some in very fragmentary form as at Lubenham, but others more complete, e.g Lutterworth and Great Bowden. Doubtless many, many others have been lost (see fig 8).

Churches and the population: dead and alive

As archaeological and structural records of society, churches are important resources, revealing much not just of the locality but also of the population that inhabited it.

Investigation has revealed that, in terms of evidence, often the longest lasting, earliest and most common example of the 'ecclesiastical'

Figure 8: All Saints, Lubenham, examples of surviving wall painting,

113

role is that of burial or cemetery use (Morris 1989, 152 Table 1). Burials can often pre-date the visible structural evidence for the first church. At Raunds, Northamptonshire, where extensive excavation was carried out in the 1970s, burials encompass the 10th century church which itself lies within the footprint of the 11th century building that we see today (Boddington 1980, cited in Morris 1989, 150). The discovery of human remains can also represent the last evidence for the presence of a long-since lost church: this was the case in the medieval heart of Leicester with St Peter's church. The location of this church was identified in 2006 in the course of building and archaeological works in advance of the Highcross shopping centre development with the discovery of the remains of some 1,300 skeletons from the churchyard (Buckley this volume and forthcoming).

While our churches may not have experienced the same degree of destruction that is often associated with building change, they have not been in any way immune from change. This change may have been planned building work, with, for example, the addition of aisles, transepts, clerestories, spires, etc., as part of the gradual growth of the church, but it can also be of a different form – the defacing of the fabric of the building in the mid-17th century at the time of the English Civil War (fig 9), or graffiti (often names or initials and sometimes conveniently with dates) engraved into internal or external stonework or into door surrounds by bored or waiting parishioners (fig 10).

One other form of medieval inscription that can be found on some churches is the 'scratch dial' or 'mass dial'. The 'scratch dial' served as a means of ensuring that the church bell was rung at the correct time to mark the canonical hours and as a call to worship and was typically inscribed on a south-facing wall or buttress (fig 11). Examples of these dials can still be found on many churches across the county, although in the course of later rebuilding and with the re-use of stone they do sometimes become relocated from their original location.

When life was lived by the rising and setting of the sun, and prior to the widespread introduction of the clock, the running of the day

Figure 9: St Peter's, Claybrooke Parva, empty alcoves where statues once stood

Figure 10: St Peter's, Claybrooke Parva, graffiti.

Figure 11: St John the Baptist, Goadby, example of a scratch dial

was dependent upon the dial, and this further reflects the key role that the church played at all levels of everyday life.

These are just small selections of the less obvious areas of interest that can be seen on our medieval churches, all of which contribute not only to the social history of the building but also form part of the record of life and the living in the parish.

Conclusion

This brief introduction to the various aspects of the church archaeology of Leicestershire merely illustrates the potential that the county's churches offer for further study. The church in Leicestershire should not be seen just as a series of examples of the artistic styles of medieval and later architecture, although this aspect is of course important. Rather it should also be viewed as a vital component of the development of the landscape and of settlement as we see there today. The building not only reflects the materials and geology from the landscape around it but also the aspirations, social conditions, prosperity and the importance of Christianity to the community for which it was built – a diminished role nowadays, perhaps, but this should not mean we neglect to explore thoroughly such a vital part of our medieval heritage.

Bibliography

Allsop, J., 1998. Ab Kettleby Church. *Transactions of the Leicestershire Archaeological and Historical Society* 72: 162.

Boddington, A., 1980. A Christian Anglo-Saxon graveyard at Raunds in P. Rahtz, T. Dickinson and L. Watts (eds) *Anglo-Saxon Cemeteries*. BAR 82, 373–8.

Bradley-Lovekin, T., 2006. *Archaeological Evaluation at St Michael and All Angels Church, Fenny Drayton, Leicestershire*. Sleaford: Archaeological Project Services.

Brandwood, G. K., 1987. *Ancient & Modern – Churches and Chapels around Market Harborough. Leicester:* Leicestershire Museums Art Galleries and Records Service.

Brandwood, N., 1990. To scrape or not to scrape? Plaster, stucco and Victorian church restorers in Leicestershire, in *Transactions of the Leicestershire Archaeological and Historical Society*. 64: 73–77.

Brandwood, G. K., 2002. *Bringing them to their knees: church-building and restoration in Leicestershire and Rutland 1800–1914*. Leicester: Leicestershire Archaeological and Historical Society.

Cantor, L., 2000. *The Historic Parish Churches of Leicestershire and Rutland. Leicester:* Kairos Press Ltd.

Coldstream, N., 2002. *Medieval Architecture*. Oxford: Oxford University Press.

Friar, S., 1998. *A Companion to the English Parish Church*. Stroud: Sutton Publishing.

Harries, J. and Hicks, C., 2001 (Revised & expanded). *Discovering Stained Glass*. Princes Risborough: Shire Publications Ltd.

Hayman, R., 2007. *A Concise Guide to the Parish Church*. Stroud: Tempus.

Herbert, A., 1941–2. Theddingworth and its church. *Transactions of the Leicestershire Archaeological and Historical Society*, 22, pt 1, 118–124.

Jones, A., 2001. *A Thousand Years of the English Parish*. London: Cassell & Co.

Miele, C., 1998. Real Antiquity and the Ancient Object: The Science of Gothic Architecture and the Restoration of Medieval Buildings in *The Study of the Past in the Victorian Age*, Brand, V (ed.) Oxbow Monograph No 73.

Morris, R. K., 1989. *Churches in the Landscape*. London: J. M. Dent.

Morriss, R., 2002. *The Archaeology of Buildings*. Tempus: Gloucestershire.

Muir, R., 1992. *The Villages of England*. London: Thames & Hudson.

Muir, R., 2007. *How to Read a Village.* London: Ebury Press

Nash, G. D., (ed.). 2009. *Saving St Teilo's – Bringing a medieval church to life.* Cardiff: National Museum of Wales.

Nichols, J., 1795–1811. *The History and Antiquities of Leicestershire.* in 5 vols, John Nichols, London. Republished by Leicestershire Library Service in 1971 in association with SR Publishers Ltd. Out of print.

Parsons, D., 1978. *A Bibliography of Leicestershire Churches: Part One: Periodical Sources.* Leicester: University of Leicester Adult Education Department.

Parsons, D., 1980. *A Bibliography of Leicestershire Churches: Part Two: Newspaper Sources.* Leicester: University of Leicester Adult Education Department.

Parsons, D., 1984. *A Bibliography of Leicestershire Churches: Part Three: Parochial Records.* Leicester: University of Leicester Adult Education Department.

Parsons, D., 1989. *Churches and Chapels: Investigating Places of Worship. Practical Handbook in Archaeology No. 8.* London: Council for British Archaeology.

Pevsner, N., 2003 revised by Elizabeth Williamson with G K Brandwood, *The Buildings of England: Leicestershire and Rutland.* 2nd edition London: Yale University Press.

Poole, G., On the churches of Leicester. *Transactions of the Leicestershire Archaeological and Historical Society,* 1, 1855–56, 1–11.

Priest, V. and Cooper, N., 2004. *Time Team Big Dig: Archaeological Investigations at Great Easton, Leicestershire.* Leicester: University of Leicester Archaeological Services Report No. 2004–144.

Rahtz, P., Dickinson, T. & Watts, L., (eds) 1979. *Anglo-Saxon Cemeteries.* BAR 82.

Rickman, T., 1817. *An Attempt to Discriminate the Styles of English Architecture from the Conquest to the Reformation.* Reprinted to the present day.

Rodwell, W., 2005. *The Archaeology of Churches.* Stroud: Tempus.

Semeonoff, R., n.d. *St Nicholas Church Leicester,* Guidebook.

Taylor, H. M. and Taylor, J., 1980 (second ed.) *Anglo-Saxon Architecture (Vols I and II).* Cambridge: Cambridge University Press.

Taylor, H. M., 1984 (second ed.) *Anglo-Saxon Architecture (Vol III).* Cambridge: Cambridge University Press.

Taylor, R. 2004. *How to Read a Church.* London: Rider.

Wells, J., Warren, S. and Buckley, R. 1990. All Saints' Church Lubbenham: An Archaeological Evaluation, in *Transactions of the Leicestershire Archaeological and Historical Society.* 64: 1–20.

Winchester, A., 2000. *Discovering Parish Boundaries.* Princes Risborough: Shire Publications.

Further Reading

Blair, J., 2005. *The Church in Anglo-Saxon Society.* Oxford: Oxford University Press.

Harbison, R., 2006. *The Daily Telegraph Guide to England's Parish Churches.* London: Aurum Press.

McNeil, T., 2006. *Faith, Pride and Works: Medieval Church Building.* Stroud: Tempus.

Scott, R. A., 2005. *The Gothic Enterprise.* London: University of California Press.

Strong, R., 2007. *A Little History of the English Parish Church.* London: Jonathan Cape.

Project Gargoyle – past, present and future

Bob Trubshaw

Introduction

Project Gargoyle was set up in 2009 by Leicestershire County Council and representatives of the Leicestershire Archaeological and Historical Society and Leicestershire Fieldworkers. The aim is to photograph all the medieval carvings inside and outside the churches of Leicestershire and Rutland. This means 'Project Gargoyle' is actually a misnomer, as the scope includes the faces and creatures depicted on corbels, capitals, arch springs (figs 1, 2,10), hoodstops (fig 6) and so forth as well as gargoyles (figs 3, 7, 8).

Figure 1: arch springer, fantastical farm animal, Beeby Church. Photo: Mike Walters

So far as anyone is aware this is the first attempt to photograph and catalogue all the medieval carvings in a county. Nation-wide projects that have previously looked at Romanesque and Anglo-Saxon carvings have, of course, already documented Leicestershire and Rutland. However there are vastly more carvings from the thirteenth to fifteenth centuries. About three hundred churches in Leicestershire and Rutland have figurative carvings – some with only a few and some with

very many. At this stage we do not know how many there are in total but a best guess is at least ten thousand.

After an initial pilot phase Project Gargoyle recruited an ever-increasing number of volunteer photographers to photograph and record carvings. This started in 2010. The total number of churches recorded is now over one hundred, which means that we are at least one-third of the way to having completed the photography phase. In practice we have probably recorded nearer to half of the carvings as, understandably, many of the photographers have chosen to visit some of the more splendid examples. The photographers are asked to record to a high standard and must have digital Single Lens Reflex (SLR) cameras with at least a 300mm lens available in order to photograph carvings high in the roof or tower for example. It will be impossible to do this project again so the pictures taken must be of as high a quality as possible though conditions in the church do not always allow the best view.

Figure 2: arch springer, face, Frisby on the Wreake Church. Photo: David Morley

Figure 3: gargoyle, north side, Orton on the Hill church. Hybrid animal. Photo: Kathy Elkin.

The sheer variety and vitality of the stone carving ranges from the recognisable to the fantastical, both animal and human, from decorative representations of plants, to scenes of everyday life, and biblical stories. Collectively they provide an excellent insight into the minds of medieval people, as many are pulling faces, tongue-poking, or depict such fantastic entities as 'green men' or dragons. Many of the carvings are human heads. Some are simple and stylised but others are more realistic. Many may be portraits of the benefactors of the church, some may err on the side of the caricature, and bring humour to the interior, of the church. True gargoyles themselves are found on the exterior of the church where they carry the rainwater from the roof away from the walls. Many, because of their outdoor location, are quite degraded (figs 3, 7). It is important to record them before further damage makes them difficult to understand or before they are removed or replaced.

Apart from these the project has revealed just how many fifteenth century wooden roof bosses have survived throughout Leicestershire. Since most of these are lost in the gloom of the roof where the light rarely is good enough to see them well it has been a revelation to see them in detail (figs 4, 5, 9). They probably were originally highly coloured, and so would have stood out much better than they do now. Sileby is one church where the roof bosses have been repainted and now make an impact (fig 5). These bosses were carved by men whose sons or grandsons may

Figure 4: 15th Century roof boss, Church Langton with possible thigh bones either side of the face. Photo: Mike Walter

Figure 5: 15th century roof boss from Sileby church, painted 50 years ago in red and gold. Photo: Steve Harris

Figure 6: mid-19th century hoodmould stop, Nailstone church. Note inward turning angle of the carving typical of church restoration at this time. Photo: Kathy Elkin.

Figure 7: gargoyle, man emptying pot, Beeby church. Photo: Mike Walters.

well have fought – or even died – at the Battle of Bosworth. And, as some of the carvings seemingly are portraits of artisans as well as patrons, we may be as near face-to-face with these people as is possible to get. Leicester and south-west Leicestershire are becoming indelibly associated with a few days in 1485; however the whole of the county shares in the heritage of that decisive century.

The project is also bringing together an increasingly interesting collection of carvings from the Gothic Revival (figs 6, 8). This is because the volunteer photographers are neither art historians nor architectural historians so – understandably – do not have the skills to decide whether a carving is wholly medieval, or a nineteenth century restoration, or a replacement. Their brief is effectively 'If it's got eyes then shoot it.' While churches known to have been built, or completely rebuilt, in the nineteenth century have been excluded from the scope of the project, in practice almost all 'medieval' churches were extensively restored in the nineteenth century. Although Victorian stonemasons lacked much of the imagination of their medieval predecessors, they were nevertheless skilled at their craft and each of them had their own style and medieval pieces were often copied. Inclusion of these carvings provides a complete corpus and allows us to investigate their work and the possible re-imagination of carvings removed during restoration or taken from 19th pattern books.

So far almost all the churches recorded have been in Leicestershire, so the proportions of churches and carvings recorded are even more impressive if Rutland is, momentarily, ignored. In practice the Rutland and east Leicestershire churches have been recorded by Lionel Wall as part of an entirely independent research project. However as we were only aware of Lionel's research during 2013 the possibilities for 'integrating' his work with Project Gargoyle have yet to be fully explored.

The photographs and associated information will form part of the Leicestershire and Rutland Historic Environment Record (HER). Although most of the effort is still focused on photographing and recording the carvings, Project Gargoyle will not stop when every church has been photographed. The intention is to create a sophisticated database, entirely separate from the HER, which can be 'interrogated' to address a wide range of research questions. The information about carvings can also be developed and enhanced by people with different areas of expertise. Researchers from different disciplines—such as art history, costume history, archaeology, architecture, church liturgy, folklore and stone carving—bring their insights to the interpretation of these sculptures.

Establishing how diverse the scope of such research and expertise might extend needs to be identified before the database is designed. The preliminary steps towards this have been set out in a discussion document called *What Can a Gargoyle Tell Us?* accessible online at www.hoap.co.uk/whatcan.pdf

Although no timescales have been set for the completion of the recording or for the development of the database, in the next few years the medieval carvings of Leicestershire and Rutland will be receiving attention in a way that none of their 'peer group' have yet to attain. More information about Project Gargoyle is online at www.leics.gov.uk/gargoyle.

Further Reading

Trubshaw, B., 2004. *Good Gargoyle Guide: Medieval Carvings of Leicestershire and Rutland.* Heart of Albion Press.

Trubshaw, B., 2007. 'Mawming and mooning – the minds of medieval masons', *Leicestershire Historian,* 43, 32–5.

Woodcock, A., 2005. *Liminal Images: Aspects of Medieval Architectural Sculpture in the South of England from the Eleventh to the Sixteenth Centuries.* Oxford: British Archaeological Reports, 386, John and Erica Hedges.

Woodcock, A., 2012, *Gargoyles and Grotesques.* Botley, Oxford, Shire Publications.

Figure 8: 19th century gargoyle, head of dragon, Little Dalby church. Photo: Bob Trubshaw.

Figure 9: roof boss, lion (?) Beeby church. Photo: Mike Walters.

Figure 10: corner arch springer, face. Rothley Court chapel. Photo: Kathy Elkin.

The medieval fortified sites of Leicestershire and Rutland

Richard Knox

Introduction

While the castles of Leicestershire and Rutland have received much study and discussion in the past, this paper aims to bring together all the evidence for these buildings and their remains into one document. In this discussion the term 'fortified site' covers all forms of castle and heavily fortified manor houses – but not those merely surrounded by fishponds or ornamental moats.

Within Leicestershire and Rutland there are nineteen sites which are widely agreed to be castle sites, one non-located (Ravenstone), plus six probable castles (all shown in fig 1) and a further six possible sites (not shown, listed in gazetteer). These latter warrant further fieldwork and documentary investigation.

The most numerous type of castle in Leicestershire and Rutland is the motte and bailey castle. This was the standard Norman fortification as depicted on the Bayeux Tapestry, and was being built in England for at least a hundred years after the Norman Conquest. These early castles comprise a large mound, the motte, built from earth dug from a circular ditch surrounding it, with an adjoining bank and ditched enclosure, known as a bailey. Initially the motte was crowned with a wooden palisade and a wooden tower, or keep. The bailey bank would also usually be palisaded. The bailey might enclose a timber or stone hall with kitchens and a chapel, as well as ancillary buildings such as stables.

The remains of many castles of this style survive in the midlands as they were abandoned or destroyed in the turbulent mid-12th and early 13th centuries before they could be developed further.

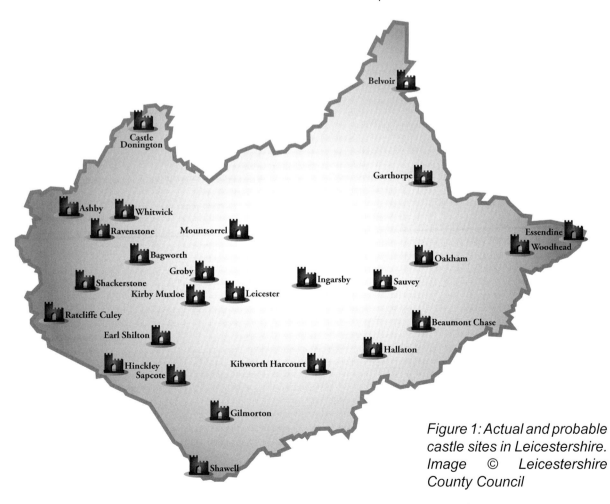

Figure 1: Actual and probable castle sites in Leicestershire. Image © Leicestershire County Council

Another early form of castle is the enclosure castle, which lacked the raised motte, but had stout bank and ditch defensive enclosures. The ditches could be water-filled by damming up adjacent streams.

Although some sites seem to have had stone walls in the later 12th century, it was during the 13th and 14th centuries, as the use of cannon developed, that all the wooden defensive buildings and walls on the surviving castles were replaced with stone. Brick was being used at the very end of the 15th century, but generally not on sites designed to withstand heavy sieges.

Castles of any type were expensive to build, both in terms of labour and materials, so they were the preserve of the rich. A 'licence to crenellate' was required from the king for the owner to legally erect a castle or to fortify a house in any way, thus allowing the crown to control the number of strongholds held by the barons. These would only be granted to nobles and gentry that the crown recognised and trusted. It was not just earls, barons and knights that occupied the castles however, the sites were often leased to, or at least run by, lesser folk, such as foresters and stewards.

Despite the obviously defensive nature of the sites and the well documented periods of military activity, and destruction or slighting at several stages of the medieval period, the reasons for their creation are in many cases debatable, and almost certainly not purely military. Castles were primarily a statement of wealth and power, functioning as family homes, estate offices and hunting lodges.

Previous research

Nichols published a list of castles in his History and Antiquities of the County of Leicester (Nichols 1811, 898), but he does not quote his sources for several of them, including Melton and 'Thorpe', leaving us tantalised and not fully enlightened. There are reports of possible castle remains in 19th century Melton and a set of earthworks at Thorpe Arnold could perhaps be construed as denuded fortifications and be the site to which Nichols referred. He also gives more in-depth details of particular castle sites within his parish histories.

The Victoria County History volumes for Leicestershire and Rutland, compiled by William Page (1907; 1908), give further documentary evidence and describe existing remains in some cases.

Leonard Cantor produced excellent discussions and accounts of the castle sites of Leicestershire in 1978 (Cantor 1978, 30–41), which, with useful additions the following year (McWhirr and Winter 1979), remained the definitive list for nearly two decades. More recently, Oliver Creighton has published two articles on the formation of the early castles of Leicestershire and of Rutland (Creighton 1997, 19–33; 1999, 21–36), which provide a clear summary of their physical description, their creation, and a discussion as to their original purpose.

Documentary evidence

The earliest and most useful medieval documentary evidence for the location of early castles in the area is a mid-12th century treaty between Robert le Bossu, Earl of Leicester and Ranulf, Earl of Chester (Douglas and Greenaway 1995, 1152–3). The treaty was made at some time between 1147 and 1153, a period of civil war in which the two earls were on opposing sides, to agree that they would not build any castles between a rectangle of existing strongholds; Hartshill (Warks), Coventry, Castle Donington, Belvoir, Oakham and Rockingham (fig 2). Mountsorrel Castle was to be passed from the Earl of Chester to the Earl of Leicester, and the latter was to keep possession of Whitwick Castle. Ravenstone Castle was to be pulled down by the Earl of Leicester, with the help of the Earl of Chester if required. The earls also agreed to combine their forces to destroy any castles built by others within this area.

Leicester Castle itself is not specifically mentioned in the agreement as it clearly would not change ownership from the Earl of Leicester, but it was still very much in existence, and had been in place since as early as 1068. This shows that the 1150s treaty should in no way be treated as a definitive list of mid-12th century castles in this area.

Documents surrounding the licence to crenellate a property can give useful ownership and dating information. Inventories, wills, royal surveys and assessments can also sometimes contain good descriptions of fortified sites. Other references for castles can be the royal record of their slighting after a siege, as at Mountsorrel and Groby.

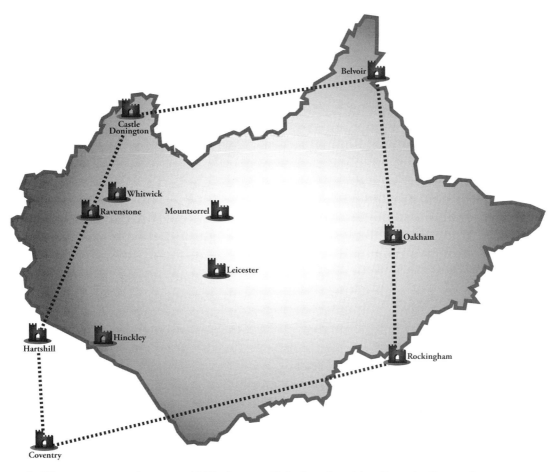

Figure 2: The agreement map c.1150. Image © Leicestershire County Council

We have information on the ownership of several local castles and in some cases we know who built them. However, due to a lack of detailed information about land ownership throughout the first hundred years of Norman rule, even with the evidence of the Domesday Book, and knowing how quickly and often some castles changed hands, it is very difficult to achieve a complete and accurate list of castle builders in the area.

There are several reasons why no documentary records are known for some of our castle sites, the most obvious being the scarcity of surviving medieval documents, due to destruction by fire, flood and ignorance. No doubt some relevant documents remain unread in libraries and collections around the world. Castles would have very few documents relating to them at the time, particularly the so-called 'adulterine' castles built without official royal licence, usually to protect particular estates or assets. Other than the bills for the building of the structures very little will have been written down about these castles, which might have been in use for only a few years.

The physical evidence
Motte and Bailey castles.
Of the 19 confirmed castle sites which survive within our study area, at least ten are, or were, of motte and bailey form. Of all these castles less than half are known to have been enhanced with stone curtain walls and keeps, the rest were either abandoned or demolished by Henry II after the 1173–4 revolt, in which the third earl of Leicester fought against the King. A developed stone castle at Mountsorrel was destroyed by King John after the 1215 revolt. Most of the surviving castles were abandoned and ruinous by the mid-14th century.

In addition to the uncontested examples, Leicestershire and Rutland have several motte-like earthwork features, which seem plausible as early castles, but lack the documentary evidence or the survival of bailey earthworks. Without undertaking invasive archaeological fieldwork on them, these cannot be confirmed as medieval fortified sites. There are several other possible interpretations for these mounds, however: medieval and early post-medieval windmill mounds, Anglo-Saxon moot mounds, prehistoric or Anglo-Saxon round

125

barrows and post medieval formal garden prospect mounds which can be up to 60m in diameter. Interpretation of these sites is usually determined by the proximity to other buildings and landscape topography, but often also by the interpreter's experience and historical inclination.

Late 12th and 13th century rebuilding in stone

Stone walls from this period are recorded on the sites of early castles at Mountsorrel, Sapcote, Oakham, Woodhead (Great Casterton) and Leicester, while licences to crenellate were granted in the 13th century at Belvoir and Castle Donington. Stone walls were probably also erected at Earl Shilton, and Whitwick in the early 13th century. Bagworth had a licence to crenellate rather later, in 1318.

Excavations on castle sites

Excavation of castle sites in Leicestershire and Rutland has been very limited and recent investigations even more so, with the exception of very minor works undertaken during ground disturbance due to new services or resurfacing works. Many of the earthworks have been Scheduled Ancient Monuments for many years, which, together with the cost of tackling the excavation of a castle site has been a barrier to many archaeological investigations. Small scale investigations have taken place at Sapcote (fig 3), Ashby, Kirby Muxloe, Oakham Leicester, and Castle Donington. A small scale excavation at Groby in the 1960s was revisited and extended considerably during a three day excavation by the 'Time Team' television programme on Channel 4 in 2010, much improving our understanding of the original castle site.

Missing castles

As well as having some earthwork remains of fortified sites with no documentary evidence, we also have sites with documentary evidence but no earthworks. Ravenstone Castle is mentioned in the 1150s agreement between the earls of Leicester and Chester and was ordered to be demolished by the Earl of Leicester. No documentary, place name or physical evidence has been recorded to conclusively locate this site within Ravenstone parish.

Sapcote Castle, for which no documentary references are known and no current earthworks remain, as the site was levelled in c.1778, makes one consider that we may have some as yet undiscovered castle sites where no form of evidence has survived. Fortunately for us the remains of the earthworks at Sapcote were described by Nichols (1811, 898) and subsequent finds of stone and pottery have led to further archaeological investigations, proving that a substantial fortified site lay within the village in the late 13th century (fig 3).

The location of fortified sites in the landscape

From the surviving earthwork evidence, albeit often rather partial, and the limited fieldwork undertaken, we have a fairly good idea of the form of the early castle sites in the area, but the on-going problem is in determining their original purpose or, perhaps, purposes. Unfortunately, the documentary evidence rarely enlightens us on this point. We therefore need to look at them in their landscape and socio-historical contexts.

The traditional view of Norman motte and bailey castles is as strongholds from which the invading Normans could both dominate and safely administrate over the subjugated Anglo-Scandinavian population, and, in part, this must be true. The spectacular positioning of Castle Donington, Belvoir and Mountsorrel Castles on natural promontories, giving extensive views of, and dominating, important roads and rivers, provide a clear indication of the motivation for their siting. However, strategic military positioning, or even practical positioning to place the castle at the heart of a particular estate does not seem to be the only motivation for the position of many of our castles.

Figure 3: Sapcote castle excavations (© Keith Hextall).

126

Castles and hunting

The location of many early castles correlates strongly with the location of the three main forests of Leicestershire and Rutland; Leicester Forest, Charnwood Forest and the Royal Forest of Leicestershire and Rutland (also known as Leighfield Forest) (fig 4). The ringing of these expanses of woodland with castles could have two reasons: the forests needed their own administration centres and, perhaps more importantly, the sites were chosen for their proximity to good hunting areas. A licence to crenellate often specified rights to hunt and keep a warren as well as the element of fortification. Castles were built by and for the nobility and the nobility loved their hunting.

Sauvey Castle and Beaumont Chase are known to have been royal hunting seats servicing Leighfield Forest. Earl Shilton's position overlooking the length of Leicester Forest indicates much the same function, although this is not backed up by the documentary evidence as at Sauvey and Beaumont Chase. Similarly, the castles at Mountsorrel, Groby, Whitwick and possibly Ravenstone may have had at least part-time hunting lodge status for Charnwood Forest.

The location of fortified sites within towns and villages.

Creighton notes that within built-up areas, be they villages or towns, the location of castles adjacent to surviving churches is very common. In some cases the castle chapel often served as – or at least later became – the parish church. At Earl Shilton the presumed pre-conquest church appears to have been enveloped and controlled by the castle of the new overlord (Creighton 1997, 31), although this church could actually be a Norman foundation. Markets are also frequently found adjacent to castles – notably at Oakham and Earl Shilton, where the markets are just outside the gates. In some cases the castle would be sited next to an existing market place, while in others the market place would be established outside the castle. The castle owners wanted to ensure control of all the commercial activities to reap maximum financial benefits, but also perhaps to stamp their mark on what were often pre-conquest civilian concerns. A close physical location would further both ambitions.

Later castles

William, Lord Hastings, a powerful and wealthy Yorkist noble during the latter part of the Wars of the Roses and in its aftermath,

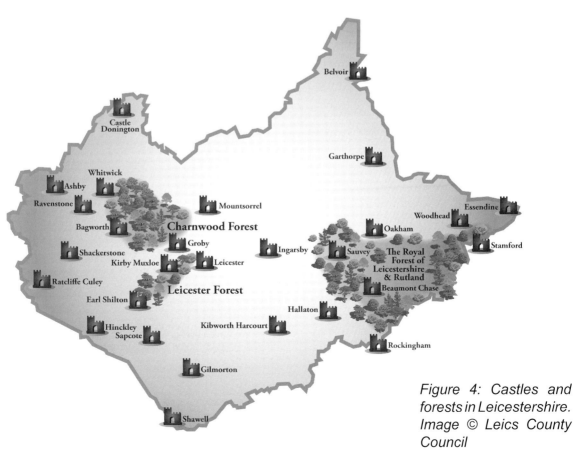

Figure 4: Castles and forests in Leicestershire. Image © Leics County Council

127

is responsible for the building of the two best preserved castles in Leicestershire. He was granted licence to crenellate four properties in 1474: Kirby Muxloe, Ashby de la Zouch, Belvoir and Bagworth. In all cases he was planning to redevelop existing buildings. Bagworth and Belvoir were already fortified, though ruinous, but at Ashby and Kirby Muxloe he was to fortify previously undefended manor houses to provide overtly high status, but also truly defendable buildings.

Hastings started work on enlarging and fortifying Ashby immediately – he had in fact started the redevelopment in 1472. He created two large towers, one of which housed a completely self-contained private residence. He may not have carried out all of his intended work at Bagworth, although very early brick work has been noted on the site, and he seems to have merely used Belvoir as a source of building stone for Ashby. He started building Kirby Muxloe Castle in 1480, before the work at Ashby was finished. Kirby Muxloe was to be a very modern fortified site, built of brick by continental workmen, and with ground level gun loops in the gate house and corner towers. However, having helped Richard of Gloucester against his major rivals for the throne in early 1483, Hastings was seen as a strong rival himself and was executed in June

the same year, leaving a large and impressive Ashby Castle to his successors, but Kirby Muxloe unfinished.

Groby Old Hall on the site of Groby Castle also received some 15th century building works, with the Greys erecting two brick towers in the mid to late 15th century, probably the earliest brick buildings in the county. Even with these towers, however, the site is unlikely to have withheld any form of serious attack and their addition merely served to elevate the status of the house .

The decline and fall of the Leicestershire castle.

The final quashing of the Yorkist uprisings by the new Tudor Dynasty at the very end of the 15th century brought about a long period of peace in most of central England. This was mirrored in the architecture of the time and Ashby-de-la-Zouch, one of only three Leicestershire castles that survived into the 16th century, was reworked with larger windows and new, even more sumptuous private apartments. The second, Belvoir Castle, was completely rebuilt as a country house in 1528, but still with some defences and Leicester Castle appears to have been relegated to the status of an estate office for the dukes of Lancaster with an assize court in the great hall. After the death

A North View of the Old Palace in Ashby de la Zouch.

Figure 5: Ashby de la Zouch castle after demolition by parliamentary forces. Picture attributed to the Countess of Huntington. (© Leicestershire County Council topographical art collection)

of John of Gaunt in 1399 the castle ceased to be the home of a great lord. The 14th century religious precinct added on to the south of the castle and surrounded by its own curtain wall with impressive gate houses, known as 'the Newarke', thrived until the dissolution of the monasteries in the 1530s, with the walls being preserved.

Of course the English Civil War in the following century saw a new need for fortified houses and castles and by this time Leicestershire had only one surviving fully fortified Castle. The strongly Royalist Ashby de la Zouch castle was besieged by Parliamentary forces during the English Civil War and its defences withstood several light artillery bombardments. After the eventual surrender of the castle to the Parliamentarians, it's defences were demolished and the Hastings's impressive tower house was blown up in 1648 to eradicate any potential Royalist stronghold (fig 5).

Belvoir Castle was another Royalist seat, and although more a country house than a castle it stood on a highly defensible site and withstood a Parliamentary siege. It was deemed enough of a threat to the Commonwealth to have its walls demolished after the Civil War. The present Castle is mostly 18th and 19th century in date (fig 6).

In May 1645, the antiquated defences of the Newarke, the strongest surviving section of Leicester's walls, posed enough of an obstacle to the besieging Royalists to incur a very heavy

and determined artillery bombardment, which breached the walls in three hours. It is likely that the walls were much reduced by development and stone robbing during the 16th century and that only part of the town and the original castle area wall were still defendable by the early 17th century. The Royalists then had to make hasty repairs to defend themselves from the Parliamentarians returning triumphant from Naseby a few weeks later. Most of the walls that survived the rigours of the Civil War were eventually pulled down in the 19th century.

The 'Magazine Gateway', two sections of the 14th century inner bailey wall, with civil war gun loops, and the 'Turret Gateway' in the Newarke are the last remnants of these defences, the latter gateway being burnt out during a riot in 1832.

Conclusion

The castles of Leicestershire and Rutland follow the general trend of central English fortified sites. The erection of the Norman castles was motivated by a need for secure centres of administration, housing of garrisons, control of major rivers and roads, proximity to good hunting facilities, a statement of intent to stay as well as of status and conquest.

The turbulent 12th and early 13th centuries saw strengthening of fortifications, sieges and slighting. Some were never rebuilt, others were recast as undefended manorial complexes, but the more significant sites were replaced by modern castles in the later thirteenth century.

THE EAST VIEW OF BELVOIR CASTLE, IN THE COUNTY OF LEICESTER.

Figure 6: Belvoir Castle. Picture attributed to the Buck Brothers (© Leicestershire County Council Topographical Art Collection)

Of all the castles of Leicestershire and Rutland, only Ashby, and arguably Belvoir, remained as true castle sites by the end of the 15th century and even these had been converted into what could be described as fortified palaces and did not survive the English Civil War intact.

This slow decline in the military and political importance of the castle has left us with a considerable array of earthwork sites and a very small collection of standing ruins. But if we are to fully understand these sites, their physical forms, date ranges and medieval function, then more fieldwork and documentary research is essential. Fortunately, virtually all of our fortified earthwork sites, be they certain or otherwise, are now Scheduled Monuments and, in theory, safe from further damage. Hopefully they will remain for future generations of archaeologists to investigate. Due to the strengthening of archaeological input into the planning process and the constant improvement of scientific archaeological techniques, we will continue to piece together the information needed in order to see the original form of these sites. With ongoing survey and excavation and a concerted effort to scour the documentary record, we should be able to learn more of the story of these important monuments and place them more securely in their medieval and landscape contexts.

Gazetteer: The castles of Leicestershire and Rutland

Much of the information in the gazetteer below is a summary from existing sources including the HER (see below) held by Leicestershire County Council and is provided as a guide to allow those interested to take their research further. Plans are shown for information only and are taken from Creighton (1997, 1999) and the drawings by Robert F Hartley held by LCC (some unpublished).

HER – The Heritage and Environment Record database is maintained by Leicestershire County Council and can be consulted by appointment. Some records are available in shortened form on the Heritage Gateway website http://www.heritagegateway.org.uk/gateway/

SMN – A Scheduled Monument Number is used by English Heritage as part of the National Heritage List for England. There may also be a Listed Building Number for a site (not given here). See:http://www.english-heritage.org.uk/professional/protection/process/national-heritage-list-for-england/

For a fast and easy way to search for information and data there is (as at 2015) an excellent private website gazetteer and bibliography for castles and other moated sites, fortified houses and defences in the UK called The Gatehouse – http://www.gatehouse-gazetteer.info/home.html run by Philip Davis. The Gatehouse is an educational resource for professionals and amateurs and aggregates data from statutory heritage organisations with direct links to those sites as well as being a resource in its own right. The site also provides links to sources for 'licences to crenellate' which is particularly useful.

The gazetteer by parish

Ashby de la Zouch: HER ref MLE15050, SMN 1013324 (fig 7)

A 13th or 14th century manor house extensively refurbished and enlarged, and then fortified between 1472 and 1476 by William, Lord Hastings. He was licenced to crenellate in 1474. By 1483 it comprised a chapel, a domestic block with a great hall, solar and service rooms, two towers, one containing a large kitchen on the ground floor and the other tower Lord Hasting's private apartments, and a curtain wall. The gardens were remodelled in the 16th century and the buildings were updated in the early 17th century. The defences were demolished after a siege during the English Civil War and the main towers were blown up in 1648.

Bagworth Moats: HER ref MLE 2688, SMN 1013324

Robert de Holand received licence to crenellate at Bagworth in 1318 (Cantor 1978, 34), but at his death in 1373 the site, referred to as a castle, is recorded as of no great value with the fishponds surrounding the mansion broken and therefore worthless. William, Lord Hastings received another licence to empark, build and crenellate at Bagworth in 1474 (Lyte 1927, 243). The surviving earthworks consist of a wide, sub-rectangular moat with a probable 19th century causewayed entrance. A triangular fishpond with an island lies to the west.

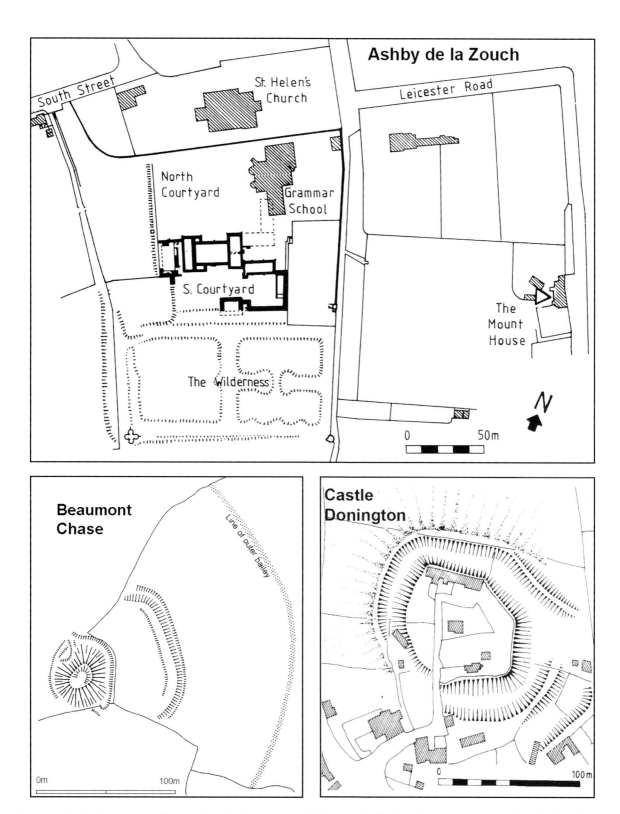

Figure 7: Ashby de la Zouch (top), Beaumont Chase (left) Castle Donington (right) (© all LCC, R F Hartley)

Beaumont Chase and Uppingham: HER ref MLE 5047, SMN 1010925 (fig 7)

A motte and double bailey castle stands on 'Castle Hill' a natural promontory overlooking the western extent of the Royal Forest of Leicestershire and Rutland. The baileys protects the eastern approach, while the natural slopes suffice on the other sides (Hartley 1983, 7). The siting of the castle overlooking Leighfield Forest and its tenancy by a royally appointed forester is a clear indication of its status as a hunting lodge and, presumably, an administrative centre for forest law. Evidence of iron working around the castle suggests an element of commercial diversification on the site, although this has not been firmly dated.

131

Belvoir Castle: HER ref MLE 3364/5, SMN None, Listed Building Nbr 1360870

Belvoir Castle stands on a natural hill, commanding views of the Vale of Belvoir and has been rebuilt several times. It was first built by Robert de Todeni, William's standard bearer at Hastings, in the late 11th century. A 13th century seal of his great-grandson, William de Aubini IV, shows a three storey, square keep with battlements, surrounded by a similarly crenellated curtain wall. (Of course this may be a standard depiction of a 13th century castle rather than a true likeness of Belvoir.) In 1247 the de Ros family took over and refortified the site. A licence to crenellate was obtained in 1267.

William, Lord Hastings acquired the site in the 1460s and he at least partly dismantled it for materials for use on his Ashby Castle development. The Manners family rebuilt the castle in 1528 but it was slighted by order of Parliament in 1649. Subsequent Manners' rebuilding on the site from 1655 was of a mansion rather than as a castle and very little of the present building is thought to date to the medieval period (Pevsner 1984, 95–101). Indeed it has changed considerably even since the antiquarian John Nichols' time due to extensive rebuilding by James Wyatt and Sir John Thoroton between 1801 and 1830 after a devastating fire.

Castle Donington: HER ref MLE 4435, SMN 1011608 (fig 7)

The original castle is thought to have been built in the early 12th century, possibly (though unproven) on an Iron Age hillfort. The site is scheduled as an enclosure castle as there is no evidence of a motte. The castle is mentioned in the agreement of c.1150. It was rebuilt in c.1278. It passed to William, Lord Hastings in 1461. It was ruinous by 1565, comprising five stone towers, a curtain wall and a dwelling house. Sir George Hastings demolished the castle in 1595 to reuse the stone to build his country house at Donington Park. Building work on the north side of the site in the 1940s revealed two thick walls, at right angles to each other, presumed to be from the keep. Sections of the curtain wall and the site of a tower, which was removed in around 1910, were also noted (Clarke 1952, 42).

In 1968–9 a section was excavated across the bailey ditch, which proved to be flat bottomed and recut more than once. The lower fill contained 14th and 15th century pottery and large amounts of building stone (Reaney 1969, 76; Creighton 1997, 34). A 30 to 40 feet deep, stone-lined well was recorded on the site in 1978. A building appraisal in 1997 recorded a surviving section of curtain wall, including a doorway and window at the back of cottages on Castle Hill (HER).

Earl Shilton: HER ref MLE 2849, SMN 1010302 (fig 8)

A large motte c.120 feet in diameter and around 10 feet high, surrounded by a wide ditch, lies just east of the 12th century church. There is no sign of a bailey bank or ditch, but the churchyard may delineate its bounds. It is believed to have been built by Robert le Bossu, Earl of Leicester, and passed to his successors. The stone folly gatehouse was built in the mid 20th century.

Essendine, Rutland: HER ref MLE 5238–9, SMN 1010693 (fig 8)

A fortified moated site with an adjoining sub-rectangular banked enclosure which acts as a bailey. The latter contains a mid 12th century chapel, now the parish church of St Mary. The moat and enclosure were once flanked to the north and south by fishponds, but only the northern pond survives. (Hartley 1983,15). A high status residence is suggested in documents from the late 13th through to the late 16th centuries, and in 1417 a description is given of an extensive manorial site (Blore 1811, 201), however there are no references to a castle here (Page 1935, 250–1). There is controversy over the founding of the castle; the Bussey family and later the de Viponts owned the land from late 1150s onwards, but it is likely to have been Walter Espec who owned the land at Domesday, and Creighton suggests that the similarity in form of Essendine to Espec's main holding, Helmsley Castle, North Yorkshire, is probably more than coincidence (Creighton 1999, 25).

Gilmorton: HER ref MLE 1535, SMN 1010495 (fig 8)

A large, flat topped motte surrounded by a dry ditch and adjoined to a later shallow moat or fishpond by a linear ditch, lies immediately west of the church. The Victoria County History plan shows a bailey bank to the north (Page 1907, 258; Creighton 1997, 25) giving the dimensions of the motte as 2.6 – 3.1m above the bottom of the ditch, with the summit measuring 27m in diameter and suggests that the motte has been lowered to accommodate a larger building than the original keep.

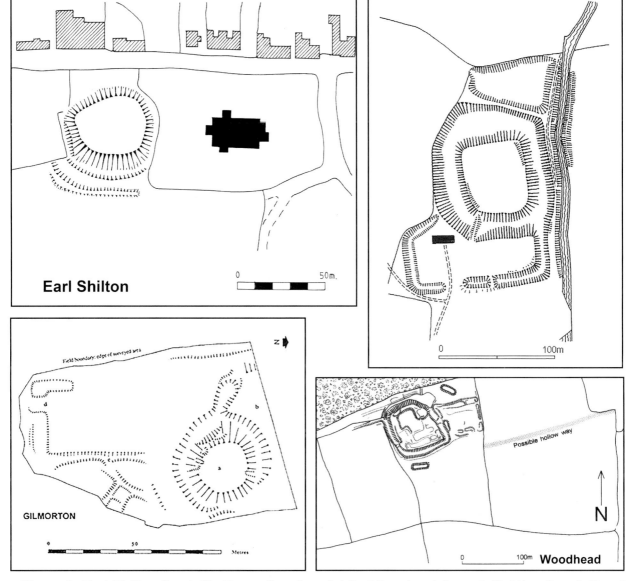

Figure 8: Earl Shilton (top left), Essendine (top right), Gilmorton (above left), Woodhead, Great Casterton, (above right).(© LCC, R F Hartley)

Great Casterton, Woodhead Castle HER ref MLE5318, SMN 1010923 (fig 8)

A stone-walled and moated site, with internal domestic earthworks and an adjacent enclosure. The site immediately abuts an area of ancient woodland to the north. There are two small fishponds, one to the north and another to the south. Although the site is very close to the strategically important Great North Road and has a small village adjacent to it, the very close proximity to the woodland strongly suggests a location motivated by hunting. It was visited by Edward I in 1290. There is no documentation for the castle until 1543, by which time it was ruinous (Page 1935, 232).

Groby HER ref MLE5047, SMN 1010193 (fig 9)

A surviving motte, *c.*30m across and 7m high, with an elongated oval bailey, which enclosed the motte and an area to the west, as shown on an estate plan of 1754. The castle is thought to have been built by Hugh de Grandmesnil in the late 11th century and was slighted by order of Henry II in 1176, seemingly by undermining the keep and removing part of the motte (Creighton 1997, 22). The Ferrers family took over the site between 1279 and 1445, when the Greys moved in. The motte ditch was filled in during the early 16th century, by the second marquis of Dorset (Nichols 1811, 631). Nichols also mentions a very ancient stone wall over 100 yards long 'above the site of the keep'. A stone wall with an arched doorway survives above ground close to the modern church. Excavations by Brian Davison in 1962/3 in advance of the A50 bypass recorded the northern bailey ditch as rock cut, 15-18m wide and very deep. The motte had been built around a thick walled, granite building measuring at least 20 by 16 feet (TLAHS 1964, 51) that may well have stood proud of the summit of the motte to provide a keep (Creighton 1997, 22). The 2010 'Time Team' excavation reopened this area and recorded steps descending into the base of the tower and revealed it's dressed stone profile. They concluded that the tower and the motte were of the same date, quashing previous thoughts that the tower might be pre-conquest (Wessex Archaeology 2011). The site remained important as a manorial centre throughout the medieval period and the plan of an impressive range of domestic buildings was recorded. To the south east of the motte, a later stone manor house was built, which includes mid 15th century brick towers, similar in style to those at Kirby Muxloe Castle, complete with diaper work seemly showing the Ferrers family crest (Dryden 1911, 103–6).

Hallaton: HER ref MLE 1628 SMN 1010487 (fig 9)
A large conical motte with a horseshoe shaped bailey to the north-west. A small ditch and bank to the south may have been dug to drain the motte ditch (Page 1907, 259–60). In 1877, curious railway engineers sank two shafts into the mound (Dibbin 1878, 316–21). They recorded the original ground surface as being 17 feet 6 inches down, and described a layer of peat and bog earth, containing leather, wood and bone fragments below the natural layer. The mound was made up of layers of clay, gravel and boulders as well as thick layers of burnt material. Metal, bone and ceramic finds were made throughout, although the upper layers were cleaner, with a somewhat gravely, yellow clay, capped with a 15 inch layer of hard chalky material. No sign of a wooden or stone palisade or tower were recorded on the motte. The engineers also sunk numerous pits within the bailey and strong evidence of iron smelting was found – although the dating for this is uncertain. A minor evaluation in 1943 revealed no new information.

Hinckley: HER ref MLE 2890, SAM 17039 (fig 9)
A motte and bailey castle, probably founded by Hugh de Grantmesnil, Earl of Leicester (Page: 1907, 257). It is mentioned in the c.1150 agreement between the earls of Leicester and Chester and the impressive, but truncated earthworks of the bailey rampart survive. The motte itself was situated on the hill top, just south of Castle Street under the present Co-op shop. By 1361 the castle is described as 'a plot', suggesting it was long out of use (Cantor 1978, 36). It was completely ruinous by the early 16th century (Chandler 1993, 282) and the 18th century saw materials stripped off the motte for road mending until a house was built on it in 1770, the footings revealing foundations of a stone bridge over the motte ditch (Nichols 1811). A watching brief during the building of the Co-op in 1976 revealed the motte ditch again (Liddle 1976, 62).

Kirby Muxloe: HER ref MLE 202, SMN 1013323 (fig 10)
Having received a licence to crenellate the existing manor house at Kirby Muxloe in 1474, William, Lord Hastings began work on his brick built fortifications in 1480, before the completion of Ashby Castle. Left unfinished by his family after Hastings' execution in 1483, the building was robbed of some of its valuable brick, but an impressive gatehouse, with low level cannon loops and the Hastings crest set into the octagonal towers survives as does one of the four intended square corner towers. The brick footings remain for the three other corner towers and three rectangular bastions set between them. The site is enclosed by an almost rectangular moat, which was recut during the excavation and restoration of the site in 1911–13. Within the curtain walls lies the stone footprint of a 13th or 14th century manor house of the Pakeman family, which the building accounts suggest was still in use during the erection of the defences (Goodall 2007, 19).

Leicester: HER apply to City Council. SMN 1012147
Motte and bailey castle built by William I and granted to Hugh de Grandmesnil soon after the conquest. Attacked and slighted in 1088 and 1101. St Mary de Castro was founded as a collegiate church in 1107. The castle was remodelled and rebuilt c.1150, including the surviving stone hall, but it was taken and the defences demolished by Henry II in 1176. Rebuilt and developed under the de Montforts and the House of Lancaster, under whom it developed into a large and important centre often hosting royalty. The walled ecclesiastical precinct, the Newarke, was developed in the 1340s and 50s. After the death of John of Gaunt in 1399 it gradually declined and was relegated by 1500 to an estate office of the Duchy of Lancaster. The Norman motte survives (although lowered in the 18th century), the 12th century great hall survived as a law court and St Mary de Castro Church is still in use. The surviving castle and the Newarke walls were damaged

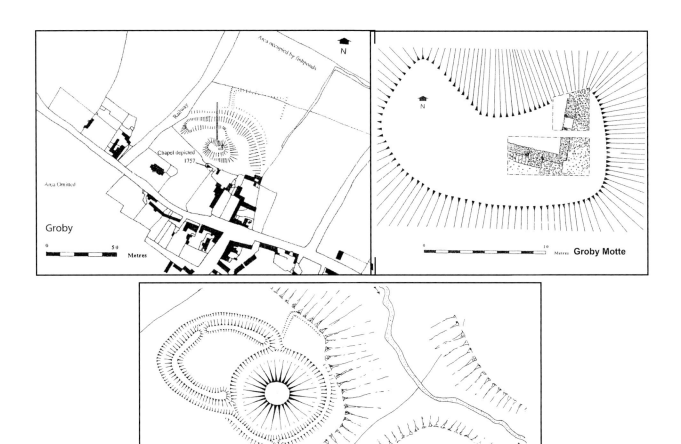

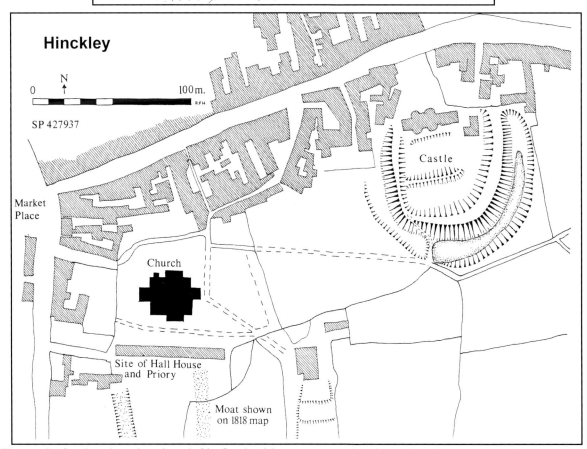

Figure 9: Groby site plan (top left), Groby Motte excavation based on Davison 1963 unpublished excavations (top right) (both © Creighton 1997), 23; Hallaton (centre), Hinckley (above) (© LCC, R F Hartley)

during the Civil War sieges of 1645 and finally demolished in the 19th century. Of the Castle and the Newarke defences only the Turret and the Magazine gateways and two short sections of wall survive (see Buckley, this volume, for an account of the Great Hall and recent work around the castle area).

Mountsorrel: HER ref MLE 714, SMN 1010188

The castle was built on a granite outcrop with commanding views of the Soar Valley and the road from Leicester to Loughborough (now the A6) in c.1080, possibly by Hugh Lupus. It is mentioned in the agreement of c.1150 and was besieged and taken by Henry II in 1174. Repair bills of the 1190s and 1200s survive. In 1215 King John granted the castle to Saer de Quincy, who then joined the rebel barons. It withstood a siege by the Earls of Pembroke and Chester, but after the collapse of the rebellion the land was given to the Earl of Chester on the condition that the castle was destroyed.

The now slight motte was on the northern end of the hill and the bailey, within which various earthworks survive, covered the rest of the summit. Some of the earthworks may be the result of quarrying. Stone footings and solid spreads of building rubble have been seen on several occasions within the area of the bailey and early medieval pottery and metal finds have been recorded on the summit during excavations by Ardron (1952). Defensive earthworks survive on the southern slopes of the hill (Hartley 1989, 10 and 25).

Oakham: HER ref MLE 5569 – 5574 & 9901, SMN (fig 10)

A motte and bailey castle was probably first built on the site after the death of Queen Edith in 1075, when William I acquired the Saxon royal estate (Page: 1908). Radford pointed out that the remains of the original motte survive inside the south east corner of the curtain wall (Radford 1955). He also suggested that the ramparts mark the original rectangular bailey. Excavations in 1953–4 (Gathercole 1958, 17–38) revealed the castle ditch to be 37½ feet wide and just over 18 feet deep and found Stamford Ware pottery in the rampart embankment.

The castle then passed to the de Ferrers family, who almost certainly built the stone, aisled great hall in c.1180 (Clough 1981). The blocked doorways in the outer walls of the hall and excavations in 1956–8 (Barber 1957, 1958, 1959) show that, at least in the 14th century, service and domestic rooms were attached to the hall in standard manorial layout. The de Ferrers may have also erected the stone curtain walls along the earth ramparts later in their lordship. The castle was granted to several different families throughout the upheaval of the 13th century. The 12th century hall has been used as a law court from at least 1229 and has survived until the present day, although the rest of the domestic buildings were pulled down in the 18th century. A description of the castle, its defences and its grounds in 1340 show it to have been in good repair at that stage but it declined during the 15th century and was ruinous (except for the hall) by 1512.

Ravenstone: HER ref MLE 4827

Extant in circa 1150, when condemned to be demolished by the Earl of Leicester in the agreement between the Earls of Leicester and Chester. The site remains unknown (Nichols 1804, 932).

Sapcote: HER ref MLE 279 & 280, SMN 1010301

A Norman motte and bailey castle, which was developed and fortified by the Basset family in the 13th century. Ralph Basset was Sheriff of Leicestershire in 1263 and effectively ran the county. Nichols describes a motte in Toot Hill Close being levelled soon after 1778 (Nichols 1811, 898). Toot Hill Close presently has an uneven surface, suggesting stone buildings below (Hartley 1989, 58 and 68) and chance encounters in the early 20th century, a watching brief in 1964 (Hawkes 1966, 69) revealed a stone line well, a cobble roadway, stone walls and building rubble all associated with 13th – 15th century pottery and tile. Excavations in 1958 recorded 13th to 18th century gardens and fishponds in a ditched enclosure to the west (Addyman 1960, 1–5). Excavations continued throughout the late 1960s and early 1970s (Hawkes 1966, 69; Smith 1968, 43; 1970, 77) revealing a late 12th or early 13th century stone curtain wall with a turret and a moat. Subsequent archaeological work on the site has continued to reveal stone and earth features (Higgins 1999, 111; Butler 2000, 251) but a coherent plan of the castle is not yet possible. There are no medieval records of a castle at Sapcote.

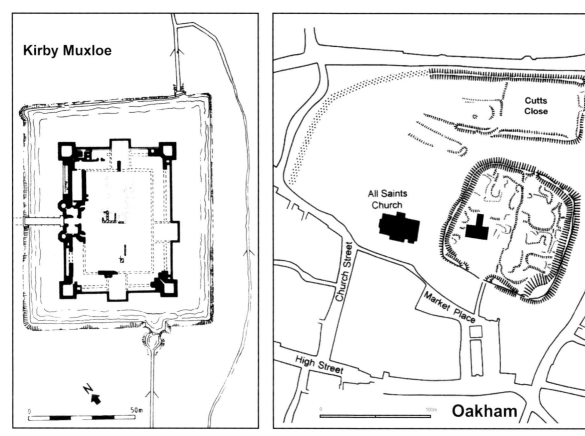

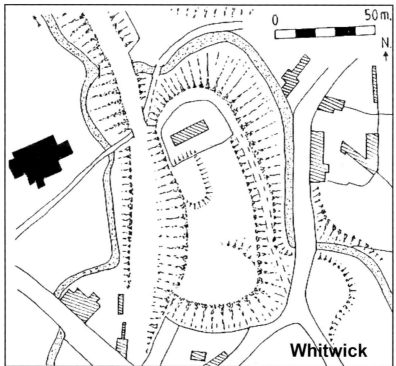

Figure 10: Kirby Muxloe (top left), Oakham (top right), Whitwick (centre above) (© LCC, R F Hartley)

Whitwick: HER ref MLE 4541, SMN 1012555 (fig 10)

Nichols (1800, 112) states that the foundations of the castle walls could still be seen in a close called Castle Hill. Fieldwork by the local vicar in 1893 (Tollemache 1893, 13–15) recorded a low sunken wall as the only remains of the castle and notes burials (presumably from a castle chapel, as it is on the wrong side for the church) to the south-east of the hill. A dam to the north west may have created a moat-like lake around the hill. In 1907 a flat topped motte *c.*8 feet high was recorded on a flat topped hill east of the church. A late nineteenth century railway line cuts

137

through the hill, damaging the site considerably (Page 1907, 261–2) although the mound was still 2-3m high when surveyed in the 1980s (Hartley 1984, 48). There is no evidence of a formal bailey enclosure, but the flat hilltop is likely to have acted as such. The castle was held by the Earl of Leicester in the mid-12th century (Cantor 1978, 38) and by William de Senevill for King John on 4th December 1204. John Comyn, Earl of Buchan lived at the castle in the late 13th century. In 1321 Henry Beaumont was given licence to crenellate the site, but the Beaumonts appear to have abandoned the site in favour of Beaumanor in the 1320s. The castle was damaged in 1331 (presumably by stone robbers), was deemed worthless in 1349, and was completely ruinous by 1427 (Farnham 1928, 231–240).

Withcote, Sauvey Castle: HER ref MLE 2675, SMN 1010303 (fig 11)

A site placed at the confluence of several small tributaries of the River Chater. There is a large sub-rectangular island within a moat–like lake, which was formed by a dam in the south east corner. The island is divided into two unequal parts by a wide, rather irregular ditch – presumably water filled at the time. The smaller section acted as the motte, and the larger as a form of bailey. It is first mentioned in 1216 when King John gave it to William, Count of Aumale. He refortified the site against the King in 1219 and surrendered it in 1220 along with Rockingham. It is mentioned as a castle several times until 1316, and was granted to successive Foresters of Leighfield Forest. Records from 1244 and 1245 show the granting of timber from the Forest and stone slate from a castle stable for the building of a chapel. This site is clearly closely related to Leighfield Forest.

Probable castle sites

Garthorpe: HER ref MLE 3813 (fig 11)

Nichols (1804, 186, 190) mentions a castle close to the watermill, in an area known as 'Castle Close'. A large, oval mound, 4 or 5 meters high, is sited adjacent to the medieval watermill site on the eastern edge of the village (McWhirr and Winter 1979, 74–5; Hartley 1987, 9 & 31).

Hungerton, Ingarsby: HER ref MLE 1704, SMN 1010839 (fig 11)

'Monks Grave' is a relatively small mound with a ring ditch, but with no bailey ditch. It is very similar in form to the Kibworth Harcourt earthwork (below). Other ideas such as a hermitage or barrow have been put forward.

Kibworth Harcourt: HER ref MLE 1772, SMN 1012568 (fig 11)

A large, flat topped mound, known as 'The Munt', lies just south of the village. It is 4m high and up to 35m wide with a flat top 25m across. A single ditch up to 2m deep and 8m wide surrounds it, with an entrance causeway to the south west. No evidence of a bailey survives.

There are records of excavations revealing stone work in an unspecified mound in Kibworth in c.1837 and 1863, and English Heritage attribute the large depressions on the north and south sides of the mound to this, but Creighton (1997, 29) thinks it is likely to have been a windmill mound close by that was actually excavated. Wood (2010, 119–20) believes that Nichol's description (1798, 639) provides fair certainty that a castle existed here with similar dimensions to Hallaton and Gilmorton.

Ratcliffe Culey: HER ref MLE3305, SMN 1010480 (fig 11)

Circular mound surrounded by ditch or moat, south-east of the Sence brook and to the east of the church. This could also be the site of a timber-framed manor house as it is surrounded by other features including a fish pond. The central mound shows no evidence of former structures and is in a typical position for an early manorial centre. Plough damage makes interpretation difficult. The Culey name may indicate a village manorial residence of the de Culeys.

Shawell: HER ref MLE 2332, SMN 1017549 (as a motte and bailey castle)

A large mound c.30 metres in diameter, with remains of a wide ditch on the south side. Page (1907, 275) considered the mound to be a large prehistoric barrow, but Cantor (1978, 35), Liddle (note in SMR 1987), Creighton (1997, 30) and English Heritage all consider it to be a castle motte. There are no records of a castle at Shawell, however, and it may therefore be the same as the site of the documented castle of the village of Catthorpe nearby.

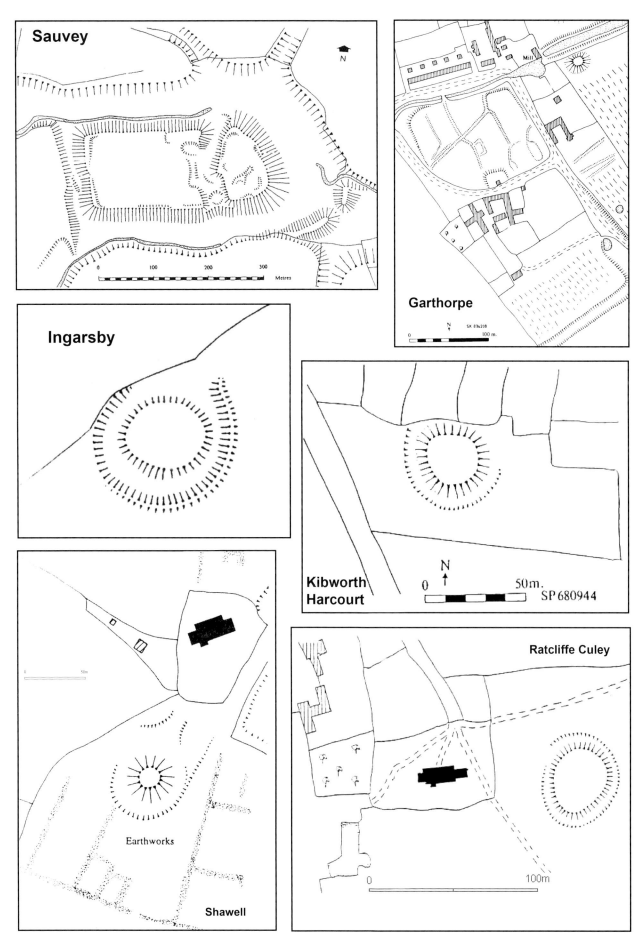

Figure 11: Sauvey (top left) (© Creighton 1997); Garthorpe (top right), Ingarsby (centre left) Creighton 1997; Kibworth Harcourt (centre right), Shawell (bottom left) (© Creighton 1997); Ratcliffe Culey (bottom right). (all others © LCC R F Hartley).

Shackerstone: HER ref MLE 3121, SMN 1008542 (motte and bailey) (fig 12)

A large, flat topped mound *c.*40 metres in diameter, with rectilinear ditches running at right angles to the north and east lies north of the church. Page (1907, 261) records a surrounding ditch 22 feet wide and describes a much destroyed but well-fortified bailey. Hoskins (1946, 9) describes it as a good example of a 12th century castle. In 1940 Frank Cotterill visited the site after a 3½ foot wide trench and square chamber were dug through the mound for an anti-aircraft position. No finds were made but the remains of a central wooden post 1 foot 2 inches in diameter were recorded. Cantor (1978, 39) knew of no records for a castle here and Creighton (1997, 27) although originally identifying the earthwork as a post medieval prospect mound changed his attribution to a castle on the basis of cartographic evidence from Peter Foss, including a map of 1785 associated with the construction of the Ashby Canal making this site more likely to be a motte and bailey (Creighton 1998, 154).

Possible castle sites

Burley, Alstoe Mount: HER ref MLE 5094, SMN 1010671

A very conical mound, set within a rectilinear bank and ditched enclosure, adjoined to the east by what appear to be earthworks of the medieval village of Alsthorpe (Hartley 1983, 12). Excavations on the mound in 1936 revealed no post holes or structures, but a quantity of Stamford Ware pottery was found (Dunning 1936, 396–411). Given the unusual form and configuration of the earthworks and the fact that the local hundred was called the Alsthorpe Hundred, and therefore probably met here, a late Saxon moot site is also a likely interpretation.

Gumley: HER ref MLE 1617, SAM 17048 (fig 12)

A large, flat topped mound, *c.*20m in diameter and surrounded by a single ditch 3 metres wide and 0.3 metres deep, stands on a thin promontory, *c.*300m south west of Gumley Hall. Old field names for the plot include 'The Mount' and 'Dane's Camp'. It is scheduled as a motte, but it could be a large barrow, possibly of middle Anglo-Saxon date (Burbidge 1993). Cantor considers it to be a Norman motte (1978, 35). Creighton regards it as a prospect mound overlooking the gardens of Gumley Hall (Creighton 1997, 29).

Launde: HER ref MLE 1841, SMN 1005493

A large, flat topped mound, with surrounding circular ditch. It is scheduled as a motte, but a 19th century field name 'Mill Close' suggests that it is most likely to be a windmill mound (Creighton 1997, 29).

Melton, The Mount: HER ref MLE 3958

A small circular mound with no associated earthworks lies off Leicester Road, south west of the town centre. A windmill is recorded as being sold in the area (Hartley 1987,11) therefore the earthwork is most likely to be a mill mound.

A castle, alleged to have been founded by Roger, Lord Mowbray, remains unlocated, although reputedly stone foundations were still visible in the King Street area during the mid-19th century (Hunt 1957).

Scraptoft: HER ref MLE 2284

A conical mound, containing a shell grotto and with a path winding up to the summit. Creighton (1997, 27) identifies it as a post medieval prospect mound associated with Scraptoft Hall.

Acknowledgements

Thanks to Leicestershire County Council/Robert F Hartley for permission to use plans from the Heritage Environment Record and to Oliver Creighton for permission to use illustrations from his papers. Thanks are also due to Peter Liddle, Kathleen Elkin and Keith Hextall for help, advice and contributions to the paper and to Alexandra Davy of Leicestershire County Council for providing images of prints from the collection.

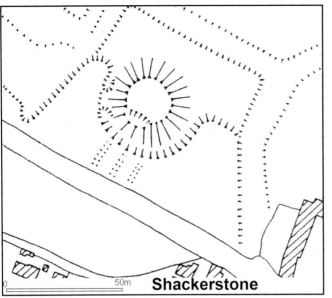 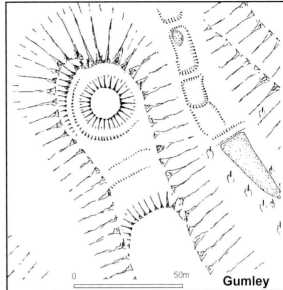

Figure 12: Shackerstone (left), Gumley (right) (© LCC, R F Hartley).

Bibliography

Addyman, P. V., 1960. 'Excavations at a moated site at Sapcote, 1958'. *Transactions of the Leicestershire Archaeological and Historical Society,* 36.

Ardron, F., 1952. *Research on the Area around Mountsorrel Castle* (Unpub handwritten notes: Leicestershire County Council Sites and Monuments Record).

Barber, J. L., 1957, 1958, 1959. 'Oakham' (note). *Medieval Archaeology* 1. 2. 3.

Blore, T., 1811. *The History and Antiquities of the county of Rutland* Vol 1. Stamford: Newcomb.

Burbidge, A., 1993. *Legends of Arthur and Camelot: Origins of Leicestershire and Northamptonshire.* Privately published.

Butler, A., 2000. 'Sapcote, Sapcote Castle'. *Transactions of the Leicestershire Archaeological and Historical Society,* 74.

Cantor, L. M., 1978. 'The medieval castles of Leicestershire'. *Transactions of the Leicestershire Archaeological and Historical Society* 53.

Chandler, J., 1993. *John Leland's Itinerary: travels in Tudor England.* Hinckley: Sutton Publishing.

Clarke T. D.-T., 1952. 'Archaeology in Leicestershire 1939–51'. *Transactions of the Leicestershire Archaeological and Historical Society,* 28.

Clough, T. H. McK., 1981, *Oakham Castle: a Guide and History.* Friends of Rutland County Museum.

Creighton, O., 1997. 'Early Leicestershire Castles, Archaeology and Landscape History.' *Transactions of the Leicestershire Archaeological and Historical Society,* 71.

Creighton, O., 1998. 'Notes: Early Leicestershire Castles: Archaeology and Landscape History'. *Transactions of the Leicestershire Archaeological and Historical Society,* 72.

Creighton, O. H. 1999. 'Early Castles in the Medieval Landscape of Rutland'. *Transactions of the Leicestershire Archaeological and Historical Society,* 73.

Davison, B. K., 1963. Excavations at Groby, Leicestershire. Unpublished site notebook, Leicestershire County Council HER.

Dibbin, H. A., 1878: No title: *Proceedings of the Society of Antiquities.* London, 2nd series, 7.

Douglas, D. C. and Greenaway, G. W., eds, 1995. *English Historical Documents, 1042–1189.* Volume 2, Land and People. Oxford: Routledge.

Dryden, A., 1911. *Memorials of Old Leicestershire.* London: George Allen.

Dunning, G. C., 1936. 'Alstoe Mount, Burley, Rutland'. *Antiquaries' Journal* 16.

Farnham, G. F., 1928. 'The Manors of Charnwood – Whitwick'. *Transactions of the Leicestershire Archaeological and Historical Society*, 15.

Gathercole, P. W., 1958. 'Excavations at Oakham Castle1953-4'. *Transactions of the Leicestershire Archaeological and Historical Society*, 34.

Goodall, J., 2007. *Ashby de la Zouch Castle and Kirby Muxloe Castle*. London: English Heritage.

Hartley, R. F., 1983. *The Medieval Earthworks of Rutland: A Survey*. Leicester: Leicestershire Museums, Arts and Records Service.

Hartley, R. F., 1984. *The Medieval Earthworks of North West Leicestershire*. Leicester: Leicestershire Museums, Arts and Records Service.

Hartley. R. F. 1989. *The Medieval Earthworks of North-East Leicestershire*. Leicester: Leicestershire Museums, Arts and Records Service.

Hawkes, C. J., 1966. *Transactions of the Leicestershire Archaeological and Historical Society*, 41.

Higgins, T., 1999. Note: 'Sapcote: Sapcote Playing Fields'. *Transactions of the Leicestershire Archaeological and Historical Society* 73.

Hoskins, W. G., 1946: *The Heritage of Leicestershire*. Leicester: Edgar Backus.

Hunt, P. E., 1957. *The Story of Melton Mowbray*. Lincolnshire: Palmers Printing and Publishing Company.

Liddle, P., 1976. Note: 'Hinckley'. *Transactions of the Leicestershire Archaeological and Historical Society*, 51.

Lyte, H. C. M., ed. 1927. *Calendar of Charter Rolls*, 6. HMSO.

McWhirr, A. D. and Winter, M. J., 1978–79. 'Medieval Castles Additional Information'. *Transactions of the Leicestershire Archaeological and Historical Society*, 54.

Nichols, J., 1798. *History and Antiquities of the County of Leicestershire, Hundred of Gartree,* 2 pt 2. London: John Nichols.

Nichols, J., 1800. *The History and Antiquities of the County of Leicestershire, The Hundred of East Goscote,* 3 pt. 1. London: John Nichols.

Nichols, J., 1804. *The History and Antiquities of the County of Leicestershire, The Hundred of West Goscote,* 3, pt. 2. London: John Nichols.

Nichols, J., 1811. *The History and Antiquities of the County of Leicester,* T*he Hundred of Spakenhoe,* 4, pt. 2. London: John Nichols.

Page, W., 1907. *Victoria County History of Leicestershire,* 1.

Page, W., 1935. *Victoria County History of Rutland,* 2.

Pevsner, N., 1984. *Buildings of England– Leicestershire and Rutland.* London, Penguin.

Radford, C. A. R., 1955. 'Oakham Castle'. *Archaeological Journal,* 112.

Reaney, D., 1969. Note: 'Castle Donington' *Transactions of the Leicestershire Archaeological and Historical Society,* 45.

Smith, S., 1968. Note: 'Sapcote'. *Transactions of the Leicestershire Archaeological and Historical Society,* 43.

Smith, S., 1970. Note: 'Sapcote'. *Transactions of the Leicestershire Archaeological and Historical Society,* 46.

Tollemache, A. F. Rev., 1898. 'Whitwick Castle'. *Leicestershire and Rutland Notes and Queries* 2.

TLAHS, 1964. Note: 'Groby Motte and Bailey excavation by Davison'. *Transactions of the Leicestershire Archaeological and Historical Society,* 39.

Wessex Archaeology, 2011. *Groby Old Hall Groby, Leicestershire Archaeological Evaluation and Assessment of Results.* Wessex Archaeology 74151.

Wood, M., 2010. *The Story of England.* London: Viking.

Ridge and furrow in southern Leicestershire

Tony Brown

Introduction

In 1733 John Crewe sold the manor of Lubenham to Samuel Wright of Islington, Middlesex, who in the following year commissioned a survey of his newly acquired property. The professionally executed document works its way through the various pieces of land belonging to the estate and concludes with the following observations:

"The open field land belonging to Lubenham lyes in three separate fields distinguished by the names of West, Middle and East fields, and are managed in such a manner that one field is always fallow, another under wheat and barley, and the third under beans and pease; and soe are annually changed. It is again divided into lands and leys, or ploughed ground and grass, which lye in furlongs that have proper names. The gleads, or low grounds that run between the furlongs and the common baulks, that lye dispersed between the land all over the fields, are calld common, or lott grass, because all persons who have a freehold in the open field have a right to a share in them, in proportion to the quantity of freehold land that they own. These gleads & baulks are their meadow ground, which they divide in the following manner."

There then follows a description of the complicated way whereby each year the meadow was distributed among the farmers and it then continues:

"The fields are again divided into yard lands which is an imaginary and uncertain measure either for quantity or value, noe two yard lands in the fields being alike" (ROLLR DE 2960).

The surveyor, James Bermingham, was describing the particular method of operating the common fields of Lubenham at that time and indicated how the component parts fitted together – plough ridges or lands grouped into furlongs, furlongs into great fields. This system of agriculture was abolished at Lubenham by Parliamentary Act in 1766 and the common fields, already in the early 17th century somewhat diminished by an earlier phase of enclosure, were replaced by the hedged fields we still have. The basic building blocks of the old system, the curved 'lands' or plough ridges, the inevitable result of ploughing in a clockwise direction using a fixed mould board plough, remained as earthwork ridge and furrow. That these ridges were what was left of an earlier system of cultivation was never really forgotten.

Allcroft mentions 'lands' or 'selions' (the Latin name for them in medieval documents) in his monumental book 'Earthwork of England' (Allcroft 1908, 611), although he did not quite interpret them correctly. Maurice Beresford re-established the connection between the ridge and furrow that could then still be seen with the strips of the pre-enclosure fields (Beresford 1949). It is pleasant to record that this was done, at least to a degree, from evidence seen in the parishes north-west of Market Harborough in Leicestershire, the subject of this paper (fig 1).

The plough ridges

The purpose of a common field system was to share out effectively the agricultural resources of a defined area and to permit a balance between arable and pasture. The practical expression of this was the yardland (Latin, *vergata*, virgate); it was this fundamental unit that defined the size of any farm in terms of its arable land, meadow and rights in other resources. These things were set out in the documents known as terriers. As an example, a long terrier of 1558–9 of four yardlands in Theddingworth, formerly the property of Catesby Priory in Northamptonshire, describes ridge by ridge 41⅝ acres in Santles Field, 35¾ acres in Nonhylls Field and 35⅛ acres in Gostyll Field. There were 6 acres of meadow and 72 'footes' (a local term for smallish pieces of meadow) – so each yardland had plough ridges with a combined area of 28⅛ acres scattered throughout the system, and also 1½ acres of meadow and 18 footes (NA SC 12/10/22).

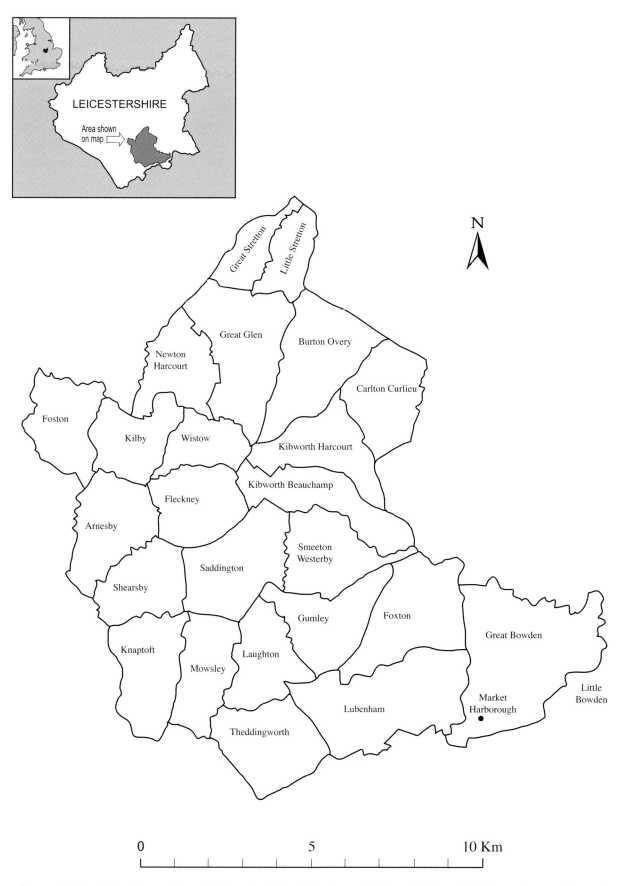

Figure 1: Parishes in southern Leicestershire. The boundaries of Kibworth Beauchamp, Smeeton Westerby, Gumley and Foxton converge on a zone of pasture, as do those of Great Glen, Burton Overy and Kibworth Harcourt.

Similarly a terrier of 1659 of two yardlands in the fields of Fleckney records 10½ acres of arable and former arable in Meare Field, 16¼ acres in Quesicke Field and 15½ acres in Holbrook Field, plus 11 poles of meadow in the Moure and 9 in the West Meadow:

> "and pasture for beaste and common for sheepe and all other profitte and benefitte belonginge to two yardland in the field and comonable places of Fleckney according to the custome" (ROLLR DE996).

A defining moment in the development of the open fields of Leicestershire was the imposition of the system of taxation set out in Domesday Book (1086), whereby townships were given assessments involving the generally duodecimal unit known as the carucate. These assessments replaced an earlier, decimal-orientated system based on the unit called a hide. Unfortunately, there is no agreement about the date at which this took place. Phythian-Adams (1978, 20) has suggested a date shortly after the conquest of Mercia by the Danes in 877, but many would now prefer a date in the later 10th century at the earliest (Roffe 2007, 195–6). In 962–3 King Edgar issued a law code in which the (carucated) territorial unit known as the wapentake, into which Leicestershire was divided, was first mentioned. All this is important for our discussion because in most of the vills studied here it was the carucage which fixed the number of yardlands a field system contained. Generally speaking the number of yardlands to the Domesday carucate was four. So Carlton Curlieu, with a total of 11¾ carucates in Domesday and 12 in the *Testa de Nevill* of 1240 (1923, 634), had 48 yardlands before its enclosure between 1599 and 1607 (Bowman 1996, 134 -5).

Plough ridges were arranged so that they fulfilled an important drainage function and ran down the slope to carry water away. In addition they were used as a method of land measurement in the setting out of common field furlongs, and it is possible to gain some insight into the way in which this was done.

The usual method of describing plough ridges in terriers was to give their areas measured in fractions of an acre, generally ¼ acre or rood, sometimes ½ acre or ½ rood and rather rarely a complete acre, the acre quite possibly originally being seen as the amount of land an ox team could plough in a day (Maitland 1897, 372–6). An example would be a terrier of 1659 describing a yardland in Mowsley, in Beesicke Field:

> "Three rood lands on Gravell Mr Byard east. One halfe acre land upon Old Flaxland Thomas Bugby west. Two rood lands upon Long William Burdet north" (ROLLR DE 66/10/24).

These very commonly encountered statements imply a level of accuracy within an acceptable range. The ridges were however very seldom exactly what the documents said they were, a point made by the following examples: "six lands by estimation an acre" (undated glebe (church land) terrier, Gumley); "three lands containing one acre by estimation, butting on the Town Hadley" (1697 glebe terrier, Fleckney). Occasionally a terrier is a good deal less informative and gives no area, simply referring to 'lands' or 'broad lands', the (presumably local) reader being expected to have in his mind what was meant.

Atterall roods and thirtyfalls

A feature of terriers relating to many parishes in southern Leicestershire is the plough ridge described as an 'atterall' rood (there are numerous variants, 'otterall', 'oderell', 'oderall,' and frequently, and possibly significantly, 'old' or even 'odd' roods are some of them). The term appears as soon as terriers begin being written in English rather than Latin, as in a late 15th century terrier of Leicester Abbey land in the fields of Kilby: "on the same furlong a node*r* (another) oderall rode Langham (the name of another tenant) lying on both sides" (BL Cotton MS Galba E III). In addition, documents relating to Great and Little Bowden, and Foxton, but not other places, have numerous examples of plough ridges referred to as 'thirtyfalls'. The term 'atterall' could be derived from the Middle English *uterage* or *outerage*, meaning 'something bigger than normal' (I am indebted to Professor Barrie Cox for this explanation). Just what the place of these things actually was in a field system is explained in a manuscript note by Rowland Rouse, the 18th century Market Harborough historian, who recorded that:

1 Thirtyfall is 30 poles
2 Thirty Falls == 1 Atterall Rood
2 Atterall (or old Roods) == 3 Roods
  (Stocks and Bragg 1926, 26).

This is confirmed by statements in 17th and 18th century terriers of land belonging to the Wyggeston Hospital "a Thirtifall is halfe an old roode or noterall roode or roode & halfe"; (ROLLR 1D50 V 35–37). The acre which theoretically lay behind all this was the acre of 160 square perches, and the thirtyfall (in Latin *tripartica*; an old rood was *roda et dimidia*) was simply thirty of them, and an old rood sixty. Atterall roods can be quite common in 17th and 18th terriers, but not everywhere; they seem to have been a localised phenomenon as none were seen in terriers relating to Great Glen, Newton Harcourt, Mowsley, and Ashby Parva for example. In Burton Overy they could be eighteen to twenty percent of the lands in some terriers but were mostly five to eight percent, but generally the figure is usually lower, three to four percent at Kilby or two to six percent in the majority of terriers at Saddington.

The situation was different at Great Bowden. Here the thirtyfall formed twenty to twenty-five percent of the lands in 17th and 18th century terriers and the atterall rood eighteen to twenty-five percent. These are in fact medieval units of measurement. For example at Kibworth Harcourt there is a *roda et dimidia* in a late 13th century terrier kept in the Merton College archives (MM 2928) and, in a long early 14th century survey of 8430 lands of the royal estate at Great Bowden, 18% were atterall roods and 28% thirtyfalls (BL Add Roll 6108).

A simple explanation for the employment of these terms would be that they present a more nuanced view of the areas of certain plough ridges. A Fleckney glebe terrier of 1697, which has references in it to the areas of lands "by estimation", makes use of the phrase "Two lands called old roods" when it comes across a pair of them. Maybe in some cases the term related to ridges originally thought of as simply 'roods', and changed when the areas of the yardlands within a particular system were being finalised and greater precision was required.

It is sometimes possible however to suspect that there was a more specific reason for the use of these terms. At Burton Overy a long Latin terrier of Leicester Abbey land contains two entries each consisting of a run of thirty lands of a rood apiece. Either in the margin or set between the lines there is a statement in a different hand that in both cases four

of these lands were roods and a half. This might be a way of correcting an earlier under-assessment, or of being able to say that both groups were to be regarded as eight acres in area rather than the slightly more awkward seven and a half (BL Cotton Galba E III). The high number of atterall roods and thirtyfalls in Great Bowden seems to be related to the clear intention shown in the 14th century survey to have big yardlands in the royal estate here. In this document these rather substantial units of tenure were specifically referred to as 'large' virgates.

The statute acre

Was there a meaningful relationship between the measurements in open field documentation and the statute acre of 4840 square yards? A statute acre was 4 perches by 40 perches, the perch (or rood or pole) containing 16½ feet (5.03 metres), and as a standardised unit of square measurement had been in existence since the 13th century. However the units of measurement out of which the acre was constructed were older than this. The perch of 16½ feet had been used at the royal residence of Yeavering in Northumbria as early as the 7th century, and the acre's breadth of four perches is present in the Burghal Hidage of the early 10th century (Jones 1979, 13; Fernie 1985, 249).

Theddingworth

Of great interest in the matter of open field measurements in southern Leicestershire is a survey of the manor of Theddingworth of 1696 (WRO CR 136 5/11). This describes the open fields, slightly reduced in area following partial enclosure in 1582, in considerable detail, giving the area of each land or group of lands in surveyed acres, roods and perches. These figures can be compared with the sizes allocated to the lands of the 44 furlongs set out in the terrier of 1558–9, which can be identified in the 1696 survey. A similar operation is possible with an unfortunately fragmentary terrier of the lands of Richard Cave of 1580 (ROLLR DE/2/53). The lands in these terriers cannot be individually placed within their furlongs, but there can be little reasonable doubt that the half acres, atterall roods, roods and half roods of the 16th century terriers can be located within acceptable limits in the 17th century survey, and that their sizes are consistent with those in the survey, where they appear with their areas carefully measured. There is nothing to suggest that Theddingworth was any different from other neighbouring parishes in the way its fields were set out and on this evidence what became the statute acre was the unit which framed the layout of the fields in this part of Leicestershire. Discrepancies are bound to exist between the areas of field systems measured in statute acres and the figures arrived at by the process of adding up the areas given in open field documentation – a standard rood was precisely 1210 square yards, but in theory a rood in a terrier could be anywhere between *circa* 900 and 1800 square yards. In addition, it is not easy to be certain about the size of a yardland in any particular place with only a few post-medieval terriers to go on and ascertaining the number of yardlands with a view to finding out what the area of the arable land of a system was, and can very often be, a matter of real difficulty.

There were places in which a different size of perch was used in the layout of the fields, leading to a variation in the size of the acre. Misterton is a large parish in the south-west of the county. It had three settlements, Misterton, Walcote and Pulteney; each with its own field system. Misterton and Pulteney were enclosed in the late 15th century, but there exists nevertheless a terrier of that period for Misterton, probably of a yardland of 22 acres and a half rood (NA SC/10/15). The ridge and furrow of Misterton is badly damaged and relatively few ridges could be measured and matched up with the terrier. But Walcote remained in common field until parliamentary enclosure in 1796, and a series of glebe terriers of early 17th – early 18th century date, looking like any other local terriers, describe 18¼ – 19½ acres, ie one yardland, much the same as the Misterton document. Measurement of the lands of this field system shows that they are much bigger than their nominal sizes and that an acre based on a rood of about 22 feet was used (figure 2 indicates how wide these lands were). In the Hundred Rolls (1279; Bod Rawlinson MS B 350) Walcote is said to have 24¼ yardlands. If, as seems likely, the yardland was about 20 acres, and if these were conceived in terms of statute ones, then Walcote would have contained only something of the order of 485 acres, instead of the 1000 it actually possessed, and the whole parish, with its 118½ yardlands, only *circa* 2,370 acres instead of *circa* 4,400. In this parish the number of yardlands to the carucate was three rather than the more commonly encountered four.

The furlongs of the common fields were set out using measuring rods or ropes. The lengths of the furlongs were variable but tend to concentrate within the range 500–700 feet, which would easily incorporate the classic 660 feet of an acre 40 perches long. As for the widths of the ridges, figure 2 consists of histograms of the widths of a large number of them in southern Leicestershire, measured either on the ground or using online mapping. The importance of the perch of 16½ feet is at once evident in Great Bowden and Arnesby – their profiles are typical of southern Leicestershire (some places have rather more double width lands, 33 feet, than these do, and there are other local variations).

Furlong division

The 1696 survey of Theddingworth enables something to be said about the way in which this measurement was actually used to set out the furlongs (fig 3). It is possible to do this because in addition to their areas the survey also gives the widths of the lands at both ends. So, the furlong called Gravel Pit Leys had 9 lands in 1696, but one of these was twice as wide as the others, so there were probably 10 lands here originally. The furlong is 10 perches wide across its northern side and 9¾ perches along the south; its length was about 41 perches (680 feet). So here was an example of a furlong with plough ridges each one perch wide and said to be in area a rood apiece, giving 2½ field acres altogether for the furlong. The 17th century surveyors made the area 1 acre, 3 roods and 8 perches. Similarly with Mill Furlong, also in Knallings Field; this was 60 perches across along the northern end and originally had 60 quarter acre lands, reduced by various amalgamations to 51. Its customary area would have been 15 acres; in 1696 it was found to contain 16 acres, 1 rood and ¾ perches. However, a land 16½ feet across did not automatically indicate a rood; Wheybrook was short, only 239 – 299 feet long (14½ -18 perches), but with a width of 41 to 42 perches had 42 lands each said to be half a rood (5¼ field acres, 5 acres and 6 perches in 1696). Another way in which ridges of this size could be formed is seen in Horspool Leys (Horse Poole Furlong), where a breadth measurement of just over 4½ perches was doubled to give nine lands each half a perch wide and 500 feet (30 perches) long. By way of contrast Gausthill (Gosthill Furlong)

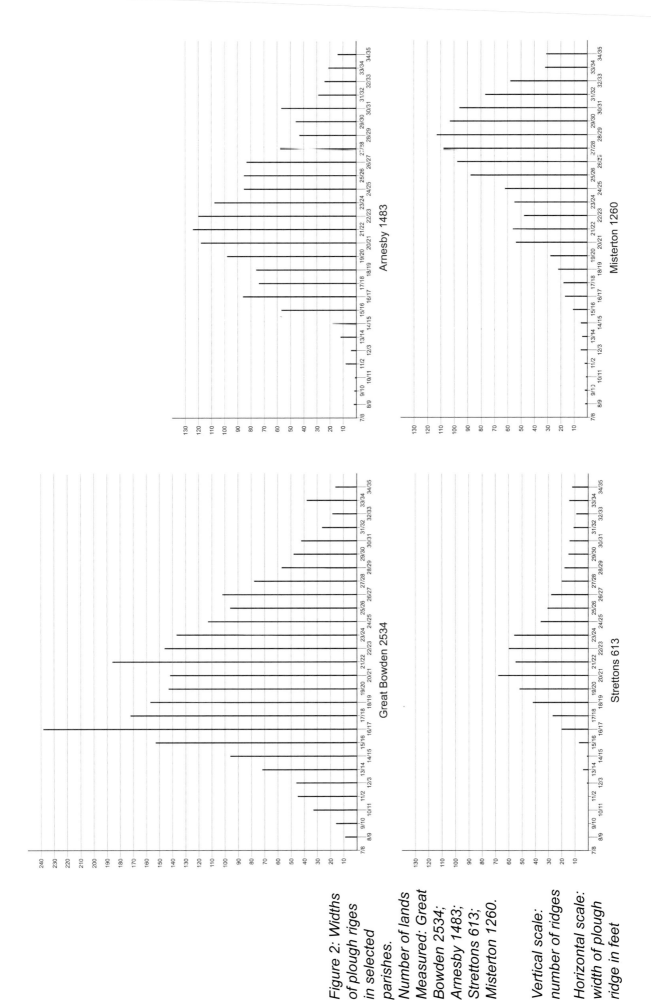

Figure 2: Widths
of plough riges
in selected
parishes.
Number of lands
Measured: Great
Bowden 2534;
Arnesby 1483;
Strettons 613;
Misterton 1260.

Vertical scale:
number of ridges

Horizontal scale:
width of plough
ridge in feet

Great Bowden 2534

Arnesby 1483

Strettons 613

Misterton 1260

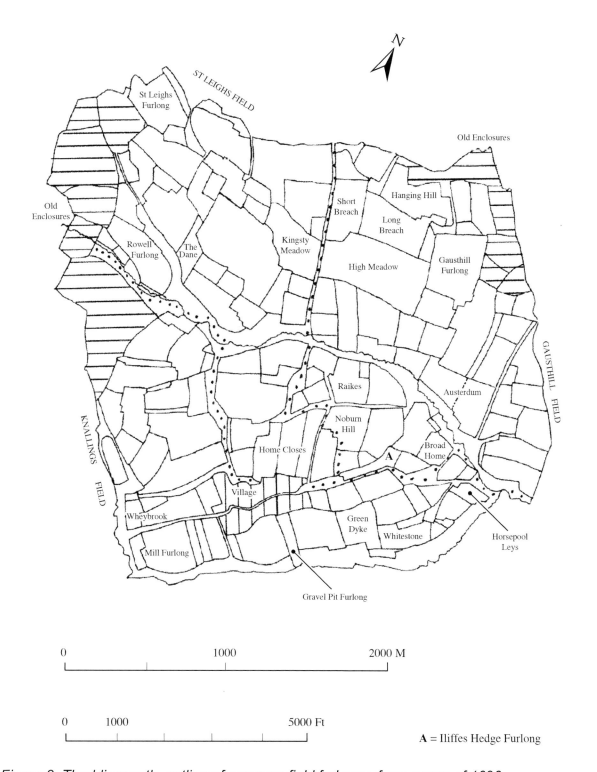

Figure 3: Theddingworth, outline of common field furlongs, from a map of 1696.

was 54 perches in breadth and 1300 feet (78¾ perches) long. Its length gave the 54 lands here an area of half an acre, giving 27 field acres, but by survey 25 acres, 2 roods, 24 perches. The actual practicalities of setting out furlongs could involve a degree of subtlety. The furlong called The Dane (St Leighs Field) had 24 lands said to be a rood apiece. It was 26 perches along the north and 24½ perches along the south. Overall its plough ridges were just over 16½ feet wide, but by way of internal

compensation there was a difference between the ridges in the short part of the furlong (17¾ feet wide) and those in the longer portion (15¾ feet). The area of the furlong using open field measurements would have been 6 acres; in the 17th century survey it comes out at 7 acres and 17¼ perches.

It might be the case that the length of a furlong was insufficient to provide lands of the desired area. The answer was to reduce the number of lands 16½ feet wide to a smaller

149

number of wider ones. Figure 2 shows that many ridges were about 22 feet across. This figure had the intelligible relationship of 1⅓ to 16½. To achieve a set of 22 foot lands all that had to be done was to multiply the number of measured perches by three-quarters. Whitestone Furlong will serve as an example. The western portion is only 260 feet (16 perches) long and 24 perches across. In order to get lands of a more acceptable area the 24 perches were reduced by three-quarters to 18, which was the number of half rood lands 22 feet wide actually there. The acre which lay behind these area measurements was the statute acre based on the perch of 16½ feet, yet this measurement nowhere appears.

Lands would vary in width depending on their position in the general shape of the furlong. Noburn Hill near the Demesne Closes in Theddingworth consisted of several distinct blocks of land. From the south was a run of 22 / 23 perches reduced by three-quarters to provide 17 lands 550 feet (33 perches) long and 22 feet across, each said to be a rood. There followed 29¾ / 30 perches, giving 29 lands 16½ feet wide and 800 feet (48 perches) long, also roods. Finally came a short run of 4¼ / 3 ½ perches, with narrow lands 9–12 feet across, rather irregular, representing the ploughing up of land taken from a trackway, a very common phenomenon.

In general the furlong shapes and the sizes of the lands within them reflected the natural topography, breaks of slope, streams, minor hills and small valleys. However, there are frequently patterns in the internal layout of furlongs that are nothing to do with a response to topographical influences. At Saddington for example there is a run of 16 lands *circa* 19 feet wide (¼ acres) marked off from the similar lands on either side by a single ridge 8 feet wide. Elsewhere very wide lands can serve to define runs of a particular type of plough ridge. At Wistow there is a furlong consisting of blocks of 10 and 12 lands (?atterall roods) 22 to 24 feet across separated by a single land just over 30 feet wide (½ acre), and another with similarly uniform runs of 8, 9, and 15 lands separated by lands like this. In many parishes there are rectangular furlongs divided into smallish groups of differently sized lands with no markers between them, as at Shearsby where there is a furlong consisting of 10 lands 20 feet wide (¼ acres) and 8 lands 16½ feet wide (?thirtyfalls), with no change in the length of the furlong to account for the difference.

Field systems – their development and some thoughts on chronology: the case of Great Bowden

One explanation for the grouping of lands of different areas in blocks within the same regularly shaped furlong comes from the 14th century survey of 18 carucates at Great Bowden, covering the land of the royal estate described in Domesday Book (Great Bowden Heritage and Archaeology 2011; fig 4). The carucates are divided into two groups, ten associated with the lord (the king and the Earl of Cornwall, who held Great Bowden from 1330 to 1336), and eight belonging to the freemen. These carucates are substantial chunks of land, not assemblages of plough ridges scattered throughout the system; the ridges are identified by their areas and furlongs, moving in a clockwise direction through the four fields. The lordly land is mostly described in decimalised units, 40 or 20 roods, 40 half acres, 10 half roods, the free land in duodecimal groupings, 32 roods and a half, 4 thirtyfalls.

The carucates were not compact blocks because four out of the eighteen were omitted. Of the free land were *terra Bonere* (Boner's land, one carucate; the name Boner occurs in a 14th century document relating to Great Bowden; Stocks and Bragg 1890, 162) and the glebe (two yardlands); of the lordly land, 2½ carucates belonging to the king, quite possibly the demesne, were absent. Also excluded from the survey were another four carucates which did not belong to the Crown, derived from land assigned to the Countess Judith in Domesday and which turn up in later medieval records as part of the group of estates known as the Honour of Huntingdon. Taking into account the reduction of one half in the assessment of the royal land at Great Bowden shown in Domesday Book, and what seems to be the return of a carucate by the Crown to the land belonging to Judith, then the original assessment for the whole of Great Bowden would appear to have been 22 carucates, which would give a yardland figure of 88, which is exactly what was said to be the case at enclosure in 1776. However, in the early 14th century the carucates and consequently the yardlands were not all of the same size; the free yardlands had 36 acres and the lord's 40. These are quite large figures.

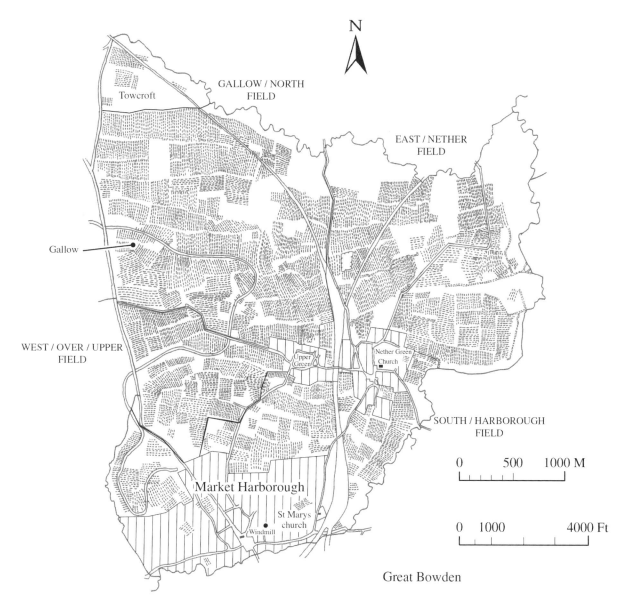

N

GALLOW / NORTH
FIELD

Towcroft

EAST / NETHER
FIELD

Gallow

WEST / OVER / UPPER
FIELD

Upper
Green

Nether Green
Church

SOUTH / HARBOROUGH
FIELD

0   500   1000 M

0   1000   4000 Ft

Market Harborough

St Marys
church

Windmill

Great Bowden

Figure 4: Great Bowden, ridge and furrow.

Quite often the furlongs are referred to as *culturae*, a term commonly used in this way in medieval documents, but here frequently also employed to indicate the subdivisions within them – "on Pylwelle Furlonge…next the *cultura* of Adam de Myners", "In both *culturae* on Wilyspyt". The *culturae* are often marked off on one side by triangular plough ridges known as gores:

"the western part of Le Nethyr Goseakyr next to a certain gore there towards the west".

The clearly defined blocks of plough ridges noticed in other parishes would be in all likelihood further examples of complicated internal tenurial arrangements similar to these.

The regularity of the way in which the holdings are set out in the survey is striking.

Time and again there is the suggestion of a planned series of furlongs with standardised acreages and internal arrangements; for example, in Seke Furlong (East Field) the freemen had 32 half roods and the earl 20 roods; in Hocstoc (South Field) the freemen had 32 thirtyfalls and the earl 20 roods. Precisely laid out furlongs like this may indeed have existed but it is possible to show that a fair number of the entries relate to portions only of larger units of land of unknown size ('in the southern part of the top of Langepole', 'the northern part of Longe Helryne').

When a holding not actually listed in the survey, but which existed at the time, such as the glebe, is added to the furlongs then the neat arrangements of acreages within them suggested by the survey can be lost. It is particularly noticeable with the lordly land just how irregular the arrangements could be – there are a very significant number of lands quite outside the range of decimalised units that characterise this part of the survey – groups of 3, 6, 18, and 19 lands are not uncommon.

It is likely therefore that what the survey shows is not the complete setting out of an entire system but rather the result of the way in which the plough ridges were distributed amongst the various carucates. This would have been done after the arable land had reached its fullest extent. A single furlong name refers to the process of expansion of the ploughed land – in the North Field some land was described as "lying towards Breck next to the king's gore". This name contains the Old English element *brec*, meaning land newly broken up for cultivation. Of greater significance is the presence in the survey of a large furlong in the north-west of the parish called Syrdaycotys (Shirtycotes in post-medieval terriers). This unusual name is derived from a set of Old English words which together signify 'fair-

Figure 5: Kibworth and Smeeton, ridge and furrow

weather shelters', a reference to the practice of creating shielings or temporary structures on pasture land in summer (Cox 2009, 176–7). The exact location of Shirtycotes is not known, but the order in which the name occurs in the survey suggests that it lay somewhere to the east or north-east of Gallow in the North Field of Great Bowden (fig 4). There is evidence therefore for the incorporation of land formerly used for pasture into what became the arable of the common fields.

The Kibworths

Seven kilometres to the north-west of Great Bowden are the two Kibworths, Harcourt and Beauchamp (fig 5). The boundary between the western parts of the two parishes works its way around and cuts through pre-existing furlongs. There could therefore have been an earlier, smaller, undivided field system here. The boundary also runs through a piece of land called the Carrs, a name derived from the Old Norse *kjarr*, meaning a damp area with brushwood on it. Both Harcourt and Beauchamp had a number of Carr Furlongs. A drift way had once run down to this zone; its funnel-shaped outline is visible in the furlong pattern, pointing not just in the direction of the Carrs but also more generally towards such significantly named furlongs as the Breach and Green Marsh. It had been ploughed up and converted into a series of small ridge and furrow furlongs called The Ridgeway.

In Kibworth Beauchamp another drift way, the northern part of which, as Weir Lane, is still in use, makes its way towards the village from the extensive low-lying and watery zone, probably originally pastureland, in the southeast of the parish. Before enclosure in 1779 this was the Nether Field, and consisted of a series of uniform, parallel sided furlongs. At Domesday there were two quite independent field systems, Kibworth Harcourt with 12 carucates and Kibworth Beauchamp with 11¾, both with 48 yardlands. This would not have been possible until the full amount of carucated land had been taken into cultivation, which would have entailed the abolition of the pasture

Figure 6: Ploughed up trackway, Burton Overy (photo by permission English Heritage (NMR) RAF Photography)

in the southeast of what became Kibworth Beauchamp and the sharing out of the rough uncultivated land in the western part of the original land unit. There is evidence here for at least two main phases in the development of the medieval field system, rather similar to what seems to have happened at Great Bowden.

Other villages

Similar observations can be made elsewhere in southern Leicestershire. At Smeeton Westerby, immediately to the south-west of Kibworth, two drift ways are visible in the ridge and furrow, leading from the settlements towards a continuation of the low lying zone seen at Kibworth Beauchamp, and as at Kibworth, ploughed up into long furlongs of a generally uniform width (fig 5 lettered A and B, east of Smeeton).

At Burton Overy at least one drift way appears in the furlongs leading away from the village towards low lying land near the Burton Brook (fig 6). At Theddingworth the track leading out of the eastern side of the village can be seen from a strip map of 1696 (WRO CR 136/M8) to have been much wider originally, having been narrowed by the creation of a furlong called Iliffes Hedge (fig 3 marked by letter A). It ran into a funnel-shaped area, also ploughed up, called Broad Home. There are several tracks and drift ways in Theddingworth which led to areas on higher ground that, when turned into common field furlongs, were given names which said something about what they were

like or their origins – Long and Short Breach; Hanging Hill Leys, from *hangende*, land on a steep slope, Gausthill Furlong, containing the Old English *gorst*, gorse; Santleys (St Leighs), a reference to its sandy nature, Rowell, from *ruh hyll*, or rough hill (Cox 2009, 270–273).

These observations can be taken to show two broad phases in the development of the local field systems, although the reality would have been much more complicated. There was a zone of arable land around the focal points that eventually became villages. Some of these inner furlongs could be relatively small, as at Laughton, Shearsby and Burton Overy (see also fig 6) and possibly retain the outlines of earlier systems. Others however were very long; at Kibworth they could run for a kilometre or more and represent substantial acts of planning, in one case clearly laid out on top of a high status Roman site, to the east of the mill mound above Kibworth Harcourt (fig 5). (Some of the furlongs north of Kibworth Harcourt have ditches underlying their headlands. This is unusual and archaeological investigation of them might throw light on when these particular furlongs were laid out). In addition, there were considerable areas of grassland of high quality near streams and rivers but also rougher grazing in both relatively high and low locations outside the arable core. This grassland could have contained places associated with the seasonal management pf grazing – Syrdaycotys in Great Bowden would have been an example; there was another furlong with this name in Newton Harcourt (Cox 2009, 300). There were Hardwicks towards the eastern boundary of Ashby Parva and in Beesicke Field in Mowsley (Cox 2009,199). The name comes from the Old English *heorde-wic* or herd farm (Cox 2005, 47). There is also the possibility of infield-outfield cultivation, in which an inner zone was kept in permanent cultivation, while some of the outlying land was ploughed up from time to time.

A context for this earlier phase of landscape organisation can be sought in the activities of the kings of Mercia in the 8th and 9th centuries (Oosthuizen 2007). Following the absorption of the Middle Anglian peoples by the Mercians and the foundation of the see of Leicester in 737, this area took on a particular significance for the Mercian royal house. Aethelbald held a council at Gumley in 749, Offa in 772 and 779 (the name could then have applied to a wider area than the present day parish); and a charter of Beortwulf was issued *aet Glenne* in 849. The attractions of hunting could have been a factor in this; the woodland at Gumley to some extent still remains, but the real purpose was for the king to assert visibly his authority over newly subordinated land and subsequently to maintain it. To facilitate this, reliable sources of foodstuff would be needed, as well as storage places and official staff to make possible these immensely important gatherings.

Some local place-names could be the result of royal interest in the area. Kibworth, Cybba's *worthy* or enclosure, might have played a significant role in these royal activities – the element *worthig* can be associated with 'a headquarters or place of status' (Faith 1997, 32–4). There are also Burton, the *burh tun* or place with or near a fortification (close to the Roman Gartree Road); Carlton, *ceorl tun*, the establishment where the freemen were, being distinguished from places more directly involved in the king's service (Faith 1997, 150–1); Laughton, *leac tun*, whose leeks had a good reputation (?in royal feasts); and Smeeton, smith *tun*, the settlement of the smiths (Cox 2009, 21, 27, 154, 245; for Smeeton, Hooke 2011, 24–5). Smeeton's association with smithing and therefore horses is of great interest; there was a Studfold (*stod-fald*, a horse enclosure, or perhaps better, the royal stud farm) beside the track that led towards Gumley (fig 5). There were many furlong names with royal associations in this area. At Gumley there was a King's Meadow Furlong; at Smeeton itself a Kingster, possibly a reference to the king's property or estate; and at Kibworth Beauchamp a whole clutch of royal furlong names, Kingsford Leys, Kingston and Kingstoke Bridge Furlong, the latter particularly significant since it could signify a royal place of assembly. There was also a Stow Meadow, another reference to a meeting place (Cox 2009, 91, 136, 248). These names all occur in the low-lying and relatively flat zones from which drift ways ran towards Smeeton and Kibworth Beauchamp. These would have been just the areas, with good access to water, to accommodate the royal, noble and episcopal retinues which could have been expected to attend the king's councils.

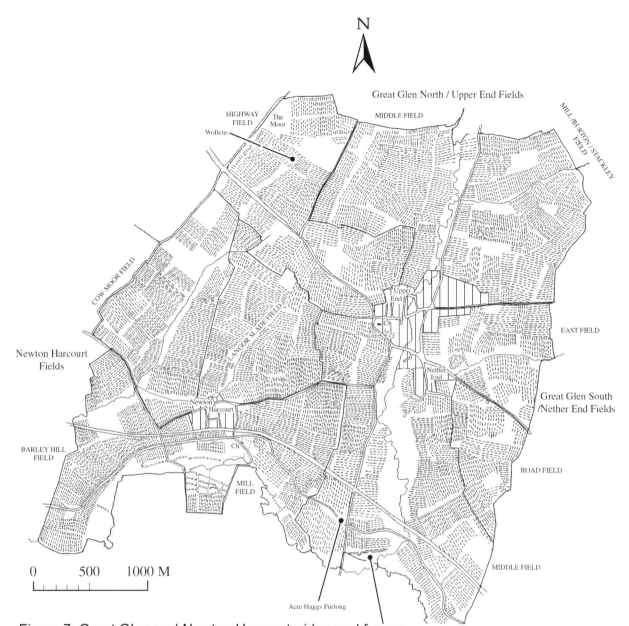

N

Figure 7: Great Glen and Newton Harcourt, ridge and furrow

The case of Great Glen and Newton Harcourt

There were two holdings in Great Glen at Domesday, with a carucage of 18¼. The Hundred Rolls are incomplete, but a reasonable interpretation would see a division into two, a demesne and villeins belonging to the principal manor on the one hand and freemen and the smaller of the Domesday manors on the other. The separation of Great Glen into two parts, the North or Upper End (a series of greens) and the South or Nether End (a street settlement) could reflect this, as would the two quite independent field systems, enclosed at different times in the 18th century (fig 7).

Newton Harcourt lies two kilometres south-west of Great Glen. The name – '*niwe tun*', the new tun – is significant. Its boundary shows

that it had been carved out of land which had at one time formed part of Great Glen. The boundary cuts through furlongs on the north, works its way around existing furlongs on the east, and cuts through another furlong at the southern end – sixteen lands of Acre Haggs Furlong in Great Glen actually lie in Newton Harcourt.

These furlongs were therefore already in place when Newton Harcourt's fields were brought into being. Newton Harcourt, along with Kilby and Fleckney, were chapelries of Wistow, Wistan's *stow*, which received its name as the place where Wistan, a representative of one of the branches of the royal house of Mercia, was murdered at a meeting in 849. This looks like the creation of a new minster church in tandem with the promotion of Wistan

155

as a saint, quite possibly for political reasons, and maybe at the expense of an older minster church at Great Glen (Parsons 1996, 26). All this probably happened before the Danish conquest in 877, which would indicate that large portions of the fields of both Newton Harcourt and Great Glen were already in existence in the late 9th century. Great Glen lost a great deal when Newton was brought into being and yet managed to have enough land for two field systems, with seven fields eventually between them, in the medieval period. The explanation would seem to be that more land was there to be added to the arable from furlongs which appear in the west and north of the parish, with such names as The Moor and Wollens, from *wald*, probably here a relatively high stretch of moorland (Cox 2009, 79–86).

Late saxon and medieval developments

The evidence from Newton Harcourt and Great Glen shows just how much land was ploughed up by the end of the 9th century. This would have been a process which continued into the 10th and 11th centuries, involving, in an agreed way, the division of possibly quite substantial areas of pasture. Some of this grassland seems originally to have been shared between communities, as is suggested by the way in which the parish boundaries of Great Glen and Little Stretton cut through the same long furlongs. Nevertheless, there may have been other factors at work to determine the way in which the boundaries of field systems were finally settled. Generally, parish and field system boundaries follow streams, tracks and prominent natural features. However sometimes there are exceptions that require explanation. The boundaries of the royal manor of Saddington follow remarkably smooth lines, except for the eastern side where there is a stream. Half way along its length the boundary crosses the stream and proceeds to work its way around and to cut through furlongs which might originally have belonged to the fields of Smeeton Westerby, rather as if the high yardland total for Saddington of 54 (13½ carucates at Domesday) was achieved at the expense of its neighbour to the east (fig 1 for the indentations in the boundary which are the result of this process).

By now the amount of land under the plough will have had the effect of so diminishing the pasture that it is easy to see how some

system of fallowing half of the arable annually and grazing its stubble could develop, with resources within each township distributed in line with the carucation. The two-field system, for which there is 12th and 13th century evidence at Fleckney, Theddingworth and Kilby (Farnham 1931, 187; Nichols 1971, 824, 877), might well have been brought into being by the time of Domesday. In that document a vill of twelve carucates in this area would be expected to have land for eight ploughs, and this is generally what is found, with many vills having the 'correct' number of ploughs and some of them one or two more.

The expansion of open field agriculture was not over in 1086. In Domesday Book Stretton appears as a member of the soke of Bowden, with an assessment of nine carucates. By the late 13th century two settlements are visible, with very similar plans, and in the Hundred Rolls very similar yardland totals (Great Stretton 22¾, Little Stretton 24, but almost 27 when it was enclosed in 1771), with plough ridges with a distinctive bias (fig 2). Two late 15th century terriers (BL Cotton Galba E III; NA SC 12/30/7) of Leicester Abbey yardlands in both Strettons show no overlap in field or furlong names, but the 17th century glebe terriers of Great Stretton have a small number of lands in the fields of Little Stretton which include lands in a Ming Field, the name of which might indicate the former existence of a shared (mingled) system. The nature of the land which had been ploughed up is indicated in the Great Stretton terrier, with such significant furlong names as Wolde, here probably a piece of open country where horses were bred and cattle kept, as the furlong names Studwoldhyll and Stok suggest (NA SC12/30/7; Cox 2009, 159–162). The growth and development of common field agriculture in southern Leicestershire spread over several centuries and probably took almost as long to complete as it did to be brought to an end by enclosure.

Changes in the open fields, in the medieval period and subsequently

The common fields of southern Leicestershire were not static but underwent changes that can be read in the archaeological record and in documents. The latter show that two-field systems had been replaced by systems with three or more fields before the end of the medieval period. Also of great significance was the trend towards the conversion of plough ridges into strips of grassland that could be fenced off to provide grazing and hay. This was something which was happening at Kibworth Harcourt in the early 14th century, where documents of this period setting out the components of certain yardlands include references to features called 'twodelrods'. There could have been quite a number of them in existence at this time – there were yardlands with as many as ten (Howell 1983, 90, 272–5). What they really represented is explained in part by a survey of 1609, which lists no less than 649 'todell' roods, arranged evenly around the three fields and 24% of the total number of lands; most furlongs had them. There are no 'todell' roods in a terrier of land in Kibworth Harcourt of 1675, but there are' leys', the universal name for grassed over arable ridges and which must be the same thing, again forming 24% of the total (ROLLR 46/28/150). At this relatively late date we will be looking at a system of convertible (or up-and-down) husbandry which involved the creation of quite considerable areas of grassed-over ridges, which could be left for a period of years before being ploughed up again.

Archaeology can document changes in the physical components of these fields. The amalgamation of individual ridges has already been commented on. A ridge could be driven through a headland to join another ridge to form what is called in terriers a 'through land'. Furlongs could be amalgamated or subdivided. At Theddingworth, Austerdum in Gausthill Field (fig 3) consisted originally of two distinct furlongs separated by a track which formed part of a north-south drift way; its southern termination continued to be marked by a triangular indentation in the field plan of 1696 (WRO CR136/M8). In the same parish the east-west furlongs Upper and Nether Raikes had a small furlong (the Furlong twixt Raikes), also running east-west, inserted between them. There are a surprisingly large number of places with evidence of cross ploughing, the ridge and furrow being turned through ninety degrees, as at Fleckney, Wistow, Newton Harcourt, and Great Bowden.

Plough ridges could be shortened and the land left unploughed and grassed over to form the features known as 'hades', which could be up to 30 metres long, with sequences of small mounds indicating stages in the process of shortening; at the end could be a prominent mound where the original turning point had been, the 'knob' of the terriers. Hades exist in a terrier of Henry VII's reign relating to Little Stretton ('cut hades'), and go on to feature abundantly in terriers of the 16th-18th centuries, as in Kibworth Beauchamp in 1712 "two half acre lands lying upon Beck with hades at both ends" (ROLLR DE 472/2).

The documentation of most open field systems will contain references to baulks. These are unploughed strips of land of varied origin. They were found in medieval documents – a deed of 1494 contains a reference to a 'common balk' in the South Field of Great Bowden (Stocks and Bragg 1890, 196). This will have been similar to the Town Baulks encountered frequently in the Theddingworth terrier of 1558 – 9; these were in the main still there in the survey of 1696 and can be understood as access ways through some of the furlongs. Elsewhere they appear as boundaries with specific functions. At Burton Overy the glebe terrier of 1601 has many entries showing arable lands in bundles of 6, 8 or 12 separated by baulks. At other places attempts were made to increase the amount of grassland by making the creation of these grass strips between each arable land a compulsory matter. Newton Harcourt field orders of 1766 are specific about baulk widths: baulks between acres should be 4 feet wide, between roods and half acres 3 feet and between roods and roods 2 feet (ROLLR DG/24/657). Flattish zones between the ridges of former furlongs still remain and could well be the result of such practices

When the long process of the enclosure of the open fields ended in the late 18th century, Leicestershire had become an area predominantly of grassland. Nevertheless, in places, ridge and furrow continued to be ploughed after enclosure had taken place. In southern Leicestershire old enclosed townships had their huge fields subdivided in the earlier 17th century into 'closes' quite often following the outlines of the former furlongs, which were ploughed up again (Goodacre 1994, 108). Flattish straight and relatively low and wide (45–50 feet) ridges in Kibworth Harcourt were the result of steam ploughing, a technique which lasted well into the 20th century, giving over 1000 years of ridge and furrow ploughing in southern Leicestershire.

Acknowledgements

This paper summarises the outcomes of a research group that met at Vaughan College in Leicester. The author would like to record thanks to the late Mrs Kay Gowland for her invaluable help in transcribing documents.

Bibliography

Allcroft, A. Hadrian, 1908. *Earthwork of England*. London: Macmillan.

Beresford, M. W., 1949. Glebe terriers and open field Leicestershire. In: W. G. Hoskins (ed) *Studies in Leicestershire Agrarian History*. Leicester: Leicestershre Archaeological Society, 77–126.

Bowman, P., 1996. Contrasting pays: Anglo-Saxon settlement and landscape in Langton Hundred. In: J. Bourne (ed) *Anglo-Saxon Landscapes in the East Midlands*. Leicester: Leicestershire Museums, Arts and Records Service, 121–46.

Bourne, J., 1996. An Anglo- Saxon estate at Aet Glenne and the murder of St Wigstan. In: J. Bourne (ed) *Anglo Saxon Landscapes in the East Midlands.* Leicester: Leicestershire Museums, Arts and Records Service, 147–64.

Cox, B., 2005. *A Dictionary of Leicestershire and Rutland Place-names*. Nottingham: English Place-name Society Popular Series 5.

Cox, B., 2009. *The Place-names of Leicestershire, Part Four. Gartree Hundred.* Nottingham: English Place-Name Society.

Faith, R., 1997. *The English Peasantry and the Growth of Lordship*. Leicester: Leicester University Press.

Farnham, G. F., 1931. *Leicestershire Medieval Village Notes. Vol. 5.* Leicester: privately printed.

Fernie, F. C., 1985. Anglo-Saxon lengths. The 'Northern' system, the Perch and the Foot. *Archaeological Journal*, 142, 246–54.

Goodacre, J., 1994. *The Transformation of a Peasant Economy. Townspeople and Villages in the Lutterworth area 1500 – 1700.* Aldershot: Scolar Press.

Great Bowden Heritage and Archaeology 2011. *Furlong and Furrow. A 14th Century Survey of the Open Fields of Great Bowden Leicestershire.*

Hooke, D., 2011. References to smithing in early place-names. *Landscape History* 32 (1), 24–25.

Howell, C., 1983. *Land, Family and Inheritance in Transition. Kibworth Harcourt 1280– 1700.* Cambridge: Cambridge University Press.

Jones, A., 1979. Land measurement in England 1150–1350. *Agricultural History Review* 27, 10–18.

Maitland, F. W., 1897. *Domesday Book and Beyond. Three Essays in the Early History of England.* Cambridge: Cambridge University Press.

Nichols, J., 1971 (originally published 1798). *The History and Antiquities of the County of Leicester. Vol. 2, Part 2, Gartree Hundred.* Wakefield: S. R. Publishers in association with Leicestershire County Council.

Oosthuizen, S., 2007. The Anglo-Saxon Kingdom of Mercia and the Origin and Distribution of Common Fields. *Agricultural History Review* 55, 153–180.

Parsons, D., 1996. Before the Parish: The Church in Anglo-Saxon Leicestershire. In: J. Bourne (ed) *Anglo-Saxon Landscapes in the East Midlands.* Leicester:Leicestershire Museums, Arts and Record Service, 11–36.

Phythian-Adams, C., 1978. *Continuity, Fields and Fission; the Making of a Midland Parish.* Department of English Local History Occasional Papers 3rd Series Number 4. Leicester: Leicester University Press.

Roffe, D., 1996. Great Bowden and its Soke. In: J Bourne (ed) *Anglo-Saxon Landscapes in the East Midlands.* Leicester: Leicestershire Museums, Arts and Records Service, 107–120.

Roffe, D., 2007. *Decoding Domesday.* Woodbridge, The Boydell Press.

Stocks, J. E. and Bragg, W. B., 1890. *Market Harborough Parish Records, to A D 1530.* London: Elliot Stock.

Stocks, J. E. and Bragg, W.B., 1926. *Market Harborough Parish Records, 1531–1837.* Oxford: Oxford University Press.

Testa de Nevill, 1923. *The Book of Fees, commonly called the Testa de Nevill. Part 2: AD 1242–1293.* London: H.M.S.O.

V.C.H. 1964. *The Victoria History of the Counties of England. A History of the County of Leicester. Vol. 5, Gartree Hundred.* London: Oxford University Press for the Institute of Historical Research.

Further Reading

Hall, D. N., 1982. *Medieval Fields.* Princes Risborough: Shire Publications

Hall, D. N., 1995. *The Open Fields of Northamptonshire.* Northampton: Northamptonshire Record Society.

Hall, D. N., 2014. *The Open Fields of England.* Oxford: Oxford University Press.

Oosthuizen, S., 2013 *Tradition and Transformation in Anglo-Saxon England: Common Rights and Landscape.* London, Bloomsbury.

Orwin, C. S. and C. S., 1967. *The Open Fields.* Oxford: Clarendon Press.

Rowley, T., (ed). 1981. T*he Origins of Open Field Agriculture.* London: Croom Helm.

Williamson, T., 2004. *Shaping Medieval Landscapes: Settlement, Society, Environment.* Macclesfield: Windgather Press.

Williamson, T., Liddiard, R., Partida, T., 2013. *Champion. The Making and Unmaking of the East Midlands Landscape.* Liverpool: Liverpool University Press.

Abbreviations

BL   British Library

      Cotton Galba E III – Robert Bruce Cotton organised his library bookpresses under his busts of Roman Emperors. The British Library holds this collection and continues this index with the original emperor name (Galba), shelf letter (E) and position of the manuscript (III) ie 3. Under this reference can be found a description of the demesne lands of Leicester Abbey as well as documents unrelated to Leicester about Christ Church, Canterbury.

      Add Roll 6108 – vellum roll containing an early 14th century survey of land in Great Bowden with a rental of 1497 at the end.

Bod   Bodleian Library, Rawlinson Manuscripts Collection

MM   Merton College Archive

NA   National Archives – SC refers to a Special Collection

ROLLR Record Office, Leicestershire, Leicester and Rutland

WRO   Warwickshire Record Office

Leicester Forest, its woodlands and parks

Anthony Squires

Introduction

Most travellers recognise the name 'Leicester Forest' as that of a service station on the M1 motorway as it skirts the western edge of the modern city. Residents of the area know it as an upmarket housing estate. Although important on a local scale, the former Royal Forest of Leicester was, it must be said, a minor property of the crown. It was largely ignored by monarchy until finally disposed of by Charles I in1628

In 1948 Levi Fox and Percy Russell published a short but admirable account outlining the history of the Forest. (Fox and Russell 1948). Since that time very little on Leicester Forest has appeared in print, yet during the intervening years our ideas of the development of landscapes, including those of royal forests, have made enormous advances. Fox and Russell had knowledge of how parks and woodlands contributed to manorial economies, but had only limited notions as to their form and how they functioned. This paper offers a brief account of the results of recent work on two key aspects of the medieval forest: the parks and the woodlands for the period up to 1628. It is hoped that it will stimulate further study of social, cultural and tenurial aspects of a landscape which has served a major provincial English settlement, Leicester, since Domesday Book (1086) and, it would appear, many centuries before that.

Any topographical study of Leicester Forest presents considerable problems, and these must be addressed at the outset. First, there are no Anglo-Saxon charters for the area of the kind that are numerous in the West Midlands and southern England. Second, later documentary evidence overall is slight, patchy and well scattered, especially for the period 1086 – 1400. Many of the documents for the later years of the Royal Forest, when it was under the control of the Earl of Huntingdon and his relatives, are contained within the Hastings Papers now in the Huntington Library in southern California and these were not available to Fox and Russell. There appears to have been only one perambulation of the Forest boundaries – that from the early 16th century and the unreliability of this was recognised even by those who drew it up. There is a very poor series of Ministers' Accounts and, because the Duchy of Lancaster lands did not technically become Royal Forest until 1399, there are no records of the Forest Eyre. This was the court administered by travelling justices to try serious contraventions of Forest Law. Also, one great handicap for present purposes is the lack of proceedings of the Swanimote Court, which tried minor matters in the forest and which would otherwise be expected to provide many details of local affairs.

The final inclosure of the Royal Forest of Leicester was conducted primarily in a spirit of speed and economy. No map of the awards has been found and very little documentation of use to the modern landscape historian has survived. The inclosure also brought about the extinction of many ancient place names including those of furlongs that can no longer be related to modern maps. This is particularly unfortunate for Lubbesthorpe, which has a wealth of early names to the mid 16th century. The earliest detailed parish boundaries are those shown on the sheets of the six inch Ordnance Survey maps of the 1880s. Unfortunately, much of the landscape of the former Royal Forest of Leicester was not surveyed adequately or at all by archaeologists before the spread of urban development which now covers much of the area. The locations mentioned in this paper have been surveyed on foot and it can be stated that, with few exceptions, they show little in terms of surviving above-surface features. After the inclosure, the landscape was cleared of its woodlands and much of it was rapidly converted to arable. Fieldwork and a search of records in the Heritage and Environment Record (HER) of Leicestershire County Council have shown that virtually nothing of relevance can be deduced from the present fauna and flora. The problems of recognising the existence of early woodland and its forms are outlined in Section VI below. The problems revisiting Fox and Russell are therefore considerable, but all is not lost!

I Background to the royal forest

The physical background

The land, part of which the chase and later Royal Forest of Leicester occupied, takes the form of a low sausage-shaped plateau some 14 miles long and 3 to 4 miles wide situated between the Rothley brook in the north and the river Soar in the south (fig 1). It borders the northern and north-western side of Leicester and extends from the present Beaumont Leys in the north-east to the village of Earl Shilton in the south-west. The surface is gently rolling and rises to a maximum height of 338 feet at Desford Cross Roads (SK456020). There are only a few steep slopes, for example at Mowmacre. Some water courses drain to the north and the Heathly Brook, however most drainage is predominantly to the south, i.e. to the river Soar; the shallow valleys providing routes to the interior.

The surface geology of the plateau is dominated by extensive swathes of boulder clay, the precise distribution of which is a key to the location and history of the woodland and, to a lesser extent, the parks. The clay is interspersed with small patches of more easily worked and better drained glacial gravels and alluvial deposits. The natural vegetation of most of the plateau is, or was, damp oakwood. Before the advent of modern agriculture, neutral grassland covered the better drained soils and small patches of acidic soil supported natural heathland, e.g. near Peckleton where patches of gorse and bracken are still visible in hedgerows

Throughout the medieval period the whole plateau presented a barrier between the town of Leicester and the north-west of the county. At the same time the heavy nature of the soils discouraged attempts at exploitation for agricultural purposes other than grazing. Lacking other significant natural resources, the economy of most of the area remained based almost entirely on trees and grass from the Norman Conquest to the early 17th century.

Forest and chase

The area under examination here has been variously known as 'the Chase of Leicester', 'Leicester Forest', 'the Royal Forest of Leicester' and simply as 'the forest' (fig 1). These terms have very often been used indiscriminately and this has given rise to confusion, at least for modern historians.

Until recently it has generally been held that a chase was an area, often well wooded but not always so, under the control of one or more lords who managed it primarily for hunting and recreation. A chase was administered under Common Law and members of local communities exercised rights in respect of collecting wood and grazing domestic stocks within its bounds. Not surprisingly, there was usually a conflict between lord and commoners over considerations of exploitation and conservation of resources.

The early names of the plateau which might give some indication of the nature of the landscape are unfortunately few. Rackham (Rackham 2003, 127–130) lists four terms which he considers are of prime importance for understanding woodland and its destruction. The Old English 'leah' names (a wood, a wooded glade, a clearing in a wood). (Cox 1971, 592) which comes down to us as the modern 'ley', are thinly scattered on the plateau. 'Hyrst', Old English 'a copse' occurs only in Sandy Hurst Wood and Hurst Common. The element 'feld', Old English 'open country', later 'open common land' and later still 'field', is found only at Glenfield. Here the settlement and some of its lands were clear of local woodland, probably much earlier than 1086. (Cox 1971, 497). The fourth and final term 'thwaite', the norse equivalent to 'leah', is found only as one of the administrative areas of the Royal Forest.

The physical nature of a Royal Forest was usually much like that of a chase but the principal difference lay in its administration. In his 'Laws of the Forest' John Manwood (Manwood 1615, 143 section 12) described it as 'a certain territory of woody ground and fruitful pastures, privileged for wild beasts and fowls of the forest, chase and warren.in the safe protection of the King'. This meant that the land, the vegetation ('vert') and the wildlife, especially the deer, were subject to a special jurisdiction. This, the Forest Law, was determined by the King and was separate from the Common Law. It was administered by a hierarchy of royal servants who supervised all aspects of the workings of the Forest including the exercising of common rights, where present, by local people. The term 'forest ring' will be used hereafter to refer to the Forest boundary and particularly that described in the interpretation by Fox and Russell in the perambulation of 1526 (see Section V below).

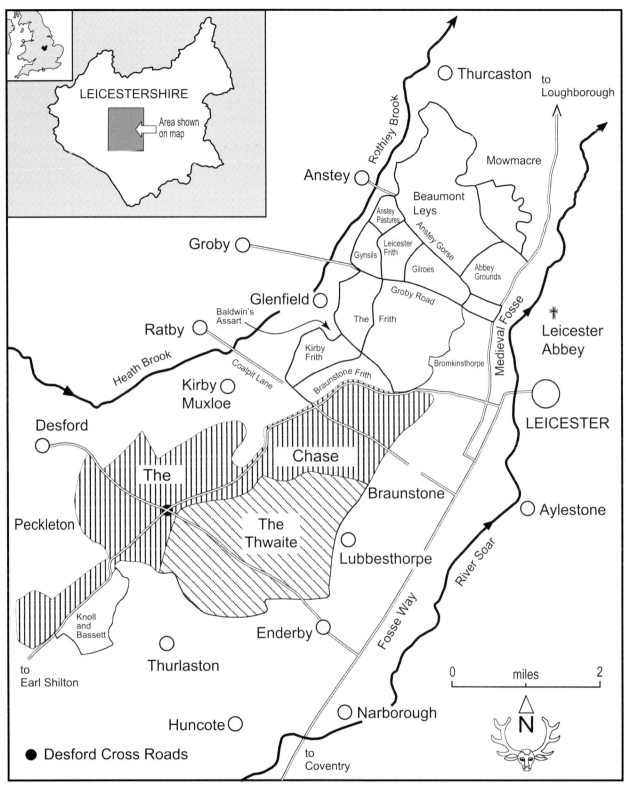

Figure 1: The Royal Forest of Leicester in relation to the plateau

Recent research is rightly questioning this rigid division (Langton and Jones 2005, xi). In it's heyday 'Leicester Forest' was administered as a chase, but the degree and nature of that administration was little short of that found in a Royal Forest. This is partly explained by the dominance over the area of successive very powerful earls of Leicester, culminating with John of Gaunt, son of Edward III. Gaunt was the greatest landowner in England and conducted himself in the manner of an overbearing monarch. After his death in 1399 and the ascent to the throne of his nephew as King Henry IV, this chase of Leicester technically came under the supposed protection of the Forest Law. Certainly a change in the landscape set in and it was one brought about by the long term incompetence, maladministration and blatant corruption of royal officials. There were, too, the increasing

163

demands from local communities in need of expanding their pasture and arable lands. At first landscape change was slow, but by the beginning of the 16th century the terminal decline in value of this royal property was well advanced.

Terms and definitions

At this point it is necessary to recognise and define two terms which, as already been noted, have been used indiscriminately by various writers, including Fox and Russell.

Acre: As Jones succinctly puts it, 'land measurement in England in the middle ages is a subject beset with pitfalls, and one in which we can rarely feel that the sources have been mastered entirely satisfactorily for it provides striking illustrations of taking the information in individual records at face value' (Jones 1979, 18). Until its standardisation at 4840 square yards by Edward I, the 'acre' was the 'customary acre'. There were many different examples of this in use over the country and their values varied widely. Adams says the Leicestershire acre was 2308 ¾ square yards (Adams 1977, 2). When this is compared to the statutory acre there is a potential error in calculations. In addition, there was usually a difference between customary and statute acres and the 'woodland' acre. As a measurement of the latter only one local record of the perch of 18 feet has been found, yet it is known from elsewhere that a perch of 16 ½ feet was widely used. Sizes of woods are given in acres, or in leagues (1.5 miles) or furlongs, and, rarely, in perches.

In order to make sense of an otherwise intractable problem a formula devised by Rackham where a recognisable length and breadth such as a league or a furlong are given (Rackham 2003, 113–4). Thus we arrive at a figure for Hereswode of approximately 6,000 acres[1].

Frith: The term 'frith' has been variously interpreted as 'wooded countryside', 'scrub on the edge of a forest' (Cox 1998, 238), 'poorly stocked woodland composed of inferior timber and scrub' (James 1981, 67) and 'land overgrown with brushwood, scrubland on the edge of forest' (Gelling and Cole 2000, 224). In the New Forest it signified 'copse wood'

1 The Rackham formula is n miles x n miles x 1.2 x 640 x 0.7, so here we have for Hereswode 7.5 x1.5 x 1.2 x 640 x 0.7 = 6048 approx. 1.2 is an adjustment factor which Rackham adopts.

(Wise 1883, 183) while in Duffield Frith it denoted a private forest (Rich 2005, 44). The diverse nature of all of these definitions is recognised and, in view of the great scarcity of documentation, endeavours will be made to interpret the 'frith' of the study area bearing all this in mind.

Woodland and parks in Anglo-Saxon England

Domesday Book provides a limited snapshot of late Anglo-Saxon England. In recent years a considerable amount of research has given valuable insights into the probable nature of pre-Conquest wooded landscapes. At this point in our narrative it is appropriate to consider some of the key points which may be considered relevant to the study of the early landscape of the former Leicester Forest.

The idea that the early Anglo-Saxon invaders found a land everywhere covered with vast tracts of forest has long been discredited. Certainly in the mid Anglo-Saxon period, much of lowland England as a whole and the East Midlands in particular were noticeably short of woodland. Much that did exist in England covered considerable areas such as the Weald of Kent. In the more sparsely wooded areas, woodland was present because it was much valued and managed for its economic, social and cultural values. Between the 5th and 11th centuries woodland, as Della Hooke points out, was, as now, 'subject to cycles of clearance and regeneration, regression and restoration reflecting [changing] economies and interests as well as management policies and techniques' (Hooke, 2011a, 144). The landscape of late Anglo-Saxon England was in many respects a 'mature' landscape and in some areas a rich one in agricultural terms.

So what was the nature of wooded landscape in later Anglo-Saxon times? Hooke, in a recent magisterial review of the evidence, makes a strong case for believing that 'natural wooded landscapes were probably a mosaic of thicker woods….. and clearings of various sizes, with the nature of the woodland also influenced by geology and the main tree species present' (ibid). By late Anglo-Saxon times in the East Midlands any connection with the 'wild wood' of post-glacial times had long been forgotten and the woodland present was all secondary woodland. The same writer mentions the importance of woodlands not only to local but also distant communities and their patterns of communication

A variety of woodlands was essential to the Anglo-Saxon economy. Some were fenced and managed as coppice for the production of underwood. Others served as areas of grazing between individual or groups of trees. Hooke suggests that the larger areas of woodland – the 'wood pastures' – were places of seasonal grazing and also for royal hunting and that they even played a part in territorial boundaries and long distance communication networks (Hooke 2011b, 114). To date, and without evidence from Anglo-Saxon charters, neither of the last two ideas has been recognised for the areas of this study. Wood pasture could remain for centuries without much or any regeneration taking place and this was most certainly the case with the landscape of Leicester Forest. Also, in some areas where little or no control of grazing existed, woodland could degenerate to heathland. In such cases and where population pressures remained high, woodland may well not have had the opportunity to regenerate leaving a landscape of gorse, bracken and heather.

The place-name evidence for woodland is mentioned below but here we note two woodland-related terms, both derived from Old English. The first is '*haga*', the exact meaning of which has been much debated. In Domesday Book '*haga*' most commonly became '*haia*' and discussion has centred on its meaning regarding an enclosure. Mileson suggests 'rather than being full enclosures, the more permanent 'hays' were probably linear or curving earth works used to retain game in certain wooded areas…to trap animals in the final stages of the hunt' (Mileson 2009, 134 in f/n). Hooke says that the evidence from Anglo-Saxon charters from other parts of the country suggests a *haga* was an enclosure into which deer could be encouraged as a readily available source of venison (Hooke 2011a, 166). Liddiard is clear: the haga must have been a deer enclosure or small hunting park (Liddiard 2007, 6–7). The distribution of the two terms in the post-Conquest West Midlands for example, was such that 'the status of the *haga* or *haia* as a deer enclosure is not in any doubt'. He also maintains that Domesday Book massively under-recorded the numbers of parks in existence at this time. *Hagas*, like woodlands, were sometimes simply omitted and elsewhere the two features were always

recorded separately. Hooke (*ibid* 167) also recognises that the Norman Kings were establishing Forest Law over areas where hunting was important in Anglo-Saxon times. Again, most of her evidence is derived from descriptions of charter boundaries, particularly from the West Midlands, a source denied us for Leicester Forest. Mileson cautions against assuming that the earliest Norman parks were simple adaptations of early 'hays'. 'Often there was a disjuncture between these features in both chronology and purpose' (Mileson 2009).

Probably the single most widely occurring place name associated with early woodland is '*leah*'. All authorities agree that in its early appearances it means 'wooded countryside'. It later came to mean 'pasture' or 'meadow' under the spelling 'ley' and was usually found in a compound form with a personal name or a topographical feature. The distribution of each example of the term backed by an early and sound pedigree is clearly important, but such meaningful data for Leicester Forest alas eludes us at present.

Other place-names indicating woodland are at present of minor importance. The term '*sceaga*' meaning 'shaw', 'a small wood' occurs only at Shaw Farm at Potters Marston, away from the plateau. The element '*feld*', Old English for 'open country', later 'open common land' and later still 'field' is found only at Glenfield. The occurrence and significance of the terms '*hangra*', 'a hanging wood'; 'holt', 'a small wood' and particularly '*wudu*', 'a wood' must await Professor Cox's forthcoming work on Sparkenhoe Hundred place-names. The few 'heathley' terms, Old Norse 'heath', 'uncultivated land' (Cox 1971, 587), for example Heathly Brook and Heathly Lodge at the Desford cross roads, place the heathland, perhaps not surprisingly, in the western section of the plateau.

Finally, the familiar Saxon 'ham' and 'ton' settlement names are virtually absent from the plateau. Similarly, ventures into the interior in the forms of '*cot*' Old English 'a cottage, hut, shelter', are similarly absent except at Westcotes. Only the Old Danish '*by*' meaning 'a farmstead' shows clearly in the names of settlements around the periphery.

The term 'park' in post-Conquest England was used to describe an enclosed hunting area. It almost invariably contained deer managed for sport, meat and social prestige. It is described more fully in Section VII.

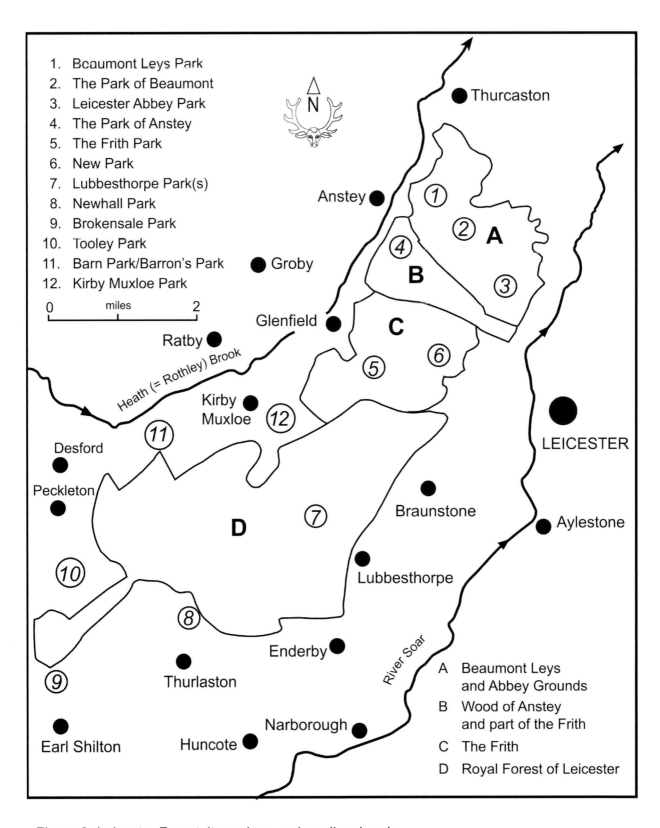

Figure 2: Leicester Forest: Its regions and medieval parks

II The plateau at the time of Domesday Book

The first written evidence for the nature of the plateau comes from Domesday Book (1086). From the data it provides, from early boundaries and from later records four areas can be recognised (fig 2). These form the basis of this paper and are referred to throughout.

Area A	The present Beaumont Leys and Leicester Abbey Grounds lying north-west of the Anstey Lane and bordering Birstall in the east.
Area B	The land between Anstey Lane and Groby Road, two roads first heard of in c1200 (Fox and Russell 1948, 60). This area later became known as Anstey Pastures, Leicester Frith and Gilroes.
Area C	The Frith: The land lying between Groby Road and Braunstone Lane.
Area D	Royal Forest of Leicester: The land stretching from Braunstone Lane to Peckleton. This is the area which is of prime interest and concern to this paper and which will form the substance of the accounts of the woodlands and parks of the Royal Forest.

Woodlands of the plateau in 1086

Several of the manors bordering the plateau possessed woodlands (fig 2). These were as follows, with their approximate acreages in descending order, again arrived at by the use of Rackham's average form factor: Thurcaston (1200); Anstey (600); Desford (300); Glenfield (270); Enderby, Huncote and Earl Shilton (each 200); Braunstone (120); Kirby Muxloe (70) and Lubbesthorpe (50).

The site of the wood of Thurcaston has already been described as a rolling and very extensive area of woodland and pasture which reached southwards from Thurcaston to the northern edge of the town of Leicester (Cabaniuk and Squires 2007, 13–19). Much of its area is shown as Area A on Figure 2. The wood of Anstey occupied part or more likely all of Area B. The wood of Glenfield lay to the south-east of the ancient village.

There may also be other areas as the problem here is probable under-recording which we meet later in section VI. The same

situation has been detected elsewhere in Leicestershire and it is suspected that woodland on Charnwood Forest was also overlooked or ignored. (Squires and Jeeves 1994, 28).

Domesday Book also records a second small wood measuring 6 furlongs by 3 furlongs, i.e. about 150 acres. This belonged to the Countess Judith and its location remains unknown. The present 'best guess' is that it lay outside the West Gate of Leicester in the manor of Bromkinsthorpe which during the middle ages was considered to be within the town (VCH Leicester IV, 375). The location of Bromkinsthorpe is now covered by the area around Braunstone Gate, Leicester, and for much of the medieval period was a liberty within the parish of St Mary de Castro, Leicester. It then became the area known as Westcotes and Danet's Hall (Tudor Road/HinckleyRoad/ Narborough Road).

All but one of the woods of Domesday Book in our study area are described simply as 'silva' and none as 'silva pastilis' (wood pasture) or 'silva minuta' which according to Rackham refers to the coppice tradition (Rackham 2003, 118). The wood of Lubbesthorpe is described as 'silva infructosa' i.e. barren woodland which in some was non-profitable. In Warwickshire, Wager considered 'silva' woods to be underwood, wood pasture or, more likely, a combination of both (Wager 1998, 11). She also considers 'silva' in the same county as 'the fortuitous record of the stage reached by the late 11th century', a description which would apply to Leicestershire equally well (ibid, 140).

It is now clear that woodland did not extend across the plateau in anything like a rolling and unbroken swathe of trees. It would appear that the woods surrounding manor settlements named in Domesday Book probably represented the best areas of tree cover and offered the better grazing. These woods were located on the plateau but were not included in whatever administration extended over the woodland called Hereswode.

The location and nature of Hereswode

There is an entry in Domesday Book for a feature called 'Hereswode'. Its size is given as 4 leagues by 1 league i.e. 6 miles by 1½ miles. Using Rackham's average form factor we arrive at a notional area of about 5,000 acres (Rackham 2003, 114).

Hereswode is described in Domesday Book as '*silva totius vice comitatus*' which has been interpreted as 'the wood of the whole people' hence 'the common woodland' and also as 'the wood of the Danish army' (Cox 1971, 104). There is a parallel here in Nottinghamshire with the Domesday wood of Sherwood which Gover maintains means 'wood belonging to the shire' and where he suggests ancient villages of the shire enjoyed swine and pasture rights and where Anglo-Saxon landowners found a common hunting ground (Gover *et al* 1940, 10).

Hereswode is one of the very few woodlands named by Domesday Book and the term is not recorded before or since. From the data of Domesday Book, knowledge of the post-conquest histories of areas A and B on Figure 2, reference to similar large scale woods of the late 11th century in other parts of England, and some, admittedly simple, calculations of acreages, a provisional conclusion can be made that Hereswode extended over Area D in Figure 2 together with some surrounding parts. It may also have extended north-eastwards into area C, i.e. land to the south-west of the main road from Leicester to Groby. It lay along the 'spine' of the plateau, over mostly clay land, heathland and other 'poor' or 'difficult' soils, ie the Chase, the Thwaite and the Frith as illustrated on Figure 1. Its boundaries were defined pretty much by the field systems of the surrounding settlements, which had almost, without exception, prospered and increased in value during the two decades since the conquest. We can picture an intermittent physical boundary of various walls, hedges and fences, made as and when required with gaps and gates to allow the passage of domestic animals to and from the interior. Only the valuable enclosed woodlands which abutted these territories would be more securely banked, fenced and ditched. In other places the open fields merged seamlessly with open land of the plateau.

That the name Hereswode did not linger beyond 1086 indicates that its identity belonged to an earlier age and that its usefulness was coming to an end. However, its land must have served a wide area as a resource for woodland and grazing. There is no evidence in Domesday Book and none for much later to suggest that any of the manors in a broad sweep south of

Leicester had, at best, anything other than only tiny quantities of woodland of their own. In this case one might ask if there is any evidence that distant woodless manors drew on the woodland and pasture of Hereswode, in a similar way in which manors in Kent and Sussex established 'dens' in the woodland of the Weald.

There is some slight suggestion in Domesday Book that this might have been the case, at least for area D. The entry for Ratby, to the north of the plateau, has some hitherto unexplained and unlocated outliers in Bromkinsthorpe, Desford, Glenfield and Braunstone. The Glenfield tithe map (ROLLR Ti/118/1) records *c*.60 acres of land to the south-east of the present Desford Cross Roads near Ashby Shrubs (the Desford to Enderby Road where it crosses the A47 Leicester to Hinckley road). The same source also marks two smaller enclosures of *c*.40 and *c*.20 acres which were similarly titheable in Glenfield. These lay on each side of a "trumpet boundary" number one (explained below and fig 3). Further anomalies are found at Kirby Muxloe where Domesday Book records 3 bovates that belonged to Lubbesthorpe. Here two freeman dwelling in Bromkinsthorpe had 5 bovates (1 bovate is about 15 acres).

However, there are no convincing signs of a pattern of drove roads of the kind found by Ford in Warwickshire and by Everitt in Kent which would have provided access to the plateau of Leicester from the south (Ford 1976; Everitt 1986). Also, there are no telltale detached parts of Hundreds, no obvious ecclesiastical dependencies, no suggestive field names and no apparent alignment of parish boundaries to suggest this. Further, there are no indications of temporary settlements except those of the men of Desford (see below and in Section III), which may have arisen from the need to manage animals brought for pasture and pannage. It is strongly suspected that the lack of records masks the presence of temporary settlements, especially on the islands of lighter soils. One such site might well have been on the glacial gravels found on both sides of the present A47 in the vicinity of the Red Cow public house in the suburb of Leicester Forest East.

A second question is whether Hereswood, including the land of the later Royal Forest (area D on fig 2) functioned as a wooded common or pasture common, the features of which were often much the same in practice. The nature of a wooded common is well demonstrated in 'The Mens' in Sussex (Rackham 2003, 175). The name here probably derives from the Anglo-Saxon word 'gemaene' (common) which Rackham presumes implied a contrast with the private woods (*ibid*). Unfortunately 'pasture', i.e. common pasture, is rarely recorded for Leicestershire by Domesday Book. (Stamp and Hoskins 1963, 21).

From our knowledge of the histories of other large Domesday woods in other parts of England and from the scanty evidence for Leicestershire, this idea of a wooded common of Hereswode would appear to be a sound one. Here we are seriously handicapped by the absence of the records, particularly those of the Swanimote Court Rolls although a late court roll of 1599, i.e. about 30 years before the sale of the Royal Forest, provides some detail. The conditions under which commoners were then required 'by law to abide' and the 'paynes' (restrictions) which governed their actions are listed (Fox and Russell, 1948, 130–32). Every man and township was to keep the forest mound, i.e. the hedges or fences, which were to be properly maintained. In particular, the inhabitants of Desford were not to 'pluck open the forest Ringe'. The inhabitants of Enderby were required to 'make their fence lawful and good against [the] wood of 'Shorte trees'. There was a problem with cattle and sheep being kept in the forest unlawfully and this was resulting in over-grazing. Also, the foraging of un-ringed pigs was adding to the agricultural and ecological decline which was by then well advanced.

A little further evidence for a wooded common is found on the sheets of the Ordnance Survey's Six-Inch sheets of the 1880s. These reveal six examples of a feature which is known as a 'trumpet' boundary (fig 3). This is usually a short narrow lane which widens abruptly at one end so that it resembles the general shape of a trumpet. Trumpet boundaries indicate access routes for stock from surrounding manors to a central area, in this case the interior of area D. One of these, TB1, indicates access from Kirby Muxloe. This feature has survived to the present as a pathway along a broad open space beside a stream and between two housing estates (SK521040). The tithe map for the same parish shows the outlines of some small enclosures to the south-west of the village.

There is also a detached outlier of the same parish, noted above, called Ashby Shrubs. However, over the area as a whole there are no other characteristic straggling shapes with concave outlines, no early 'common' names are evident and no suggestive field patterns survived to the 1880s. The years following the final inclosure and sale of the Royal Forest brought about a complete transformation of the ancient landscape, particularly with the loss of the trees and woods and the rights of common associated with them.

Although generations of noble earls of Leicester hunted over all four areas of the plateau, their influence over what had been the Domesday Wood of Thurcaston, in area A, slowly declined. Its subsequent history in the hands of the Knights Hospitaller to the early 16th century has been described elsewhere (Cabaniuk and Squires 2007, 13–14).

Area B, it will be recalled, was the site for the larger of the two woods given for Anstey. The names of the villagers open fields are 'Stocking Field ('stocking', land cleared of trees) and Horse rood ('rod', a clearing) are possible alternatives for the site of this wood, but further evidence is lacking. The woodland of area B, much of it wood pasture, had been partly assarted (the clearing of forested land) by 1265, and this area has come down to us under the name Anstey Pastures (Courtney 2003, 41–42; see also the park of Anstey below in section VII). The middle portion on figures 2 and 3 was known as The Marclose in the early 14th century, and more recently (and confusingly) as Leicester Frith (Cox 1998, 189: fig 1). The whole site of area B is defined by the two ancient roads of Anstey Lane and Groby Road and I agree with Fox and Russell that it was not co-extensive with the Royal Forest in 1526 (Fox and Russell 1948, 21).

III The administration of the plateau 108• – 1399

It is difficult to account for the early political administration of areas A to D since all sources are post-Conquest. However, there can be little doubt that in late Anglo-Saxon times this wooded landscape provided wood and pasture for local people (and possibly others from further afield) and was a place for hunting by the nobles and others of the ruling elite. In 1204 the Earl of Leicester claimed 'that his men dwelling in the forest to wit the men of Desford, Bagworth, Glenfield and Thurcaston

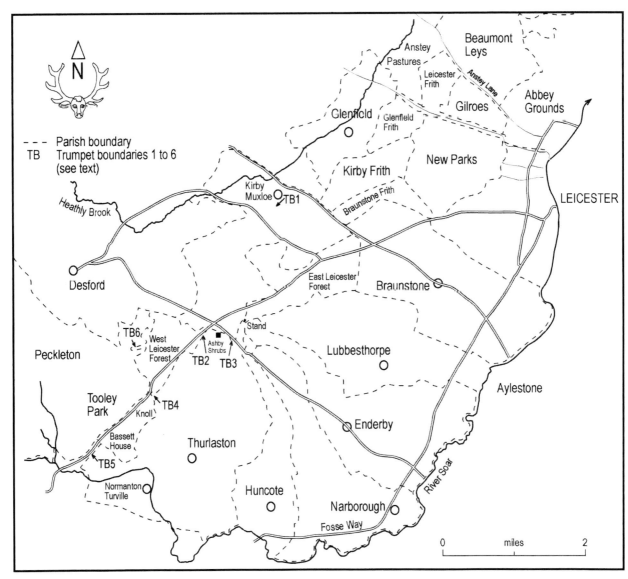

Figure 3 Parish and trumpet boundaries in the 1880s

are able to have common of pasture and the other easements belonging to them as they are accustomed to have in the forest and in the woods, whence the Earl of Winton ought to have nothing but the hunting' (Hastings MSS Vol.1, 34–42). Such disputes were not uncommon in 13th century England.

In 1086 the land of the plateau was under the control of Hugh de Grandmesnil, although it does not appear to have any discernible tenurial connections to his surrounding manors. Thereafter, the lands descended through the Beaumont Earls of Leicester to 1206 and to the de Montfort Earls of Leicester to 1265. In that year the Earldom of Leicester and in 1267 the Earldom of Lancaster were bestowed by King Henry III on Edmund his brother. Ownership of the plateau lands continued with the earls and later dukes of Lancaster. Their lands in Leicestershire were just one element of the many ducal estates

extending across the country. The Leicester property was administered from Leicester Castle, which allowed a tight control of the area. This reached a high point under John of Gaunt (died 1399). In that year Henry of Bolingbroke, his nephew and successor in the dukedom became King Henry IV and areas C and D became *de jure* royal forest.

The parish boundaries

It is now necessary to consider the origins of the parish boundaries shown on the sheets of the first editions of the Six Inch Ordnance Survey and plotted on Figure 3. Fox and Russell took the view that these had been laid down at the time of the 1628 Inclosure and that they demonstrated how the commissioners in charge had allocated to each parish the acreage stated in this Award (Fox and Russell 1948, 108–09). At first sight this seems plausible, but since no map has been found to show the details, it must remain conjecture. A document in the Hastings MSS in the Huntington Library in California headed 'The Contents of several grounds within the Forest or Chase of Leicester taken out of thereto' is dated 1621 and lists the names of men who had 'acquired' royal land by means that are not stated. The names Hastings, Quarles and Stafford appear there and in the Inclosure Award. We can reasonably account for the areas given in both documents by considering that the Award was simply legalising possession of lands which these men already enjoyed in 1621 i.e. before enclosure. This 'theft by stealth', Mileson points out, was rampant in England. 'Where royal pressure became less regular office holders might take over effective ownership, milking the profits and perpetuating park and forest jobs simply to maintain their own privileges (Mileson 2009, 147).

A very different view of the origin of these odd parish boundaries is offered here. Clearly, those of Lubbesthorpe, Enderby, Narborough and Huncote (and possibly Thurlaston), all settlements to the north of the river Soar and south of the forest ring, are the sign of a designed landscape, but not of 1628. These boundaries did not develop slowly or organically over a long period. The purpose of the planning was to formalise the sharing of limited woodland and grazing. At a time when there was little or no need to introduce restriction, animals were turned out onto the plateau to graze as and where they would. From time to time a 'drift' or 'round up' would take place and individual animals would be claimed by their owners. When pressures on resources became too great, it was necessary to impose restrictions on the demands of the inhabitants of individual manors. It was at this point that common rights were established and the sharing of resources placed on a regular footing. Stamp and Hoskins state that the process of the appropriation of common land to particular manors was in operation at the time of Domesday Book but was largely completed by the 13th century (Stamp and Hoskins 1963, 34). The Statute of Merton (1236) which permitted inclosure of common land and waste by lords if sufficient land remained to satisfy the needs of tenants, certainly aided the process. Neilson adds that early common rights were often brought to an end by the growth of lordship and a growing desire and ability of lords to partition areas of waste (Neilson 1942, 58).

The signs of such early designs on the landscape are a familiar occurrence in other parts of Leicestershire and across England. Rowley, for example, describes a particularly interesting example in the Clee Hills in Shropshire (Rowley 1965–68, 48–67). From the summit of Clee Hill lines radiated out systematically dividing the hillsides into segments according to the noble owner's perception of the needs of the inhabitants of the surrounding manors. This resulted in a pattern of parish boundaries which is very much like those in the southern half of area D of Leicester Forest (fig 3). Foard studied Rockingham Forest where the geology and topography are remarkably similar to that of the plateau at Leicester (Foard 2001, 46). He found that detached blocks of woodland were allocated in the medieval period to resolve disputes over common rights, rather than being associated with the original creation of townships by the fragmentation of Anglo-Saxon estates in the mid to late Saxon period. Hooke found that on some Anglo-Saxon landscapes partition had been taking place until the late 12th century and that some parishes show long, thin tongues of land stretching into much of the woodlands (Hooke 1998, 161–62).

We can account for the apparent anomalies at the northern tip of the parish boundaries in area D by taking account of the arrival of the King's Stand (see Section VIII below) in the early 17th century. However, there still remains the matter of who carried out the reorganisation of the landscape. His action was to have a major influence on the development of area D, including the woodland of the Royal Forest, for the following three centuries.

Hugh de Grandmesnil must be a prime suspect for the extension of manorial boundaries. However, there appears to be no manorial connection between the areas of Hereswode covered by area D and the surrounding manors, most of which de Grandmesnil held. One assumes it was sufficient for his tenants to graze their stock and take wood with only the minimum regulation necessary to preserve the noble sport, i.e. there was no need to extend manorial boundaries onto the plateau provided the interests of hunting were not prejudiced.

The activities of the Beaumont earls on their Leicestershire estates cannot be accounted for and they must at least remain suspects.

171

In 1266 Edmund, Earl of Leicester and the king's brother, was given the power to administer his forests, i.e. those at Needwood, Blackburn, Duffield Frith and Leicester as though they were Royal Forests, i.e. under the terms of Forest Law. Here was power indeed, particularly as exercised later by John of Gaunt, Duke of Lancaster. However, the year 1266 appears rather late for manorial regulation of the nature we are attempting to account for here.

An understanding of reorganisation of manorial/parish boundaries in area D must be seen against other events taking place on the plateau. In area A, Simon de Montfort sold 320 acres of his noble wood at Beaumont to Leicester Abbey in c.1240. In so doing he effectively broke up his park of Beaumont (fig 4; Cabaniuk and Squires 2007, 13–19). At about the same time he also gave to Leicester Abbey his valuable wood of 'Doveland' (described below in section VI) in Bromkinsthorpe manor. Again, and at about the same time,

he granted to the Abbey of Leicester the assarts of 'Oselishawe' and 'Langbreche' (fig 5 – Olishawe, Langbrake). The establishment of most of the parks around the periphery of area D meant that access to much of the land they enclosed was no longer available to commoners. The dates of emparkments are considered below. The making of Frith Park, if the dates are correct, was a major upheaval to tenants' activities in area C. The early 13th century was a period of rising population in many parts of England, which produced an increased demand for grazing and woodland products. The formal attribution of wooded areas on the plateau in area D at least helped those manorial lords who were feudal under-tenants to more easily manage their properties. With these considerations in mind the it is believed that the evidence for manorial reorganisation points to the first half of the 13th century and to the activities of Simon de Montfort (1208–65) who entered his Leicestershire lands after 1230.

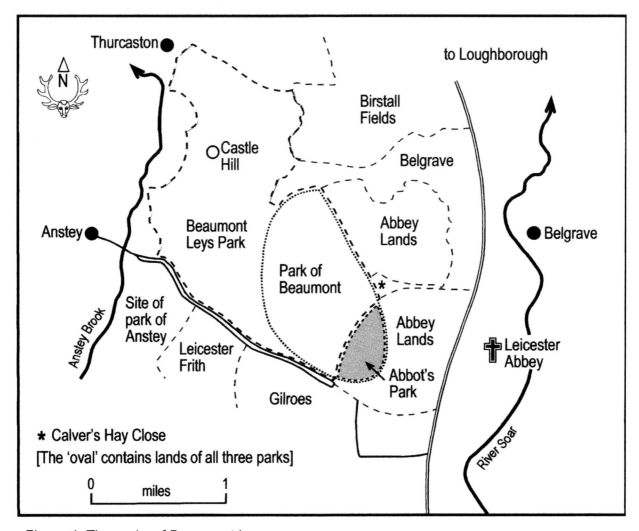

Figure 4: The parks of Beaumont Leys

172

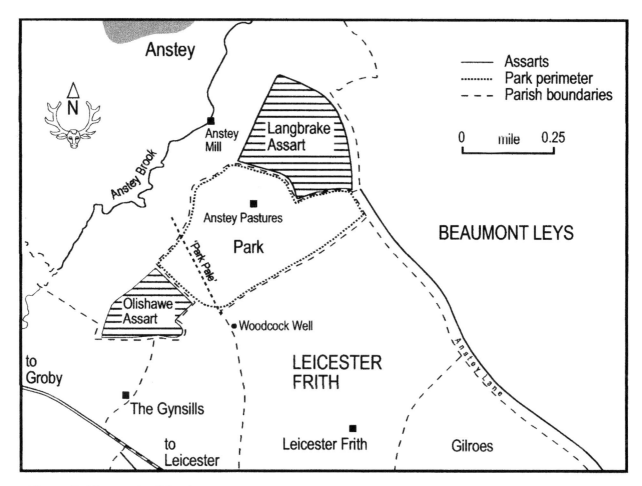

Figure 5: The park of Anstey

Lubbesthorpe

Before closing this section it is worth remarking that the manors which have most obviously been reorganised all drain south to the River Soar. At the same time Desford, Kirby Muxloe and Glenfield to the north, together with Peckleton to the west appear to have escaped the same level of change, yet they all depended on the plateau for wood and grazing. We can reasonably assume that the creation of Barn Park at Desford and Tooley Park at Peckleton (see Section VII below) solved de Montfort's problem in the north-west of the forest. Thurlaston to the south-west, including Normanton Turville, was a large manor and there may have been no need to redefine its boundaries in the early 13th century.

Lubbesthorpe parish (figs 3 and 8) is a special case both within this southern 'block' of parishes and within the bounds of the Royal Forest. The element 'thorpe' means a secondary Scandinavian settlement (Cox 1971, 515) or hamlet and it alone was within the forest ring. In 1303 Lubbesthorpe had been a populous village of 31 families. The Poll Tax of 1377 assessed 12 households and the tax quota for 1445 indicated poverty had

set in. The village had been deserted by the middle of the 16th century. (Parker 1947, 78). A considerable area of its former open field system, the contentious 'Lubbster Closes' of the perambulation of 1526, together with the other lands (supposedly a total of about 300 acres), lay within the forest ring. The furlongs of the open fields had been enclosed at sometime between 1471 and 1550. Finally, the parks, fishpond and warren, all medieval creations, also lay well within the forest ring. Seen in the context of the whole of area D Lubbesthorpe appears something of an anomaly.

IV The Frith (area C)

Area C was bounded by the two ancient routes across the plateau of the Groby Road and Braunstone Lane (fig 8). It was regarded from early times as a 'defensa' area, i.e. a place where deer were given special protection in the breeding season (Fox and Russell 1948, 31). The area has come down to us simply as 'The Frith'. Sometime in the 13th century it appears to have become separated from area B, probably on account of its creation as a park. This may have been at the hands of Simon de Montfort. For this reason it is convenient to outline its history to 1526 in this section.

173

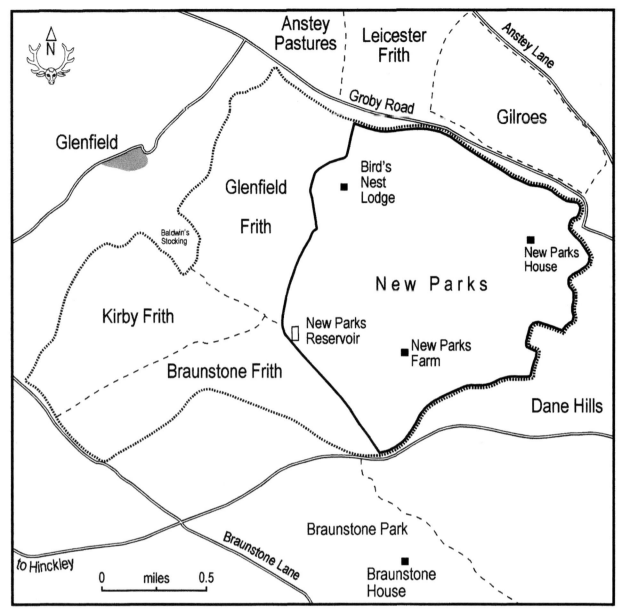

Figure 6: New Park and the Frith

Throughout the 14th century the Frith/area C, was a place where deer could always be found and where prime oak woodland enabled noble lords to dispense gifts of timber to favourites and 'worthy causes'. In 1364 King's Wood, today the site of Meynell's Gorse, was described as 'so full of wild animals of the Duke of Lancaster that it made no value of the pasture of Wheatcroft', which lay on the opposite side of the Braunstone Lane (Fox and Russell 1948, 71). In 1381 Henry Ballard shared with one unnamed other the post of parker of 'the park called the frith'. The Frith lay within easy reach of Leicester Castle, the administrative headquarters of the Leicestershire estates of the Honour of Leicester. An account for the manor of Heathley (sic) in 1406 included the lease of '30 acres of border meadow, 20 carucates of land and the crops and branches

of 23 oaks' preserved in the Frith. There was an additional income from wood sold by the cartload, from logs carried away by the buyers and from bark sales. Much wood was used for the 'reparation and maintenance of the palings there' (DL29/198/3116). The Frith was therefore a place of profit as well as pleasure and in 1444 Henry VI settled it on his intended consort as part of the marriage settlement (Nichols 2/1/783).

The stewardship of the Frith Park was given by Edward IV to William Lord Hastings as part of his stewardship of local duchy lands (Nichols 1/2/380). Again in 1499 Edward, son of the said William, received profits from trees in the park which remained pailed and contained deer (Nugent Bell 1920, 34–35). But by that year the end of the Frith Park was in sight. Henry VIII sent commissioners

174

to conduct a survey of the property. They reported that they found it 'well replenished with deer' for they saw 'by estimation 1000', which is an unlikely figure. There was 'great plenty of wood called old stand but little timber or none'. They noted that lopping and cropping of the main trunks was likely to produce an income of £40 a year indefinitcly and added that if the trees were to be removed and the land given over to grazing, a sizeable income could be assured. At the same time they warned that any such move would mean that the town of Leicester and adjoining villages 'would be greatly hurt and in a short time would likely to decay' (DL43/14/6).

The King now regarded the Frith Park as an expensive luxury and within a short time its 1,584 acres were divided into two unequal parts. The larger was sub-divided into three areas and allocated to the villages of Glenfield (290 acres), Kirby Muxloe (244 acres) and Braunstone (238 acres), (Fox and Russell 1948, 134). It is likely that the new Glenfield Frith, now built over, is on the site of the Domesday woodland (c.270 acres) of that manor.

The smaller of the two parts of the divided Park was retained by Henry who created a new park, now covered by the New Parks housing estate (DL43/6/1, bundle 6 No.1). A description of 1606 simply records 'the King's new park in the frith, from the gate next to Leicester from the pale towards Groby, contained 7 furlongs and comes to in acres 303 acres, 3 roods, 6 foot, price 2s the acre'. (DL43/6/1). Leland records in 1538 that it had a good pale (Chandler 1993, 281). There is no record of the monarch having hunted here or even having visited. Instead, the park was later leased to various persons well placed in royal circles who lost no time in exploiting its resources. A survey of 1606, when it was in the hands of Lord Cobham, referred almost exclusively to the value of its meadow and its grazing for sheep, cows and horses (Nichols 2/1/784). This was entirely in line with the duchy's policy at the time which enabled lessees to sub-enclose for sheep and cattle (Somerville 1953, 307). There is no mention of woodland or a royal visit. The area had been allowed to quietly dispark and one is left wondering why the king created a park here in the first place.

The approximate boundaries of the New Park are shown on Figure 6. The site of Birds Nest Lodge together with a section of its moat, survive today as a public open space. Apart from a short section of bank, which may or may not be a remnant park pale, along the line of the present road 'Park View', nothing more appears to have survived in the way of above surface features.

It is significant that records for 'the frith' for the years 1399–1526 make no reference to it forming part of the Royal Forest yet, as we have seen, it became technically 'royal' in 1399. At the time of its first record as a park in 1297 it was up and running and had been so for many years. The interesting point now is to try to determine when it was emparked and became separated from area D. Since there is no record of this we can make an informed guess, which then leads to an interesting line of thought.

From our knowledge of other medieval parks (royal and otherwise) in Leicestershire (Cantor and Squires 1997, 9–19; 77–78) and elsewhere in England we may postulate this most likely occurred at some point between the years 1200 and 1250, the golden age of park creation (Cantor and Hatherley 1979, 79). If we nominate, say 1250 as our latest date we have a period of about 50 years (1250 – 1297) which we can probably add to the Frith park's existence within its later known boundaries as shown on Figure 6. We may now suggest that the Frith park remained unchanged in outline for almost 300 years (c.1250 to 1526). Further, the creation of the Frith park appears to have been just one of a series of developments on the plateau, already mentioned, in the mid 13th century, which collectively were to shape the landscapes until the next series of major administrative changes three centuries later. We must also remain aware that the land of area C may once have been part of 'Hereswode'.

V The Royal Forest (area D)
The development of area D 1086 – 1399
Mention has already been made that human influences on the landscape of the plateau, including area D, took place from outside rather than from within. In 1086 almost all the surrounding settlements had prospered and increased in population during the 20 years since the Conquest and their open field systems had reached the limits of cultivation against the plateau. Thurlaston manor was

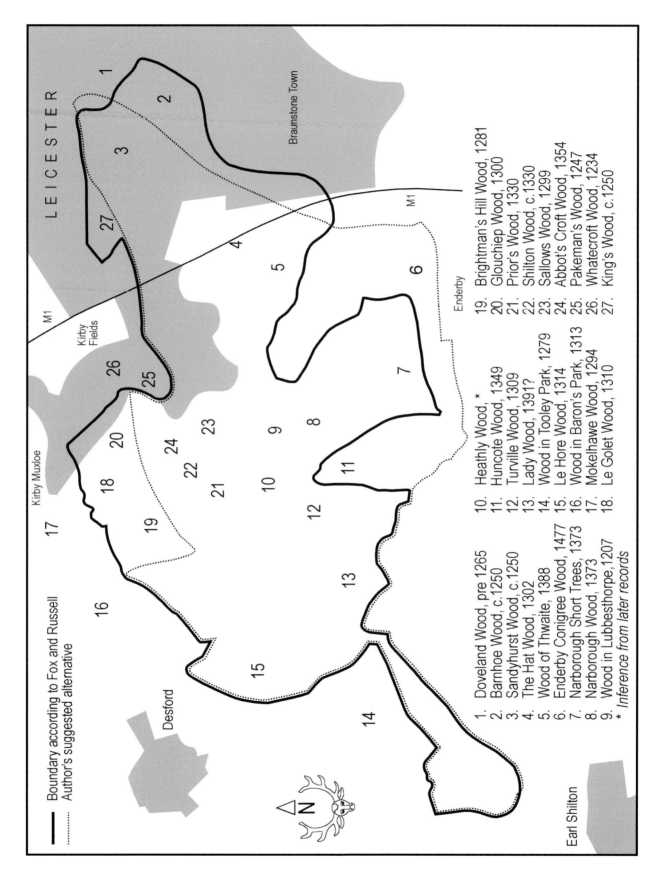

*Figure 7: The
Royal Forest
of Leicester;
its boundaries
and medieval
woodlands*

LEICESTER

Braunstone Town

M1

Kirby
Fields

M1

Kirby Muxloe

Desford

Enderby

Earl Shilton

N

Boundary according to Fox and Russell
Author's suggested alternative

1. Doveland Wood, pre 1265
2. Barnhoe Wood, c.1250
3. Sandyhurst Wood, c.1250
4. The Hat Wood, 1302
5. Wood of Thwaite, 1388
6. Enderby Conigree Wood, 1477
7. Narborough Short Trees, 1373
8. Narborough Wood, 1373
9. Wood in Lubbesthorpe, 1207

10. Heathly Wood, *
11. Huncote Wood, 1349
12. Turville Wood, 1309
13. Lady Wood, 1391?
14. Wood in Tooley Park, 1279
15. Le Hore Wood, 1314
16. Wood in Baron's Park, 1313
17. Mokelhawe Wood, 1294
18. Le Golet Wood, 1310

19. Brightman's Hill Wood, 1281
20. Glouchiep Wood, 1300
21. Prior's Wood, 1330
22. Shilton Wood, c.1330
23. Sallows Wood, 1299
24. Abbot's Croft Wood, 1354
25. Pakeman's Wood, 1247
26. Whatecroft Wood, 1234
27. King's Wood, c.1250

* *Inference from later records*

perhaps the exception. It was large in size and had increased little in value. From the late 11th century it was developed by various feudal tenants and late in the 14th century, probably by 1373, Sir Robert de Swillington, the Earl of Leicester's Master Forester, built his moated dwelling of Newhall (Armitage-Smith 1911, 163–64; see also fig 9).

The pressures on the unenclosed plateau of area D are readily identifiable and little different from those affecting large wooded areas in other parts of England. The demands were for underwood, timber, grazing for domestic stock and pannage for pigs in autumn. Those commoners claiming such rights came also from the town of Leicester. The attempts to meet these demands and at the same time preserve the landscape for the benefit of the deer, kept the earls of Leicester in constant struggle with their tenantry and others.

The granting of assarts was seen as one way of solving the claims of the more important individuals. Royal favourites also benefited. Assarting meant the enclosing of an area of land with a definite physical boundary so that the recipient could make his profit at least with no further reference to the common rights. A particularly large assart was granted at Glenfield in 1358 to one Baldwin. It became known as 'Baldwin's Stocking' and its boundaries are still detectable in the road system at Glenfield which still follows the boundary (fig 6). In a grant of 1307 the Earl of Lancaster granted Thomas Malore permission 'to enclose with a ditch and hedge 24 acres (measured by the perch of 18½ feet) of land adjoining the waste of 'Neustocking'. The ditch was to be 2½ feet deep and the hedge 2½ feet high, never exceeding five feet so that his wild beasts may enter and leave at their will' (Hastings MSS vol. 1, 23–24). A similar grant in 1345 by the Earl of 80 acres to Simon Pakeman – this was the origin of Pakeman wood shown as 25 on Figure 7 – included a similar restriction (Fox and Russell 1948, 46). Trees within assarts could only be felled with the approval of the relevant forest officers.

The scarcity of records is surely failing us here, but it is noticeable how little assarting appears to have been taking place. Also, there are no records for the creation of purprestures. These were illegal inclosures on someone else's property, or the erection, without permission, of buildings where none had

been before. The perpetrators were usually prosecuted in the Swanimote courts and such sites might be allowed to remain permanently on payment of the appropriate fine. There is no evidence for any such sites in area D.

Another notable feature is that there is no mention of the typical and essential crafts and industries such as hurdle making and tanning which one would expect. There appear to have been no forges and even the making of charcoal appears to have left no trace when there was an active market for the product in 15th century Leicester (Bateson 1901, 294–95). Occupational surnames for people in the surrounding villages from the 14th century from lay subsidies and poll tax returns are virtually nil. In Roman times pottery had been produced at Potters Marston and the revival of this in the medieval period is reflected in a grant of 1309 for life by the Earl of Leicester to John Curteys, his potter, of 45 acres of waste in the forest of Leicester at a place called Turville Wood (fig 7; DL25/961). The fuel came from within the bounds of the Royal Forest but the manufacture of the pots took place outside the forest ring.

One gains the impression that by the end of the 14th century there has been remarkably little development within the forest ring since the late 12th century and that the landscape had not changed substantially in character. Apart from Lubbesthorpe, there appears to have been no settlement of any degree of permanence, no attendant churches (or even chapels), few assarts and, again with the exception of Lubbesthorpe, no open fields. The few known medieval pottery scatters support this view. There are no 'green' names and few early 'common' names to suggest organic growth of any kind. Drifts are not mentioned and neither is 'stint', which is the rationing of grazing. Of the typically Norman features, the castles of Leicester, Groby, Earl Shilton and possibly Sapcote were outside the forest ring as were the enclosed parks with the exception of Lubbesthorpe. There were no moated sites or fortified manor houses within the ring. No monastic houses were founded here; there were no monastic granges and no new monastic grants were made after 1265. There is a dominant sense of 'emptiness' within the forest ring; it seems to have been a 'special' place and in detail contrasted sharply with Charnwood Forest a few miles to the north. At the same time we should not see Leicester Forest, area D, as a trackless wilderness. Routeways connected areas of grazing and wound round parks and enclosed woodlands. One also wonders if this huge clay plateau, covered with grass and trees and little else, effectively held back the development of the town of Leicester in the same way that Sherwood Forest restricted Nottingham and Lancaster Forest the town of Lancaster (Short 2000, 135).

The bounds of the royal forest

The bounds of a Royal Forest were essentially a judicial ring around an area of land, its course usually plotted by the use of existing features on the landscape. For the extent of the Royal Forest of Leicester we must rely on the details of the perambulation of 1526, vague and varied documentary references to small sections of the perimeter, mention of landmarks being within or without the Forest and to field survey.

The only known perambulation of the Forest was in existence in 1526 and the details have been plotted on Figure 7. Fox and Russell based their views on 'the general extent of the forest in the 14th century, from deductions from the parish boundaries as they existed before the changes in the 19th and 20th centuries and from information given in the Inclosure Award. (Fox and Russell 1948, 64). They also drew on the details of the original document of 1526 which is among the duchy records in The National Archives (DL/39/5/14).

The perambulation was drawn up as part of an enquiry into the boundaries and state of the landscape prior to the major reorganisation of duchy lands north of Leicester and elsewhere in the country. The handwriting produces certain problems in transcription. A good many of the place names, although legible, cannot be located from modern sources. Further, the compilers were uncertain as to whether or not certain areas – particularly the 'Lubbers Closes' – were within the Royal Forest. An alternative view of the boundaries is presented (fig 7) based on the findings of Fox and Russell but particularly on my own interpretation of the details in the perambulation and from a copy now in private hands. Although the two views differ markedly in places, the approximate area enclosed in both cases is about 4,500 acres. We must also allow that the document may well be a rehash of the bounds of a much earlier

survey, the original of which has not survived, or at least has not been found. One sees here at Leicester a situation similar to that found by Stamper in the Royal Forest of Pamber (Hants), where the 'economic forest' recorded in the Forest Proceedings existed with a larger 'legal forest' laid out by a perambulation but answerable to the Court of Chancery (Stamper 1983). Pettit notices that 'by the 16th century the importance of perambulations was only nominal' and that there existed a Forest and a Forest Proper (Pettit 1968, 7).

VI The woodlands of the plateau

Putting aside these lines of enquiry for the time being, we now move on to examine the woodlands of the plateau, over which the Royal Forest extended and listed on Figure 7.

The problems of interpreting records of medieval woodland are well known (Squires TLAHS 69, 1995, 86–89; Wager 1998, 1–9 and others). Some 'woods' may be enclosed or open or the tree cover so limited as to scarcely merit at least to modern eyes the term 'wood'. Also, woodlands of less than two acres are seldom recorded (Rackham 2003, 137). A wood may change its name to reflect a change of ownership, including when it is divided between an owner's heirs. A wood may be let in parts to persons whose names linger on long after their connection with the wood has ceased.

Woodland is recorded only when it has value; even then it may escape the records. Moreover, woods were not planted; land simply 'tumbled down' to woodland by natural regeneration. The origins of a wood are therefore seldom recorded. When a wood is cleared it is more likely to appear in the manorial records under the term 'assart', 'stocking' and 'stubbing'. The sparse records for Leicester Forest make no mention of the Black Death (1348) and the possible expansion of woodland on a landscape devoid of the activities of a sizeable percentage of the earlier human population.

The documentary records for woodland in area D are meagre and must be augmented by those from the 17th century and later. I have worked through many of the Duchy of Lancaster records and other woodland records in the The National Archives; the Hastings manuscripts in the Huntington Library; the major collections in the Record Office for Leicester, Leicestershire and Rutland, and particularly the Winstanley Papers (ROLLR 16D66 and DG5) and the details provided by the sheets of the first edition of Six Inch maps of the Ordnance Survey. In 1565 Roger Taverner conducted a major survey of all the royal woods in the counties south of the Trent. Unfortunately, the details for Leicester Forest have escaped entry (on TNA LRRO 5/39) and have not been found elsewhere.

Figure 7 brings together the data from all available sources but this list of woodlands is probably far from complete. There were certainly other groups of trees which today we would recognise as 'woods'. The inadequacies of Domesday Book as a record of the woodland of its time have long been recognised. The collection of data depended on the filling in of forms which, according to Rackham, were changed twice for woodland during the survey (Rackham 2003, 111). Leicester was part of 'circuit four', along with Northamptonshire, Oxfordshire and Warwickshire (Welldon Finn 1963, 39). The commissioners for this circuit clearly did not pay attention to recording woodland in the ways their colleagues did on the other circuits. Hooke points out that woodland 'put outside the manor' or 'having passed into the King's hands' may well have gone unrecorded in Domesday Book (Hooke 1998, 150).

Foard writing of Rockingham Forest (Northants) reports a similar situation and says the woodland in the heart of the Forest was 'significantly under represented' (Foard 2001, 44). He adds that Domesday Book appears to omit without comment some lesser woods that, from 13th century records, were known to have been present. Rackham says that half the woodland in the late 11th century was systematically omitted from Domesday Book (Rackham 2003, 120). Wager, from her work in Warwickshire, also suggests that woodlands recorded for the first time in the 12th, 13th or even 14th centuries may have existed at the time of Domesday Book (Wager 1998, 13). She also notes that for Warwickshire, and presumably other counties, Domesday Book excluded 'groves'. Bearing these points in mind and the nature of the management of area D from 1086 to about 1250, outlined above, one wonders if most of the woods in area D were present in 1086 and just how many woodlands were subsumed under the title 'Hereswode'. It is suspected that a great many were and this

points to the fact that Hereswode appears to have been extra manorial and therefore there were no manors or persons to which all its assets could conveniently be ascribed.

Plotting woodland sites in Leicester Forest against soils produces a tight correlation between permanent woodland presence and boulder clay. In Rockingham Forest Foard states that the geology was the primary determinant of woodland in Anglo-Saxon times and reminds us that the survival of woodland into the post-Conquest period was influenced by a range of political, tenurial and management factors. Also, the woodland at Rockingham 'almost without exception' lay on the least productive land (Foard 2001, 41). The sites of both Doveland Wood (1) and The Hat Wood (4) (see below and on fig 7) appear to have been typical of damp oak woodland. Of the remaining woods 21 were located wholly or mostly on the clay. Only the woods of Sandyhurst (3); Huncote (11); Le Hore (15) and Pakeman's Wood (25) were situated on lighter and better drained soils. Given that the great majority of woodland sites provided a major deterent to cultivation it is hardly surprising that woodlands proved to be an enduring feature of the local medieval landscape.

Two woodlands stand out as worthy of special mention since they were particularly prominent features of the landscape to 1628. Doveland Wood (1) in Bromkinsthorpe manor is first heard of in 1255 when it was sufficiently valuable for Simon de Montfort to grant it to Leicester Abbey as 'a plot of woodland and open country called Doveland with its gate as it is presently enclosed' (Charyte's Rental, a 15th century list of the possessions of Leicester Abbey). A survey of the royal woods in 1554 found Doveland to contain 45 acres of coppice of which 15 acres were of 13 years growth, 20 acres of 10–11 years growth and 10 acres of 8–9 years growth. It was clearly well-managed and valuable woodland. (TNA E315/462 item 4). After the Inclosure of the Royal Forest it became part of the Winstanley estate and disappears from the records as a wood when the later park of Braunstone was first laid out. Doveland lay to the north-east of the modern park and in the neighbourhood of the present Gooding Avenue. One wonders if it was the Domesday wood of the Countess Judith, mentioned earlier.

The woodland called 'The Hat' (4) occupied a position in the manor of Lubbesthorpe adjoining the manor of Braunstone and within the forest ring. The first mention is in the reign of Henry III (1216–72) when the hospital of St. John granted to Walter de Cobyngton permission to take 'in the common wood of Lubbesthorpe' sufficient wood for his domestic needs (Hastings MSS, Vol.1, 59). Roger de Zouche held 'the wood of Lubbesthorpe' in 1302 (Cal. Pat. R. 1301, 27) and in 1482 William Lord Hastings died owning of 40 acres of the same wood (TNA N4/1/38). His descendant Henry, Earl of Huntingdon, held the wood in 1581 when it was composed of 'diverse oaks, thorne and other kinds of wood' and where the coppice underwood was of 'sundry years growth' (Parker 1947, 220). Later, in 1606, Sir George Manners held Lubbesthorpe and was condemned by local people 'for cutting down the vert of the forest in a place called the Hatte and that unseasonable time' (DL44/679). Further cutting took place in 1624 when Thomas Dilks 'did put in cattle not commonable, viz horses; beasts and sheep to the destruction of the covert and great disturbances of his majesty's game' (DL44/1062). By 1628 the wood had been virtually lost and what remained vanished shortly afterwards. It is suspected that this site was that of the Domesday Wood of Lubbesthorpe.

VII The parks

Parks were common features of the medieval landscape. Much research has been carried out over the last three decades into their forms, how they functioned and their social and economic significance. Many parks contained deer but they also met a number of other needs and aspirations of their owners. These are well summed up by Jones and Page as 'profit, prestige, pleasure and patronage' (Jones and Page 2006, 113). Twelve parks are known for the area of the plateau (listed on fig 2). First, we consider a few important general points about medieval parks and then move on to examine briefly each in turn.

The typical post-Conquest park was an area specially set aside and with a boundary composed of an internal ditch and a fence-topped bank. Rackham says about 50% of parks contained some form of internal compartmentalisation (Rackham 2003, 195). This allowed such profitable activities as growing wood, breeding rabbits in warrens,

managing fishponds as well as maintaining stocks of deer. Most parks were expensive to establish and they were expected to pay the costs of their maintenance.

Many parks were located on poor soils although Mileson makes the point that powerful lords were able to empark land that had recently been under the plough, meaning someone had forfeited his arable (Mileson 2009, 53). Parks expanded and contracted to reflect the economic circumstances and social aspirations of their owners. Most rich men had parks and some of them had many. Financial considerations were often outweighed by the social element of ownership. Herring says parks made the unequal power relationship of feudal society concrete: the carefully located high bank and fence, stopped up roads re-routed along the outside of the pale and the locked gate all went to make social inequality permanently visible (Herring 2007, 60).

The parks of the study area were all up and running before they are first recorded. Parish boundaries may have been laid out along already existing earthworks of perhaps pre-Conquest enclosures such as the hays, previously mentioned. Hoppitt remarks on how few boundary earthworks she found in parts of Suffolk and wonders if large woods were fenced and managed as parks (Hoppitt 2007, 163). This is interesting in view of the fact that all the known parks of Leicester Forest (except those at Lubbesthorpe) lay outside the forest ring, within which there were many anciently established woods.

Finally, there has developed a recent awareness that many parks were part of much larger and grandiose designed landscapes. No evidence for this in the area of the plateau has been discerned thus far.

Beaumont Leys Park, the park of Beaumont and the park of the abbey grounds.

The histories and topographies of these three parks (fig 4) have been described elsewhere (Cabaniuk and Squires 2007, 11–19) but a resume is offered here.

Area A in Figure 2 was described by Domesday Book as the wood of Thurcaston. Within this huge area a park, the 'park of Beaumont' i.e. park number 2 on Figure 2, is noted in Charyte's Rental of Leicester Abbey. It had been created at some time before 1240, the year in which Simon de Montfort effectively severed it in two when he sold about 320 acres of his 'noble wood of Beaumont' to Leicester Abbey. This move enabled the abbot to establish what was later to develop into the extensive Abbey Park, i.e. park number 3. (This early park should not be confused with the modern 'Abbey Park', which is a 19th century creation and is now run by the City of Leicester). The remnant of the park of Beaumont together with its surrounding land was re-enclosed as late as 1482 when Edward IV created Beaumont Park, i.e. park number 1. The name of the creator of the park of Beaumont and the date of its establishment are not known. It may have been created by Simon de Montfort after 1230 only for him to break it up only ten years later. A date earlier than 1230 is therefore indicated. One suspects this park originated as a Saxon hunting ground, a hay unrecorded by Domesday Book. Its position can be seen to have had a strong influence on the development of the landscape from the mid 13th century, or earlier, to the dissolution of the monasteries in the 1530's and beyond.

The park of Anstey

The sole record for the park of Anstey (fig 5) comes from the Rental of Leicester Abbey. Here the compiler states 'we have a view of frank pledge of all our tenants.....between the great northern parietum ('wall', 'dividing wall', 'boundary') and the park of Anstey' (Nichols 1/2/appendix 76). The date is presumably pre-1341 when the first Rental was drawn up rather than that of 1477 when Abbot Charyte brought the list of the Abbey's holdings up to date. There is no indication that the Abbey held this park because, as already noted, the monks were developing a park (park number 4 on fig 2) on their home demesne (Squires 2006, 90–91).

The most likely creator of the Park of Anstey is Simon de Montfort who had already granted the assarts of Langbroke and Olishawe (Courtney 2006, 41–43). This was in exchange for the Abbey relinquishing their pasture rights in the Earl's enclosed woods which lay between the Anstey and Groby roads, i.e. the area of what later became known as Marclose and later still, Leicester Frith (fig 5). By emparking as he did, the earl was preserving a section of the northern part of the wood of Anstey.

A further assart of Freeboroweholme is described as lying below the 'defensive' pallisade on the south side of the mill. This appears to be marked by the surviving bank and ditch which editions of Ordnance Survey maps have labelled 'park pale'. Excavations of this feature have revealed that it extends at least 60 metres north of Gynsil Lane (Leicestershire Museums Archaeology Sheet LE 397). This lane appears to be an old route partly created by assarting from Anstey to join that village with Glenfield. Its route avoids the flood plain of the Anstey brook over which only one bridge was needed. If, as Courtney suggests, the whole of Mill Field rather than just the areas of Langbroke and Olishawe to the east of Gynsil Lane originated as an assart, the supposed site of the park became part of the common field system between the years 1341 and 1477 (Courtney 2003, 42–43).

The location of the park was probably as shown in Figure 5. There is still a routeway leading from Anstey village called Park Road. It reaches the mill as a footpath and meets the Gynsil Lane in the region of the park. The extension of the 'park pale' earthwork into Mill Field suggests it originated as an assart bank. The section south of Gynsil Lane, which extends to Woodcock Well, may have been adopted as a length of the pale of the park of Anstey.

The Frith Park and New Park

These parks have already been described above.

Lubbesthorpe Park(s)

The first mention of a park at Lubbesthorpe (fig 8) is in 1348 when William la Zouche granted to Roger and Felicia la Zouche certain rents of the manor, together with a vivary (fishpond) and 'all the ancient park' (Farnham LMVN 1933, 5,262). There is no record of any deer, although the park appears to have survived the Black Death in 1348. The perambulation of the Royal Forest in 1526 mentions 'Lubbster park' and in a list of 'rent of lands' in Leicester Forest (1528) there is only a pasture called 'Old Park' (ROLLR DG5/544).

Field name evidence locates the general area of the park(s) as lying adjacent to the Warren and close to the Hat Wood. The archaeological remains of the park are very poor and are shown on Figure 8. There is the dam of a fishpond immediately to the east of Old House, which Hartley illustrates (Hartley 1989, 69). This may well have been within one of the two parks. It also seems likely that the new park was simply an extension of the 'ancient' one. All four features: wood, park, warren and lawn occupy the boulder clay which extends across the parish north-west of Abbey Farm. This landscape does not offer any features along which a pale line could be placed to noticeable advantage.

Newhall Park

The first record for Newhall Park (fig 8) occurs in a letter of 1373 from John of Gaunt, duke of Lancaster, to Robert de Swillington, his chief forester of the Chase of Leicester. (Armitage-Smith 1911, vol 2, 163). Swillington's term of office spanned the two decades after 1371 and he was probably the builder of the New Hall sometime before 1370 (Fox and Russell 1948, 38). His Inquisition Post Mortem (IPM), taken in 1391 states he held a moiely, i.e. half, of the manor of Newhall and 'a hall, rooms, granges and other houses' together with arable, meadow, a wood with pasture and other lands in Thurlaston and elsewhere, but there is no mention of a park (Farnham LMVN 1933, 5, 296)

The other half of the manor of Newhall was held by the Turvilles. When William Turville's widow died in 1474 she held the manor of Newhall, but her IPM does not mention a park (*ibid*, 299). Her son John held the office of Keeper of Barrons Park, i.e. Barn Park,

in 1496 along with [the woods of] Stratho, Swynhills and La Hore (wood number 15 on fig 7) in the Forest of Leicester. On the death of John in 1507 a long list of his possessions fails to mention any park (Cal. IPM Hen VII, Vol III, 122). John's son William received a licence from King Henry VIII to enlarge and enclose his park of Newhall. The park is mentioned by the commissioners perambulating the border of the Royal Forest in 1526. Saxton's map of 1576 shows the park as still enclosed. It is also shown on the 'anonymous' map of Leicestershire of 1602 and Speed's map of 1611. When Edward Turville died in 1620 he held the manor of Thurlaston called Newhall and a free park called Newhall park (Farnham LMVN, 1933, 5, 303). Two years later Burton describes it as disparked and in 1630 it was divided into closes (Burton 1662, 6). Nichols writing in 1811 claimed the boundary banks were still visible (Nichols 4/2/1003).

The present site of New Hall retains a large water-filled moat which presumably enclosed Sir Robert de Swillington's New Hall. However the name New Hall and the lateness of this date for moat construction suggests there may have been an earlier building on this site. Of the Turville mansion only a few fragments of the wall remain, which Pevsner found 'quite untelling' (Pevsner and Williamson 1992, 409).

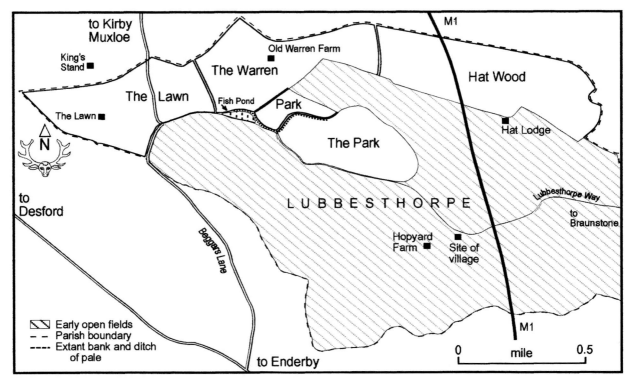

Figure 8: Lubbesthorpe in the middle ages

182

Figure 9: Thurlaston and New Hall parks

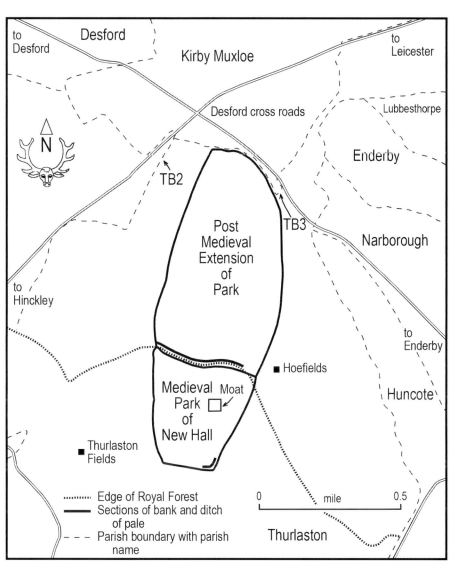

To the south-west of the moat is a collection of earthworks including a large square pond surrounded by a level terrace on three sides and two large fishponds, now drained. In addition, there is a level area divided by faint rectilinear banks and ditches which are probably the remains of a formal garden. These have been mapped by Hartley (Hartley 1989, 70). All of these features were the work of generations of the Turvilles.

The perambulation of the Royal Forest in 1526 stated that the forest ring ran '…. to Nabill [Narborough Hill] corner which is next to corner of Sir William Turville's park, newly enclosed, and from there to Howfield [Hoefield] gate and from there to New Pool within the said park' (DL39/5/14). The 'New Pool' appears to be the large fishpond to the east of the Hall. This description, taken with the extent of earthworks (which are probably remnants of the medieval pale), makes it clear that the site of the medieval park contained the moat and occupied the area shown on Figure 6. This lay adjacent to and outside the forest ring. The park 'new enclosed' was an extension of the medieval park northwards. That Henry VIII had permitted Sir William to empark land within the forest ring may give an indication of the esteem in which Sir William was held and/or how little he valued his Forest of Leicester. Alternatively, it was a reward for Turville administration of the western end of the Royal Forest.

The park contained deer and woodland. This presumably was the 'Turville Wood' noted throughout the 14th century (fig 7, wood number 12). Fox and Russell, describe the wood in 1319 as 'between the hermitage [now lost?] on the one side, Enderby way on the other and abutting on the wood of Huncote' (fig 7, wood number 11; Fox and Russell, 1948, 30). This places Turville Wood in the northern section of the extended park.

The western edges of both parks followed an ancient routeway from Thurlaston in the direction of Desford. Its broad features in places suggest a drove road from the south onto the plateau. The northern edge of Sir William's extension is marked by the parish boundary and the eastern edge is suggested by a long hedgeline which follows the 'Howfield gate'. Nichols claimed the park extended over 200 acres, but this was not so (Nichols 4/2/1003).

Brokensale Park

Brokensale lay in the parish of Normanton Turville in the manor of Thurlaston. The single medieval reference to the park records that in 1279 among Radolphus Turville's possessions was a park called Brokensale. Nichols identified this with Brackenholme (Nichols 4/2/1003). Since no alternative derivation has

183

been found the following description is based on this remark.

'Brackenholme' almost certainly refers to the land around the present Bracknell's Barn (fig 10). According to Fox and Russell (Fox and Russell, 1948, 26) it was an area of some 90 acres enclosed from the forest at an early date. It first enters the records when Edmund, Earl of Leicester, purchased from Nicholas Turville his (Turville's) 'right and claim of all his woods in the forest of Leicester except Brackenholme....' (Nichols 4/2/1003). The site was at least partly wooded and contained a lodge and a moated site, now ploughed out (Hartley 1989, 59). These three features go some way to suggest the presence of a medieval park. Also, field survey suggests a probable line for the southern boundary. Here the line of the pale would have run along a contour which separates the park from the floodplain of the river Soar. Elsewhere a continuous hedge line was a possible eastern boundary. A possible western edge may have been the trumpet-shaped parish boundary mentioned under Tooley Park.

There is no documentary or archaeological evidence for a second park in Normanton Turville. The present Normanton Park is believed to be a post medieval creation and contains the site of the lost village of Normanton Turville. It would appear that Brokensale and 'the park of Normanton Turville' are one and the same.

Tooley Park

Tooley Park (fig 10, number 14 on fig 7), occasionally referred to as 'Shilton Park' enters the records in 1279 when Edmund, Earl of Leicester had 'a wood, a free chase and a park called 'Thorland' (Tooley), (Farnham LMVN MSS version in ROLLR). An extent (valuation) in 1297 of Edmund's manor of Earl Shilton noted that 'the park of Tolowe' was not included 'because the bailiff of the earl has all his animals at his will there' (ibid). The following year Edmund's widow Blanche received the park as part of her dower (Cal. Close R. 1296–1302, 161).

Earl Shilton was a demesne manor of the earls of Leicester and remained so until 1362. There was a castle in the town from which the park was administered. The account by the reeve of Earl Shilton for the period 1361–62 mentioned the cost of repairing the fence of the park was 31s 7½d (a little over £1.58)

(TLAHS 22 1938–39, 346). Adequate fencing was an important concern since the park was a popular grazing ground for the earls' animals throughout the 14th century (ibid 307). At the same time John of Gaunt granted oaks to his tenants 'so that they could make a fence at Tooley Park' against escaping deer, which were damaging their crops. George Hastings was given the keepership of the park – a mere sinecure – in 1507 (Fox and Russell 1948, 76–77). A building called 'Tooley Lodge' is mentioned in 1526 (TLAHS 12, 1921, 152). For that year Fox and Russell (p134) give the reported area of the park as 475 acres but its true acreage was 450. The reported annual rental was £24.

A description of the park in 1526 survives as part of the perambulation of the Royal Forest and allows an impression of the nature of the landscape. The perimeter of the park was '50 furlongs, every furlong 40 poles and every pole, 18 feet'. This works out at a little over 4 miles. The length of the park within the pale was 9 furlongs and the breadth was 5 furlongs 'which maketh in acres within the ground 360' (DL39/5/14). The true area is almost 40 acres fewer.

In 1526 the park remained well wooded. Allmans wood stood within the pale with wood worth £200 and pasture £20 yearly. It was noted that if the deer 'be ridde' and the woodland felled the grazing in the wood would be worth £30 yearly and would support 200 bullocks. The best of the woodland in the park produced 70 loads of timber at 12d the load and 15 loads of underwood [from coppice] at 6d each year. Values of other areas – unintelligible to the modern researcher – are given (DL39/5/14). The king had the herbage of the park which was valued at 60s yearly (ibid). George Vincent was the 'Forester' of the park in 1566 and was entitled to reasonable estovers out of the wood to maintain and run his messuage [dwelling] in Peckleton. He also had pannage for 40 pigs within the park (TLAHS, 17, 1932–33, 138–40). On the eve of the inclosure of Leicester Forest there were 200 deer present.

Sir Henry Harrington occupied the park in 1606 when it was claimed it extended over 410 acres. It contained 112 dotterells [old and much decayed trees] worth 6s 4d each; 180 timber trees worth 13s 4d each; 4,800 'young oaks' at 2s or 2s 6d each and 5,800 ashes at 2s each (DL44/711). Another survey 2 years

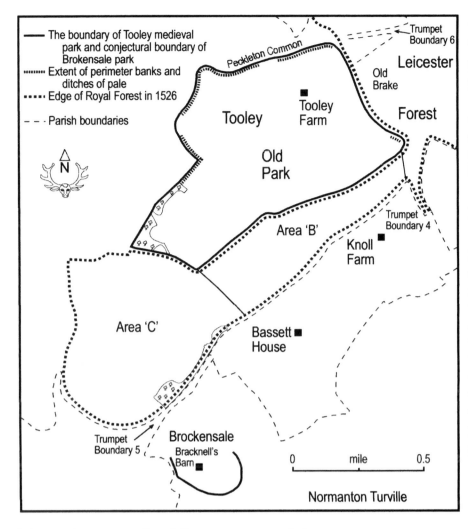

Figure 10: Tooley and Brokensale parks

Map legend:
— The boundary of Tooley medieval park and conjectural boundary of Brokensale park
······· Extent of perimeter banks and ditches of pale
·—·—· Edge of Royal Forest in 1526
– – · Parish boundaries

N

Peckleton Common

Trumpet Boundary 6

Old Brake

Leicester

Forest

Tooley

Tooley Farm

Old Park

Area 'B'

Trumpet Boundary 4

Knoll Farm

Area 'C'

Bassett House

Trumpet Boundary 5

Brockensale

Bracknell's Barn

0   mile   0.5

Normanton Turville

likely that the additional land came from area B. In 1842 the area of the park was given as 630 acres and this expansion was probably accounted for by the land of area C.

Barn Park

Barn Park (fig 11 and No 11 on fig 2) sometimes known as Barron's Park or the park of Desford, is first recorded in 1298 in the IPM of Edmund of Lancaster, Earl of Leicester and brother of King Edward I. He had the manor of Desford 'including a park' where the pasture was worth 20s yearly and the pannage 10s yearly (Cal IPM Edwl, vol 3, 209). Five years later, Thomas, Earl of Leicester and Lancaster, held the park

later and supposedly of the same area, lists 2,102 timber oaks worth a total of £494, 1,086 decayed fuel oaks worth £204-1s and 270 'small beeches' worth £252-12s-4d (British Library Additional MSS 38444). The reader must make what he will of these figures. By 1616 the lodge was much decayed but deer were still present (DL968).

If the Figure of 410 acres quoted above in 1606 is even approximately correct, the park appears to have expanded during the period 1526–1608. The survey of 1526 was of the old park; Figure 10 shows the boundary and areas where the banks and ditches of the medieval pale survive. The survey of 1606 reflected the expansion.

The mention of so many old and decaying trees, which were a characteristic element of the landscape of much of the Royal Forest in 1526, suggests the expansion of the park had been achieved by taking in land from the Forest. If so, it means that the boundary of the Royal Forest in the Tooley area at the time of the Inclosure in 1628 was different from that described a century or so earlier. It seems

and complained that persons had broken into it and had done damage (Cal Pat R, 1301–07, 270). By 1313 the pannage of the park was worth nothing and no deer were present 'because of the depasturing by the lord's colts and foals' (DL29/1/3). In addition, oaks had to be felled for fencing the park. Income from 'crops' and bark produced £6-3s-9d and the sale of nuts 2s-9d. (DL 29/1/3). A few years' later repairs to the pale around the park cost 16d (TLAHS 19, 1936–37, 265). An outbreak of murrain among the deer at Tooley Park in 1373 caused John of Gaunt, who held the park, to ban hunting until the situation improved (Armitage-Smith, 1911, vol.2, 208). Murrain appears to be a general term, possibly covering more than one disease.

'Le Barnpark' is mentioned in 1392 as having been assigned to Agnes, wife of Simon Pakeman (1306–76), a senior officer of the Earls of Lancaster (Fox and Russell, 1948, 65). A valuation of the park in 1399 records an income of £6-5s-4d from faggots [bundles of small branches] and the cost of maintaining the pale fence was 58s 10½d (DL29/278/11987).

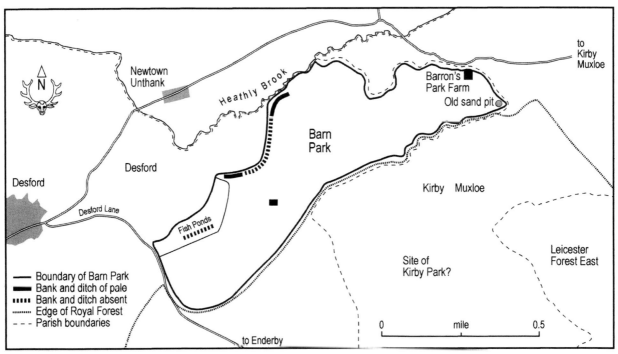

Figure 11: Barn or Barron's Park

The first recorded keeper of the park was John Turville, who had pasture for a bull, 12 cows, a boar and 12 pigs (Farnham LMVN 1933, 5, 19). A number of 15th century documents record the sale of woodland products from the park. For the construction of his castle at Kirby Muxloe, William Lord Hastings took 59 loads of wood and 40 logs in 1480 and 30 loads of wood the following year. In addition, 'rods' were also cut for the making of hurdles for the platforms of the scaffolding at the castle (TLAHS 11, 1915/16, 215).

Those boundaries of the early park can be readily followed today (fig 11) From the western-most tip by the Desford Lane the line follows a minor stream and a series of fishponds to a point north-west of Park House. From there it turns abruptly east then north-east to meet the Heathly brook. After a short distance it moves eastwards again along the Desford parish boundary as far as Barron's Park Farm. Thereafter, from the 'Old Sandpit' on the first edition of the Six Inch Ordnance Survey sheet the line is the Desford/Kirby Muxloe parish boundary; but it breaks away a little south-east of Park House to eventually reach the Desford Lane.

There is no evidence to suggest that over the years the park has contracted or expanded beyond the boundaries shown on Figure 11. The documentary record post 1628 is good and tends to confirm the long continuity of these boundaries. The archaeological evidence produced by field survey is highlighted in the earthworks and fishpond shown on Figure 11. Hartley has mapped these in detail (Hartley 2008, 14).

Kirby Muxloe Park

There are curiously few records of the park of Kirby Muxloe (fig 12 and number 12 on fig 2) and nothing before 1474 when King Edward IV gave William Hastings licence to empark 2,000 acres there (Cal. Chart. R. (1427–1516), 242). Such a grant can be seen less as a practical proposition and more as a reward, a badge of honour even, from the monarch to a man in recognition of faithful service rendered over many years. The area Hastings did empark is that shown in Areas A, and B on Figure 12. Area A was originally all or part of Whatecroft Wood, sometimes known as Whatecroft Coppice, first heard of in 1234 (fig 7, wood number 26). Area B can also be identified with the park when in 1626 land in Kirby Common, i.e. Kirby Frith, was described as adjacent to Wheatcroft Park (ROLLR DG5/527). Leland in 1558 noted Kirby Muxloe park as 'four miles from Leicester besides Leicester Forest' (Chandler 1993, 281). Saxton shows the enclosed nature of the park on his map of 1576.

The park at Kirby Muxloe is an example of a feature which documentary resources refer to as 'little park' and it is clear it lay adjacent to the manorial residence, in this case the putative 'castle'. These parks were landscaped for mixed leisure interests and often resembled

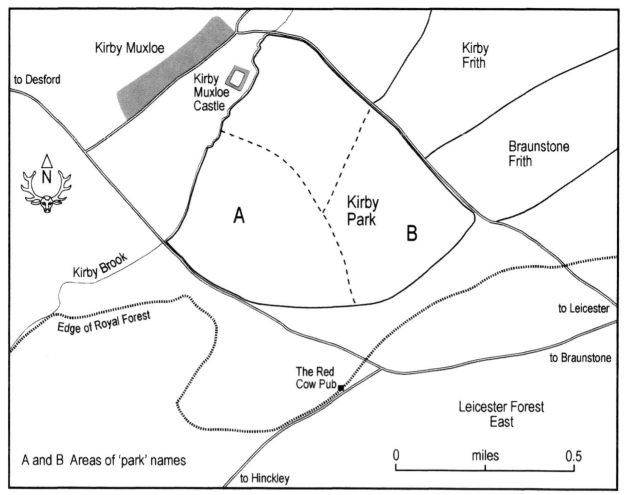

Figure 12: The Park of Kirby Muxloe

gardens rather than a normal park. They were often moated around or well fenced in order to keep the deer out (Mileson, 2009). It seems likely that Lord Hastings did not live long enough to enjoy his creation.

After the death of Sir Henry Hastings in 1630, the park was bought by Sir Robert Bannister and later it passed to William Wollaston, esq. (Nichols 4/2/ 624). However, it is doubtful if it survived the Civil War as anything more than an agricultural estate.

The parks: a summary

The parks of the plateau, including area A, present a diverse collection of sites in terms of size, location, longevity and functioning and as a group are difficult to analyse. Here we examine the parks in area D only, i.e. parks numbers 7 – 12 on Figure 2. Perhaps the most obvious feature is that they all lay outside the forest ring, a matter taken up again below.

The second point that must be made is that the parks when first recorded, were up and running, as discussed above in the case of Frith Park. The only exception is Kirby

Muxloe park. One might quite reasonably date their origins to the first half of the 13th century. Tooley Park, Barn Park and Frith Park enclosed land on which Domesday Book says there were more than 200 acres of wood. This is consistent with the notion that the Normans emparked most of the Domesday woodlands of 200 or more acres across the rest of the county (Squires 2004, 150) At the same time one wonders why other large woods were not emparked. As already noted, Hoppitt points out that in Suffolk fenced woodland could have functioned in the manner of, but without the status of, a 'park' and generated no records as such (Hoppitt 2007, 154). Perhaps this was so at Enderby, Huncote and Braunstone, each with 200 acres of Domesday woodland? It would appear that the emparking by lords was primarily a matter of rescuing the best woods and pastures which otherwise faced unknown futures in the face of the increasing demands of commoners.

In area D Barn and Tooley Parks were the two major parks in all respects. They were created from the demesne lands of the Earl of

Leicester's manor of Desford and Earl Shilton (parish of Peckleton) respectively. Normally, a licence to empark was required from the crown. This condition hardly applied in area D at least, since a succession of earls were sufficiently powerful to grant themselves and their lordly feudal tenants 'permission' to go ahead. The sole exception was at Kirby Muxloe where more research is needed into the precise area which was emparked. Barn Park and Tooley Park are also interesting in that they functioned as grazing areas for the horses of the earls and dukes of Lancaster, and as such were two of a string of parks including those at Duffield Frith and Needwood Forest (Wiltshire and Woore 2005, 97). Interestingly, Short points out that one effect of the creation of deer parks in the medieval period was to fossilise prehistoric Roman and Anglo-Saxon landscapes (Short 2002, 123). Such features could remain present until disparking allowed the landscape to be fully worked again. In such a dreary landscape as that of the modern Leicester Forest, perhaps efforts should be directed towards a detailed archaeological survey of both Barn and Tooley parks before they are engulfed by housing?

The anomaly of the position of the park(s) at Lubbesthorpe (fig 8) once again draws our attention to the 'forest ring' and the origin of that line. We can accept that its course was laid down after the parks of Tooley and Barn had been established but was this also the case at Newhall? Was the line there laid out and Newhall park established on its southern edge or was Newhall Park there originally and the 'ring' drawn to prevent possible further expansion northwards? From her work on Suffolk parks, Hoppitt (Hoppitt 2007, 152) suggests that parish boundaries were defined when woods and parks were already part of a local landscape. At Newhall one can see that the forest ring was established to check the advances of the ambitious Turvilles.

Finally, it can reasonably be claimed that the forest ring of area D was laid down to recognise park boundaries and other enclosures secured during the mid 13th century and we are led once more to Simon de Montfort, second Earl of Leicester, as the most likely reformer.

VIII The Duchy lands 1399 – 1628
Change in the Duchy lands 1399 – 1526
For perhaps half a century after they became

'royal' the Duchy lands were administered efficiently before change set in. The chief problems were firstly the lack of any real interest on the part of the crown. This approach was also found in other properties, e.g. Needwood Forest which was also too far away from the capital and, as there was no royal 'house of access' near it, 'the king had no pleasure in the game of deer there' (VCH Staffs 2, 352). The second problem was the granting for life of the office of chief forester to court favourites and/ or local magnates whose land holdings and social position in a particular area were such that their involvement in the forest could not be overlooked. Such men found themselves with what in some cases meant a free hand to enrich themselves at the crown's expense and to the detriment of the forest economy and landscape.

Hastings and Greys
The landscape of Leicester Forest was particularly unfortunate to be the battle ground of the ambitions of two families of more or less equal power and prestige c.1500. Worse, there was a deep animosity between them which reached back more than two centuries and to the highest levels in the royal court. The problem has been described in some detail (Fox and Russell 1948, ch4; Squires 2002). We may simply note here that after the elevation by Edward IV of William Hastings to the rank of baron and William's spectacular rise to power on the ancestral estates north-west of Leicester (and beyond), the various members of the family came to occupy a grip on Leicester Forest. This was during the early years of the reign of Elizabeth and at a time when the fortunes of the Greys were at their lowest. At the same time, the Hastings were enclosing their Forest manors of Kirby Muxloe, Enderby and Braunstone. The demand for grazing rose and their tenants' beasts were turned onto the Royal Forest in increasing numbers. As we have seen, Lord Hastings removed much wood for his castle building at Kirby Muxloe; one wonders what (if any) payment the crown received in return. The Greys had adopted a similar approach to removing woodland in that part of the Duchy lands i.e. area C (fig 2) which they regarded as their fiefdom. It was hardly surprising if lesser mortals followed their lead and that the landscape suffered accordingly.

In 1523 the Crown, in the form of Chancellor Wolsey, sought to defuse the problem by, as a first step, having a survey made of the Royal Forest and Duchy Lands. This was carried out by independent commissioners who clearly did visit the scene. 'The forest' they claimed 'was a fair and goodly ground well replenished by deer' and they reported that they saw 200 in a wood 'above Huncote'. However, they could hardly ignore the signs of a century and more of decline of the royal property. The King's woods in the forest they reported were all decayed and wasted…. and the woods that were left were growing on other men's grounds and not upon the King's'. The royal woods had been laid waste 'by reason of the Newark and the Bede House [in Leicester]. The occupants have been taking 200 loads of wood a year by lop and top, but for the last 12 years have been taking the bodies as well' (DL43/14/6).

This was just one of the abuses the commissioners noted. Such was the devastation of the woods and the spread of grassland they were moved to report that since 'all the king's part of the forest is so wasted and is now a goodly pasture' the crown would receive more income from it as a sheepwalk. But they also added that 'for the salvation of the game [it would be necessary] to nourish wood again in 3 or 4 suitable places' (DL43/14/6). Any sales of wood for the king have left no record. The contrast here is with the Royal Forest of Leighfield in Rutland which at the same time was also under the supervision of the Hastings family. There the Forest was comparatively well run, with woods enclosed and properly fenced. Warrants for sales were issued and returns made to the Exchequer (Squires in prep for Rutland Record).

The adjudication between the interests of the two noble families provides more detail. In the Frith (area C, fig 2) all cattle were to be taken out. Pigs and sheep had been removed previously because the damage they were causing was such that it could no longer be ignored. After several other observations the report closed with a caution that 'if all the king's woods in the Frith and Beaumont Leys (area A) are sold, the king's town of Leicester and all his mills and tenants therein [and elsewhere] shall in a short space be utterly decayed' (DL3/16/3).

The once well-wooded landscape was in rapid decline. An early 17th century survey of the woodlands of the Swinhill, Sallows (wood 23 on fig.3), Sandyhurst (No. 3), King's Wood (No. 27) and 'Coppice Bushes' (unlocated) – a total area of 245 acres – records 'some oaks, many doded oaks, thornes and some poles' (Hastings MSS). This was a sad state of affairs indeed.

Leicester Forest 1526 – 1628: the closing years.

The deterioration of the landscape of area D can be matched with that of other Royal Forests since Tudor monarchs seldom hunted far from the capital. However, the first Stuart King, James VI and I, suddenly took an interest in this distant property. In 1606, the third year of his reign, he commissioned a survey of Leicester Forest, or what was left of it, to determine (1) the metes and bounds of the Forest, (2) the spoil and encroachment in the royal woods, (3) the extent of the underwood and thicket, (4) the abuse caused by the over-grazing of sheep and the damage done by rabbits in the warrens.

The King's choice of commissioners was as unfortunate as it was unavoidable. They were headed by Henry Hastings, Earl of Huntingdon. He was also Chief Forester and in 1605 had been granted licence to kill 80 bucks and 40 does annually, fish in his majesty's fishponds, take partridges and pheasants and have 32 loads of firewood worth £16 per year (Nichols 3/2/593). The remaining commissioners included Walter Hastings of Braunstone and several other family members; truly a 'mafia' of the times.

The enquiry continued on a farcical note when no jurymen could be found who knew the Forest's metes and bounds. Nevertheless, the commissioners continued on the basis of the details in 'an ancient document remaining in Mr. Gerrard's office' (Fox and Russell, 1948, 93). The metes and bounds it described were presumably those laid out in the mid 13th century.

The sheer level of the scandal of the maladministration of the Forest over the previous century or so and the sad rundown state of the woodlands could hardly be hidden from the monarch. As to the first item 'many thornes have been cut to the hurt of the game and it is recommended no more shall be cut' (DL44/660). Witnesses accused Sir Walter Hastings of cutting down trees and coppice in Narborough Wood and of cutting down thickets and enclosing the same at the value of £5 every acre'. Sir Henry Hastings was presented for 'cutting down the forest… to the number of 500 trees…and in a short time there will be nothing left to shroud the deer in' (Hastings MSS). Likewise, Sir George Manners of Lubbesthorpe cut down 30 acres of the vert (greenery) in a place called The Hat and that at an unseasonable time. There were other presentments for cutting wood and turning the ground into pasture for sheep (DL44/679 and Hastings MSS).

Other early 17th century surveys present a similarly depressing picture. The grounds within the royal forest belonging to the king extended over 1600 acres of which 300 were not enclosed. This is not surprising in view of the areas 'taken out of the forest' which we have noted above. The number of timber trees remaining in the Forest was 3055 and these were worth £667-10s. At an average of a little over 4 shillings each the value of these was moderate to low. 'Decayed fuel oaks' numbered 1170 and these were worth only 3s 6d each (British Museum Add MS.38444). A survey of the woods under the care of George Cater produced an average of all manner of trees and only 8 trees per acre.

From this data and the foregoing remarks we can deduce that much of the remaining woodland was concentrated in the western part of the Forest. A great preponderance of 'young oaks' suggests some coppicing, the few timber trees a shortage of middle aged specimens and the few 'doderels' a grassy scene on which they alone stood.

The commissioners established that there were four rabbit warrens. Three of these in total extended over 100 acres 'to the utter exile of his majesty's game'. (Fox and Russell, 1948, 97). The commoners complained bitterly that the rabbits escaped and destroyed the vegetation for their grazing animals (Hastings MSS). It was even worse for any possibility of woodland regeneration; but no direct action was taken to remedy this situation.

The King's Stand
In his bout of unexplained enthusiasm King James decided he wished to hunt in this Forest of Leicester and ordered a stand to be constructed. In the manner of the times, instead of chasing deer he preferred to have the deer driven past where he was seated so that he minimised the discomfort and maximised his chances of making a kill. The site in the Forest is still marked on modern Ordnance Survey maps as 'King's'Stand' (SK 513019; see fig 3). Local landowners in the area agreed to 'give up' land: Lord Huntingdon 120 acres; Walter Hastings 40 and George Quarles 65. This was probably land they had recently 'acquired'. At the same time the parish boundaries were re-adjusted to accommodate the scheme. In the event the King never did visit his stand. This was probably on account of the onset of his chronic ill health including tuberculosis. In 1613 the Spanish ambassador sent home 'the King grows too fat to be able to hunt comfortably' (Cal. SPD 1611–18, 199). Two years later he was dead.

It is from the time of this rather sad effort to restore the spirit of the sport of kings from an age long passed, that a picture of the nature of Leicester Forest – or rather that part which the king owned – emerges. It is one predominantly of rolling wet grassland, largely devoid of trees except for ancient hulks, the 'doded oaks' which were probably in no one's interest to remove. There were in places groups of ancient oaks, mostly old pollards, which were the survivors of what once was substantial woodland. But the most striking feature of this almost savannah-type landscape was the large numbers of sheep, cattle, horses and of course the rabbits, which had escaped from their warrens. Elsewhere, on 'other men's lands' there were more trees in woods open or fenced, but the signs of the forthcoming crisis were there to be seen.

IX The end of Leicester Forest
In 1626 the crown realised there was little purpose in maintaining the Royal Forest. It was run down to the point where the tree cover barely provided shelter for the deer and where, in any case, land carrying the lingering woodland was worth much more as sheep pasture. Such coppices which remained had high maintenance costs and the demand for underwood for charcoal making was falling as the coal trade in Leicester was developing. (Stocks 1923, 168). The crown, in the person of Charles I, was in need of ready cash and was no longer prepared to do battle with the increasing demands of the commoners and the unauthorised grazing.

The end came quickly and Nichols prints the details of the Inclosure document (Nichols 4/2/781–95). The new owners of the lands had no hesitation in realising the costs of their purchases by felling the trees, fencing their plots and transforming what had been an open scene into what is the undistinguished agricultural landscape (minus the obvious urban developments) we see today.

Conclusion

The decline and decay of Leicester Forest from the early 15th century has much in common in pattern and process with other similar properties of the crown. However it is in the early years from 1086 to the end of the 14th century, when the area was supposedly a chase, which are of particular interest.

It is suggested the 'Hereswode' of Domesday Book occupied an area south-west of the present Groby Road and within and around the area which is shown as Royal Forest on Figure 2. This Hereswode may also have extended over all or part of area C but the admittedly scanty evidence suggests otherwise. Within this imprecise area, but not manorially part of it, lay the woods attributed by Domesday Book to the surrounding settlements. Hereswode was therefore most likely that area of the plateau where its woodlands were missed or more likely ignored.

In the early years after the Conquest the land of Hereswode was used communally as grazing, wood pasture and for woodland products. Eventually the need for regulation along with the creation of the parks saw the emergence of 'rights' with the re-organisation of the parish/manorial boundaries in the mid 13th century at the hands of Simon de Montfort, 2nd Earl of Leicester.

Derived from the perambulation of 1526, the line of the 'forest ring' probably reached back to the mid 13th century. It appears to have enclosed an area from which almost all of the familiar features of Norman occupation are missing. Preliminary assessment from the records of the Heritage and Environment Record for the late Anglo-Saxon period tends to confirm this. One wonders what the woodland of Hereswode tells us about late Anglo-Saxon boundaries. Also, bearing in mind the location of these woods on the watershed of this 'lonely' and 'silent' area, what can one hypothesise about the plateau with its woodlands as marking an even earlier boundary? It would be very surprising if the woodlands of the plateau did not once contain at least some of the 'hays' of the Anglo-Saxon hunting elite. Identifying these and relocating them to post-conquest parks would make an interesting line of research.

There is a very urgent need for more fieldwork, field walking and excavation before the apparently unstoppable urban advance destroys all. In the meantime, the opportunities for further research on the 'Royal Forest of Leicester' and its surrounding areas hardly need highlighting.

Bibliography

Adams, I. H., 1977 *Agrarian Landscape Terms: A Glossary for Historical Geography.* London: Institute of British Geographers. Special Publication 9.

Armitage-Smith, S., 1911. *John of Gaunt's Register. Volume 2.* Camden Third Series Vol XXI. Royal Historical Society.

Bateson, Mary, 1899. *Records of the Borough of Leicester II, 1327–1509.* C J Clay and Sons. London.

Bowman, Paul and Liddle, Peter (eds) 2004. *Leicestershire Landscapes.* Leicestershire Museums Archaeological Fieldwork Group. Monograph No. 1.

Burton, William, 1622. *The Description of Leicestershire.*

Cabaniuk, Stefan and Squires, Anthony, 2007. *Beaumont Leys and Its Parks.* Leicestershire Historian 43.

Cal. Chart. R., *Calendar of Charter Rolls,* HMSO.

Cal. Close R., Calendar of Close Rolls, HMSO.

Cal. IPM, Calendar of Inquisitions Post Mortem, HMSO.

Cal. Pat. R., Calendar of Patent Rolls, HMSO

Cal. SPD., Calendar of State Papers Domestic, HMSO.

Cantor, L. M. and Hatherley, J., 1979. *The Medieval Parks of England.* Geography. Vol 64, part 2.

Cantor, Leonard and Squires, Anthony, 1977, *The Historic Parks and Gardens of Leicestershire and Rutland.* Kairos Press. Newtown Linford.

Chandler, John, 1993. *John Leland's Itinerary: Travels in Tudor England.* Sutton Publishing, Stroud, Gloucestershire.

Charyte's Rental – a rental book for the possessions of Leicester Abbey from the time of William Charyte, a Canon of Leicester Abbey, compiled circa 1477. Now in the Bodleian Library Oxford (Laud MSS 625). Analysed by Professor R H Hilton in '*The economic development of some leicestershire estates in the fourteenth and fifteenth centuries*' Oxford 1947. Excerpts were also printed in John Nichols '*The History and Antiquities of the County of Leicester*' in 4 volumes. 1795–1815.

Courtney, Paul, 2003. Between Two Forests: The Social and Topographical Evolution of Medieval Anstey. *Transactions of the Leicestershire Archaeological and Historical Society*, 77.

Cox, Barrie, 1998. *The Place-Names of Leicestershire: Vol XXV 'The Borough of Leicester'.* The English Place-Name Society: Nottingham.

Cox, Barrie, 1971. *The Place Names of Leicestershire and Rutland.* Unpublished Phd thesis. University of Nottingham.

DL, Papers of the Duchy of Lancaster held in The National Archives, Kew, London.

Everitt, A., 1986. Continuity and Colonisation: The Evolution of Kentish Settlement, Leicester.

Farnham, G. F., 1933. *Leicestershire Medieval Village Notes.* Privately printed.

Foard, Glenn, 2001. Agriculture and Industry in Rockingham Forest. *Medieval Archaeology, XLV.*

Ford, W. J., 1976. Settlement Patterns in the Central Region of the Warwickshire Avon. In: Sawyer, PH (ed) 1979. *English Medieval Settlement.* Edward Arnold.

Fox, Levi and Russell, Percy, 1948. *Leicester Forest.* Edgar Backus. Leicester.

Gelling, Margaret and Cole, Ann, 2000. *The Landscape of Place-Names.* Shaun Tyus. Stamford.

Gover, J. E. B. et al., 1940. *The Place Names of Nottinghamshire. English Place Name Society, Vol XVII.* Cambridge University Press.

Hastings Manuscripts, 1928. *A report on the Manuscripts of the Late Reginald Rawdon Hastings. Vol.1.* HMSO. (These papers now form part of the Hastings Collection in the Huntington Library in San Marino, California).

Hartley, Robert F., 1989. *The Medieval Earthworks of Central Leicestershire.* Leicestershire Museums Service, Leicester.

Hartley, Robert F., 2008. *The Medieval Earthworks of South-West Leicestershire.* Leicestershire Museums Archaeological Fieldwork Group. Monograph number 2. Leicester.

Herring, Peter, 2007. Historic and Archaeological Survey of Cornish Deer Parks. In: Rotherham; Ian (ed) 2007. *The History, Ecology and Archaeology of Medieval Parks and Parkland.* Wildtrack Publishing, Sheffield.

Hooke, Della, 1998. *The Landscape of Anglo-Saxon England.* Leicester University Press.

Hooke, Della, 2011a. The Woodland Landscape of Early Medieval England. In: Higham N.J. and Ryan M.J., 2011, *Language and Landscape in Anglo-Saxon England,* Boydell Press, Woodbridge, Suffolk.

Hooke, Della, 2011b. *Trees in Anglo-Saxon England.* Boydell Press. Woodbridge, Suffolk.

Hoppitt, Rosemary, 2007. Hunting Suffolk's Parks: Towards a Reliable Chronology of Emparkment in: Liddiard, Robert (ed), 2007. *The Medieval Park: New Perspectives.* Windgather Press, Bollington, Macclesfield.

James, N. D. G., 1981. *A History of English Forestry.* Basil Blackwell. Oxford.

Jones, Andrew, 1979. Land Measurement in England, 1150–1350. *Agricultural History Review, Vol. 27.*

Jones, Richard and Page, Mark, 2006. *Medieval Villages in the English Landscape: Beginnings and Ends.* Windgather Press, Bollington, Macclesfield.

Langton, John and Jones, Graham (eds), 2005. *Forests and Chases of England and Wales c1500 to c1850.* St. John's College Research Centre: Oxford.

Liddiard, Robert (ed), 2007. T*he Medieval Park: New Perspectives.* Windgather Press, Bollington, Macclesfield.

Manwood, John, 1665. *A Treatise of the Laws of the Forest.* 3rd edition. (available as a free Google ebook, 4th edition 1717).

Mileson, Stephen, 2009. *Parks in Medieval England.* Oxford University Press, Oxford.

Neilson, N., 1942. Early English Woodland and Waste. *Journal of Economic History, Vol. II.*

Nichols, John, 1795–1811, *The History and Antiquities of the County of Leicester,* in eight volumes, London, John Nichols. reprint by S and R Publishers, Wakefield (referred to as 4/2/nnn where 4 is the volume number and 2 is the part number, followed by the page).

Nugent-Bell, Henry, 1821. *The Huntingdon Peerage.* London. 2nd edition.

Parker, L. A., 1947. *The Tudor Enclosure Movements in Leicestershire, 1485–1607.* Unpublished Phd thesis located in the Record Office for Leicester, Leicestershire and Rutland.

Pettit, Philip A. J., 1968. *The Royal Forest of Northamptonshire: A Study In Their Economy 1558–1714.* Northamptonshire Record Society, Northampton.

Pevsner, N. and Williamson, E., 1992. *The Buildings of England: Leicestershire and Rutland.* Reprinted with corrections 2nd edition. Penguin Books, London.

Rackham, Oliver, 2003. *Ancient Woodland.* 2nd edition. Castle Point Press, Colvend, Dalbeattie, Kirkudbrightshire.

Rich, Brian, 2005. in: Wiltshire, Mary, et al, *Duffield Frith: History and Evolution of the Landscape of a Medieval Derbyshire Forest,* Landmark Publishing, Ashbourne.

Rowley, R. T., 1965–68. The Clee Forest: A Study In Common Rights. *Trans. Shropshire Archaeological and Natural History Society. Vol. LVII.*

Short, Brian, 2000. Forest and Wood Pasture in Lowland England. In: Thirsk, J (ed) *Rural England: An Illustrated History of the Landscape,* Oxford University Press.

Somerville, Robert. 1953. *History of the Duchy of Lancaster. Vol 1, 1265–1603.* Council of the Duchy of Lancaster, London.

Squires, Anthony and Jeeves, Michael, 1994. *Leicestershire and Rutland Woodlands Past and Present.* Kairos Press, Newtown Linford.

Squires, Anthony, 1995. A Provisional List of the Medieval Woodlands of Leicestershire (excluding Rutland) c.1200 – c1530. *Transactions of the Leicestershire Archaeological and Historical Society,* Vol LXIX

Squires, Anthony, 2002, *The Greys: A Long and Noble Line.* The Silk Press, Hale, Cheshire.

Squires, Anthony, 2004. Parks and Woodland in Medieval Leicestershire. in: Bowman, Paul and Liddle, Peter (eds) *Leicestershire Landscapes,* Leicestershire Archaeological Fieldwork Group, Monograph No 1. Leicester.

Squires, Anthony, 2006. The Landscape of Leicester Abbey's Home Demense Lands to the Dissolution. In Story J, Bourne J, and Buckley R, (eds) *Leicester Abbey: Medieval History, Archaeology and Manuscript Studies.* Leicester Archaeological and Historical Society, Leicester.

Stamp L. Dudley and Hoskins, W.G., 1963. *The Common Lands of England and Wales*. Collins, London.

Stamper, P. A., 1983. *The Medieval Forest of Pamber, Hampshire*. In: Landscape History 5.

Stocks, H., 1923. *Records of the Borough of Leicester IV,, 1603–88*. Cambridge University Press, Cambridge.

Wager, Sarah, 1998. *Woods, Wolds and Groves: The Woodlands of Medieval Warwickshire*. British Archaeological Reports. British Series 269, Oxford.

Welldon Finn, R., 1963. *An Introduction to Domesday Book*. Longmans.

Wiltshire, Mary, et.al. 2005. *Duffield Frith* Landmark Publishing. Ashbourne.

Wiltshire, Mary and Woore, Sue, 2009. *The Medieval Parks of Derbyshire*, Landmark Publishing, Ashbourne.

Wise, John, 1883. *The New Forest: Its History and Scenery,* 5th edition, Gibbings.

Abbreviations used in the Text

DL, Duchy of Lancaster (see bibliography).

HER – Heritage and Environment Record, held by Leicestershire County Council.

LMVN – Leicestershire Medieval Village Notes (Farnham – see bibliography).

ROLLR Record Office for Leicester, Leicestershire and Rutland (located in Wigston Magna).

TLAHS Transactions of the Leicestershire Archaeological and Historical Society.

TNA - The National Archives, Kew, London

VCH Leics – 1958, *The Victoria History of the County of Leicestershire*, Volume IV.

VCH Staffs – The Victoria History of the County of Staffordshire Vol 2.

Coal mining in medieval Leicestershire

Robert F Hartley

Introduction

There is a fair amount of documentary evidence for coal mining in medieval England, including several references in Leicestershire, which will be discussed below, but it has always been difficult to picture the scale and nature of the industry. The discovery of dated coal mine workings in a modern opencast excavation at Coleorton between 1988 and 1995 for the first time allowed us to see the layout of 15th century mines and some of the artefacts used by the miners. The archive and finds are of national importance for the way they allow us to understand the industry at a specific place within a set period of time in the medieval period.

The coalfield area and county boundaries

The coalfield area of North West Leicestershire extends over the county boundary into Derbyshire, and by looking on both sides of the border we can obtain a larger sample of documentary evidence about coal mining. In addition, we need to note that prior to about 1890 the boundary was extremely convoluted (fig 1). The parish of Donisthorpe was minutely subdivided, while several places now well within Leicestershire, including Measham, Stretton en le Field, Oakthorpe, and parts of Packington and Ravenstone were isolated parts of Derbyshire. All these islands were transferred to Leicestershire, while Netherseal

Figure 1: Area of outcrop of the Coal Measures and the Derbyshire / Leicestershire boundary in the medieval period.

and Overseal were given to Derbyshire in exchange.

The main published source of information on the coalfield (Owen 1984) covers both counties together, and for the purpose of setting the documentary background I shall do likewise.

Outcropping coal seams and early mining areas

Figure 1 also shows the area of outcrop of the Coal Measures within which the coal seams are found. The lowest and oldest seams outcrop at the north-west, the highest and most recent seams at the south east. The seams then descend gently below other rocks in a south easterly direction, which is why the coal was mined at greater depth in the 19th and 20th centuries around Coalville, Bagworth and as far south as Desford.

The parishes where we have medieval documentary references to mining are shown on Figure 2. In the case of Breedon we know there is no coal in the parish, and the references must be to the daughter settlements of Staunton Harold, Worthington or Newbold. The coal seams do not outcrop in the vicinity of Ashby de la Zouch, so the coalfield is divided into three distinct mining areas, centred respectively on Newhall (Derbyshire), Oakthorpe (formerly in Derbyshire), and Coleorton.

Figure 3 shows the way in which the thickest and best seams outcrop, and includes the names of these seams. There were particularly good reserves of coal in three areas. The first is the triangle of land between Bretby, Stanton and Newhall, the second is the parish of Oakthorpe, and the third is the area where the parishes of Staunton Harold, Worthington, Coleorton and Swannington

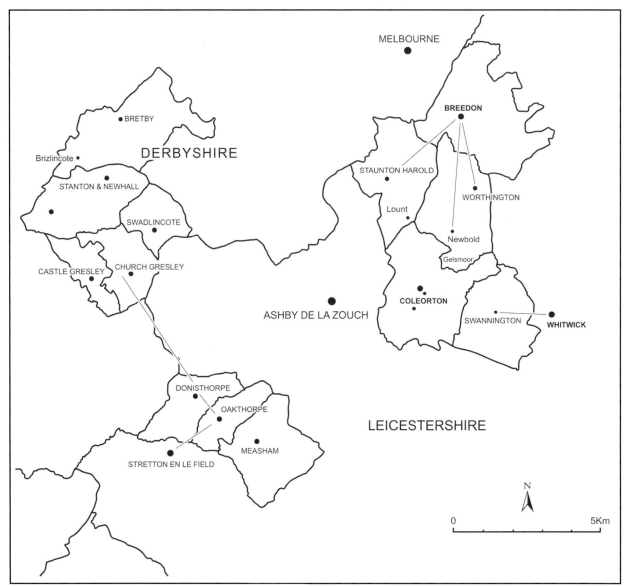

Figure 2: Parishes with documentary references to coal mining in the medieval period.

meet. All of these, with probably a few other thinner seams, were being worked to some extent prior to 1500.

Documentary references to coal mining within the area

The few fragmentary records we have are dictated by the chance survival of certain collections of documents. The records of three local abbeys – Burton on Trent, Leicester and Garendon – are particularly important.

The document which provides the earliest published reference cannot now be located, but is believed to state:- "Philip, son of Eilnod gave to Rudolf, son of Gerbold", a piece of ground worth 2s per annum "where coal is gotten". This was at Swannington in 1204 and if this quotation is authentic it is one of the earliest references to coal mining anywhere in England.

Swannington

This hint of early mining at Swannington is followed by a case in 1293:- Roger Godberd claimed to be Chief Lord of Swannington, and thereby to have total right to the waste there. This was disputed by Alan Talbot, a free man of Swannington, who claimed that he was also a Chief Lord and that as a free man he was entitled to an acre of the waste including the underlying coal. At the hearing it was established that according to "the custom of the said vill" each freeman was entitled to a part of the waste proportionate to his (land) holding, and also had the right to dig for coal. (Farnham 1930–3, Vol. IV, 192).

This record is important, as it shows that the coal reserves on the waste (later known as Swannington Common) were recognised as a common resource for the freemen of the

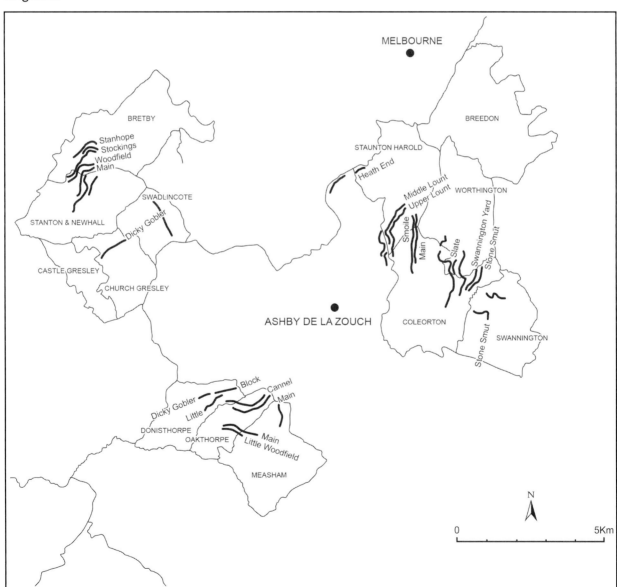

Figure 3: Outcrops of the thickest and most valuable coal seams in the coalfield.

197

village, and that the practice of digging out the coal probably originated within Anglo-Danish society, predating the more hierarchical "feudal" system of laws brought in by the Normans. The area of coal seam outcrops seems to have been deliberately set aside as "waste" or common pasture for livestock, within which the diggings for coal (providing they were fenced off) would cause little disturbance.

In the 14th century there are indications that coal mines were starting to be seen as a source of private profit, for in 1321 Henry Bloodles of Worthington purchased property at Swannington including a coal mine (VCH Leics Vol 3, 31, Farnham 1930–3, Vol 4, 195). In 1369 Edmund Blackfordebi granted land and tenements at Swannington including a coal mine to Thomas Blackfordebi (VCH Leics Vol 3, 31, Farnham 1930, Vol 4, 195). Owen considered it likely that these mines would have been "on or close to Swannington Common..... where the Stone Smutt Rider and the One Foot seams outcropped" (Owen 1984).

Coleorton

To the west of Swannington lies Coleorton, which must have had just as much mining activity but for which no medieval references survive. There were two village foci within this parish – Overton Quartermarsh and Overton Saucy. By the 1420s the original village of Overton Saucy was being referred to as "Coal Overton", later written down as "Cole Orton". We now know from archaeological evidence (which will be reviewed below) that there was a sophisticated and large-scale coal mining industry here by the 1450s, with every sign that it had been developing for many decades previously. The fact that there is no medieval document mentioning this industry shows how little reliance can be placed on documents to tell us about the work and life of the common people.

It is only in 1498 that we have any direct documentary clue to the industry, and that is just a reference to two "collyers", Thomas and Robert Pocock, of Overton Saucy, being charged with cutting down trees and underwood to the value of 40 shillings on the property of John Beaumond in Overton Quatermarsh (Farnham 1930–3, Vol 2, 77).

By the second quarter of the 16th century Swannington and Coleorton were supplying coal to villages as far afield as Frisby and Galby, 10 miles south-east of Leicester (Hoskins 1944–5 171–210), and it was quite usual for tenants even further south, in the Welland Valley (on the Brudenell estates), to pay part of their rents by bringing loads of coal from the North West Leicestershire pits. During this century there are increasing references to the mining activities of the Beaumont family as the whole business of coal mining increases in scale during the Elizabethan "Industrial Revolution".

Breedon, Staunton Harold and Worthington

The parish of Breedon on the Hill (with its chapelries of Staunton Harold and Worthington), adjoined the north side of the Swannington and Coleorton common lands and their inhabitants also seem to have exploited the coal seams. Two small hamlets – Lount (Staunton Harold) and Newbold (Worthington) came into existence during the medieval period as common-edge settlements presumably housing a growing number of coal miners and their families.

At Worthington (presumably at the south end of the parish near Lount) in 1270 Ralph Bozun and his wife granted their lands and the coal mines which they contained to the monks of Garendon Abbey (Nichols 1804, 731). Some references to coal mining at Breedon on the Hill must surely concern Worthington. For example in 1300 Isabel de Hastings was responsible for working coal and iron ore at three places in Breedon parish, one of which was Gelsmoor (Farnham Vol 2, 30). The iron was probably coming from Cloud Hill, and the coal from Newbold and Gelsmoor.

Oakthorpe

In the western part of the Leicestershire coalfield the seams outcrop to the west of Ashby de la Zouch, near Oakthorpe village (in Derbyshire until the late 19th century). There is a reference to "Colpytsyche" at Oakthorpe in 1412, perhaps referring to a drainage channel or sough from a coal mine (Derbyshire Deeds, DD6783). Leicester Abbey had lands in Oakthorpe and was supplying loads of coal – presumably from its mine there – by 1393 (Owen 1984). A Rental, probably from 1477, confirms that the Abbey certainly owned a mine at Oakthorpe by that date (Nichols 1804, 1031). There are more complete details in the early 1500s:- in 1503 William and Robert Gresley leased to John, Abbot of Leicester and John Blount various lands, with the underlying coal. The following year the Abbot leased Mease Croft in Oakthorpe and the underlying coal. (Derbyshire Deeds, DD6786, 6791–3).

There are other possible mining areas in medieval Leicestershire, including Alton Grange, Coal Pit Heath at Packington, Ravenstone, Heather and Normanton, but as yet with no documentary or archaeological confirmation.

Medieval mining landscapes, Coleorton, Leicestershire

Despite the vast amount of published documentary material, prior to the discoveries outlined below, from the Lounge Opencast Site at Coleorton, very little was known in detail about coal mining methods before the 18th century. The archaeological importance of this site lies primarily in the fact that some of the early underground workings and artefacts were closely dated by analysis of tree-rings in the oak pit props. These dates allowed us to define one area of mid-15th century workings, and other areas of early-16th century workings, and as a result to understand some of capabilities and methods of Leicestershire coal miners at that era. A second advantage of this site was that it was worked in a way which exposed large areas of ancient mine galleries at one time, allowing them to be viewed to some extent in context.

The opportunity

In the mid 1980s British Coal Opencast put in a planning application for an opencast site north-east of Ashby de Zouch. They gave the site the codename "Lounge", presumably derived from the nearby hamlet of Lount. The site was a big one by British standards, involving the excavation of 2.5 Km^2 of countryside to expose parts of ten seams of coal. A modern opencast mine is highly-mechanised and uses large, high-capacity machines for excavating the overburden and removing it to tipping grounds. When old coal workings are uncovered there is only a brief period to make observations and retrieve finds before the coal itself is dug out and the working area moves onwards.

On the Lounge site several factors were favourable to the recovery of information and artefacts. To begin with we had lots of

help from British Coal Opencast, they were operating a big site where large areas of old workings were cleared out before extraction of the solid coal, and several members of the Museum Service staff were available to visit at regular intervals. I had a remit to record the County's archaeology, Stuart Warburton and colleagues were preparing display material for the proposed Snibston Discovery Park three miles away at Coalville, while John Crocker, a senior officer with the National Coal Board, had taken early retirement on grounds of ill-health and was also able to visit the site in connection with his intended publication on the history of Coleorton Hall and its owners..

On the earliest phases of the opencast site (1988–1990) we were able to make observations and retrieve finds, and also find storage space for them and commission some conservation work. A most important discovery from this period was the Coleorton Coat (L.A30.1992), a woollen coat which, on stylistic grounds, appeared to date between the 15th to the 17th centuries. There were also several single-ended picks, wooden shovels, three-legged stools, and parts of small sledges which we presumed had been used to move baskets of coal underground.

In the extension area (Area C) we found well-organised pillar and stall workings 30m below the surface. Descending to them through the overburden were timber-lined shafts with jointed oak frames. There were large numbers of pit props made from complete sections of oak tree trunks and late in 1990 John Crocker suggested we could have these dated by analysis of the growth rings. The results obtained by Robert Howard of Nottingham University were remarkable – the oak trees from which the props were cut had been felled in 1450, 1453 (two), 1455, and 1463. These dates immediately led us to reinterpret the importance of the Coleorton coat, which had been found in workings not far away, and probably dating from the 1530s at the latest. It could now be seen as one of the earliest pieces of working clothing ever found.

This information propelled our little project into national significance, and I arranged a press day. The story was carried the following day by the Times, Guardian, and most fully by the Daily Telegraph. To allow them to illustrate their article I provided an isometric drawing to give an idea of the appearance of the workings, the shaft and the pit-top (fig 4).

Further research and exhibitions

The Museums Service was now in a favourable position to promote the archaeological importance of existing and potential finds from the opencast mine. With a planning application being submitted at the same time to extend the site we were able to anticipate the likely presence of further early workings and plan our activities accordingly.

We had publicity, staff and buildings resources, and a demonstrable purpose for our activities. Good publicity is good for getting backing from councillors; staff could record and retrieve items, which could then be stored in the Snibston buildings. The new displays at Snibston would be directly improved by the addition of these high-profile discoveries. Bob York and a colleague from the staff at Snibston carried out a rather arduous excavation of most of a mine shaft as the overburden was removed around it, so that the components could be used to make an authentic reconstruction of a 15th century mine for the displays at Snibston.

Meanwhile, I was able to spend some time studying the landscape around the opencast site for more clues. With John Crocker's help I had access to a range of very detailed vertical air photos, on which there was a great deal of evidence of old mines. The evidence was in two forms – soilmarks and earthworks. Soilmarks in ploughed fields showed areas of dark colouration where mine spoiltips had been. Earthworks provided better-preserved evidence with the shaft hollows and spoil tips still in existence. With the evidence from the opencast site we could now understand the spoil tips and soil marks as the surface evidence not of shallow "bell pits" for local households, but of mine shafts, up to 30m deep, and producing thousands of tons of coal per year.

Coleorton has an unusual field pattern because in the 18th century large areas of common were divided up into smallholdings for the miners. These plots are not worth ploughing, but were used to graze livestock, and a vast amount of earthwork evidence survives. However, some old mining areas were allowed to regenerate back to woodland, so the earthworks are hidden from the aerial view. In this case I had to battle with the vegetation and attempt to plot the features on a large-scale map. To some extent we were also able to use documents and field names to help in understanding the historical development of the parish.

When British Coal applied for permission to extend the opencast once more in 1991, archaeological sites had been established as "a material consideration in the determining of planning applications" and we were able to impose some conditions on the developer. We asked British Coal to fund a more detailed survey of the areas they wanted to mine. They lent me two of their surveyors for a day with laser survey equipment to establish more accurate locations for the shafts in Birch Coppice.

Probably for the first time anywhere we also imposed conditions on recording and retrieval of finds likely to be made in the workings, over 30m below the surface. They agreed to pay a site archaeologist, and to contribute to our likely conservation costs.

In the event, only part of the site was opencasted. Birch Coppice was saved because of its value as a wildlife reserve. However, several more areas of early workings were uncovered, and numerous finds added to our collections, although nothing from this later part of the site could be accurately dated, and the finds appeared to be from the 16th and 17th centuries.

Review of the finds

Unfortunately, with the ending of the opencast work in 1992, the impetus to interpret and conserve the finds lapsed. Many had been acquired for possible use in major displays at Snibston which did not come to fruition, and they had been temporarily stored in parts of the Snibston Colliery buildings, while others had been transferred to the Archaeology store at Humberstone Drive in Leicester. No funding was available for staff to work on them, and they were in danger of losing their documentation and the contexts which gave them archaeological value. With the break-up of the former Leicestershire County Council in 1997, most of the finds would need moving from sites in the City of Leicester to new storage within the smaller administrative area of the County.

In 1999 I was given curatorial responsibility for all of the Technology collections in the County Museums Service collections, by then focused on Snibston Discovery Park. John Crocker and I realised that there was still an outstanding need to identify and label all the remaining finds from the Lounge site, many of which had been acquired and stored without being properly accessioned into the Museum Service collections. It was not an easy task. John wrestled with reconciling incomplete and inaccurate lists. I had to organise the moving of virtually every item, from several sites in Leicester and within Snibston Discovery Park. The task took two or three years to complete to a situation where everything was documented and housed in reasonably good storage conditions. John believed there were 480 items (plus two missing). I now think there are over 500, but in some cases it depends on how you count pieces which are component parts or fragments.

A summary of the finds, with their Accession Numbers is set out below. The Accession numbers indicate how some items were collected for the Technology collections (L.T) while others had been included in Archaeology (L.A) as we obtained dating evidence and became more aware of their antiquity.

Summary of finds from Lount Opencast Mine

L.A90.1987	Pottery, surface scatter
L.A91.1987	Pottery, surface scatter
L.T58 1989	Finds from Area "B" as follows :-
	1. Probably from old workings in Upper Main/High Main; wooden spade, 2 wooden hooks, sycamore bowl, 5 single-ended picks, 5 parts of wooden sledges (corves), parts of 5 wooden stools.
	2. Probably from Middle Lount seam and associated with early 19th century Spring Wood Colliery; 2 double ended picks, one double-ended sledge hammer, two sections of shaft curbing.
	3. Probably from 1920s adit working; small mine-tub.
	4. Several other stray finds
L.T64.1990	Finds from Area "C", Upper Main pillar and stall workings:- numerous shaft timbers, pit props (some dated to 1550-1563 period), parts of coal basket, wooden hook, leather boot.
L.T3.1991	Wooden spade
L.T10.1991	19th/20th century spade
L.A30.1992	Woollen coat, 16th cent
L.A31.1992	Boots and other pieces of leather
T.C.1603	Fragments of fabric
L.A87.1992	Sherd of Medieval Sandy Ware pottery
L.A88.1992	Fragments of Black Ware pottery
L.A91.1992	Fragments of Cistercian Ware pottery
L.A61.1994	Finds from shaft excavation
L.A113.1992	Finds from Area "F" as follows:- 66 pieces of wood, including shaft frames, pegs, wedges, parts of stools, 25 parts of corves, 40 wickerwork samples, 2 wooden spades, 3 wooden hooks, 1 handle from wooden hook
L.A114.1992	Finds from areas "F" and "J" including 8 timbers from possible sough.
L.A115.1992	Finds from Area "H" including 6 corf runners and several parts of stools.
L.A116.1992	Finds from areas "C" and "D", shoes etc
L.A62.1994	Late 17th cent long coat
X.W62.1998	24 pieces of wood and 2 bricks

The larger finds are currently (Sept 2013) in store in the Main Store at Snibston Discovery Park, and the smaller and more sensitive items in the Sensitive Store at the Collections Resources Centre, Barrow on Soar. Some items are also on display, mainly at Snibston. They are safe and tidy, but still await detailed study and analysis. There are comprehensive files of information, with drawings and detailed lists, now brought together in the archives of the County Council's Archaeology collections at the Collections Resources Centre.

A picture of the industry

The finds and field notes allow us to reconstruct something of the appearance of 15th century coal mines for the first time (fig 4.) The industry was well organised, with sufficient demand for its coal to justify the expense of sinking carefully-constructed timber-lined shafts to depths of at least 30 metres. The shafts were about 1.5m square internally, with horizontal oak frames every metre or so down, and smaller branches pushed up and down behind them as "bratticing" to prevent the surrounding material from collapsing into the shaft.

They were mining in the Upper Main and High Main Coal Top and Bottom seams, which in this area form a single layer of coal about 3m thick. Within the seams, the miners were removing the middle 1.5 to 2m of coal, leaving the top and bottom coal as a roof and floor to retain the softer coal measures above and below.

Several shafts would have been in use at any one time, with specialist teams of miners working respectively on shaft sinking and setting out the underground working. We have evidence of approximately 300 shafts in the area around the Lounge site, with the earliest dated one of 1450 being at the south end of the area, and with the more northerly ones dating from the 16th century, created in a gradual process of extraction of the coal over more than 100 years. This might suggest that three or four new shafts were being completed each year, providing full-time employment for a shaft-sinking team. At the surface another two teams, woodmen and carpenters, must have been scouring local woodlands for suitable timber, and shaping it in a workshop of some sort to make shaft timbers which would interlock together, and props of the right length to support the roof in the particular areas being worked.

Once the shafts had reached the coal seam and galleries had been dug out into it, the miners could begin digging the coal, using single-ended picks to break it out, and one-piece wooden shovels to lift it into baskets or "corves" These corves comprised an oak platform with iron-shod sledge runners under each side, and a body of stout basket work with sides 60 cm long and 60cm high. They would have been used to move the coal underground and were probably then wound up the shaft and emptied at the surface. Underground the men were wearing leather turnshoes and at least one had a good-quality but now quite old woollen coat for work wear.

At the surface the coal was sold, and carried away in carts or horse-panniers for use over an area extending up to 40 miles away. There was in particular a long-established trade to Leicester, involving the carriers in an overnight stay just west of the town, and the coal was sold the following morning on the Coal Hill, just by the East Gate of the town. A toll was payable at the North Bridge of Leicester, and to avoid this, carriers heading further afield would have used routes such as the Coalpit Lane which runs through the south end of Wistow parish and heads for the south east of the county. By the 18th century the transporting of this coal was notorious for the damage it caused to the County's roads, especially where streams were crossed, and it may not be coincidence that there are early "packhorse bridges" over the Rothley Brook at Thurcaston and Anstey and over the River Soar at Aylestone, on routes which might well have been used by the coal trade.

Preserving the landscape

Following the underground discoveries a study was made of the adjacent landscape, and it proved possible to identify numerous mine sites surviving as earthwork or soil mark features. The Coleorton area is now recognised as one of the most important surviving early coal mining areas in Britain. In the late 1990s English Heritage were reviewing historic mining sites under their Monuments Protection Programme. Based on my recommendations, in 2001 they moved to schedule five areas of historic mining remains in Coleorton, in total covering nearly a square kilometre as follows:

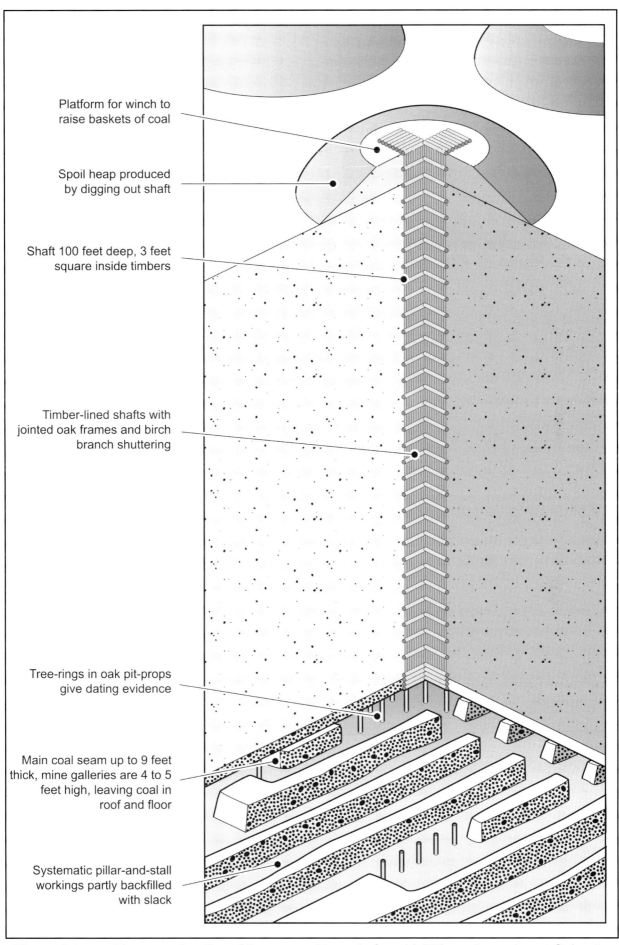

Platform for winch to
raise baskets of coal

Spoil heap produced
by digging out shaft

Shaft 100 feet deep, 3 feet
square inside timbers

Timber-lined shafts with
jointed oak frames and birch
branch shuttering

Tree-rings in oak pit-props
give dating evidence

Main coal seam up to 9 feet
thick, mine galleries are 4 to 5
feet high, leaving coal in
roof and floor

Systematic pillar-and-stall
workings partly backfilled
with slack

Figure 4: Isometric reconstruction of the general layout of a mid-15th century mine at Coleorton,
at Grid Reference SK3896 1784, approximately 700m north of Coleorton Hall.

1. & 2. *Rough Park and Birch Coppice*

Shaft mines likely to be of 15th/16th century date, well preserved in woodland. The workings will be in the Main Coal at depths of 30–40 metres.

3. *Newbold Hurst*

Shaft mines likely to be of 16th century date, sunk to workings in the Main Coal at depths in excess of 30m, well preserved in woodland.

4. *Farm Town*

Small pits on the outcrop, with very little spoil material, possibly "bell pits". Date unknown, probably medieval. Well preserved in old pasture land.

5. *Lount Wood*

Area of numerous small excavations representing possible "bell pits" on outcrop of Upper Lount coal. Date unknown, probably medieval and perhaps from early in the period. Well preserved in woodland.

Details of these sites are maintained on the Historic Environment Records database at County Hall, Glenfield, Leicester.

Conclusion

The Lounge Opencast Site demonstrated the degree of survival of pre-Industrial Revolution coal mines in the local coalfield, and for the first time allowed us to understand some of the mechanics of 15th and 16th century mines in this area. It yielded a large number of finds, which are currently in store but are worthy of further study. As a result of the discoveries, five areas of the Coleorton landscape have been given statutory protection.

The totality of the landscape of this small coalfield has been recognised as having great potential importance because it preserve a vast amount of evidence of mines from the 15th century or earlier, to the 20th century. These remains are primarily underground, but at the surface are numerous earthwork features, and also cottages and smallholdings which include mine sites and miners' housing from the early 18th century onwards. The landscape is threatened by modern "gentrification", but it is hoped that measures can be introduced into the planning system to give the whole area the conservation status it deserves.

References

By far the easiest source to search is Owen, who includes very full references to numerous earlier publications. The publications by Hartley, R. F. in 1994 and 2006 have additional photographs of the excavations and drawings of the finds.

Derbyshire Deeds, Derbyshire Record Office, Matlock.

Farnham, G., 1930–33. *Leicestershire Medieval Village Notes* (6 Volumes) Leicester: privately printed.

Hartley, R. F., 1992. 'Coleorton'. In: *Current Archaeology* 134.

Hartley, R. F., 1994. 'The Tudor Miners of Coleorton, Leicestershire'. In: *Mining Before Powder*. Peak District Mines Historical Society.

Hartley, R. F., 2006. 'Lounge Site Revisited: Medieval Mining Landscapes at Coleorton, Leicestershire'. In: *Mining in the Landscape*. NAMHO Conference Proceedings.

Hoskins, W. G., 1944–5 'A Short History of Galby and Frisby'. In: *Transactions of the Leicestershire Archaeological and Historical Society* 22, 171–210

Nichols, J., 1804. *History and Antiquities of the County of Leicester*, Vol 3, pt 2, 'West Goscote Hundred'. London: John Nichols.

Owen, C., 1984. *The Leicestershire & South Derbyshire Coalfield.* Moorland Publishing/ Leicestershire Museums Service

Victoria County History of Leicestershire, Vol 3, 1955. London: University of London Institute of Historical Research.

Archaeology and medieval Leicester

Richard Buckley

Introduction

The aim of this article is to review the results of fieldwork on medieval sites within the City of Leicester since the excavation of the Austin Friars site in 1973–6 (fig 1.1; Mellor and Pearce 1981) and to show how our knowledge of the archaeology of the medieval borough has advanced. The article will include a brief account of the investigation of medieval sites in the city before 1973, whilst the evidence from more recent work will be discussed under a series of thematic headings. These will consider the transition from Roman to medieval Leicester, the development of medieval urban topography; town life and industry; the high-status sites of Leicester Castle (fig 1.2) and the Newarke (fig 1.3); and evidence for religious buildings such as Leicester Abbey, the churches of St Peter (fig 1.4) and St Michael (fig 1.3) and the chapel of St Sepulchre.

The article is based on the work of many archaeologists and the sheer volume of data means that that it is only possible to give a fairly cursory account of the results of some important projects. It is hoped that this summary will at least provide pointers to more detailed published and unpublished (grey-literature) accounts which exist.

Medieval archaeology in Leicester 1840–1990

Inevitably, perhaps, archaeological attention in the 19th and early 20th centuries concentrated largely on Leicester's Roman past, rather than on its development in the medieval and later periods. Certainly the more visible manifestations of the medieval town, its few surviving buildings, were not universally valued. By the mid 19th century, many must have been in a poor state of repair and large numbers were demolished and replaced with new brick structures, reflecting the town's increasing prosperity. The few buildings that remain today, such as for example the Guildhall (fig 1.16) and Newarke Houses Museum (fig 1.11d), only survived as a result of the campaigns of the Leicestershire Archaeological and Historical Society.

Unfortunately, the latter was not successful in saving one notable building, the late medieval Wyggeston's Hospital (fig 1.14), whilst the considerable number of commercial and domestic timber-framed buildings, recorded in 19th-century photographs and engravings (Courtney and Courtney 1995) had largely gone by the early 20th century. As late as the 1940s and 50s, buildings such as St Mary's Vicarage in the Newarke (fig 1.11c), probably the house of the Dean of the Newarke College, was partially demolished and there are also (unconfirmed) reports of the destruction of timber buildings within what is now St Nicholas Circle in connection with the construction of the inner relief road and elsewhere as part of the slum clearance (Clarke 1957; Clarke and Simmons 1960). Admittedly, most of these domestic structures were by then probably in a poor state of repair and not up to modern standards, but unfortunately were swept away with little thought given to making a permanent record for future generations. It is in no small measure due to the considerable efforts of architects such as Henry Goddard, Thomas Fosbrooke, Albert Herbert and Waller K Bedingfield that any drawings and records survive at all of some of Leicester's more significant medieval buildings.

Leicester's two major surviving medieval monuments, the Castle (fig 1.15) and Abbey, have attracted interest from a comparatively early period, perhaps by virtue of their association with important personages or historical events. In the 1840s, the historian and editor of the Leicester Journal, James Thompson, undertook excavations at the site of Leicester Abbey which were continued in the 1850s by the Nevinsons under the auspices of the Leicestershire Architectural and Archaeological Society (Buckley 2006). At the same time, prompted by major alterations to the Great Hall, Thompson wrote a short book on Leicester Castle which includes a good description of the surviving evidence for the medieval Great Hall and John of Gaunt's cellar (Thompson 1859). In the early 1920s, research excavations resumed at Leicester Abbey, under Fosbrooke and Bedingfield, culminating at the end of the decade in the stripping of the entire plan of the claustral buildings under the direction of the latter, in connection with the conversion of the site into a public park (Buckley 2006, 6–8). Although these are often referred to as archaeological excavations, and consequently judged rather harshly as a result in terms of recording, it is clear that the prime objective was to strip pernicious weeds from the area of the proposed park (Bedingfield 1931). The recording of abbey building plans should in many respects be viewed as a useful by-product for which we should be grateful to Bedingfield for his foresight.

The first truly archaeological excavation in Leicester was that of the Jewry Wall site by Kathleen Kenyon between 1936 and 1939 (fig 2.1). In her own words, this represented 'the first opportunity for the investigation of any extensive area within the Roman city' (Kenyon 1948, 1). Due to damage from deep basements, the medieval levels here were restricted to pits and fragments of a structure built into the northern portico of the baths. Hence the lack of much detail on the medieval levels in the report is more a result of the extensive damage that had occurred from cellarage rather than an unwillingness to give them due consideration. The volume includes specialist reports on medieval pottery, tile and small finds. In 1939, sections were cut through Newarke Houses Garden (fig 2.2) revealing the line of the castle bailey ditch, and further excavations were undertaken next to the Turret Gateway in Castle View (1951), across the eastern town defences on Churchgate (1950) and inside St Margaret's Church in 1946–9 (fig 2.3; Clarke 1952). The report includes medieval pottery descriptions and drawings. The northern town defences were sectioned in 1952 and the comparatively scanty record of medieval finds suggests that the prime objective was to elucidate the Roman sequence for the defences (Goodchild 1953). Further small-scale investigations took place in the 1950s, with major excavations at Blue Boar Lane in 1958 in advance of the construction of the inner relief road (Wacher 1959) but with little mention in the surviving accounts of discoveries dating to the medieval period.

Excavation was almost continuous throughout the 1960s with many small sites examined with extremely limited resources

in the western part of the town, published collectively in the 1980s and 90s (Clay and Mellor 1985; Clay and Pollard 1994). With the exception of the discovery of the Southgates medieval kiln (Hebditch 1967–8), the medieval levels were mostly represented by pits and structural fragments. In her retrospective on 25 years of archaeology in Leicestershire, the Senior Field Archaeologist of Leicestershire Museums Service, Jean Mellor, acknowledged that the majority of excavations before 1971 had concentrated on an examination of the Roman levels, often to the detriment of the medieval deposits: 'Regrettably, in the context of large scale destruction of Roman deposits by the construction of the inner ring road and limited resources, the medieval levels were not afforded the attention they deserved' (Mellor 1992). The turning point came in 1971 when the decision was taken to proceed with full excavation of a site in St Nicholas Circle (fig 2.4), close to the frontage of the medieval High Street (later Highcross Street and now St Nicholas Place). Although located above the south range of the Roman forum, this site also lay in the heart of the medieval town and 'a determined effort was made to examine all the medieval deposits as well as the Roman' (Mellor 1992, 94).

The site revealed extensive evidence of medieval burgage plots[1] separated by stone boundary walls, with considerable evidence of back yard activities (Kipling 2010). Large assemblages of finds were also recovered, including significant quantities of medieval and post-medieval pottery and small finds. The following year a narrow trench was excavated on the west side of Southgates (usually referred to as the 'Newarke Houses Car Park' site; fig 2.5), revealing a series of medieval burgage plots together with a section through the castle bailey ditch and evidence for the robbed town wall (McWhirr 1972, 64–5). In 1973–6, the site of the Austin Friars near West Bridge (fig 2.6) was excavated and a major post-excavation programme was put into effect immediately afterwards. The report (Mellor and Pearce 1981) represents a significant milestone in the archaeology of medieval Leicester with a detailed consideration of all classes of finds, including the pioneering work of Deborah Sawday and Rosemary Woodland

---

1 A long narrow plot within a borough, usually with buildings on the street frontage, held by a tenant in return for payment of rent to the lord.

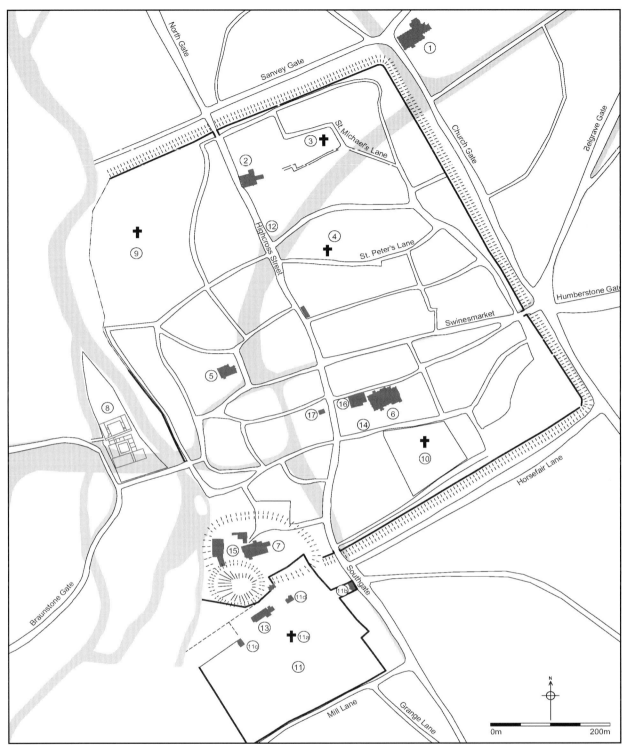

Figure 1: Medieval Leicester showing principal buildings referred to in the text. (Drawn by M. Morris)

Key: Churches: 1. St Margaret; 2. All Saints; 3. St Michael; 4. St Peter; 5. St Nicholas; 6. St Martin; 7. St Mary de Castro

Friaries & religious precincts: 8. Austin Friars; 9. Blackfriars and church of St Clement; 10. Greyfriars; 11. The Newarke and church of the Annunciation of the Blessed Virgin Mary (11a), Newarke Gateway (11b), St. Mary's Vicarage (11c) and Wygston's Chantry House (11d)

Hospitals: 12. St John's Hospital; 13. Trinity Hospital; 14. Wygston's Hospital

Other buildings: 15. The Castle; 16. The Guildhall; 17. Wygston's House

(Grey background line through centre of city is route of modern road system)

in classifying the medieval and post-medieval pottery by fabric and form, leading to the development of a dated type series. The excavation report also contained the results of detailed analysis of building materials, small finds, leather, wood, animal bone, human bone and environmental remains and represented in many ways a starting point for future analysis of medieval sites in Leicester.

For most of the 1980s, little excavation took place within the historic core of Leicester and its suburbs: comparatively few sites were developed and those that were, were mostly cellared. A small excavation on Causeway Lane in 1980 (fig 2.7; Buckley 1980; Connor and Buckley 1999) revealed extensive pitting of the 12th–13th centuries, and amongst the pottery assemblage were several sherds of hand-made early Anglo-Saxon pottery, unfortunately residual in later contexts, but significant in pointing to activity of this period in the vicinity.

The 12th-century Great Hall of Leicester Castle (fig 2.8) had been studied in the 1960s by Walter Horn, who carried out a programme of radiocarbon dating with a view to confirming the date of the surviving roof. Results were mixed, but suggested that much of the upper structure was later medieval work rather than 12th century (Horn 1970; Leicester City Museum Service (LCMS) archive). In the early 1980s, tree-ring dating of the arcade posts was undertaken, providing an estimated felling date of c.1150 (Laxton 1981–2) and a major programme of architectural recording of the roof followed during the repairs of 1984. This led to a new interpretation of the form of the 12th-century hall as summarised below (Alcock and Buckley 1987). A number of watching briefs (Mellor 1984–5, 98; Mellor 1986, 88; Liddle 1986, 92–3) and a small-scale research excavation (Buckley 1987, 92) were also carried out at the castle in the 1980s. Later in the decade, the long-awaited excavations in advance of the construction of the Shires shopping centre were undertaken in 1988–9. These comprised two sites, one on St. Peter's Lane (fig 2.9) which revealed extensive pitting and robbed Roman structures (rather than the hoped-for site of the lost church of St Peter) and Little Lane (fig 2.10) where the medieval levels consisted of pits and robber trenches to the rear of properties fronting on to the medieval Swinesmarket (now High

Street). Long-running excavations such as these provided the opportunity for extensive sampling of deposits and on-site sieving to recover environmental remains, masterminded by Angela Monckton (Monckton this vol.). Post-excavation analysis of the results continued immediately afterwards, with further revisions to the medieval pottery fabrics by Deborah Sawday, following her major programme of work on the 1971 and 1973 St Nicholas Circle sites. In 1989, investigations took place within a 12th-century undercroft[2] in Guildhall Lane, first discovered in the 19th century (fig 2.11), with the aim of recording the structure and sampling archaeological deposits inside to assess evidence for its date (Hagar and Buckley 1990, 99–101). The site within which this building lies was subsequently excavated in 2003 in advance of the construction of the new BBC building (Kipling 2010).

The first site in the City to be excavated under the terms of the 1990 Planning Policy Guidance Note 16 (Archaeology and Planning) was Causeway Lane in 1991 (fig 2.7), adjacent to the small site of 1980 previously referred to (Buckley 1980). The post-Roman levels here included further evidence for probable Anglo-Saxon activity in the vicinity, for the re-use and later robbing of Roman structures and of course the ubiquitous pitting as found on most medieval sites in the city. Again, an extensive environmental sampling programme was put into effect and with secure funding in place, specialist analysis of the results came to fruition in 1999 with the publication of the excavation report (Connor and Buckley 1999).

The effect of the new planning guidance was to create a significant increase in fieldwork projects in the city. This led to large-scale excavations at Bonners Lane in 1993 (fig 2.12; Finn 2004) and the discovery of the first early Anglo-Saxon structure in Leicester, together with important evidence for the development of the south suburb in the medieval and post-medieval periods. Other important sites investigated between 1990 and 2008 with medieval levels included Bath Lane (fig 2.13; Cooper 1993a); High Street (fig 2.14; Cooper 1993b); Bowling Green Inn, Oxford Street (fig 2.15; Higgins 1997a); Westbridge Place (fig 2.16; Higgins 1997b); Friar Lane (fig 2.17; Gnanaratnam 1998); Oxford Street and York Road (fig 2.18; Gossip 1998, 1999a/b); St

2   A cellar or storage room beneath a building

208

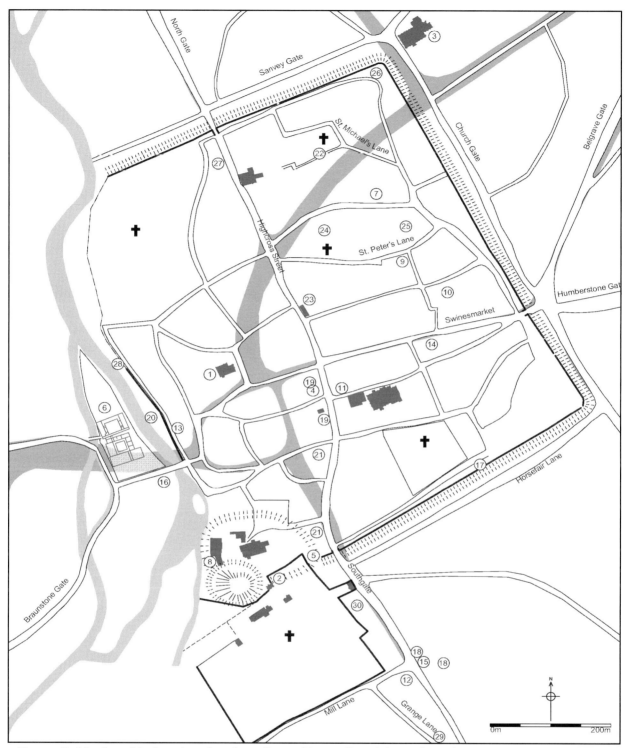

Figure 2: Medieval Leicester showing sites with medieval deposits referred to in the text in order of first mention. (Drawn by M. Morris.)

Key to sites, with museum accession numbers (where known).
1. Jewry Wall site 1936–9; 2. Newarke Houses garden A39.1939; 3. St Margaret's Church; 4. St Nicholas Circle A302.1971 and A295.1973; 5. Newarke Houses Car Park A263.1972; 6. Austin Friars A389.1973; 7. Causeway Lane A475.1979 & A1.1991; 8. The Great Hall and John of Gaunt's Cellar, Leicester Castle A33.1992; 9. St Peter's Lane (Shires) A40.1988; 10. Little Lane (Shires) A39.1988; 11. 9 St Nicholas Place A4.2003; 12. Bonners Lane A168.1993 13. Bath Lane A28.1992; 14. High Street (Cameo) A14.1992; 15. Bowling Green Inn A7.1996; 16. Westbridge Place A139.1996; 17: Friar Lane A49.1997; 18. Oxford Street and York Road A54.1997, A139.1996; 19. St Nicholas Place/Applegate A10.1999; 20. Westbridge Wharf, Bath Lane A16.2003; 21. Castle Street A7.2004; 22. Vine Street A22 and A24.2003; 23. Freeschool Lane A8.2005; 24. Vaughan Way A2.2003; 25. East Bond Street A5.2006; 26. Sanvey Gate A21.2003; 27. Great Central Street A13.2006; 28. Bath Lane, Merlin Works A29.2006; 29. Grange Lane A3.2005; 30. Oxford Street, DMU James Went Building A11.2006

Nicholas Place/Applegate (fig 2.19; Meek 2000); Infirmary Road (Taylor 2000); 9 St Nicholas Place (fig 2.11; Kipling 2004; Kipling 2010); Westbridge Wharf, Bath Lane (fig 2.20; Cooper 2004); Castle Street (fig 2.21; Score 2010). Many of these projects were undertaken in connection with the construction of high-rise blocks for apartments or student accommodation.

The western extension to the Shires Shopping centre to create Highcross Leicester led to a series of trial trenching projects in 2003–4, three large excavations, at Vine Street (fig 2.22; Higgins 2007), Freeschool Lane (fig 2.23; Coward 2007) and Vaughan Way (fig 2.24; Gnanaratnam 2004, 2009) and a smaller one at East Bond Street (fig 2.25; Tate 2007). Nearby, the construction of a block of apartments on Sanvey Gate led to major excavations (fig 2.26; Jarvis 2005, 2006) whilst important investigations were also undertaken on Great Central Street (fig 2.27), including the Highcross Street frontage, in advance of the construction of another block (Thomas et al 2007; Tate 2008). At the time of writing, the latter has not been constructed, a victim of the 2008 economic crash. Similarly, further excavations were carried out on the Bath Lane Merlin Works site (fig 2.28), but again no new buildings followed and the post-excavation analysis was not commissioned as a result (Kipling 2008).

In the south suburb, there was an excavation on Grange Lane (Thomas 2006) and on the site of De Montfort University's James Went Building on Oxford Street (Jones 2009a, Morris 2010). Apart from large excavations, many smaller interventions, such as watching briefs and evaluations, were also carried out during the period 1990–2008 and are detailed under the relevant year in 'Archaeology in Leicestershire and Rutland' published in the *Transactions of the Leicestershire Archaeological and Historical Society*. It is perhaps worth noting that despite the comparatively large number of investigations undertaken over the past 20 years, the south-east quarter of the historic core of Leicester still remains largely unexplored. This area, bounded by High Street, Gallowtree Gate, Horsefair Street, Millstone Lane and Southgates is of a very different character to the north-east and north-west quarters which contained predominantly 19th and 20th-century industrial buildings, many of

which were demolished following the decline in manufacturing industry. Much of the south-east quarter is occupied by the market place, whilst surrounding streets largely follow the medieval pattern and retain narrow burgage plots occupied by retail premises. Hence only rarely do opportunities present themselves for archaeological investigation in this area and when they do, they are frequently very small 'keyhole' excavations. At the time of writing, one exception has been a small research excavation at Greyfriars in 2012 which revealed evidence for the church, chapter house and cloister walk of the Franciscan friary.

Discussion of medieval themes
Early-Middle Anglo-Saxon Leicester
Until comparatively recently, there was only very limited archaeological evidence for occupation in Leicester between the 5th and 10th centuries AD. Antiquarian records indicated early Anglo-Saxon burials outside the east and west gates of the town, the latter at Westcotes perhaps high status in view of their association with weaponry (Clough et al 1975, 62).). Within the walls, dark earth deposits which had accumulated over the latest Roman levels had been noted in excavations at St Nicholas Circle in the late 1960s, whilst quantities of hand-made pottery were recovered from this and a number of other sites, particularly in the north-east quarter of the walled area. From the 1988 Shires St Peter's Lane excavation (Lucas and Buckley 1989) came pottery and a triangular bone comb of late 4th to 5th-century date (fig 3). Pottery was also recovered from the 1988 Shires Little Lane excavation, whilst the 1991 Causeway Lane site produced pottery, a 5th-century brooch fragment and a bone pin-beater used in weaving for compacting weft threads (Connor and Buckley 1999, 253). Unfortunately, all of the material was residual in later contexts, but it did appear to suggest a dispersed settlement of early Anglo-Saxon date within the walls based on comparison of the density of pottery per square metre with the rural Anglo-Saxon site of Eye Kettleby (Connor and Buckley 1999). In 1993, Leicester's first domestic Anglo-Saxon structure was discovered outside the south gate, adjacent to the Roman Tripontium Road, on the Bonners Lane site (Finn 2004). It was of unusual form, having a sunken-featured interior surrounded by substantial posts, suggesting a type of hall/sunken-featured building hybrid. The site

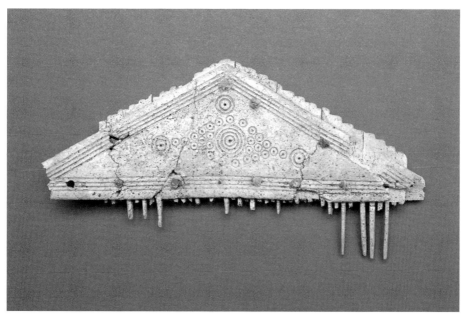

Figure 3: Anglo-Saxon bone comb from St Peter's Lane.

also produced early Anglo-Saxon pottery and objects associated with textile manufacture, including a spindle whorl, bone pin-beater and bone comb, the latter originally thought to be 5th–6th century, but now dated to the 7th century AD (Ian Riddler pers. comm.). Close to this site, the fragmentary remains of two further sunken-featured buildings were discovered on the east side of Oxford Street (Gossip 1998, 1999a). Taken together, the evidence suggested an extra-mural settlement of rural character in the early Anglo-Saxon period, although its relationship with the apparent activity within the walls remained uncertain.

The boom in development in the first decade of the 21st century provided the opportunity to investigate a number of large sites within the walls, particularly in the north-east quarter. Two of the 2003–6 Highcross Leicester sites, Vaughan Way and Freeschool Lane, both revealed for the first time intra-mural structural evidence of the early Anglo-Saxon period. A dark-earth deposit containing Anglo-Saxon pottery was found at Freeschool Lane sealing a number of hearths, cut into the latest metalling of the Roman north-south street to the east of the macellum. The hearths were of unknown function and were dated by coins to the late 4th century, although radiocarbon determinations suggest this could be extended into the 5th century. Micromorphological analysis of the dark earth indicated that the deposit initially comprised dumped building and domestic deposits, later changing in composition, with the inclusion of burnt daub deposits, coprolites and bone, perhaps suggesting timber structures and domestic activity in the immediate vicinity (Coward and Speed 2009).

Subsequently, the eastern gable wall of the Roman macellum (market hall) in the insula to the west collapsed, sealing the dark-earth and street metalling (fig 4 overleaf). Cut into the top of it was a two-post sunken-featured building (SFB) of early Anglo-Saxon form, although unfortunately with no finds from the primary fill to confirm the dating (fig 5 overleaf). The later fills, believed to be slumped midden deposits from higher in the sequence, contained Saxo-Norman pottery. Another two-post SFB was discovered further to the east, outside the main excavation area, just 25m from the findspot of the triangular comb from the 1988 Shires St. Peter's Lane excavation. It contained early Anglo-Saxon pottery including one roughly scored sherd that is believed to be late 5th to early 6th century in date. To the north, on the Vaughan Way site, the fragmentary remains of two more sunken-featured buildings associated with hand-made pottery were discovered. Taken together, the four SFBs and the possible disturbed one indicated by the comb and pottery from Shires St Peter's Lane, all lie on, or very near to, the line of projected Roman streets, are close to one another (100m apart or less) and are in a part of the town that the Highcross Leicester excavations suggest was relatively un-developed in the Roman period, perhaps indicating it was deliberately targeted by the early Anglo-Saxon settlers.

Figure 4: Freeschool Lane: collapsed east wall of the Roman macellum with Anglo-Saxon sunken-featured building cut into it. View east.

Figure 5: Freeschool Lane: detail of Anglo-Saxon sunken-featured building cutting collapsed wall. View east.

Tantalising evidence of a pit containing Anglo-Saxon pottery close to a group of undated post holes on the Sanvey Gate site (Jarvis forthcoming) may suggest that there were also halls, as one might expect on a settlement site of this period. Detecting and dating such remains, particularly in an urban context, is extremely difficult and at Vine Street, two sides of a large post-hole structure in the corner of insula IV dated to the late 3rd century or later could in fact be of the early Anglo-Saxon period. The posts would have been about 0.2m across, spaced at 1–1.5m

intervals, and a building a minimum of 10m by 5.5m is indicated. Placed centrally within the postulated structure was a large oval of vitrified soil, indicative of a sizeable fire, surrounded by trampled clay. Dating has proved inconclusive – the post-holes cut the mid 3rd century street metalling, but contained only residual 2nd to 4th-century pottery. Post-holes rarely contain dating evidence contemporary with their use and are more likely to contain finds deriving from deposits into which they were cut. Hence, it is entirely possible that structural features cutting the latest Roman deposits on a number of sites are in fact early Anglo-Saxon, as has been suggested for Causeway Lane (Connor and Buckley 1999, 83).

The possibility that evidence for early Anglo-Saxon activity exists elsewhere within the walls should not be discounted, as the present finds distribution pattern may be rather biased due to the disproportionate amount of investigation the north-east quarter has received. To the south, at 9 St Nicholas Place in 2003, for example, dark earth deposits were found sealing Roman street-metalling and the environmental samples produced both cereal and weed seeds, thought to be more indicative of rubbish deposits or dumping of waste rather than gradual accumulation (Monckton 2009). At Castle Street in 2005, a group of Anglo-Saxon pottery and a bone pin-beater could indicate another disturbed SFB, again close to the line of a Roman street (Score 2010).

By AD 679, the Mercian see centred on Lichfield was partitioned and a bishopric was established at Leicester, with Cuthwine as the first bishop; it subsequently underwent an uncertain period but was then re-established in 737 (Kirby 1965–6, 2). On the assumption that a cathedral was established during this period, perhaps on the site of the present St. Nicholas Church (Kenyon 1948), it is possible that this became a focus for periodic fairs and markets and maybe settlement, although evidence for this in the archaeological record is currently lacking. Current thinking dates the handmade Anglo-Saxon pottery from Leicester to the 5th–7th centuries and there is as yet no evidence for imported middle Anglo-Saxon pottery such as Ipswich Ware from Leicester. This does not necessarily indicate a hiatus in activity as it is considered possible that the period was aceramic (Cooper 2009).

Saxo-Norman Leicester and the development of urban topography

Ealheard may have been the last Saxon bishop of Leicester and probably fled to Dorchester on Thames in 874 before the Danish conquest was complete in 877 (*ibid*, 2) when Leicester became one of the 'five boroughs' of the Danelaw (Ellis 1976). Until recently, the only evidence for late Saxon Leicester amounted to the double-splayed windows in the nave of St Nicholas Church and chance finds of bone and metal objects principally along the line of the medieval High Street (now Highcross Street).

Streets

The influence of relict Roman structures on the development of medieval urban topography in Leicester has long been acknowledged – the substantial Roman defences and gates in particular effectively restricting access points to the town, whilst elements of the more substantial masonry buildings such as the forum, baths and macellum must have influenced not only the development of routes through the town, but also that of the medieval plot layout. Mostly, the Roman streets themselves appear to have disappeared – in places under collapsed walls such as that of the macellum, and elsewhere beneath silts and dark earths. On the rare occasions that Roman and later streets appear to coincide, rather than indicating continuity, this is more likely to be due to other factors such as substantial standing Roman walls preventing the development of alternative routes. The earliest element of the post-Roman street pattern is probably the medieval high street – now Highcross street – taking the shortest distance between the north and south gates whilst respecting the eastern side of the forum (Buckley and Lucas 1987). Paul Courtney suggested (1998) that the most likely pattern for settlement in the later Saxon period is for properties along the principal north-south and east-west streets – present Highcross Street/ Southgate Street and High Street respectively.

Whilst much of the medieval street pattern must have developed in the Saxo-Norman period, archaeological evidence for this is largely absent and the earliest documentary references are from the 12th–13th centuries. With the exception perhaps of the principal medieval thoroughfares of Swinesmarket and Highcross Street, it is highly likely that as elsewhere most streets remained unmetalled until at least the later medieval period. Hence, primary datable archaeological deposits such as metalling episodes may not exist in the majority of cases and where they do, are likely to have suffered severe truncation from modern service trenches and road resurfacing. Where medieval streets have gone out of use, opportunities have arisen for some archaeological investigation. When the Shires shopping centre was extended across the line of East Bond Street, limited excavation revealed some patchy cobbling thought to be that of the medieval Parchment

213

On Bath Lane, the excavation of the Merlin Works site revealed evidence for a cobbled lane leading towards the river, immediately outside the southern wall of the Blackfriars precinct (Kipling 2008). On the site of the Roman macellum on the west side of Highcross Street, a putative road consisting of cobbles in a dark-grey silt may represent part of the medieval or post-medieval Blue Boar Lane (Derrick 2004, 149). To the south, gravel surfaces which may relate to the medieval Hotgate (later Bakehouse Lane) were revealed in an evaluation in 1999 (Meek 2000, 228). Watching briefs on service and other trenches dug through modern road lines have on occasion revealed possible medieval metallings, as at Humberstone Gate (Warren 1998, 162)

Plot development

Comparatively little excavation has taken place close to medieval street frontages in Leicester, largely due to the lack of opportunity to investigate sites where this crucial area has not been destroyed by extensive cellarage. Hence, most archaeological data relating to the development of the town in the medieval period derives from features such as pits and wells in backyards rather than from structures.

Lane, a theory supported by the lack of other medieval features such as pits or structures (Higgins and Lucas 1996, 115). The Highcross Leicester excavations at Vine Street (Higgins et al 2009) revealed the remains of at least two lanes of rough cobbles under the line of the modern Elbow Lane (fig 6) and Grape Street, the former defined by a roadside ditch. These sealed robber trenches of Roman structures dated to c.1150–1250 (Higgins 2007, 201). They went out of use comparatively quickly, perhaps due to the overall decline of the north-east quarter from the 14th century onwards, and were sealed by garden soils. Despite this, the routes must have persisted in some form as they survived as streets into the modern period.

The 1971 St Nicholas Circle excavations examined a series of medieval plots with stone boundary walls a little way back from the Highcross Street frontage (Kipling 2010). Interestingly, the work produced sparse evidence of intensive 12th-century occupation which may indicate the persistence of large plots or communal areas at least on the axial streets into the 13th century, before they were subdivided into the more typical narrow burgage plots (Courtney 1998, 119).

Figure 7: Freeschool Lane, view west towards the Highcross Street frontage.

Across the road from this site, in 2003, a site at what is now 9 St Nicholas Place examined part of the corner of Highcross Street and Guildhall Lane (Kipling 2010). Although medieval archaeology on the Highcross Street frontage had been destroyed by 19th-century cellars, evidence emerged at the rear for the early development of plots. Here, later property boundary walls defined five or six medieval tenement[3] plots, two of which (plots 4 & 5) seemed to have resulted in the subdivision of one large plot with frontages to both Highcross Street and Guildhall Lane. The latter was occupied by a 12th-century stone undercroft, probably located at the rear of a large high-status tenement, perhaps owned by a wealthy merchant (*ibid* 142). Apart from this subdivision, there was otherwise little evidence to suggest that the plots had changed since they were set out perhaps in the Saxo-Norman period (Kipling 2010, 140).

To the north, excavations in 2003 on the site of the former Cameo Cinema in High Street revealed an 11th-century pit suggesting some activity in the area at this date (Cooper 1993b, 89). Deposits of the 11th century may have been truncated by a cultivation horizon of the 11th–13th century, possibly representing ridge and furrow (*ibid* 90) and a possible north-south ditch may point to early plot boundaries for such cultivation activities. This may support the idea that away from the focus of major Roman public buildings, there were perhaps large open areas of accumulated cultivation soils which formed a focus for post-conquest settlement (Kipling 2010, 138–9).

Just two significant frontages, both on Highcross Street, have been investigated: the Freeschool Lane site (fig 7; Coward and Speed 2009) and Great Central Street (Tate 2008). The former was excavated in 2006

and produced evidence for the truncated remains of Saxo-Norman timber structures close to the street frontage. This is the only place in Leicester where structures of this period have been discovered so far and the site is also notable in producing 116 sherds of Leicester ware, the first sizeable assemblage in the town of products from the late Saxon pottery kiln found on Southgate Street in 1967 (Hebditch 1967–8, 5–9). Thereafter, occupation continued here in a series of narrow burgage plots defined by stone boundary walls which were subject to repair and alteration throughout the medieval and post-medieval periods (Coward and Speed 2009). Due to the continuity of alignment, it was not possible to identify whether the earliest plots were wider and later became subdivided. At the Great Central Street site, a significant proportion of the Highcross Street frontage was occupied by a high status stone building presenting its long side to the street. This would appear to indicate a wide plot which was perhaps not subdivided until much later on, probably after the demolition of the structure (Tate 2008, 279–81). The building is a possible candidate for the medieval vicarage of All Saints Church which lies opposite (P. Courtney pers. comm.).

Away from the axial streets, large-scale excavation of medieval deposits has only taken place so far in the north-east quarter of the town. At Causeway Lane (Connor and Buckley 1999), regular linear alignments of pits at right angles to the medieval St John's Lane point to the establishment of plots by the 11th–12th century. The presence of wells and cess pits

3   Tenement: usually property with buildings on it

215

suggests intensive domestic and commercial activity in a series of plots based on a unit of measurement of one pole (16ft 6in, 5.03m). Determining precise widths for the plots is fraught with difficulties due to the complete lack of evidence for boundaries which here must presumably have been of timber. However, the excavator postulated a combination of one and two-pole properties (Connor and Buckley 1999, 80) with a suggestion of some fluidity in the precise boundary line indicated by dating differences (*ibid* 85).

Also in the back lanes area of the north-east quarter, a number of pits containing Saxo-Norman pottery at Vine Street point to some occupation in the 10th–11th centuries, although this was not particularly dense (Higgins *et al* 2009). In the 12th–13th centuries, the Roman town house and adjacent warehouse on this site were extensively robbed, with some walls possibly retained for re-use in medieval structures. As previously noted, streets had been laid out here by this time and a series of large land divisions fronting on to them seem to have been established, each containing a structure of timber or masonry with associated pits and wells. The size of the plots and the dispersed nature of activity contrasts considerably with the narrow burgage plots encountered on Highcross Street. At both Vine Street and Causeway Lane, there is some evidence to suggest the reuse of surviving Roman structural elements in medieval domestic buildings (Connor and Buckley 1999, 86).

Vine Street and Causeway Lane contrast with the Shires site of St Peter's Lane where although there was intensive pit digging in the 12th–13th centuries, the distributions were not only irregular but the ovoid form of the features was also unlike the more normal range of cess pits and wells encountered in domestic plots. It is suspected that the pits were perhaps associated with gravel quarrying and there is no evidence for rubbish pits, cess pits and wells until the very late medieval period (Buckley and Lucas 2007).

The Highcross site of Vaughan Way was mainly concerned with the excavation of St Peter's Church and its graveyard, although a small number of features of the Saxo-Norman and High Medieval periods (*c*.1100–1400) indicate domestic activity relating to plots on medieval St John's Lane (now Causeway Lane) and St Peter's Lane (Gnanaratnam 2009).

From the archaeological evidence we have so far, some variation can be seen in the pattern and intensity of medieval settlement in different parts of the town. Unsurprisingly, archaeological evidence from the medieval High Street (now Highcross Street) and Swinesmarket (now High Street) indicates that the principal commercial streets of the borough have the most concentrated occupation leading to a considerable build-up of complex archaeological deposits and a long-lived pattern of narrow burgage plots defined by masonry walls, frequently with evidence of many rebuilds. In the rear of properties are the usual range of back-yard features, including rubbish pits, wells and cess pits, and on occasion features with a more specialised industrial function. Away from the principal axial streets, other sites, such as Newarke Houses Car park to the west of Southgates (Mellor 1971–2, 64–5), have also revealed narrow plots and stone boundary walls, some of which had been rebuilt on more or less the same line on many occasions.

By contrast, although the north-east quarter sees intensive settlement in the 11th–13th century in regular plots, some perhaps as narrow as 1 pole in width, in the first half of the 14th century, there is apparently a hiatus. At this time, pit digging seems to have stopped completely suggesting a sudden decline in the occupation of this part of the borough. Whilst it could be argued that an absence of pits could merely indicate a change in methods of rubbish disposal, the disappearance of cess pits is surely more significant as they represent an essential amenity of every residential plot. Certainly such features continue to be constructed in the later medieval and post-medieval periods elsewhere in the town. The sites of the north-east quarter are also similar in that there are deep deposits of 'garden soil' overlying all earlier features and in places reaching a depth of over 2m. It can be assumed therefore that this part of the town suffered a dramatic decline in the late 13th-early 14th centuries, from which it did not recover until the late 18th century. This may in part have been due to famine in the earlier part of the century, the population decline presumably exacerbated by the effects of the Black

Death in 1348–9 when it has been said that a third of the population of Leicester was taken (Kelly 1877, 398).

The character of occupation in archaeological terms of certain parts of the town, most notably the south-east quarter and the area of the Saturday Market, remains unknown for the obvious reason of lower levels of modern development in this area. The presence of larger numbers of high-quality buildings in this zone and the survival of narrow medieval plots means that future large-scale excavation is rather unlikely and we must be content with evidence from small key-hole investigations. However, one would imagine intensively occupied narrow burgage plots as seen on the principal streets of the medieval borough.

Suburbs

It is only really in the south suburb that any large-scale archaeological investigation has been undertaken during the period under review and includes sites at Bonners Lane (Finn 2004), Oxford Street (Gossip 1998, 1999a, 1999b) and Oxford Street De Montfort University (DMU; Morris 2010). Apart from the early Anglo-Saxon activity noted above, this work has also provided archaeological evidence for settlement in the 12th–13th century along both sides of what is now Oxford Street, with backyard activity to the rear. Whilst the earliest documentary references for occupation in the south suburb are from 1200, archaeological evidence suggest that settlement could have been established as early as the 11th–12th century, but seems to have declined from the mid 13th century. After this period, much of the area may have reverted to agricultural use, with evidence of large-scale crop processing being undertaken on the Oxford Street DMU site in particular (Radini 2010) (fig 8). The earliest medieval buildings in the south suburb are of earth-fast timber construction, found at Bonners Lane and at Oxford Street DMU and at the former site were later replaced with stone-footed structures (Finn 2004, 63). To the rear are the usual range of yards, cess pits and wells, the contents of which help to characterise the nature of domestic occupation, together with other features pointing to industrial activity in the suburb, in particular tanning, metalworking and crop processing (see below).

Excavations on Oxford Street in advance of the construction of De Montfort University's new Business and Law Building in 2006–8 also revealed some evidence for plot divisions in the form of ditches and fence lines, although it was difficult to tell whether this was a result of deliberate planning or piecemeal development.

Figure 8: Oxford Street De Montfort University building: possible corn drier

A major change in land divisions must have occurred with the establishment of the Newarke precinct in 1330–1, but the boundaries of this do not seem to have been formalised until its walls and gates were constructed in the early decades of the 15th century. Archaeological evidence from this site indicated that the walls did not result from a single building campaign, but were constructed in stretches, perhaps as the college acquired parcels of land (Morris 2010). Activity continued between the Newarke wall and the Oxford Street frontage on this site during the late medieval period, with possible evidence for brewing.

Town defences

Since the publication in 1987 of the current state of archaeological knowledge of the town defences (Buckley and Lucas 1987), further investigations have taken place across the line of the northern and western town walls (Cooper 1996; Cooper 2004, Jarvis 2006, 219; Kipling 2008; Wardle 2008), together with smaller investigations revealing traces of the town wall robber trench of the southern and eastern

defences in Berridge Street (Gnanaratnam 1998, 158) and the Market Place (Derrick 2001, 132). The most significant discovery, however, has been that of the western defences – long suspected from small observations and from medieval documentary sources (Lucas 1978–9) but never confirmed with any confidence. Excavations at the Westbridge Wharf site in Bath Lane in 2003 revealed the Roman rampart and town wall footings together with rare evidence for possible refurbishment of the town wall in the medieval period (fig 9). A substantial chunk of displaced Roman town wall core was encountered and a parallel trench had been excavated to the south of the observed wall and infilled with stone rubble and capped with stiff clay (Cooper 2004, 144–5). In view of the documented destruction of the town and castle defences on the orders of Henry II following the sack of Leicester in 1173 (Fox 1942), it has been suggested that the displaced core fragment resulted from the undermining of the footings, with the parallel footings representing reinstatement of the town wall later in the medieval period (Cooper forthcoming). That the curtain walls of the castle were also slighted at this time is suggested by the discovery of rubble of this period in the fill of the bailey ditch (Clarke 1952, 25; Buckley and Hagar 1992, 180).

The Merlin Works site on Bath Lane, immediately to the north of Westbridge Wharf, revealed further evidence for the line of the town wall. Here, a route seems to have been created through it in the medieval period to provide access to the river. This was marked by a lane of crude cobbling immediately outside the southern wall of the Blackfriars precinct and was probably an extension of Friars Causeway (Kipling 2008, 278). Also on this site, there was evidence for a large rectangular masonry structure apparently used as a cess pit and thought to be the documented public latrine constructed in 1342–3 (*ibid*). Further north still along Bath Lane,

Figure 9: Westbridge Wharf. The town wall robber trench under excavation. View south.

Figure 10: Section through the town ditches at Sanvey Gate. View north-west

evaluation by Birmingham Archaeology the same year confirmed that defences ran at an oblique angle across the north-west corner of the town, presumably respecting the line of the river Soar and perhaps also an area of marshy ground (Wardle 2008, 279).

The documentary sources show that although the four town gates survived until 1774, the town wall, whilst maintained during the medieval period, finally fell into disuse towards the end of the 15th century and was then thoroughly robbed of its stone in the 16th and 17th centuries (Buckley and Lucas 1987, 63). However, the sources also suggest that the ongoing maintenance was against a background of illicit removal of stone, such as when Geoffrey the Baker admitted breaking the stone of the town wall to sell it in 1291 (*ibid*, 61). Evidence of early robbing of the wall has come from a small-scale investigation of the northern defences on Cumberland Street in 1997 (Cooper 1998). Here, the town wall robber trench contained pottery of the 12th–13th century and was cut by a circular pit containing mid 13th-century pottery This led the excavator to suggest that most of the wall was robbed in the 13th century, leaving just its front (i.e. northern face) intact (*ibid*, 98).

The eastern end of the northern defences was examined in 2005 (fig 10; Jarvis 2005 and 2006), and showed that quantities of building materials, presumably robbed from Roman structures, had been dumped into the partially silted Roman town ditch in the 12th century. The latter seems to have been infilled relatively early, whilst the inner ditch may have been maintained at this time, as indicated by a 12th-century re-cut. A 4.5m-long section of the Roman town wall apparently collapsed during this period and a localised area of its footings was robbed. As noted above, evidence of a breach of the town wall at such an early date is of particular interest and it is again tempting to associate it with the documented destruction of the castle and town defences in 1174. The medieval town ditches at Sanvey Gate contained some preserved organic material, including bone, insect remains, seeds, leaves, twigs, and even worked leather and timbers.

High-status and religious buildings
Leicester Castle, The Great Hall and John of Gaunt's Cellar

As a result of major repairs to the 12th-century Great Hall in 1985–6, necessitating the erection of scaffolding inside to the level of the ridge, the opportunity was taken by the author to commission a full survey of the timber roof structure. The aim of the project was to clarify the dating and form of the building, which had earlier been subject to some discussion between Walter Horn and J.T. Smith (Radford *et*

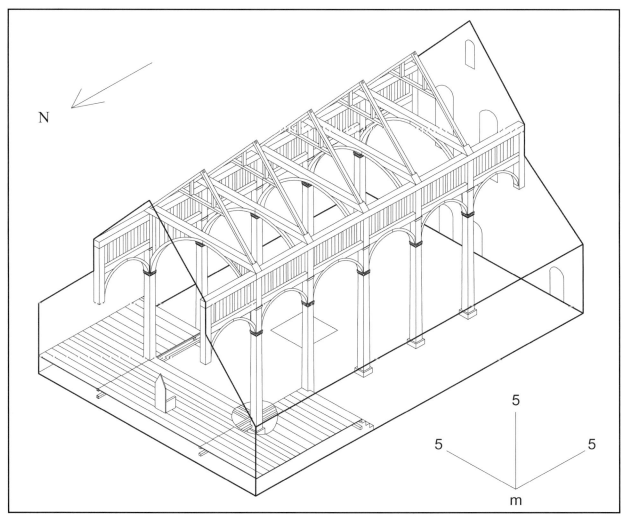

N

5
5   5

m

Figure 11: Reconstruction of the 12th-century timber frame of the Great Hall, Leicester Castle (drawn by R Buckley).

al 1973, 82, n7). The hall is a rectangular stone building 24m (79ft) long and 17.5m (57ft) wide, originally divided into a nave and two aisles by two longitudinal rows of five oak arcade posts, most of which only remain as fragments. Stylistically, the windows and the scalloped capitals of the arcade posts date the hall to the mid 12th century, whilst a detached capital was dated to *c.*1150 by dendrochronology in the early 1980s (Laxton *et al* 1981–2, 80). Although Horn had suggested that the present roof structure, of tie beam, principal rafter and purlin construction, was original, J.T. Smith regarded it as a reconstruction of the 14th century, due to the fact that a tie beam cuts across the two 12th-century windows at the southern end of the hall (Radford 1955, 183, note.1).

In 1985, an architect, Nick Klee, prepared drawings of the timber frame (Alcock and Buckley 1987; in archive, LCMS) whilst an extensive dendrochronological survey involving taking 25 samples from the roof

was carried out by the Nottingham University Tree Ring Laboratory (*ibid* 73–4; Liddle 1986, 92). The latter confirmed that the roof in fact dates to the early 16th century and it may be significant that in 1523, the royal commissioners added a memorandum to their report on the condition of the castle that 100 oaks should be taken from Enderby wood for its repair (Fox 1942, 146). Analysis of the results of the architectural survey by Dr Nat Alcock led to a new interpretation of the form of the 12th-century hall (fig 12; Alcock and Buckley 1987). He concluded that it was originally 'a magnificent clerestoried structure' with longitudinal arcades, composed of timber Romanesque style semicircular arches, with larger transverse arches spanning the nave. The spandrels of the northernmost nave arch seem to have been infilled with planking which was perhaps decorated, signifying its position at the high end of the hall and effectively framing views of the dais from the low end. The base of the western arcade post which supported this arch, together with its

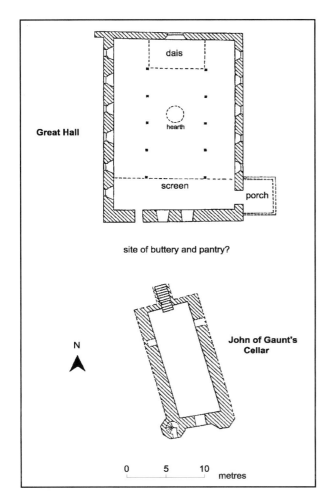

Figure: 12: Leicester Castle, plan of the Great Hall and John of Gaunt's Cellar (drawn by D. Mackie).

sandstone plinth, was rediscovered in 1996 by Neil Finn whilst exploring one of the 19th-century heating ducts beneath the floor of the Great Hall. Significantly, the base of the post contained paired mortises (with traces of original incised marking-out lines) which are tentatively interpreted as having taken a series of horizontal timbers supporting the dais at the high end of the hall. The dais seems to have occupied the entire northern bay of the hall and was presumably accessed via steps from the aisles, the latter providing clear service routes from the kitchen at the southern end of the hall. Also in 1996, small areas of plaster were removed to inspect the surviving timber arcade posts of the west aisle which had been embedded in masonry during alterations of 1821. Although it was hoped that there would be evidence for the form of the 12th-century aisle roofs, in the event the posts were found to have been trimmed longitudinally in 1821, destroying all surface treatment and jointing on the west face (Finn and Buckley 1997, 104).

In 1994, a watching brief was maintained during re-paving works in Castle Yard (Mackie and Buckley 1994). Adjacent to the southern end of the Great Hall, and running at right-angles to it, an insubstantial 0.4m-wide stone wall foundation was observed, associated with a 60mm thick mortar floor. Its position, coinciding precisely with the southern bay of the hall where the entrance is presumed to have been, suggests that it is probably the wooden porch referred to in the building accounts of 1377–8 (Fox 1942, 143). Also uncovered were the foundations of the original east wall of the Great Hall, taken down in about 1695 when the present brick façade was constructed.

A small evaluative excavation was undertaken in 1986 in the gardens of Castle House, immediately adjacent to the north wall of the Great Hall, with a view to locating evidence for a solar block. Documentary sources refer to a staircase leading to the Great Chamber from the high end of the hall (Fox 1942, 144) and there are indications of two blocked doorways on the external face of the north wall. However, the fieldwork showed that the ground sloped away sharply adjacent to the north wall of the hall, leaving no room for an attached structure in this position. It must instead have been to the east, at right angles to the hall, perhaps approached via a pentice[4] (Buckley 1987, 92).

To the south of the Great Hall was the service block, of which only the undercroft known as John of Gaunt's Cellar survives today (fig 12). In 1992–3, a full stone-by-stone architectural survey of the interior and southern external elevation of this building was undertaken (Buckley 1993). This confirmed that it was of two phases, as suspected in the 19th century (Thompson 1859). The original structure was probably built as the undercroft to a detached kitchen at broadly the same time as the Great Hall in the mid 12th century. It certainly seems to respect the defences of the motte and bailey castle which are likely to have gone out of use in the late 12th–13th century. The western (riverside) walls of both the hall and undercroft may well have utilised the stone curtain wall thought to have been built in the early 12th century by the Robert de Beaumont, first Earl of Leicester (Fox 1942, 135). In the early 15th century, the undercroft seems to have been extended southwards

4   Covered walkway

221

and furnished with a replacement four-centred arched vault in finely cut ashlar. This was found to be covered with mason's marks, of 13 main types, which presumably represent a tally of the stones dressed by individual masons (Buckley 1993, 87). Documentary sources indicate that a tower or chamber was built over the wine cellar between 1400 and 1410 (Colvin 1963, 702) and this almost certainly refers to John of Gaunt's Cellar. The southern elevation of the undercroft had two polygonal towers added, the western one containing a newel staircase providing access to the upper floors of the block. In form, these towers are similar to those on the Newarke Gateway (c. 1400) and Turret Gateway (1422–3; Fox 1942, 154), built in connection with the enclosure of the Newarke precinct, and there are also links between the three structures in terms of masons' marks.

The medieval kitchen and associated ground-floor structures were demolished in the 18th century and the only evidence we have for them is from engravings of the period. A stone-lined drain leading eastwards from the site of the castle kitchen across Castle Yard was revealed in the 1994 repaving works whilst excavations in 1996 above John of Gaunt's cellar provided only fragmentary indications of structures which had existed here. Buildings between the kitchen and the hall, such as a buttery and pantry, must have been destroyed by the construction of the transverse cell block on the south side of the hall in the mid 19th century (Finn and Buckley 1997, 103).

Other features

The bailey ditch of the first castle at Leicester – thought to have been established in c.1068 – was discovered in 1939 when it was sectioned in the gardens of Newarke Houses Museum (Clarke 1952). Part of the ditch was subsequently observed during redevelopment of the Everards Brewery site in 1966 (Clay & Pollard 1994, 43) and again in 1984, when reconstruction of the garden wall of Castle House revealed a partial section through it (Liddle 1986, 98). In 1991, rebuilding of outbuildings to the east provided the opportunity to excavate a section through the upper levels of the ditch, and as at Newarke Houses 1939, extensive deposits of sandstone rubble (Buckley and Hagar 1992, 179–80) were encountered in the upper fills. This included blocks of stone with mortar adhering

to them and was dated to the 12th century by pottery from deposits both above and below. The deposit is interpreted as evidence to confirm the documented destruction (or more likely, slighting) of the castle defences after the sack of Leicester in 1173 (Fox 1942, 136).

Several other watching briefs were undertaken between about 1980 and the present on minor works within the castle, including one in 1982 during the rebuilding of a retaining wall in Castle View adjacent to the motte which confirmed extensive slippage of the motte and also produced a single unstratified and undated human skeleton (Mellor 1981–2, 85). Others included refacing of the boundary wall between St Mary de Castro and Castle View (indicating that it had a stone core beneath a facing of brick); in Castle View itself revealing a stone wall (Knox 1995, 129); on the motte (Harvey 1996, 167) and during the provision of disabled access to Castle House. The latter revealed tantalising evidence of structures between Castle House and the Great Hall, perhaps remains of the solar block or other chambers mentioned in the documentary sources (Fox 1942; Reilly in archive, LCMS). Apart from features already referred to above, during the 1994 repaving of Castle Yard (Mackie and Buckley 1994, 119–24) the remains of a stone structure were revealed in the roadway adjacent to St Mary de Castro, to the north and south of which were four undated burials (presumably medieval): three of children and the fourth was not excavated. Their position suggests that they may pre-date the establishment of a route through the Turret Gateway to the Newarke in the early 15th century. In the northern area of Castle Yard, a stone-lined drain containing 12th–13th century pottery was cut by a later stone structure of probable medieval date which is likely to be associated with a range of buildings at right angles to the northern end of the Great Hall, linking to what is now Castle House.

St Peter's Church

The former St Margaret's Baths site on Vaughan Way was excavated in 2003–6 and revealed the remains of St Peter's Church and its graveyard, containing over 1300 individuals, together with an adjacent group of high-status buildings (fig 13). The church, thought to have been one of the six mentioned in Domesday Book for Leicester, had been demolished in 1573 and the walls thoroughly robbed of their

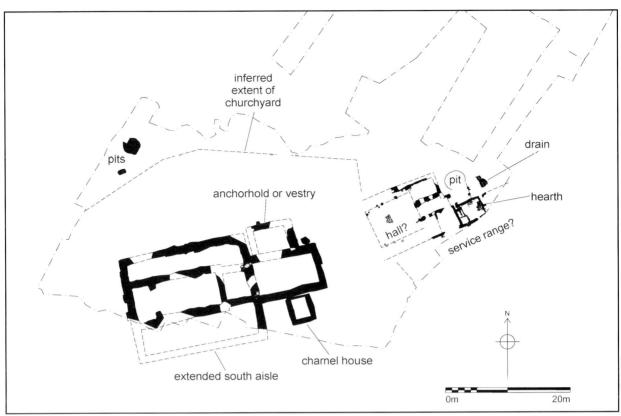

Figure 13: St Peter's Church and adjacent domestic building in the late medieval period (drawn by A. Gnanaratnam).

Figure 14: The site of St Peter's Church under excavation. View west. The robber trenches of the church show as parallel strips of pale material (above the 2 seated figures).

stone, thereby preventing precise dating of the construction phases. However, radiocarbon dating of some of the earliest burials suggests that the graveyard was in use in the late 10th to mid 11th century. These were charcoal burials, a tradition which is thought to stretch from the late Saxon period through to the 12th century (Thompson 2004, 231) and some three hundred are known nationally (Holloway 2008, 136). The first identifiable church was a three-cell masonry building, of which the central and eastern cells at least appear to be contemporary. Whilst it is possible that this building is of the same period as the earliest burials, it is thought more likely that is of early Norman date and perhaps replaced a timber predecessor.

A small rectangular cell was subsequently added to the west end of the nave and the discovery of a bell casting pit inside it, with an archaeomagnetic date of 1150–80, suggests that this was a bell turret. The casting of bells inside church towers is a well-known phenomenon and was normally undertaken for the purely practical reason that it would have been very difficult to manoeuvre a completed bell into the building via narrow doorways and then hoist it into position. Also in this period, probably post-dating the bell-casting pit, north and south aisles were added to the nave, the south perhaps c.1190 and the north c.1220 and the chancel was enlarged. In the south-west corner of the site, a communal grave re-using a pre-existing quarry pit contained at least

22 individuals, radiocarbon dates from two of these suggested interment in the second half of the 12th century. The grave appears to indicate multiple deaths resulting from a single event, perhaps a highly infectious disease. During this period, the northern boundary of the graveyard moved, with burials found overlying earlier pits with unstable fills, causing some slumping.

Between about 1250 and 1400, the chancel was enlarged, encroaching upon a north-south street to the east which had by now become disused. The enlargement of chancels is a common occurrence in the 13th century, when they were frequently widened to match the width of the nave due to the increased visual importance of the ritual of the Elevation of the Host. A number of burials were cleared before the floor make-ups were laid and probably before construction commenced. Cutting the backfilled bell-casting pit at the west end of the nave was a male burial with a coin of Edward I (1272–1307) in its mouth and in the nave was a probable high-status burial containing a papal bulla of Pope Innocent VI (1352–62).

The late medieval period, c.1375–1550, saw further alterations, with the widening of the south aisle and the addition of a room on the north side of the chancel, most likely a vestry or very possibly a cell for an anchorite. The latter may be suggested by an adjacent pit containing finds suggestive of the disposal of domestic waste. To the south of the chancel was a charnel house (fig 15), probably built initially to accommodate burials disturbed by one of the church building phases – possibly the widening of the south aisle –and then used over an extended period of time. The church continued to be used in the first half of the 16th

Figure 15: St Peter's Church: the charnel house under excavation.

224

century, with records of repairs and burials, but was probably ruinous by 1555.

Throughout the history of the churchyard, the majority of individuals were buried without coffins and instead are assumed to have been simply shrouded and placed in an unadorned grave without any grave goods. There was some evidence for coffins, indicated by the shape of the grave, the presence of nails or the movement of skeletal remains during the decomposition of burial and coffin. A number of burials showed evidence for the individual being laid on a bed of charcoal or ash as part of the interment ritual, regarding which there is much speculation over the symbolism. Other burials had stones laid on them, on either side of the head or as grave linings; again the reason for this ritual is by no means certain.

To the east of the church, a large sunken-floored building interpreted as an undercroft or cellar and a possibly contemporary cross wing were constructed in about the mid 12th century and indicate a high-status residence, perhaps associated with the church (fig 13). The robber trenches suggest that the latter was a substantial stone building, perhaps of two storeys, whilst the slender robbed walls of the undercroft may indicate that it had a timber superstructure. A later modification was the addition of an internal earth ramp retained by a pair of walls providing access between the undercroft and the cross wing. To the west of the cross wing there may have been an ancillary structure, as shown by a series of beaten-earth floors, the limits of which were marked by a north-south street established during this period, providing access from St Peter's Lane. The undercroft was probably demolished between the mid-12th and early 13th century, but the adjacent stone cross wing appears to have remained in use, until it was itself pulled down in the second half of the 14th century.

After a period of disuse, marked by pits and deposits of garden soil, another high-status building was constructed, tentatively identified from the very fragmentary evidence as hall and service range. The hall seems to have been aisled with a central hearth, possibly with timber walls in its earliest phase (for which no evidence survived) and with an adjacent building of post-hole construction. The walls of the hall were apparently later replaced in stone, and the service range was both enlarged and rebuilt with mud walls on insubstantial masonry foundations. The plan of this is difficult to interpret, but it may well have been of typical medieval form: a central passage flanked by buttery and pantry, leading to a kitchen. This block seems to have been a long-lived structure, based on evidence for many rebuilds and repairs. One of the rooms had a stone-lined pit or tank from which clay and slate-lined drains ran to the north and south, together with at least one hearth and may have been the kitchen. In view of its position, it is tempting to see this hall and service block as the vicarage of St Peter's mentioned in later documentary sources. If so its precursor, the undercroft and cross-wing, could represent an earlier phase of this building, demolished as a wider programme of church-funded building works in the later 13th century which included the construction of the new chancel and vicarage.

St Michael's Church
Until recently, little was known about another lost church in the back lanes of the north-east quarter of Leicester, St Michael's, which had been demolished in the 15th century. Janet Martin speculated that it had been founded before the Conquest and that like St Peter's, it was probably part of the original endowment of St Mary de Castro and later Leicester Abbey (Martin 1990, 21). Burials had been found on the east side of Vine Street in the 1950s (*ibid* 25, n.32) and again when a large site on Vine Street was investigated during 2003–6 as part of the Highcross Leicester development. This excavation is known mainly as the site of a large Roman courtyard house, to the east of which was a substantial rectangular stone building, perhaps a warehouse, constructed in the 3rd century AD (Higgins *et al* 2007). The discovery of large numbers of burials in the vicinity of this building indicated that in the medieval period, the area was in use as a graveyard, almost certainly that of St Michael's. Whilst the possible Roman warehouse is an attractive candidate for the church, its north-south orientation suggests that this was not the case. Instead, the church is more likely to be a small rectangular building with masonry footings found just to the north, probably constructed in the latter half of the 12th century at the earliest. A porch was added to its western end in *c.*1250–1400

and in the main part of the building, possible make-up deposits signified a raised floor level. There were ten inhumations inside the church, including two males in the porch which may represent high-status burials. Some 218 inhumations were assigned to the period 1250–1400, all apparently interred without coffins. The comparative lack of intercutting has been taken as an indication that there was no great pressure on space and that the parish was perhaps not densely populated. A small four-post structure in the graveyard may have been the support for a cross or possibly the footings of a lychgate. Later in this period, there seems to have been a hiatus in burial activity and indications of a change of use for the southern portion of the graveyard, where there was a natural accumulation of soil before the next interments took place. Subsequently a small timber structure was erected, possibly part of a wider complex of structures and boundaries extending to the south and perhaps indicating habitation within the graveyard. This could relate either to the Gild of St Michael's, known to have been associated with the church in the late 14th century, or to the documented residence of an anchorite. The continued absence of burials or other features within the Roman warehouse building may suggest that the walls were re-

Figure 16: Carved boss in the roof of the north aisle of All Saints Church; 15th century.

used for a structure associated with the church in the medieval period, perhaps the vicarage recorded in 1221–22 (Martin 1990, 21).

St Mary's Vicarage

The former St Mary's Vicarage in the Newarke was subject to an historic building survey in 2005 (Finn 2005). Much altered in the 19th century and partially demolished in the 20th, this stone building was probably constructed in the late 14th century to accommodate the

Figure 17: Great Central Street, showing foundations of possible vicarage. View south-east.

dean or one of the canons of the College of the Annunciation of the Blessed Virgin Mary (dissolved in 1547). It is a compact variant of the typical medieval hall plan with opposed doorways in the east and west walls defining a cross passage, a door at the west end of which seems to have led to a newel staircase, a fragment of which survives. The northern room was heated by a fireplace in the north wall and this, together with elaborately moulded beams of the first floor frame above indicate it was of high status. By comparison, the beams supporting the first floor in the chamber on the south side of the cross passage only had plain chamfers. A wide portion of the west wall appears to have incorporated a passageway and possibly a small chamber, perhaps a garderobe.

The first floor seems to have been divided into three rooms (indicated by mortices in the floor frame), two of which were heated. These would have served as private accommodation and garderobes were probably provided at this level too, with shafts within the thickness of the walls.

It seems likely that the building was originally only two stories high, with a shallow-pitched and lead-covered roof like other buildings in the Newarke.

All Saints Church, All Saints Vicarage and the Cross Keys Inn

Following the theft of lead from its roof and the subsequent scaffolding of the interior to facilitate repairs, the author took the opportunity in 1987 to organise a photographic survey of the carved roof bosses (fig 16; LCMS Accession No. A5.1987). The shallow-pitched roofs of the north and south aisles are dated to the 15th century and have cambered tie beams, each with many carved bosses, a significant proportion of which are representations of faces. These are of particular interest as caricatures by the carver perhaps of inhabitants of the medieval town and include members of both sexes with a variety of different hairstyles.

An excavation on the west side of Highcross Street in 2007, just south of the site of the north gate, revealed evidence for occupation on the principal thoroughfare of the medieval borough (fig 17; Tate 2008, 279–80). On the frontage was a substantial late-medieval cellared stone building presenting its long side to the street. This had a semi-circular projection on its rear wall, probably to accommodate a newel staircase providing access to upper floors. Although detailed

Figure 18: Remains of 12th-century undercroft 9 St Nicholas Place. View west.

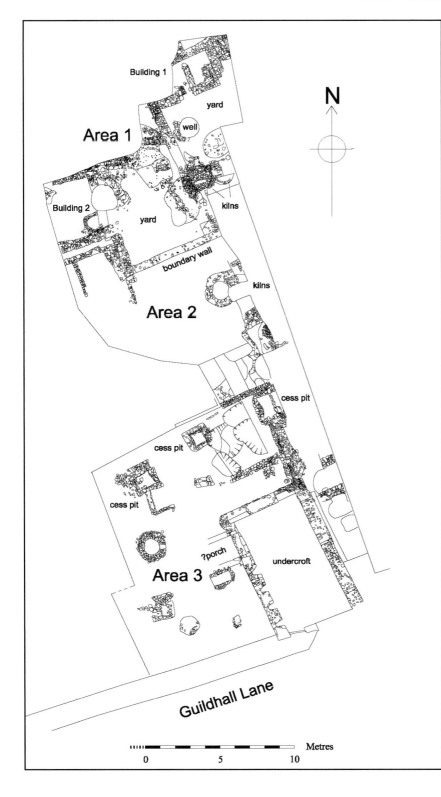

Building 1

yard

well

Area 1

Building 2

yard

kilns

boundary wall

kilns

Area 2

cess pit

cess pit

cess pit

?porch

undercroft

Area 3

N

Guildhall Lane

Metres

0   5   10

Figure 19: 9 St Nicholas Place: plan of principal features (drawn by R. Kipling).

an important crown-post roof building immediately to the north of All Saints' Church. Dendrochronological dating indicated a felling date of about 1335 making it the earliest surviving domestic building in the city (Hartley 1988).

St Sepulchre

In 1999, investigations by Archaeological Project Services at Leicester Royal Infirmary revealed 20 burials, perhaps in family plots, associated with the medieval church of St Sepulchre which had been founded in the 12th century but was ruinous by the 1570s (Taylor 2000, 225).

12th-century undercroft, Guildhall Lane

This rare survival of an intact medieval undercroft on Guildhall Lane (fig 18) was first noted in the 19th century, when the artist John Flower was advised of its existence by the Sexton of St Martins whose 16th-century timber-framed house lay above it (Thompson 1845). It was photographed in 1861 when the latter was demolished and remained largely forgotten thereafter until the late 1980s when

analysis of the results of this excavation have yet to be undertaken, it is suspected to be a high-status medieval building, probably two stories and possibly even the vicarage of All Saints' Church opposite.

Across the road from this site in 1986, a watching brief was maintained by Fred Hartley and David Smith during the renovation of 107–109 Highcross Street (known as the Cross Keys in the 19th century, and possibly before),

it was rediscovered by the Leicestershire Museums Archaeological Survey Team. In the early 1990s, detailed drawings of the structure were prepared and evaluative excavations undertaken with a view to establishing a date for the structure (Hagar and Buckley 1990). In 2003, the site of 9 St Nicholas Place was redeveloped for a new BBC building, leading to the demolition of the 19th-century brick vaults above the undercroft and providing the opportunity to excavate the medieval levels of the site (Kipling 2010). The undercroft, which runs at right angles to the Guildhall Lane frontage, is constructed of random mortared granite and re-used Roman tile, and measures about 8.5m long by 4.5m wide internally and 2.5m deep. In the west wall, there are the remains of four round-headed windows with sloping sills and splayed jambs, some of the arches constructed of Roman tile. In the east and north walls are square niches lined with Roman tiles. The 2009 excavations (fig 19) showed that the building was constructed between the first quarter of the 12th to mid 13th century and cut through Anglo-Saxon dark-earth deposits and underlying Roman street metallings (Kipling 2010, 129–31). The building was presumably of two stories and is thought to have been used for the storage of the goods of a wealthy merchant, whose adjacent domestic accommodation perhaps fronted onto Highcross Street, although no evidence for this survived. Access originally seems to have been via an external ramp or flight of steps to a wide doorway in the west wall, facilitating the passage of goods in and out of the building (*ibid* 141). The undercroft and associated accommodation is thought to have occupied a single large plot of land, perhaps one of the late Anglo-Saxon *hagae*[5] which had not yet been subdivided.

Early in its life, the undercroft underwent a number of alterations, suggesting that by the 13th century it was no longer used for the storage of valuables and had been subdivided internally, partly for the stalling of domestic animals but also to accommodate internal cess pits, perhaps serving the rooms above (*ibid* 142). During the construction of the new BBC building, the undercroft was preserved *in situ* beneath it.

Leicester Abbey

Although the precinct walls of Leicester Abbey, to the north-east of the medieval town, survived the Dissolution, most of the claustral buildings had probably been demolished by the late 16th century, with the exception of the gatehouse, farm buildings and a few other structures, many of which appear on 18th-century engravings (Buckley 2006). Limited investigations were undertaken on the site in the 19th and early 20th centuries, but it was not until the major excavation campaign of 1929–32 as part of the conversion of the

5   Anglo-Saxon estate boundary

Abbey Grounds into a public park, that the full plan of the claustral buildings was revealed. This work was directed by the architect of the park scheme, W.K. Bedingfield, and whilst no excavation report was ever produced, plans of what was found survive in the Leicestershire Records Office. Bedingfield published a summary of the results and a plan indicating his interpretation of the function of the various buildings (Bedingfield 1931).

In 2000, ULAS and the School of Archaeology and Ancient History at the University of Leicester embarked upon what was to become a ten-season project at the site to assess the survival of archaeological remains, clarify the plans of particular buildings and provide training opportunities for undergraduate students (Buckley 2006). Initially, attention focused on Cavendish House, (fig 20) a mansion of the 16th–17th century, which was thought to have been constructed on the site of the medieval abbey gatehouse. This indicated that the latter probably started off in the 12th or 13th century as a simple rectangular structure with a gate-hall flanked by small chambers. It was then significantly enlarged in the 14th–15th century with the addition of polygonal turrets at the corners and on either side of the gate-hall (Buckley 2006). Further information on the appearance of the building comes from the Buck Brothers engraving of 1730 and from a description by the Crown Commissioners in the 1530s (Fox 1938). The latter makes reference to glazed windows and chimneys, indicating an unusually high level of comfort for a monastic building, perhaps suggesting that by this time it had become the Abbot's lodging. The secular function of the building may also explain why the gatehouse was chosen for conversion into a mansion by the Hastings family in the second half of the 16th century. Further trenches were examined in 2000 within the cellars beneath the dormitory and in the eastern cloister walk, where a comparatively large area of medieval tiled floor survived intact. In general, the impression was that only destruction deposits had been removed from the site during the large-scale excavations of the 1920s–30s, leaving earlier levels substantially intact, although most of the walls had probably been robbed.

From 2002–5, our excavations concentrated on an examination of the suspected site of the kitchen (fig 21) revealing it to be a large

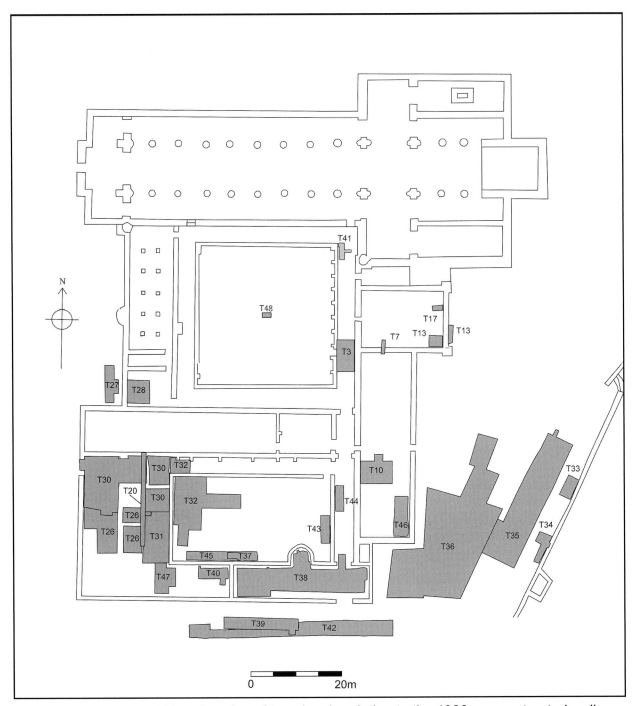

Figure 20: Leicester Abbey, location of trenches in relation to the 1930s reconstructed walls.

Chapter House: T7, T13 and T17; East Cloister Walk: T3, T41and T44; Cloister Garth: T48; West Range: T27 and T28; East Range: T10 and T46; Kitchen: T20, T26, T30, T31 and T32; Infirmary: T33, T34 and T36; Guest Range: T37- T40, T42-T43

detached structure measuring approximately 39 feet (11.88m) square internally with walls 4ft 4in (1.32m) thick, except for the west wall which had been refaced, increasing the thickness to about 5.7 feet (1.74m). The external corners appear to have been buttressed, whilst the internal corners showed evidence for superimposed burnt deposits and stone arch abutments, indicating the presence of corner fireplaces, some of which contained circular hearths or ovens. Hence the kitchen

was octagonal internally and square externally and was similar to the surviving Abbot's kitchen at Glastonbury Abbey (fig 20). Outside were cobbled yard surfaces and a complex of stone-lined and capped drains of different phases, taking rainwater from the roofs of the buildings and flushing some of it through the interior of the kitchen, presumably to provide a ready source of water for cleaning fish and other foodstuffs. Environmental evidence from the kitchen is discussed elsewhere in this volume by Angela

Figure 21: Leicester Abbey: plan of the excavated remains of the kitchen (top) compared with the Abbot's Kitchen, Glastonbury (bottom). Drawn by R.Buckley.

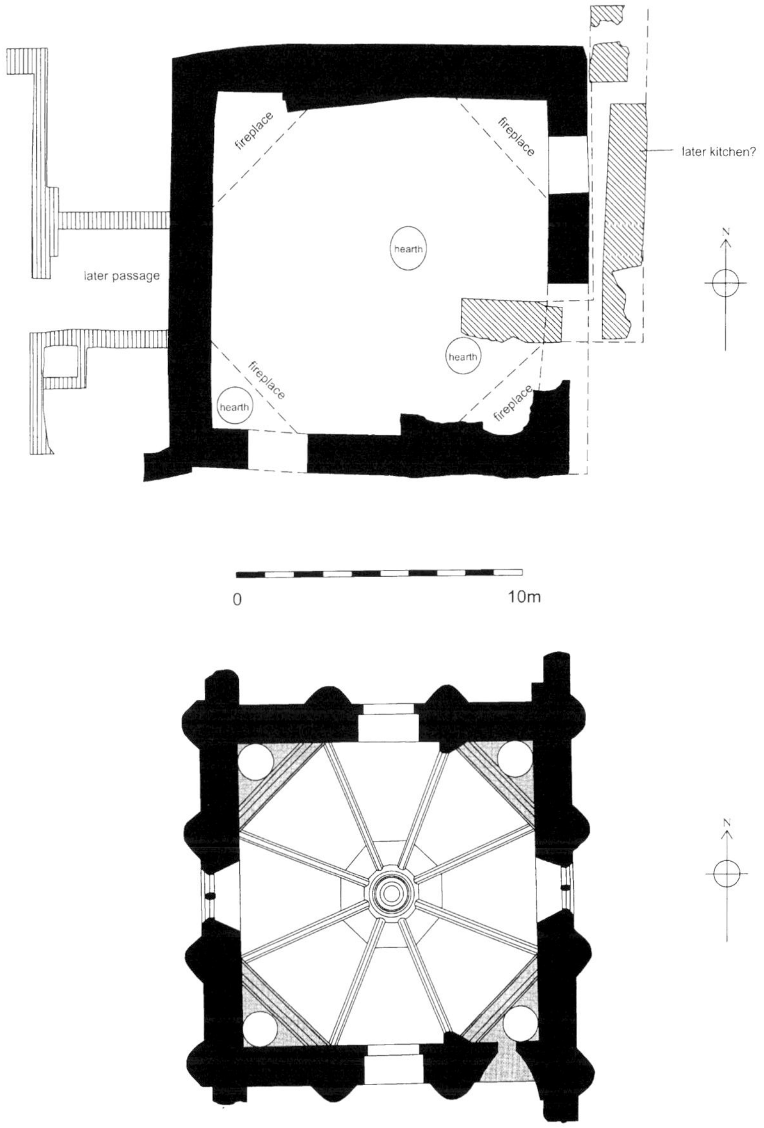

Monckton. The discovery of a lead pipe indicates that a supply of fresh water was also available. Later in the medieval period, a passageway marked by two substantial walls was added to the west side of the kitchen, probably to provide access to a range of buildings which is yet to be revealed by excavation. Peter Liddle (this vol.) suggests that this could be the King's Tower referred to in the Crown Commissioners' Survey. An unexpected discovery during the final stages of excavation was that the kitchen had been demolished in the medieval period and replaced by a rectangular building constructed against the south wall of the refectory; whether or not this was also a kitchen remains uncertain.

A range of buildings against the eastern precinct wall which appear on the surviving Bedingfield archive plans and interpreted as the site of the infirmary (Liddle 1995, 7), were investigated in 2006–7 (fig 22; Hyam and Jones 2009). Evidence for a large rectangular hall with surviving mortar floors laid over a number of earlier floor levels was identified, with further rooms and open areas to the north, lying above the line of the abbey main drain. The latter discharged into the Soar via an arch in the precinct wall and although it may originally have taken effluent from the reredorter (latrines at the south end of the dormitory), it was filled-in at some point during the medieval period. This may have resulted from a remodelling of the dormitory and reredorter block by extending it southwards, suspected from Bedingfield's excavation plans. To the west of the hall was a walkway which

presumably provided access to ranges of buildings to the west and a large rectangular stone platform, perhaps the foundation for a tower.

The final two seasons of excavation on the site focused on an examination of the site of the suspected guest hall which lay just to the west of the infirmary and south-east of the kitchen (Hyam and Jones 2010). This appeared on the Bedingfield plan as a rectangular structure with a projecting semi-circular bay in its north wall, originally thought to be the window referred to in the Crown Commissioners' survey of the 1530s (cf. Buckley 2006, 67). Unsurprisingly, perhaps, the excavations showed that the plan and sequence of buildings in this area was in fact much more complex and indicated that the guest hall was almost certainly at first floor

231

Figure 22: Leicester Abbey: the infirmary. View north.

Figure 23: Leicester Abbey: architectural fragments from earlier cloister arcade recovered during a watching brief on the reconstruction of 1930s walls.

level, above a covered west-east walkway and a series of rooms which were probably garderobes. At one end of the hall was a cross wing with a heated chamber at ground floor level, indicated by the base of brick fireplace at the end wall. The Crown Commissioners' survey describes an 'entree leydyng furth of the cloyester in to the hall and chaumbers, and other houses of offyce buylded square about a yarde adjoynyng to the seyd cloyester parte stone and parte tymber' (*ibid*, 67). Taken together, the archaeological evidence from the infirmary and guest hall excavations seems to bear this out, suggesting what is in effect a subsidiary southern cloister with covered walkways providing access between different buildings. The walkway running north from the guest hall seems to have been contemporary with a lead water pipe running under its floor. The pipe trench cut surfaces and other deposits pre-dating the walkway, and it seems quite likely that the guest hall complex was constructed later on in the life of the abbey.

A number of archaeological watching briefs were undertaken at Leicester Abbey between 2000 and the present, many concerned with minor works which produced little new archaeological information. However, the low walls which were constructed in the 1930s to mark out the plans of the principal claustral buildings were extensively rebuilt between 2005 and 2007 and archaeological monitoring enabled the recovery of inlaid floor tile and architectural fragments re-used in their construction (Jones 2009b). An area of well-preserved walling in the north-east corner of the cloister revealed the in-situ base of a cluster of five columns from the cloister arcade. Other fragments found in the vicinity (fig 23) indicated that a Romanesque cloister arcade of the 12th century had been demolished in the 14th century and replaced with a Gothic traceried arcade, requiring additional buttressing on the inner wall, facing the cloister garth (Alexander 2007, 2009). A small stone tank uncovered in the western cloister walk was almost certainly the laver shown on Bedingfield's excavation plan. Further medieval wall foundations were encountered in the west and south ranges, including one which appeared to indicate that the refectory continued further west than previously supposed (Jones 2009b).

Industry in Leicester

Archaeological investigations in Leicester since about 1980 have provided considerable information on trade and industry in the medieval town to supplement the body of information available in the published Borough Records (RBL), summarised in Victoria County History of Leicestershire Vol. 4. Substantial assemblages of animal bone, industrial residues and pottery have come from rubbish deposits from the larger sites whilst extensive sampling for the recovery of plant remains has now become the norm (Monckton, this volume) and has furnished new information on brewing and crop processing in particular.

Artefact manufacture

Evidence for the manufacture of bone pins and knife handles during the medieval period had been found on St Nicholas Circle in 1971 (Kipling 2010). On the Shires Little Lane site, a pit of *c*.1475–1550 contained an abnormally high number of goose wing bones, representing the separated wing tips of 70–80 birds, which suggests the use of feathers for arrow flights, quill pens and brushes. It may be significant that an arrowsmith ('arwesmyt') appears in the borough records for 1318 (RBL I). Further manufacturing waste from this pit may be indicated by 21 sheep horn cores and six antler fragments (Gidney 1991a).

On Sanvey Gate, (Jarvis 2006), a pit containing almost exclusively cattle horncores may suggest waste from the workshop of a tanner or hornworker, most likely the latter (Browning forthcoming).

Skin processing

Tanners' workshops were frequently located next to rivers as large quantities of water are required for the processing of animal hides into leather. At Westbridge Wharf, Bath Lane, the animal bone evidence suggested the dumping of waste from the processing of cattle hides by the tanners and sheep hides by the whittawyers working close to the river in the medieval period. Hornworking may also have taken place in the vicinity (Browning 2010). On the Merlin Works site immediately to the north, a yard area to the south of the precinct wall of the Blackfriars contained several small stone-lined tanks, some of which contained degraded lime, often associated with the work of the fellmongers who removed hair from the skins of sheep (Kipling 2008, 275–

278). Over the yard was a deposit containing organic waste, with considerable quantities of animal bone including butchery waste. Also on Bath Lane, an evaluation by Birmingham Archaeology identified an area of medieval industrial features possibly associated with tanning (Wardle 2008, 279).

Whilst a good supply of water was essential for hide processing, not all workshops were near the river and some must have relied upon wells, such as the whittawyers who seem to have been operating in Leicester's south suburb during the medieval and post-medieval periods. Here, at Bonners lane (Finn 2004), a pit containing the feet of 28 sheep was interpreted as evidence of the waste from the workshop of a light leather manufacturer such as a fellmonger, whittawyer or glover (Baxter 2004, 143). Similar activity is suggested on the De Montfort University Business and Law site to the north, where medieval and early post-medieval pits contained unusual concentrations of sheep bones (Morris 2010).

Other sites in the town have produced possible evidence of waste from skin processing. On Vine Street, the animal bone elements of sheep/goat recorded in Phase 8 (1100–1250) were interpreted as waste from horn and skin working rather than from the utilisation of the complete carcass. It is considered more likely that goats were brought into the town primarily as skins, for the preparation of goat leather and horn-working. Similarly, at Causeway Lane, an assemblage dominated by lamb metapodials was taken to be evidence of waste from skins rather than meat, the bones representing either complete lambskins or leg skin used in trimming garments (Gidney 1999, 323). Also at this site, metapodials from infant lamb and one kid, as well as foetal calf bones, suggesting parchment production, were recovered (Gidney 1999, 328).

Considerable evidence has also emerged for the use of the skins of other animals in medieval Leicester. The partial skeleton of a horse was found in a pit at 72 St Nicholas Circle dated to c.1100–1250 (Score 2006) and a number cut marks on the skull may suggest removal of the hide for leather. A late-medieval deposit from Vaughan Way contained a large number of cat metapodials from at least four cats and fine cut marks suggested skinning,

perhaps indicating debris from a small cottage industry. On the Shires sites of Little Lane and St Peter's Lane at least 26 partial cat skeletons were recovered from medieval deposits, suggesting exploitation for their skins (Gidney 2007, 460). Also on these sites, there appeared to be a correlation between the pits used for the disposal of horse, dog and cats (Gidney 1991, 9), which may all have come under the auspices of the whittawyer. At Causeway Lane, evidence of large numbers of cat bones with knife marks from medieval and post-medieval phases suggested that the occupants of one of the plots specialised in procuring cat skins, and some pelts may have been brought in with the head and possibly paws still attached (Gidney 1999, 327). At the Austin Friars site, where there was extensive evidence for leatherworking from waterlogged deposits, an offcut comprising the nose and upper lip of a dog suggested the use of dogskin for the manufacture of items of clothing (Allin 1981, 167).

Metalworking
A building with masonry footings on the frontage of Highcross Street (Highcross Freeschool Lane site) contained a 3m sub-square and c.3.0m deep pit with near-vertical sides which may originally have functioned as a cellar. By the 12th–13th century, after it had partially silted up, a series of superimposed hearths inside it suggest a change to an industrial function, probably metalworking, based on evidence for temperatures in excess of 1500°C being achieved. Elsewhere on this site, secondary ironworking is indicated by the presence of redeposited ferrous slag. Limited evidence for ironworking has also been identified on the Vine Street site, with ferrous slag, including smithying hearth bottom, recovered from a pit and adjacent robber trench. Also on this site, metalworking waste from pits dated to the mid 13th century suggested copper-alloy working in the vicinity and included part of the base of a clay mould used for casting a copper-alloy object, possibly a cauldron or bell. This activity may have taken place nearby, where a bell or cauldron casting pit was found together with an adjacent hearth-furnace, possibly housed within a sub-rectangular timber structure (Higgins et al 2009). As noted above, at Vaughan Way the western bell turret contained a 12th-century bell-casting pit. This consisted of a sub-circular pit containing many burnt clay

fragments and evidence for *in situ* burning. It has been interpreted as a pit for casting a bell by the lost-wax process – the mould of wax encased in earth (perhaps a mixture of loam and dung) would have been heated over a flue to fire it and cause the wax to run off, thereby creating a void into which the molten bronze was poured. An archaeomagnetic date of AD 1150–1180 (GeoQuest sample 10,001) was obtained for the stone lining of the flue. Whilst there was no evidence for the hearth used for melting the bronze, waste material including dross and an ingot fragment was found in the vicinity.

Evidence for copper-alloy working has also been found at Great Central Street, including a crucible and a possibly contemporary stone-lined hearth (Tate 2008), Causeway Lane (Connor and Buckley 1999, 88) and at 72 St Nicholas Circle there is a crucible from deposits of *c.*1100–1250 (Score 2006, phase 7).

Lime burning and brickmaking

Evidence for medieval lime kilns has been found on a number of sites in Leicester. At St Peter's Lane (fig 24; Shires) and nearby at Vaughan Way (Highcross Leicester), both dated to the 11th–12th century and both close to St Peter's church. These consisted of large pits containing partially burned limestone, some of which was blue lias, probably from the Crown Hills area of Leicester. The St Peter's Lane site also produced significant quantities of stone-dressing debris of this period and taken together, the evidence may suggest related activity in a builders' yard, perhaps associated with one of the many building phases of St Peter's. Similarly, a 13th-century lime kiln from Vine Street (Higgins *et al* 2009), together with other industrial features, has been interpreted as evidence of an area of open ground, again perhaps used as a builder's yard, but this time in connection with extensive renovation and rebuilding from the late 13th century onwards at nearby All Saints Church (Collinson 1950, 120). Excavations on Bath Lane in 2003 also revealed evidence for a lime kiln, probably of 12th to 13th-century date (Cooper 2010; Sawday 2010).

Evidence for brickmaking in Leicester in the late medieval and post-medieval periods is known principally from cartographic evidence. 'Bricke Close' is shown on the 1613 William Senior map of Leicester Abbey and is probably the site of the kilns for the nearby Abbot Penny's wall (Buckley 2006, 24). In the vicinity of modern Newarke Street, the William Stukeley map of 1722 is labelled 'brick kilns where antiently was a Roman pottery', while Robert's 1741 map shows a brickworks at the end of Hangman's Lane (near the junction of modern Newarke Street and Welford Road). The archaeological evidence for this industry consists of two post-medieval brick kilns found during excavations on Newarke Street in 2002 (Derrick 2002). Both

Figure 24: St Peter's Lane (Shires), remains of probable lime kiln.

235

Brewing

Evidence for medieval brewing has now come from a number of sites in Leicester, with malting ovens from Vaughan Way (Highcross; Gnanaratnam 2009), Oxford Street/ Southgates DMU (Morris 2010), possibly Great Central Street (Tate 2008) and on the Highcross Street frontage (Freeschool Lane; Coward and Speed 2009). The latter site lay within the commercial heart of the medieval borough, just to the north of the Wednesday Market, and had extensive evidence for brewing on a semi-commercial scale. Here, one of the plots had been subdivided longitudinally with a stone wall in the 14th century and the area was occupied by a series of malting ovens (fig 25) and stone hearth bases (fig 26), probably for heating mash in metal vessels. This brewery, together with associated environmental evidence, is described in more detail elsewhere in this volume by Angela Monckton.

Horticulture

Environmental evidence for horticulture in the medieval town is described elsewhere in this volume (Monckton), but it is noteworthy that much of the north-east quarter was under cultivation from about the mid 14th century onwards, probably following a major decline in the population. The archaeological evidence, found on almost all sites in this area, consists of substantial homogeneous deposits of dark-brown sandy loam, frequently referred to as 'garden soil' which can reach up to about 2m in thickness. Whilst the formation processes for this deposit are still imperfectly understood, the Shires and Highcross excavations have shown that it represents a gradual accumulation as buried ground surfaces can sometimes be identified (with difficulty) within it. Removal of the garden soil generally shows that underlying Roman and medieval deposits have suffered major truncation (unless preserved in a hollow) suggesting that the land was under the plough. Hence, the garden soil deposit probably

Figure 26: Freeschool Lane: malting oven. View east.

were updraught kilns of an L-shaped design with two stoke-holes positioned at the end of each flue and thought to date to the late 16th-early 17th century. A thin deposit of lime on the floor of the kilns suggests that lime burning had taken place as well as brick production.

represents a mixture of ploughed-up earlier deposits mixed with dumped organic waste. It is hoped that future environmental analysis may provide confirmation of this interpretation.

Outside the walls, two sites on Newarke Street (Cooper 1996 and Derrick 2002) revealed evidence for medieval bedding trenches, the one on the latter site probably of 12th to 13th-century date. The trenches are thought to have been dug to receive manure or compost, probably for small-scale production of garden produce as suggested for similar features at Usk (Courtney 1994, 14–16).

Conclusion

Unlike many other historic towns and cities in Britain, Leicester's success as an industrial centre from the early 19th century has meant constant change, with continuous cycles of demolition and redevelopment leading to the disappearance of almost all visible traces of the medieval borough. This lack of visible testimony of course makes it extremely difficult for anyone interested in the past to gain a real feel for what it would have been like to have lived in a middle-ranking town such as Leicester during the medieval period. Until recently we have had to rely to a great extent on documentary sources and historical accounts, with the inevitable bias this brings by concentrating on higher-status buildings and people.

Since the pioneering excavations of the early-mid 1970s at St Nicholas Circle and the Austin Friars, our knowledge of the archaeology of the medieval borough has increased significantly, largely as a result of the implementation of new planning guidance in 1990 (PPG16 'Archaeology and Planning'). Enshrined in this guidance was the principal that developers should pay for the archaeological investigation of sites which would be destroyed or damaged by their proposals. Whilst an element of developer funding had been in place before this (Shires 1988–9), most projects had only been possible through grant aid from English Heritage (and its predecessor bodies). Such funding as there was did not enable the completion of the detailed analysis of the results of some important investigations of medieval sites, such as the tenements at St Nicholas Circle in 1971 (Mellor 1992), although a summary of the phasing has now been published (Kipling 2010). The important and well-preserved late medieval pottery assemblages from this site (Sawday pers.

comm.) remain a priority for future publication. The publication of the Shires excavations too remains outstanding, a casualty of the closure of Leicestershire Archaeological Unit in 1995 and the local government reorganisation which followed. Some funding from English Heritage has enabled most of the analysis to be finished and the intention is to publish the results in conjunction with those from the Highcross Leicester project 2003–6. Developer funding, whilst not without its problems, has allowed large areas to be looked at, not only within the walls but also in the south suburb. The availability of street frontages has continued to remain elusive, mostly due to the presence of 19th-century cellars, but the Highcross Leicester project enabled the excavation of several properties fronting on to the principal commercial street of the town, modern Highcross Street.

How has this upsurge in investigation changed our view of the character and development of the borough in the post-Roman period? Most significantly, perhaps, new light has been shed on the processes of decay of the Roman town and its reoccupation in the early Anglo-Saxon period, both inside and outside the walls. This provides a vivid picture of a scatter of sunken-featured buildings and perhaps halls amongst the Roman ruins within the walls, but also clustering of similar structures outside the south gate. We cannot yet say whether such occupation continued into the Middle Anglo-Saxon period, as there is a dearth of artefacts datable to this period. What can now be confirmed, however, is that there is tangible archaeological evidence for the late Saxon borough in the form of fragmentary timber structures found on the Highcross Street frontage on the Freeschool Lane site (Coward 2009). This confirms the view of Paul Courtney who, on the basis of artefact distribution, believed that modern Highcross Street and High Street would be the most likely focus for late Anglo-Saxon activity (1998, 137). Archaeology has also made a major contribution to what we know about the way in which the medieval town plan developed during this period within the constraints of the walls of the former Roman city. For example we are now beginning to detect tangible evidence for the influence exerted by surviving Roman ruins on the evolving street pattern, with upstanding structures being respected by particular routes.

The town defences, consisting of the patched up Roman walls, gates and re-cut ditches, continued to influence the pattern of development throughout the medieval period, the borough authorities ensuring that the gates were maintained as the principal point of access, not only for security, but also for the collection of tolls which were important for the town's continuing prosperity. Once within the town, there was a marked contrast in the built environment between the principal commercial streets (High Street and Swinesmarket) and the areas behind them, known as the back lanes. Excavations in the latter areas, particularly the north-east quarter, has given the impression of plots with timber buildings on the frontage, the backyards containing the usual range of cess pits, wells and occasionally industrial features. Plot boundaries in this area must have been marked by timber fences or mud walls as generally no physical evidence has survived for them, the plot divisions being inferred from pit alignments. It is likely that animals were kept in the backyards which, to modern eyes, must have been rather squalid – most plots in this area had cess pits and wells in close proximity, whilst in others, there is also evidence for the dumping of large quantities of animal-bone waste from skin processing. The area was punctuated by two open spaces – the graveyards of St Michael's and St Peter's, the latter with an adjacent high-status hall or vicarage, but otherwise must have been quite densely occupied until decline set in from about 1300.

By contrast, the frontages of the principal commercial thoroughfares had structures of higher quality, including public and religious buildings – many of which are recorded in later illustrations. Excavation at a number of sites has demonstrated more continuity of occupation, leading to the construction of permanent stone boundary walls which were regularly rebuilt or patched up. The plots themselves exhibit a much greater variety in the character of activity, both domestic and commercial, with complex changes in tenancy, as shown by plot divisions. In many respects, this contrast between the commercial streets and the back lanes in terms of status continued right through into the 20th century (Newitt 2009).

Whilst archaeology has been successful in providing new insights into the plans and architecture of high-status buildings and sites – most of which were well constructed in stone – it can contribute comparatively little to our knowledge of the appearance of ordinary domestic buildings. Most of these would have been timber-framed or even of mud and of those surviving into the 19th and early 20th centuries to be recorded in drawings and photographs, almost all would have been the better-constructed examples of 15th century or later date. Hence the appearance of houses and commercial premises dating before then, or those of more lowly status, is largely guesswork. We can perhaps assume that the overall look of the town was very much as described by later authors. In the early 16th century, John Leland said: 'The Hole Toune of Leircester at theis Tyme is buildid of tymbre' (Ellis 1976, 82) and a century later, John Evelyn noted 'the old and ragged Citty of Leicester, large & pleasantly seated, but despicably built, the chimney flues like so many smiths' forges' (Ellis 1976, 87). The writers make comparatively little comment on the better-built stone churches and religious buildings which must have stood out in stark contrast. Other accounts in the Borough Records and elsewhere give the impression of the rural character of the town, with many mature trees and animals being allowed to run loose in the streets, most of which were unlikely to have been paved.

The backyards of many burgage plots have now been excavated, both on the principal commercial streets, but also in the back lanes area of the north-east quarter, and detailed analysis of environmental and artefactual data has allowed us new insights into food and drink and making a living in the medieval borough. The inhabitants too and their places of worship have also been subject to study through work at Leicester Abbey and at the lost churches of St Peter's and St Michael's. The two latter sites have together provided one of the largest assemblages of secular medieval burials to be analysed in the region.

Finally, the investigation and recording of many of Leicester's few remaining medieval standing buildings and the integration of the results with those from archaeological investigation have provided new information on nationally significant buildings such as the Great Hall and John of Gaunt's Cellar at Leicester Castle and the gatehouse at Leicester Abbey.

Acknowledgements

I am especially gratefully to the many archaeologists who have supervised projects in the city or undertaken specialist analyses over the past thirty or more years, upon whose work this summary is based: Lynden Cooper, Nick Cooper, Paul Courtney, Jennifer Browning, Aileen Connor, Jon Coward, Mick Derrick, Neil Finn, James Gossip, Tony Gnanaratnam, Jules Hagar, Tim Higgins, Andy Hyam, Steve Jones, Roger Kipling, John Lucas, Dave Mackie, James Meek, Angela Monckton, Mathew Morris, Debbie Sawday, Vicki Score, Gavin Speed, John Tate, John Thomas and Sally Warren. Thanks also to Patrick Clay, Peter Liddle and Chris Wardle for commenting on this paper and last but not least, to Jean Mellor and Terry Pearce for ensuring that the archaeology of medieval Leicester began to receive the attention it deserved.

Bibliography

Alcock, N. and Buckley, R., 1987. 'Leicester Castle Hall', *Medieval Archaeology* 31, 73–79.

Alexander, J., 2007. *Leicester Abbey Loose Architectural Stones Report* 1. Unpub. archive report.

Alexander, J., 2009. *Leicester Abbey Loose Architectural Stones Report* 2. Unpub. archive report.

Allin, C., 1981. 'The Leather', in J. E. Mellor and T. Pearce *The Austin Friars, Leicester.* Leicester. Council for British Archaeology.

Bedingfield, W. K., 1931. 'Presidential address', *Transactions of the Leicester Literary and Philosophical Society* 32, 5–24.

Baxter, I., 2004. 'Animal, bird, reptile and amphibian bones' in N. Finn *The Origins of a Leicester Suburb: Roman, Anglo-Saxon, Medieval and Post-Medieval Occupation on Bonners Lane*, 132–148. BAR (Brit. Ser.) 372. Oxford: Archaeopress.

Browning, J., 2010. 'The Animal Bones' in L.Cooper, 2010 *An Archaeological Excavation at Westbridge Wharf, Bath Lane Leicester NGR: SK 5811 0444 centre.* Unpublished University of Leicester Archaeological Services Report 2010–229.

Buckley, R., 1980. 'Causeway Lane' in P.Liddle (ed) 'Archaeology in Leicestershire and Rutland 1979–80' *Transactions of the Leicestershire Archaeological and Historical Society* 55 (83–97).

Buckley, R., 1987. 'A trial excavation at Leicester Castle' in P. Liddle (ed) 'Archaeology in Leicestershire and Rutland 1986', *Transactions of the Leicestershire Archaeological and Historical Society* 61, 97 (88–99).

Buckley, R., 1993. 'John of Gaunt's Cellar, Leicester Castle' in R. Buckley (ed) 'Archaeology in Leicestershire and Rutland 1992' *Transactions of the Leicestershire Archaeological and Historical Society* 67, 86–87 (73–115).

Buckley, R., 2006. 'The archaeology of Leicester Abbey' in J. Story, J. Bourn and R. Buckley (eds) *Leicester Abbey, Medieval History, Archaeology and Manuscript Studies*, 1–67. Leicester: Leicestershire Archaeological and Historical Society.

Buckley, R. and Hagar, J., 1992. 'An excavation in Castle Gardens, Leicester' in R. Buckley (ed) 'Archaeology in Leicestershire and Rutland 1991' *Transactions of the Leicestershire Archaeological and Historical Society* 66, 179–80 (172–93).

Buckley, R. & Lucas, J., 1987. *Leicester Town Defences: Excavations 1958–1974.* Leicestershire Museums Publication 85.

Buckley, R. and Lucas, J., 2007. *Excavations at Little Lane and St Peter's Lane (Shires) Leicester.* Unpub. ULAS Archive Report 2007–147.

Clarke, D T-D., 1952. 'Archaeology in Leicestershire 1939–51' *Transactions of the Leicestershire Archaeological and Historical Society* 28, 17–48.

Clarke, D T-D., 1957. 'Slum Clearance' & 'Leicester, Belgrave Gate' in 'Archaeology in Leicestershire 1956–7' *Transactions of the Leicestershire Archaeological and Historical Society* 33, 59 (59–65).

Clarke, D T-D. and Simmons, J., 1960. 'Old Leicester: an illustrated record of change in the City' *Transactions of the Leicestershire Archaeological and Historical Society* 36, 45–48.

Clay, P. & Mellor, J. E., 1985. *Excavations in Bath Lane, Leicester.* Leicestershire Museums, Art Galleries and Records Service Archaeol. Rep. 10.

Clay, P. N., and Pollard, R. J., 1994. *Iron Age and Roman Occupation in the West Bridge Area, Leicester. Excavations 1962–1971.* Leicester: Leicestershire Museums, Arts and Records Service.

Clough, T. H. McK., Dornier, A. and Rutland R. A., 1975 *Anglo-Saxon and Viking Leicestershire.* Leicester: Leicestershire Museums, Art Galleries and Records Service.

Collinson, H., 1950. 'A Description of the Fabric' in P. Hepworth, 'All Saints, Leicester: A Short History of the Church and Parish' *Transactions of the Leicestershire Archaeological and Historical Society* 26, 93–132.

Colvin, H. M., 1963. *The History of the Kings Works. Vol. 2 The Middle Ages.* London: HMSO.

Connor, A. and Buckley, R., 1999. *Roman and Medieval Occupation in Causeway Lane, Leicester.* Leicester Archaeology Monographs 5.

Cooper, L., 1993a. 'Bath Lane' in R. Buckley (ed) 'Archaeology in Leicestershire and Rutland 1992' *Transactions of the Leicestershire Archaeological and Historical Society* 67, 83–86 (73–112).

Cooper, L., 1993b. 'An evaluation and excavation at the Cameo Cinema, 40 to 50 High Street, Leicester' *Transactions of the Leicestershire Archaeological and Historical Society* 67, 88–93.

Cooper, L., 1996. 'A Roman cemetery in Newarke Street, Leicester' *Transactions of the Leicestershire Archaeological and Historical Society* 70, 1–90.

Cooper, L., 1998. 'New evidence for the northern defences of Roman Leicester: an archaeological excavation at Cumberland Street' *Transactions of the Leicestershire Archaeological and Historical Society* 72, 92–109.

Cooper, L., 2004. 'Bath Lane, former Harding's Dye Works in R. Buckley and S. George (eds) 'Archaeology in Leicestershire and Rutland 2003' *Transactions of the Leicestershire Archaeological and Historical Society* 78, 144–5 (143–178).

Cooper, L., 2010. *An Archaeological Excavation at Westbridge Wharf, Bath Lane Leicester NGR: SK 5811 0444 centre.* Unpublished University of Leicester Archaeological Services Report 2010–229.

Cooper, N., 2009. 'The Anglo-Saxon pottery' in J. Coward and G. Speed 2009 *Urban Life in Leicester: An Archaeological Excavation at Freeschool Lane.* Unpub ULAS Report.

Courtney, P., 1994. *Report on the Excavations at Usk 1965–1976: Medieval and Later Usk* (ed. W. H. Manning)

Courtney, P. and Courtney, Y., 1995 *The Changing Face of Leicester.* Stroud: Alan Sutton

Courtney, P., 1998. 'Saxon and Medieval Leicester: The Making of an Urban Landscape' *Transactions of the Leicestershire Archaeological and Historical Society* 72 110–145.

Coward, J., 2007. 'Freeschool Lane/Highcross Street' in S. Bocock & N. J. Cooper (eds) 'Archaeology in Leicestershire and Rutland 2006', *Transactions of the Leicestershire Archaeological and Historical Society* 81 181–190 (173–235).

Coward, J. and Speed, G., 2009. *Urban Life in Leicester: An Archaeological Excavation at Freeschool Lane* Unpub. ULAS Report 2009–140.

Derrick, M., 2001. '65 Market Place' in R. Buckley 'Archaeology in Leicestershire and Rutland 2001 'Transactions of the Leicestershire Archaeological and Historical Society 75, 132 (129–162).

Derrick, M., 2002. *An Archaeological Excavation at 21–27 and 29–33 Newarke Street, Castle Ward, Leicester (SK 5857 3041)* Unpub. ULAS Report 2002–195.

Ellis, C. D. B., 1976. *History in Leicester.* Leicester: Leicester City Council.

Finn, N., 2004. *The Origins of a Leicester Suburb Roman, Anglo-Saxon, Medieval and Post-Medieval Occupation on Bonners Lane.* BAR 372.

Finn, N., 2005. *The Former St. Mary's Vicarage, The Newarke, Leicester: Historic Building Record and Excavation* Unpub. ULAS Report 2005–137.

Finn, N., and Buckley, R. 1997. 'Leicester Castle' in R. Buckley (ed.) 'Archaeology in Leicestershire and Rutland' *Transactions of the Leicestershire Archaeological and Historical Society* 71, 103–4 (86–130).

Fox, L., 1938. *Leicester Abbey.* City of Leicester Guidebook.

Fox, L., 1942. 'Leicester Castle', *Transactions of the Leicestershire Archaeological and Historical Society* 22, 125–170.

Gidney, L. 1991 *Leicester; the Shires 1988 Excavations: The animal bones from the post-medieval deposits at St. Peter's Lane.* AML Report 131/1991

Gidney, L., 1999 'The Animal Bones' in A. Connor and R. Buckley (eds.) *Roman and Medieval Occupation in Causeway Lane, Leicester.* Leicester: University of Leicester. Leicester Archaeology Monographs No. 5, 310–333

Gidney, L. 2007. 'The animal bone' in J. Lucas and R. Buckley *Excavations at Little Lane and St. Peter's Lane, Leicester (Shires) 1988–9* Unpub. ULAS Report: 2007–147, 463–488.

Gnanaratnam, A., 1998. 'Friar Lane' in R. Buckley (ed) 'Archaeology in Leicestershire and Rutland 1998' *Transactions of the Leicestershire Archaeological and Historical Society* 73, 158 (156–195).

Gnanaratnam, A. 2004. 'Vaughan Way, St Margaret's Baths' in R. Buckley and S. George (eds.) 'Archaeology in Leicestershire and Rutland 2003' *Transactions of the Leicestershire Archaeological and Historical Society* 78, 157 (143–178).

Gnanaratnam, A. 2009. *The Excavation of St. Peter's Church and Graveyard, Vaughan Way, Leicester 2004–2006.* Unpub. ULAS Report 2009–156.

Goodchild 1953. 'Leicester city wall in Sanvey Gate: excavations in 1952'. *Transactions of the Leicestershire Archaeological and Historical Society* 29, 15–29.

Gossip, J., 1998. 'York Road/Oxford Street' in R. Buckley (ed) 'Archaeology in Leicestershire and Rutland 1998' *Transactions of the Leicestershire Archaeological and Historical Society* 73, 159–60 (156–195).

Gossip, J. 1999a *Excavations at Republic Car Park, Oxford Street, Leicester.* Unpub. ULAS Report 99/112

Gossip, J. 1999b. *Excavations at York Road, Leicester.* Unpub. ULAS Report 99/111.

Hagar, J. and Buckley, R., 1990. 'A twelfth-century undercroft in Guildhall Lane, Leicester' in P. Liddle (ed) Archaeology in Leicestershire and Rutland 1989' *Transactions of the Leicestershire Archaeological and Historical Society* 64, 99–101 (93–108).

Hartley, R. F., 1988. '107–109 Highcross Street (The Cross Keys Inn)' in P. Liddle 'Archaeology in Leicestershire 1987' *Transactions of the Leicestershire Archaeological and Historical Society* 62, 83–5 (72–93).

Harvey, D., 1996. 'Castle Gardens, Leicester' in R. Pollard (ed.) 'Archaeology in Leicestershire and Rutland 1995', *Transactions of the Leicestershire Archaeological and Historical Society* 70, 167 (154–179).

Hebditch, M., 1967–8. 'A Saxo-Norman pottery kiln discovered in Southgate Street, Leicester 1964' *Transactions of the Leicestershire Archaeological and Historical Society* 43 , 5–9.

Higgins, T., 1997a. 'Leicester, Oxford Street' in N. Cooper (ed) 'Archaeology in Leicestershire and Rutland 1996' *Transactions of the Leicestershire Archaeological and Historical Society* 71, 104 (86–130).

Higgins, T., 1997b. 'Leicester, Westbridge Place' in N. Cooper Archaeology in Leicestershire and Rutland 1996' *Transactions of the Leicestershire Archaeological and Historical Society* 71, 104–5 (86–130).

Higgins, T., 2007. 'Vine Street' in S. Bocock & N.J. Cooper (eds) Archaeology in Leicestershire and Rutland 2006, *Transactions of the Leicestershire Archaeological and Historical Society* 81, 192–205 (173–235).

Higgins, T and Lucas, J., 1996. 'New Bond Street, Leicester: the Shires Churchgate extension' in R Buckley (ed) 'Archaeology in Leicestershire and Rutland 1995' *Transactions of the Leicestershire Archaeological and Historical Society* 69, 113–116 (97–136).

Higgins, T., Morris, M. and Stone, D. 2009. *Life and Death in Leicester's North-east Quarter: Excavation of a Roman Town House and Medieval Parish Churchyard at Vine Street, Leicester (Highcross Leicester) 2004–2006.* Unpub. ULAS Report 2009–134.

Holloway J., 2008. 'Charcoal burial: A minority burial rite in early medieval Europe' in E. Murphy (ed) *Deviant Burial in the Archaeological Record.* Exeter: Oxbow. 131–147.

Horn W., 1970. 'The potential and limitations of radiocarbon dating in the Middle Ages: the art historian's view', 23–87 in R. Berger (ed.), *Scientific Methods in Medieval Archaeology,* Berkeley: University of California Press, 1970.

Hyam, A., and Jones, S., 2010. 'Leicester Abbey' in J. Thomas (ed) 'Archaeology in Leicestershire and Rutland 2009', *Transactions of the Leicestershire Archaeological and Historical Society* 84, 242–6 (338–341).

Jarvis, W., 2005. 'Sanvey Gate' in N. J. Cooper (ed) 'Archaeology in Leicestershire and Rutland 2004', *Transactions of the Leicestershire Archaeological and Historical Society* 79,144 (141–154).

Jarvis, W., 2006. 'Sanvey Gate' .in N. J. Cooper (ed) 'Archaeology in Leicestershire and Rutland 2005', *Transactions of the Leicestershire Archaeological and Historical Society* 80, 219 (215–250).

Jones, S., 2009a. 'Leicester, Oxford Street, De Montfort University' in T. Higgins and N. Cooper (eds) 'Archaeology in Leicestershire and Rutland 2008', *Transactions of the Leicestershire Archaeological and Historical Society* 83, 246–50 (242–271).

Jones, S., 2009b. *An Archaeological Watching Brief During Restoration Works at Abbey Grounds, Abbey Park, Leicester NGR: SK 58 05 (area).* Unpub. ULAS Report 2009–180.

Kelly, W., 1877. 'Visitations of the Plague at Leicester' *Transactions of the Royal Historical Society* 6, 395–447.

Kenyon, K. M., 1948 *Excavations at the Jewry Wall Site, Leicester.* Oxford: Rep. Res. Comm. Soc Antiq. London 15

Kipling, R., 2004. '9 St Nicholas Place' in R. Buckley and S. George (eds) 'Archaeology in Leicestershire and Rutland 2003' *Transactions of the Leicestershire Archaeological and Historical Society* 78, 143–178.

Kipling, R., 2008. 'Bath Lane (former Merlin Dye Works)' in N. J. Cooper & D. Randle (eds) 'Archaeology in Leicester, Leicestershire and Rutland 2007', *Transactions of the Leicestershire Archaeological and Historical Society* 82, 275–278

Kipling, R., 2009. *An Archaeological Excavation at 9 St. Nicholas Place, Castle, Leicester (NGR: SK 5840 0448 centre)* Unpub. ULAS Report 2009–110.

Kipling, R., 2010. 'A medieval undercroft, tenements and associated buildings at 9 St Nicholas Place and related sites, Leicester'. *Transactions of the Leicestershire Archaeological and Historical Society* 84, 117–149.

Kirby, 1965–6. 'The Saxon Bishops of Lindsey (Syddensis), Leicester and Dorchester', *Transactions of the Leicestershire Archaeological and Historical Society* 41, 1–8.

Knox, R., 1995. 'Castle View, Leicester' in R. Buckley (ed) 'Archaeology in Leicestershire and Rutland 1994', *Transactions of the Leicestershire Archaeological and Historical Society* 69, 129–30 (97–136).

Laxton, R., *et al* 1981–2. 'Tree ring dates – results from Leicestershire' in P. Liddle 'Archaeology in Leicestershire and Rutland 1982' *Transactions of the Leicestershire Archaeological and Historical Society* 57, 78–80 (78–93).

Liddle, P. 1986. 'Archaeology in Leicestershire and Rutland 1985' *Transactions of the Leicestershire Archaeological and Historical Society* 60, 78–95.

Liddle, P. 1995. 'The archaeology of the abbeys and priories of Leicestershire'. *Transactions of the Leicestershire Archaeological and Historical Society* 69, 1–21.

Lucas, J., 1978–9. 'The Town Walls of Leicester: Evidence for a West Wall' *Transactions of the Leicestershire Archaeological and Historical Society* 54, 61–68.

Lucas J. and Buckley, R.J. 1989 'The Shires excavation – Interim report' in P. Liddle 'Archaeology in Leicestershire and Rutland 1988', *Transactions of the Leicestershire Archaeological and Historical Society* 63, 105–6 (105–120)

Mackie D. and Buckley, R., 1994. 'Castle Yard, Leicester' in R. Buckley 'Archaeology in Leicestershire and Rutland 1994' *Transactions of the Leicestershire Archaeological and Historical Society* 69, 119–124 (97–136).

Martin, J., 1990. 'St Michael's church and parish, Leicester', *Transactions of the Leicestershire Archaeological and Historical Society*, 64, 21–5.

McWhirr, A., 1972. 'Archaeology in Leicestershire and Rutland 1973'. 1999' *Transactions of the Leicestershire Archaeological and Historical Society* 48, 59–64.

Meek, J., 2000. St Nicholas Place in R. Buckley (ed) (Archaeology in Leicestershire and Rutland 1999' *Transactions of the Leicestershire Archaeological and Historical Society* 74, 223–9 (223–260).

Mellor, J. E., 1971–2. 'Southgate Street' in A. McWhirr *Archaeology in Leicestershire and Rutland 1970–2*', TLAHS 57, 64–5 (62–76).

Mellor, J. E., 1981–2. 'Leicestershire Archaeological Field Unit Annual Report 1982' in P. Liddle 'Archaeology in Leicestershire and Rutland 1984' *Transactions of the Leicestershire Archaeological and Historical Society* 84–6 (78–93).

Mellor, J. E., 1984–5. 'Leicestershire Archaeological Unit Annual Report 1984', in P. Liddle 'Archaeology in Leicestershire and Rutland 1984' *Transactions of the Leicestershire Archaeological and Historical Society* 59, 97 (86–103).

Mellor, J. E., 1986. 'Leicestershire Archaeological Unit Annual Report 1985' in P. Liddle 'Archaeology in Leicestershire and Rutland 1985' *Transactions of the Leicestershire Archaeological and Historical Society* 60, 87–90 (78–95)

Mellor, J.E., 1992. 'The first twenty-five years: archaeology in Leicestershire 1965–1990' *Transactions of the Leicestershire Archaeological and Historical Society* 66, 92–103.

Mellor J. E., and Pearce, T., 1981. T*he Austin Friars, Leicester.* London: Counc.Brit. Archaeol. Res. Rep. 35.

Monckton, A., 2009. 'The environmental material' in R. Kipling 2009 *An Archaeological Excavation at 9 St Nicholas Place, Castle, Leicester (NGR: SK 5840 0448 centre)* Unpub ULAS Report 2009.

Morris, M., 2010. *Life in the Suburbs: The Archaeological Excavation of Iron Age to Post-medieval occupation beneath the PACE and Hugh Aston Buildings, De Montfort University, Leicester (2006–2008) SK 584 040.* Unpub. ULAS Report 2010–134.

Newitt, N., 2009. *The Slums of Leicester* Derby: Breedon Books.

Radini, A., 2010. 'The environmental evidence' in M. Morris 2010 *Life in the Suburbs: The Archaeological Excavation of Iron Age to Post-medieval occupation beneath the PACE and Hugh Aston Buildings, De Montfort University, Leicester (2006–2008) SK 584 040.* Unpub. ULAS Report 2010–134.

Radford, R. A., 1955. 'Oakham Castle', *Archaeological Journal* 112, 181–184

Radford, R. A., Jope, E. M. and Tonkin, J. W., 1973. 'The Great Hall of the Bishop's Palace at Hereford', *Medieval Archaeology* 17, 78–86.

RBL *Records of the Borough of Leicester, vols 1–7*, edited by M. Bateson, R.B. Stocks and A. Chinnery. Leicester 1901–74.

Sawday, D., 2010. 'Post-Roman pottery' in L. Cooper 2010 *An Archaeological Excavation at Westbridge Wharf, Bath Lane Leicester NGR: SK 5811 0444 centre.* Unpublished University of Leicester Archaeological Services Report 2010–229.

Score, V., 2006. *Archaeological Excavations at 72, St. Nicholas Circle, Leicester SK 5832 0432* Unpub. ULAS Report 2006–113.

Score, V., 2010. 'A Roman 'delicatessen' at Castle Street, Leicester'. *Transactions of the Leicestershire Archaeological and Historical Society* 84, 77–94.

Tate, J., 2007. 'East Bond Street – Highcross Quarter' in S. Bocock & N. J. Cooper (eds) 'Archaeology in Leicestershire and Rutland 2006', *Transactions of the Leicestershire Archaeological and Historical Society* 81, 177 (173–235).

Tate, J., 2008. 'Great Central Street' in N. J. Cooper & D. Randle (eds) 'Archaeology in Leicester, Leicestershire and Rutland 2007', *Transactions of the Leicestershire Archaeological and Historical Society* 82, 279–80 (275–298).

Taylor, G., 2000. 'Infirmary Road, Leicester Royal Infirmary Victoria Building' in R. Buckley (ed.) 'Archaeology in Leicestershire and Rutland 1999', *Transactions of the Leicestershire Archaeological and Historical Society* 74 224–225 (223–259).

Thompson, J., 1845. Letter in Proceedings of the Committee. *Archaeology Journal,* 1, 390–1.

Thompson, J., 1859. *Leicester Castle.* Leicester: Crossley and Clarke.

Thompson, V., 2004. *Dying and Death in later Anglo-Saxon England.* Woodbridge, Suffolk: Boydell Press.

Thomas, J., 2006. Grange Lane, in N. J. Cooper (ed) Archaeology in Leicestershire and Rutland 2005, *Transactions of the Leicestershire Archaeological and Historical Society* 80 p.217 (215–250).

Thomas, J., Tate, J. and Parker D. 2007. 'Great Central Street, no. 71, (former 'Pretty Legs')' in S. Bocock and N. J. Cooper 'Archaeology in Leicestershire and Rutland 2006', *Transactions of the Leicestershire Archaeological and Historical Society* 81, 179–181 (173–235).

Wacher, J. S. 1959. 'Leicester Excavations 1958' in D T-D Clarke (ed) Archaeology in 'Leicestershire and Rutland 1958' *Transactions of the Leicestershire Archaeological and Historical Society* 35, 78–80 (78–86).

Wardle, C., 2008. Bath Lane, Blackfriars' in N. J. Cooper & D. Randle (eds) Archaeology in Leicester, Leicestershire and Rutland 2007, *Transactions of the Leicestershire Archaeological and Historical Society* 82, 279.

Warren, S., 1998. 'Humberstone Gate, Leicester' in R. Buckley 'Archaeology in Leicestershire and Rutland 1998' *Transactions of the Leicestershire Archaeological and Historical Society* 72, 162 (156–195).

Food for the people of medieval Leicester: the evidence from environmental archaeology

Angela Monckton

Introduction

Food remains recovered as a result of environmental sampling during archaeological excavations have been analysed in order to contribute to the understanding of life in the past. Excavations in Leicester during the last 20 years have been extensively sampled, and tonnes of soil have been processed by wet sieving and flotation on fine meshes for the recovery of tiny remains of plants and animals, adding to the evidence from the larger animal bones and oyster shells recovered by hand.

The remains recovered from samples included small animal bones including those of fish, fish scales, shell of various kinds, insect remains, together with charred cereal grains and seeds which would not be found otherwise. Small samples have also been taken to examine them for microscopic remains such as pollen and parasite ova, together with samples for the analysis of soil and sediments in order to recover evidence of the surroundings and living conditions. The results from sampling have provided evidence of foods available to the people in the town and countryside as well as some evidence of the environment and economy in medieval times.

Extensive sampling was carried out for the first time in Leicester on the Shires excavations in 1988–89, at Little Lane and St. Peter's Lane, recovering a wide range of remains. The results showed that charred plant remains were common but often present at a low concentration (Moffett 1993, Monckton 1995). More selective bulk sampling was carried out at Causeway Lane and Bonners Lane in order to extend this information (Monckton 1999, 2004a). This was continued on other sites in the town, particularly for the recent Highcross Excavations which included the sites at Freeschool Lane, Vaughan Way (St Margarets Baths site), and Vine Street (Buckley forthcoming) and some of these results are described below. Excavations in local villages have also been sampled but these have usually been only small interventions;

although evidence is accumulating more is required. It is hoped that comparison of plant remains from the town with those from the villages will contribute to an ongoing study of how the people were provided with food and other commodities.

This paper describes the remains of actual food ingredients recovered from medieval deposits in Leicester and its locality, and concentrates mainly on plant remains, particularly the staple cereals, to expand on earlier reviews of environmental archaeology (Monckton 1995, Monckton 2004b). Much of the data is in archive reports so the sites with charred plant remains are listed at the end of this paper in Table 4. The village sites are described by John Thomas (this volume) and Leicester sites by Richard Buckley (this volume).

It is intended that the sample data will be studied and recorded on a database for the museum service in a project at ULAS (Radini in progress). The available foods are summarised from some Leicester excavations and are listed in Table 1. The crops, food plants, cultivated plants and some of the weeds are shown in Table 2.

Phases

The common phasing established for the Leicester Highcross excavations is used: Saxon AD *c.*450–850, Saxo-Norman 850–1150, earlier medieval *c.*1100–1250, medieval *c.*1250–1400, late medieval *c.*1400-1500, post-medieval 1500–1750, modern 1750-present. The site phases are usually dated by pottery styles using pottery terminology for the region (Sawday and Davis 1999), some overlap occurs but samples are usually from selected datable contexts.

Preservation in the soil

Most of the sediments in Leicester are free-draining, 'dry' rather than waterlogged, and animal bones are generally well preserved on the sites, including fish remains recovered from sieved samples. Plant remains such as seeds and cereal grains that are burnt can become charred and so do not decay and are preserved in most types of deposits within the city and have also been recovered from excavations in the local villages. These remains generally represent plant products such as cereals, which come into contact with fire during their processing, use or disposal; they can provide information about plant materials used or consumed on the site. Plants such as legumes, which may not require parching in their processing, and vegetables, which may not be allowed to go to seed are not often preserved, so more extensive sampling is required to increase the chance of their recovery. Other remains including charcoal, oyster shell, and eggshell have also been found, typically in rubbish pits and these provide evidence about food preparation, cooking, and foods available in the past. Evidence of other activities has also been found from some deposits particularly from charred cereals in malting kilns.

Some remains were found to be preserved by mineral replacement, usually called mineralisation, which occurs in conditions found in cesspits where sewage and latrine waste was dumped, and the organic remains become impregnated with calcium salts which preserve them in a semi-fossilised state. Mineralised food remains include fruit stones and pips which often occur together with small fish bones which passed through the gut and were then deposited in the pit as sewage. These pits also preserved microscopic eggs of human gut parasites confirming their use as cesspits, with occasional finds of coprolites (mineralised faeces) adding to this evidence for the disposal of human waste. Mineralised remains of flies including the latrine fly, were also preserved showing the putrid conditions in the pits (Skidmore 1999).

Material preserved by waterlogging is more rare in the town although some pollen was recovered from the wells and deeper pits (Greig 1994, 1999). More extensive waterlogged deposits have been found occasionally such as at the Austin Friary which provided some additional evidence of the surrounding environment (Mellor and Pearce 1981).

Food for the people

The available food as found from remains in sieved samples and hand-collected bones and shell is summarised by period below with examples from some sites shown in Table 1 opposite.

Cereals

At the Saxon site at Eye Kettleby free-threshing wheat was found, most probably bread wheat, as a change from spelt (a glume or husked wheat) which was cultivated in the Roman period. Barley was the most common cereal found there and is the cereal most tolerant of damp growing conditions. In Leicester the deposits associated with the Saxon building at Bonners Lane produced only a small number of grains of free-threshing wheat and barley, and little was found in samples from a single small pit of Saxon date at Causeway Lane. Saxon deposits at Freeschool Lane have yielded similar evidence for bread wheat grains and barley. Saxo-Norman deposits from both Leicester (at Freeschool Lane) and the villages also contain bread wheat, barley, oats and a little rye, with wheat as the most numerous cereal.

In post Norman Conquest deposits in Leicester in addition to bread wheat a second type of wheat called rivet wheat has also been found and they occur together in samples dating from the 11th–13th century from the Shires and Causeway Lane excavations (Moffett 1993, Monckton 1999), and in late to post medieval contexts from the Shires and at Bonners Lane (Moffett 1993, Monckton 2004a). Both are productive cereals although rivet wheat was not so good for bread making unless mixed with other cereals, but it could have been used for pottage, which was a thick soup and a staple medieval food. Rivet wheat has long straw which is useful for thatching. These cereals are distinguished by their chaff, and identifiable chaff (rachis) of bread wheat together with that of rivet wheat has been found at a few sites outside Leicester (see below).

Bread wheat was favoured for milling to use as flour for bread making, although the whole grain was also used in frumenty (boiled cracked wheat) and pottages. Other cereals found at this time include barley and oats, both often used for brewing (see below), as well as for porridge, pottage and griddle cakes; rye was also used as a mixed grain for bread making.

Period	Cereals	Vegetables and Garden.	Fruit and Nuts	Meat and Game	Poultry and Game	Fish	Seafish and Shellfish
Saxon	Bread wheat Barley	Peas/ Beans	–	Cattle Sheep Pigs	Fowl Goose Duck Woodcock	Pike Perch Salmon Eels	Herring
Saxo-Norman	Bread wheat Barley Oats, Rye.	–	Hazelnuts Bramble Elder.	Cattle Sheep Pigs	Fowl	Carp family	Herring
Earlier medieval c.1100–1250	Bread wheat Rivet wheat Barley Rye Oats	Beans Peas Cult. Vetch Leeks Flax	Hazelnuts Sloe Apple	Cattle Sheep Pigs Rabbit	Fowl (eggs) Goose (eggs)	Eels Salmon Pike Tench Perch	Herring Thornback Cod Ling Mackerel
Medieval c.1250–1400	Bread wheat Rivet wheat Barley Rye Oats	Beans, Beans/ Peas Cult. Vetch Flax Opium-poppy	Hazelnuts Apple	Cattle Sheep Pigs Hare Rabbit	Fowl (eggs) Goose (eggs) Duck (eggs) Teal Swan	Eels Perch	Herring Thornback Cod Ling Haddock Oysters
Late medieval	Bread wheat Rivet wheat Barley Rye Oats	Beans Peas Cult. Vetch Flax Leeks Violet Mustards	Hazelnuts Blackberry Raspberry Figs	Cattle (+ dairy) Sheep Pigs Fallow Deer Hare Rabbit	Fowl Goose Duck Teal Woodcock Pigeon Swan	Eels Grayling Pike Dace Chub Tench Perch	Herring Thornback Cod Ling Mackerel Plaice Haddock Oysters Mussels
Post-medieval	Bread wheat Barley Rye Oats	Beans, Peas, Flax, Dill, Hops, Asparagus, Opium-poppy, Marigold, Columbine.	Hazelnuts Bullace (plum) Blackberry Raspberry Apple Figs Grape	Cattle (++dairy) Sheep Pigs Fallow Deer Hare Rabbit	Fowl Goose Duck Woodcock Pigeon Swan Turkey	Eels Salmon Pike Gudgeon Roach Tench Perch	Herring Thornback Cod, Ling Mackerel Plaice Haddock Gurnard Whiting Turbot Smelt Oysters Mussels

Table 1: Foods available in Leicester by period, examples of Saxon from Bonners Lane, Saxo-Norman from St Nicholas Place, earlier medieval to post-medieval from the Shires.

Source of information: Saxon period Bonners Lane (in Finn 2004), Saxo-Norman period in St Nicholas Place (Kipling 2009), earlier medieval to post- medieval the Shires excavations 1988–9, plant remains (Moffett 1993), animal bones (Gidney 1991–93), fish remains (Nicholson 1992), shellfish (Monckton 1994). The additional evidence for eggs is from Causeway Lane only (Boyer 1999). (Thornback = Thornback ray).

Fruit and nuts

At Anstey samples contained some hazel nutshell as evidence of gathered food, and charred fragments of hazel nutshell have been found on most sites throughout the medieval period in the town and in the country. They are not numerous but are a common find so must have been a popular gathered food.

Figure 1: Fruitstones from Freeschool Lane: mineralised plum and cherry stones

Only hedgerow fruits have been recovered occasionally from the villages. In contrast cesspits from the town and southern suburb have preserved a wide range of fruit remains (fig 1).

From *c*.1100 AD onwards in the town at the Shires and Causeway Lane the range of fruits included sloe, wild plums, blackberry and elder probably gathered from hedgerows, with probable orchard fruits of damson, cultivated plum, apple and pear; grapes and figs could both have been imports. At St Nicholas Place abundant remains from a cesspit within the undercroft included gathered plant food represented by hazel nutshell, sloe stones, blackberry and elder, with occasional fig seeds.

A greater variety of fruit remains was recovered from late medieval cesspits, cultivated fruits including apples and plums, with strawberries of the wild type which can also be grown in gardens, and figs also very numerous as imports. Both quantity and variety of fruit increased in the late medieval period, including the strawberry and very abundant figs, perhaps related to better-off people. More of this evidence has been recovered

from Freeschool Lane (Radini 2009). The York Road site also shows this domestic evidence with abundant fruit remains found in a late medieval cesspit there. Domestic and other activity in the southern suburb increased into the post-medieval period: cesspits at Bonners Lane and the Bowling Green Yard contained numerous fruit pips of figs and blackberry together with sloe, apple and grape. Grapes may have been imported, possibly as raisins, but local cultivation is a possibility.

Vegetables

In deposits from Leicester throughout the medieval period peas and beans were found (Moffett 1993, Monckton 1999). Food evidence from hearths of a *c*.1250–1400 phase are associated with brewing at Freeschool Lane and included abundant charred legumes, peas, beans and vetches from the hearths, probably from brewing vessels. The legumes in these deposits may be included incidentally as domestic waste burnt with the fuel, but the presence of so many is noteworthy and suggests that legumes were being consumed or processed on the site. It is possible that this was waste from drying legumes for winter storage using the same kilns as for malting (Radini 2009). Late medieval deposits from Bonners Lane contained numerous peas and beans and it was suggested that these were perhaps used as animal food for pig keeping there (Baxter 2004); this may also be the case at Freeschool Lane (Browning 2009). Few legumes have been found in samples from the villages although Anstey village deposits also contain possible edible legumes and fodder vetch. Elsewhere in England, legumes have been noted as being rare in charred deposits (Moffett 1994) as it is not necessary to process them by heating, however, because they have been found abundantly in Leicester it is suggested that they may have been parched by fire for winter food, and accidentally burnt in the process.

Other evidence for vegetables included leeks (Moffett 1993) found from a charred seed, and flax/linseed which has edible seeds (Table 1). Some of the Brassica seeds found could be from vegetables but they could not be identified further, they may be from cultivated plants such as cabbages and mustards, and some of this group are wild plants which are could be used as salads or added to pottage. Many wild plants have edible leaves, particularly

248

the young leaves of fat-hen and sorrel which would have been consumed in spring; they are a source of vitamins after the winter. Seeds of such plants are very common in all periods although it cannot be demonstrated that they were used as food.

Garden plants and herbs

These are rare finds, a few large post-medieval rubbish pits and a well at the Shires contained charred grains of cereals from domestic rubbish along with seeds of additional plants including dill, hops, asparagus and marigold which are all useful and were possibly garden plants (Moffett 1993). The fewer large pits and a stone-lined well may suggest that there were fewer properties in the area of the Shires at this time, possibly with large gardens, and at least one such residence is known on High Street from the 17th century (Courtney 2000). Pollen from a well at St Peters Lane included borage as a possible garden plant with edible flowers (Greig 1994). Opium poppy is an ornamental plant as well as having seeds that were used as food flavouring, a source of edible oil, and possibly for medicinal use; these seeds have been found in some of the cesspits. Mint has recently been found at Freeschool Lane which may have been used as a herb.

Fish

Other food remains included abundant fish bones and scales recovered from samples mainly from cesspits, with a scatter of scales found in many deposits in the town. Without sieving only a few of the larger bones are recovered by hand such as at the Austin Friars, while results from the Shires samples showed that a wide range of fish were consumed in Leicester in the Roman period, and increasingly throughout the medieval periods. A higher proportion of sea fish was found compared with Roman deposits, and there were more large sea fish, indicating fishing with improved technology in deeper waters during the medieval period (Nicholson 1992).

Freshwater fish; grayling, pike, gudgeon, tench, perch and salmon were consumed, as in the Roman period, with the addition of roach, chub and dace in medieval times. Seafish in the Roman period included herring, smelt, gurnard and flatfish from inshore waters, with the addition of cod, haddock, ling, mackerel, plaice, turbot and thornback ray in medieval times (Table 1). Herrings and eels were the most common fish consumed in both Roman and medieval times in Leicester (Nicholson 1992). Similar results were found from Causeway Lane and at both sites the fish consumed were generally smaller; fish were not cheap and larger fish were consumed at the Austin Friary suggesting that the townspeople of the north east quarter were selecting more affordable cheaper fish (Nicholson 1999).

Samples from Leicester Abbey (figs 2a, b, c) contained fish bones of sea fish including numerous herrings, with cod and plaice, as well as freshwater fish including perch with eels. Numerous scales of the carp family from

Figure 2b: Fish remains from Leicester Abbey: herring vertebrae

the fills of drains in the kitchen area suggested that fish were an important part of the diet, perhaps because of wealth or for religious reasons. Sea fish such as herring would have been brought to Leicester preserved, probably salted, and the whitefish was probably dried and brought from the coast by carters at increased cost to cover transport (Dyer 2002). Freshwater fish would have come from rivers and fish ponds, whilst eels would have been

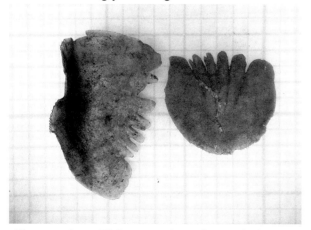

Figure 2a: Fish remains from Leicester Abbey: Perch Scales

trapped in the rivers - eel traps are known from the Trent (Cooper 2000). Fish remains are rare on the village sites but characteristic of urban deposits of both Roman and medieval times.

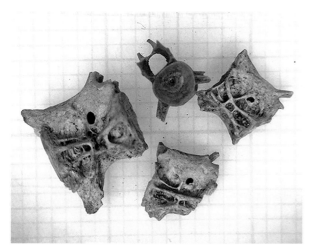

Figure 2c: Fish remains from Leicester Abbey: Eel vertebrae

Shellfish

Oyster shells from the Shires were analysed and found to be from managed oyster beds as the shells were regular in shape, but they were smaller and distinct from the Roman oysters so were from a different source (Monckton 1994). Other oyster shells found in Leicester at Causeway Lane in medieval deposits were found to be identical to the Roman shell so were judged to be residual (Monckton 1999b), and this was also the case at Vine Street (Hill 2009). Oysters seem much less common in medieval Leicester than in Roman times in the town. Other shellfish include mussels and occasional whelks. More oyster shell, together with whelks, was recovered from the Austin Friary than elsewhere in the town; this shows abundant supplies brought from the coast. However, techniques of analysis were not available at the time to investigate this further (Mellor and Pearce 1981). Oysters can survive for up to two weeks if kept cool and moist which allows time for transport. Shellfish and preserved sea fish may have been brought on the return trip from the east coast when exporting materials such as wool and cloth from Leicester and its area.

Eggs

Fragments of eggshell were found in pits of the medieval phases at Causeway Lane and identified as coming from hen, duck, goose and possibly pheasant, as evidence that the eggs were consumed (Boyer 1999). Further evidence for chickens kept for their eggs was from the bones of hens in egg-laying condition found in medieval pits at the Undercroft at St Nicholas Place (Baxter 1992). Eggshell from the Highcross sites will be identified in due course but less shell has been recovered overall from these excavations.

Poultry and Game

At Bonners Lane in the Saxon period bones of domestic fowl, goose, duck and woodcock were found and similar domestic and wild fowl were consumed in the late and post-medieval periods with the addition of hare and rabbit in the post-medieval period (Baxter 2004). Similar evidence has been found at sites in the town (Gidney 1999). A detailed comparison of the consumption of game and poultry is being made with the Highcross sites (Browning forthcoming).

Dairy

The evidence for dairy produce is indirect consisting mainly of the bones of calves used for meat as found in the late medieval and post-medieval periods at the Shires. Slaughter of calves increased over time and is evidence for milk production because the cows would have continued to produce milk after removal of the calf as they do today. Butter pots are know in the post-medieval period from elsewhere in the midlands but have not yet been found in Leicester. It is assumed that milk, butter and cheese were consumed at times but the evidence is difficult to find. Milk would not have kept long but cheese and butter could be stored for later use.

Meat

The consumption of beef, mutton and pork is seen throughout the medieval periods in the town (Table 1) and evidence of the butchery trade has been found at the Shires (Gidney 1991–93). In the late medieval period in the north east of the town there is little evidence from Causeway Lane, while at the Shires rubbish pits contained bones of larger sheep kept for wool before being used for meat, and calves used as veal suggesting the development of dairy products (Gidney 1991, 1992). In contrast in the southern suburb at Bonners Lane there is abundant domestic rubbish and even evidence of pigs being kept in back yards. This was apparently not always successful as several whole skeletons of a pig and piglets were found in a pit and are thought to have died of disease (Baxter 2004). Pig keeping was also suggested at Oxford Street from the find of neonatal piglets (Browning unpublished).

Post-medieval evidence from the north east of the town from a rubbish pit at Causeway Lane showed that an improved breed of pig was being introduced (Gidney 1999). The study of animal bones is a large subject providing evidence for stature, age profiles, and butchery, and the variety of meat and animal products used over time: evidence is accumulating from the many Leicester excavations because animal bones have been recovered from most previous excavations as hand-collected material. The evidence for the recent Highcross sites will be compared with the rest of the town (Browning forthcoming). Little evidence has been found at present from animal bones in the villages to suggest where animals were raised for meat for the town.

Drinks

Ale is known from documentary sources (Dyer 1989) as a medieval staple drunk by men, women and even children of all classes, and large quantities of various strengths were produced regularly because ale does not keep well. Ale can be produced from any cereal, or mixture of cereals, and in Leicester oats formed a high proportion of the grain in the deposits of charred germinated grain presumed to be malt (marked 'M' in Table 4).

The earliest evidence is from Saxo-Norman deposits of oats probably for brewing at Freeschool Lane. Deposits c.1100–1250 from Vine Street also contained mainly oats with some germinated, similar remains were found from a possible malting kiln at Vaughan Way and in the suburbs at Grange Lane, while at Oxford Street, also in the suburbs, a deposit of mainly barley with moderate germination is also thought to be brewing waste. Remains of charred oats from c.1250–1400 were probably waste from the brewing process, were found from the Undercroft at St Nicholas Place, and at Vaughan Way. With the possible exception of the kiln at Vaughan Way, all these probably represent small scale domestic brewing of ale, possibly sold by householders to local people.

Large scale brewing was found in deposits with a high proportion of oats from Freeschool Lane from a stone-lined malting kiln c.1250–

1400 confirmed as malt from the high percentage of oat germination. The oats were mostly mixed with wheat or barley (Table 3). Water would have been available from wells or purchased from watermen, but may have been less safe to drink than ale which was boiled during preparation (see below). Herb teas may have been made from some of the plants found (Table 2). Wine was mainly an imported drink, known from documentary sources.

Other evidence from plant remains
Interpretation of samples

As well as providing evidence of the plant foods consumed (Table 1 and 2) samples can be investigated to find evidence of food production and trades. The types of plant remains in the samples can also indicate activities on sites and contribute to the characterisation of different areas of the town.

Charred plant remains representing cereal waste included cereal grains, chaff and weed seeds. After identification they were counted to find the proportions of each which can indicate the stage of cereal processing (van der Veen 1992). Deposits with a high proportion of grains represent the clean cereal product ready for use, while deposits with a high proportion of chaff and weed seeds represent waste from various stages of cereal processing and cleaning. Bread wheat, barley and rye are free-threshing cereals which are easily threshed from the chaff, so chaff would not be expected to be found with the grains far from where the cereals were grown and this is an unexpected find in the town. It must be remembered that straw was used in the town for animal bedding and other purposes and may be a source of chaff and weed seeds but is unlikely to be rich in grains.

Domestic occupation has been found to be typified by a low density scatter of charred cereal grains and weed seeds and occasional chaff fragments, with low numbers of charred items per litre of soil, probably representing waste mainly from food preparation (Table 4). This occurs on most types of sites where people lived and worked. Richer burnt deposits of grain can result from accidental fires during storage or use so deposits of clean grain can potentially occur at many sites where there was domestic occupation. However, cereals require processing for a variety of reasons

	Saxon	Saxo-Norman	Medieval Rural	Medieval Urban	Post-Med	Botanical name
CEREALS						
Wheat free-threshing grain	++	++	++	++	++	*Triticum* free-threshing
Wheat free-threshing chaff	+	+	+	++	++	*Triticum* free-threshing rachis
Bread wheat, chaff	+	+	+	++	++	*Triticum aestivum* s.l. rachis
Rivet wheat, chaff			+	++	+	*Triticum turgidum* type rachis
Spelt, chaff	1 r	1r	-	2r		*Triticum spelta* L.
Barley, grain	++	++	++	++	++	*Hordeum vulgare* L.
Barley, chaff	+	+	+	+	+	*Hordeum vulgare* L. rachis
Rye	+	+	+	++	++	*Secale cereale* L.
Oats	+	+	+	++	++	*Avena* sp.
LEGUME CROPS						
Beans or Peas	+	+	++	++	++	*Vicia/Pisum*
Beans				+	+	*Vicia faba* L.
Peas				+	+	*Pisum sativum* L.
Cultivated Vetch			+	+	+	*Vicia sativa* ssp sativa (L.) Boiss.
IMPORTS						
Fig			+/+*	+/+^		*Ficus carica* L.
Grape (m)				+	+/+*	*Vitis vinifera* L.
GATHERED or GROWN						
Hazel nut shell	+	+	+	++	+	*Corylus avellana* L.
Fruit stones, Sloes (m)	++	+		++	++	*Prunus* sp.
Bullace and Damson (m)				+		*Prunus domestica* L.
Apple or Crab Apple (m)				++	++	*Malus* sp.
Hawthorn	+					*Crataegus* sp.
Blackberry				+	+	*Rubus fruticosus* agg.
Elder	+	+	+	++	++	*Sambucus nigra* L.
GARDEN PLANTS						
Columbine					+*	*Aquilegia* sp.
Opium Poppy (m)				++	+*	*Papaver somniferum* L.
Borage (pollen)					P	*Borago officinalis* L.
Violet				+*		*Viola* cf *odorata* L.
Flax or Linseed	+			+		*Linum usitatissimum* L.
Grape (pollen)					P	*Vitis vinifera* L.
Wood Strawberry					+*	*Fragaria vesca* L.
Mint				+		*Mentha* sp.
Dill					+*	*Anethum graveolens* L.
Hop					+*	*Humulus lupulus* L.
Pot Marigold					+*	*Calendula officinalis* L.
Asparagus					+*	*Asparagus officinalis* L.
Leek				+	-	*Allium porrum* L.
CROP WEEDS						
Black bindweed			+	+	+	*Fallopia convolvulus* (L.) .
Cleavers	+	+	++	++	+	*Galium aparine* L.
Corn cockle		+	+	+	++	*Agrostemma githago* L.
Stinking Mayweed	+	+	++	++	++	*Anthemis cotula* L.
Other weed seeds	++	++	++	++	++	Weed seeds

Table 2: List of selected plants from Leicester, Leicestershire and Rutland by period.

Key: Remains are seeds in the broad sense unless stated, taxonomy after Stace (1991). r = residual?, + = present, ++ = found on over half the total sites of that period. Medieval includes earlier to late medieval periods (c.1100–1500). * = seeds from the Shires (Moffett 1993), P = pollen from the Shires (Greig 1994). (m) = mineralised. Remains are charred unless described otherwise.

from threshing on the farm to cleaning before consumption, so when grains and cereal waste seeds and chaff are found in comparatively larger quantities agricultural or commercial activity could be indicated by the higher densities of remains per litre of soil (Table 4).

Other activities include malting which is indicated by germination of the grains although germination can occur after a wet harvest or in poor storage conditions so the proportion of germinated grains is considered. Modern malting results in over 70% germination of the grains but lower levels have been found in some medieval deposits, perhaps because the cereals were less uniform (Moffett 1994), and poor preservation and damage by burning makes this more difficult to recognize. A further consideration is that oats can be used ungerminated to add to other malted grains to strengthen the brew (Amsterdam Museum 1994).

Domestic waste

By examining the type and density of charred plant remains in samples differences have been found between some areas of the town, and on the village sites. In Leicester a low density scatter of remains including cereal grains and weed seeds together with sparse chaff has been found in samples from the Shires and Causeway Lane. This is thought to represent waste from food preparation of whole grain for foods such as pottage (Moffett 1993), with the weeds from the final cleaning of the grain and a few spilled grains burnt in the hearth. Hearth cleanings containing this waste were dumped or accumulated in features on the site. Little grain would be expected in domestic contexts because in the medieval period bread flour is likely to have been produced by mills and bread purchased from bakers (Dyer 1989).

A similar low density scatter of charred plant remains has also been found in floor deposits and features associated with medieval buildings at Vine Street and Vaughan Way from the Highcross excavations, Leicester Abbey kitchen area, and also from some of the village sites (Table 4). At Anstey a low density scatter of remains was found on the house platform as evidence of the domestic activity there. Examples of village excavations which have produced only evidence of domestic activity from sparse charred plant remains with little or no chaff are Freeby, Barrowden, Claybrook Hall, and Stapleton (Monckton

2004c), although investigation of other parts of these villages may produce different types of evidence if the opportunity arises to investigate them.

A second type of domestic waste occurs in cesspits used for the disposal of sewage shown from the microscopic eggs of parasites of the human gut and they also contain fruit stones and pips together with fish remains as evidence of diet and intense domestic occupation. Cesspits have been found at the Shires and Causeway Lane associated with a scatter of charred plant remains, and have now also been found on other sites in the town and suburbs as evidence of domestic occupation. However, cesspits are uncommon finds on rural sites, perhaps because middens were used instead with the waste used to manure the fields, and this may be one of the reasons that finds of fruits and fish remains are rare outside the town.

Gardening

Although the evidence for garden plants, herbs and vegetables is based on only a few seeds it is probably significant because these remains are less likely to be preserved. Most of this evidence is from the post-medieval features at the Shires (Table 2), and may represent a garden there with pollen of borage and grape found in a well (Greig 1994), and seeds of garden plants in pits (Moffett 1993). Peas and beans are present throughout the period and could be field crops or grown in gardens, as could flax. It is likely that there were gardens in the town and surroundings and the produce contributed to the diet of the inhabitants (Dyer 2006). Ornamental flowers such as columbine would have been appreciated then as they are now and they are shown in many medieval illustrations. There are also likely to have been orchards for fruit in the locality.

Agriculture: crops from the countryside

In contrast to the samples with a scatter of charred cereals as domestic waste (see above) some samples with very abundant charred plant remains have been found at some sites. At Anstey samples from an earthworks ditch contained a high density of charred plant remains including chaff and weed seeds interpreted as evidence of the processing of cereals nearby as an agricultural activity on that part of the site. Chaff is more diagnostic than grains and the chaff of bread wheat showed that this was a crop grown there. A number of these agricultural type assemblages with abundant chaff have been found in samples from some of the villages (marked 'A' in Table 4) showing the cereals cultivated and their processing. Anstey and Wyfordby have only bread wheat chaff, while a few others have a second type of wheat called rivet wheat (see above under Cereals). The occurrence of rivet wheat as well as bread wheat is of interest because both types of wheat have been found together in some deposits in Leicester.

Of the sites examined so far in Leicestershire and Rutland only the village sites of Saxby, Old Dalby and Whissendine have produced both rivet and bread wheat chaff, and both have been found at Sherrard Street in Melton Mowbray (Table 4). Rivet wheat is now known from an increasing number of sites in the midlands from the early medieval period onwards (Moffett 1991) and with the earliest find being from Higham Ferrers in Northamptonshire with a Late Saxon date (Moffett 2006). The evidence at present suggests that this crop was introduced and spread in use during the medieval period. All the local sites which have produced rivet wheat outside Leicester to the present are in Rutland or eastern Leicestershire which is on productive agricultural land, and may possibly have supplied these cereals through local markets (Monckton 2007).

The other cereals, barley, oats and rye have all been found to be abundant on some sites in the town and suburbs although they are not abundant in samples from the countryside with few exceptions; post-medieval remains of a barley crop at Whissendine (Table 4), and a deposit containing numerous rye grains has been seen from Coleorton which may be of maslin. Some medieval crops were grown as mixtures: oats and barley were grown as 'dredge' used as stock feed or for brewing, and wheat and rye were grown together as 'maslin' (Greig 1991), a mixed grain, usually wheat and rye. However, it is difficult to prove this from samples because cereal may have been mixed in use or disposal, a few exceptions have been found in Leicester (see below).

The weed seeds found with the cereals can indicate the type of land cultivated. More intense cultivation of the clay soils began in the Roman period and continued in the Saxon period as shown by the presence of the arable weed, stinking mayweed (fig 3), found

at Eye Kettleby. The weeds found at Anstey in medieval contexts for example, include cleavers and corn cockle which are typical of autumn sown crops such as wheat and rye, while stinking mayweed again indicates the cultivation of heavy clay soils. The increase in the occurrence of this latter weed in medieval times is thought to be related to the use of the mould board plough (Greig 1991). The presence of leguminous weeds with the crop may indicate that it was grown after fallow or following a fodder crop, because some of the legumes are the size of cultivated vetch, perhaps suggesting this fodder crop was grown as part of a crop rotation system. These remains give a glimpse of what was growing in the village field system.

Figure 3: Mayweed with poppies

Crop remains found at Bonners Lane, Leicester, in a late medieval sample contained abundant barley grains with numerous seeds of vetches and tares together with stinking mayweed which became a very troublesome weed of claylands by late medieval times (Jones 1988). Other weeds which are characteristic of spring sown crops include black-bindweed found with barley, oats and the legume crops seen at Freeschool Lane (Radini 2009). An ongoing study of crop weeds may reveal more evidence about the sources of cereals for the town (Radini in progress).

Cereals traded in Leicester

Surprisingly, some rich deposits of charred cereals from the town have been found which appear to be 'agricultural type' assemblages of grains, chaff and weed seeds as crop remains (marked 'C' in Table 4), and are similar to some found in the countryside. Such samples do contain numerous grains and appear to be threshed but uncleaned cereal product rather than simple cereal waste. However it

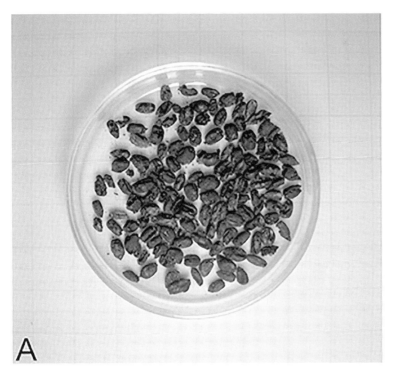

Figure 4: A: Maslin from Vaughan Way. B: charred rye and wheat grains. C: rye and bread wheat chaff (rachis).

is possible that they consist of grains mixed with cereal cleaning waste because cereal cleanings were often used as fuel in ovens and kilns for processing cereals. Cereals may have been dried in a kiln for storage if gathered wet or parched to facilitate milling (Moffett 1994, 2006). These may also represent commercial activities concerned with cereal supply and cereal cleaning, perhaps by corn traders. This certainly shows that uncleaned cereals were brought into the town, possibly some were grown in the town fields nearby. Some deposits show other trade activities associated with brewing with evidence of malted (germinated) grain. Different cereals or mixtures of cereals, were used for brewing on different sites at different times.

Saxo-Norman deposits from the town include partly-cleaned wheat grains with numerous seeds at Vaughan Way, and oats (probably for brewing) at Freeschool Lane with chaff and weed seeds present. Deposits of c.1100–1250 from Vine Street and Vaughan Way contained cereal cleanings from bread wheat crops, including rivet wheat at the former site as also found in the suburb at Grange Lane (Table 4). Also at Vaughan Way, a very rich deposit of a mixed crop of bread wheat and rye was found in a pit pre-dating part of the cemetery. This consisted of equal amounts of the two grains, with both types of chaff equally well represented together with

some arable weed seeds (fig 4). This is good evidence for the cereals being grown together as 'maslin' and the crop being brought to the town uncleaned but probably threshed. The cereal is all charred and may have been burnt accidentally.

Other crops were used for brewing. In the c.1250–1400 deposits at the Undercroft at St Nicholas Place, at Vaughan Way, and at Freeschool Lane, deposits containing oats have been found. The oats at Freeschool Lane had a high percentage of germination and were from a kiln, so there is good evidence these were malted grains for brewing ale. The former two deposits also contain a moderate amount of germination so may similarly represent waste from the brewing process (Table 3). There is some evidence for the use of a mixed crop of oats and barley, or 'dredge', used for brewing in this period at Freeschool Lane (Radini 2009). In the late medieval period at Bonners Lane rubbish pits contained such abundant charred barley grains that they must have been waste or accidental loss from some commercial use, however no kiln was found. Hulled barley was prepared for human consumption by parching and rolling to remove the papery hulls although this could not be demonstrated from the remains. Grain may have been prepared for sale at the site (Monckton 2004a).

255

The sites with evidence of cereal cleaning and processing at Vine Street and Vaughan Way are close to the areas of domestic occupation at Causeway Lane and the Shires where no evidence of cereal processing or brewing was found. So these two former sites may represent trade activities to supply the people living in the north east of the town with cereal grain as food and ale to drink. In earlier medieval times brewing was probably carried out in domestic kitchens to sell to people nearby whilst later brewing could be on a more commercial scale (see below). Corn suppliers may also have worked from their back yards, possibly cleaning grain for market as may be the case of the maslin crop at Vaughan Way.

The quantities of uncleaned cereal in the town suggest that it was grown nearby because transport was expensive (Dyer 2002) so it would have been uneconomic to transport cereals containing waste: an alternative explanation is that the waste may have bulked up the product for sale by the farmers and then been cleaned later during food preparation for use or sale to purchasers. However, Leicester had a system of town fields (Billson 1920) and some of the cereals are likely to have been grown nearby.

Baking and Cooking

There is little evidence for bread making because common ovens were used for most of the period which have not been excavated. It is known that the mills were controlled by the Lords of Leicester (Fox 1935) as were the bread ovens, and bakers were highly regulated by law (Billson 1920). Flour and bread would leave little archaeological trace although some cereal waste may be found. The only evidence for cooking may be suggested from some of the hearths found near houses and charred cereal remains in rubbish pits, probably removed from domestic hearths and dumped, which show food grains and legumes possibly to make pottage.

In the later medieval periods some households may have acquired individual bread ovens (Dyer 1989). The only possible bread oven bases found associated with cereal remains are post-medieval at Bowling Green Yard in Leicester and at Sherrard Street, Melton Mowbray, although ovens can be used to bake other foods such as pies and puddings. Unfortunately there is little to suggest what was cooked or whether it was for the household or for sale. There is little evidence at present to show how meat and fish and other foods were cooked although much is known from documentary sources. The only good evidence for a kitchen is from Leicester Abbey (Buckley 2006) with evidence of hearths and drains, however, only remains of food ingredients were found including cereals, legumes, fish and meat bones in the deposits.

Brewing

The site at Freeschool Lane is the first in Leicester providing substantial evidence for malting and brewing from the presence of charred cereal grains with a high percentage of germination in what are clearly malting kilns of c1250–1400 date. The evidence is extensive from the plant remains and from the remains of purpose built kilns so must have been carried out on a commercial scale (Coward and Speed 2009). The kilns found here consisted of conical pits lined with stone, presumably set in the floor of the building, with an elongated flue where the fire was set, presumably outside the building. They had lost the upper structures which would have supported the grains during heating over the conical chamber. However, it is known from documentary records that the grain was placed on matting of straw or horse hair over the heat. Fragments of burnt straw matting were found here which probably held the grain (Radini 2009), presumably the matting was supported on beams or slats over the heat. It must have been difficult to regulate the heat; fires were a common occurrence in towns (Dyer 1989). Even during successful runs of the kiln some grains would fall into the fire, or be included with cereal waste burnt as fuel, and so may be preserved by charring. The remains in the kilns are likely to be from the last few uses of the kilns: other features on the site contain dumps of charred remains which also provide evidence of brewing and the cereals used.

The process of brewing starts with preparing malt from germinated grain, firstly by soaking the grain, draining off the water, then piling the grain on a floor in a warm place to sprout turning the starch to sugar by the action of enzymes. This was carried out in a building, perhaps the upper floor of the brewhouse, because it takes several days and the grain must be turned to keep the germination even. When the cereal sprout was about the same length as the

Site Phase	Feature	Items/ litre	%Wheat	%Rye	%Barley	%Oats	%Germ*
Saxo-Norman							
Freeschool Lane	Layer G5008	1460	-	-	9.7	90.3*	30%
c.1100–1250							
Vine St	Pit G562	520	7.3	-	9.2	83.5*	15%
Vaughan Way	Kiln 525	43	20.1	3.4	0.7	75.8*	22%
Oxford Street	Hearth F51	255	1.3	-	85.1*	13.6	37%
Grange Lane	Kiln 302	579	50.9	1.2	2.4	45.5*	38%
c.1250–1400							
Vaughan Way	Oven 5487	5000	3	-	3	94*	36%
Undercroft	Pit F100	703	43.1	1.6	0.8	54.4*	18%
Freeschool Lane	Kiln 5987	601	11.1	2.2	30.8*	55.9*	76%
Freeschool Lane	Kiln 6064	43	-	-	29*	71*	63%

Table 3: Cereals for Brewing: Grains used for malt: the density of remains in the sample (items per litre of soil), followed by the proportions of each type of grain of the total identifiable grains, with the proportion of germinated grains.

*Key: %Germ = percentage of germination, * = the cereals showing germination (malting). Source of information: as Table 4.*

grain, as found in some of the samples (Radini 2009), the grain was heated in a kiln to stop germination by parching or lightly roasting, and then the grains are roughly ground and the malt sugars extracted in hot water.

From elsewhere it is known that extracting the malt from the grain was carried out in large cisterns, probably made from lead, installed over a hearth to heat the water. Only the remains of the hearth bases were found at Freeschool Lane. After extraction, the liquid was tapped off or bailed out and cooled, then fermented with yeast in a vat, barrels or troughs. Once the yeast was established some would be saved for future use; yeast was also used by bakers so the two trades were often connected. After fermentation of the sugars to produce alcohol the yeast settled out and the ale could be tapped off into barrels and sold. The drink produced here would have been ale, as elsewhere in medieval England at this time, in contrast to beer which is flavoured with hops which were not regularly used in England until late medieval times (Dyer 2002).

Ale does not keep well so would have been sold and consumed soon after it was ready. Herbs were sometimes used to flavour ale and include some members of the daisy family, sloe, elder, blackberry and mint (Behre 1999). Although these plants were represented on the site it cannot be shown from the evidence that they were actually used.

The cereals used here were mixed but contained a large proportion of oats (Table 33) which, it is of interest to note, were the main cereal used for brewing in the medieval period on the Continent where it was mixed with about 25% wheat, and / or barley (Amsterdam Museum 1994, 63). This seems to be the case in Leicester where oats are the most abundant cereal and were commonly used in some of the regions of England (Dyer 2002), and charred oats have often been found associated with medieval kilns (Moffett 2006). Germinated oats were also found as probable brewing waste in deposits at Vaughan Way and the Undercroft at St Nicholas Place (Tables 3 and 4). Barley became popular for brewing in the late medieval period particularly when hopped beers were produced, and barley is most commonly used today.

Ale was an important part of the medieval diet and is said to have been safer to drink than water because it was boiled in the process: a number of grades of ale were produced with weaker ale brewed for women and children.

Towns had a large demand for ale and brewing on a commercial scale would have been needed to supply the people and the site at Freeschool Lane was certainly one source of supply.

Conclusions

Charred cereal remains from the villages show that bread wheat was cultivated widely in the two counties with rivet wheat only found in north east Leicestershire and Rutland, although more samples are needed to investigate the distribution further. Barley was also common, with oats and rye found occasionally. Some rich samples representing agricultural waste were found from some areas of the villages in contrast to a scatter of domestic waste from food preparation.

In the town a similar scatter of domestic waste includes all the above cereals, while some samples similar to agricultural waste have also been found showing that uncleaned cereals were brought to the town and cleaned for use and supply to the townspeople. The question of whether the cereals were grown nearby in the town fields or transported uncleaned requires investigation. Evidence for brewing has been found from small scale activity in the Saxo-Norman period at Freeschool Lane, increasing in the period c.1100–1250 at Vaughan Way and Oxford Street, and then on a commercial scale at Freeschool Lane with kilns dating from c.1250–1400. The grains used for malting were mainly oats with some wheat and/or barley. Domestic occupation at the Shires and Causeway Lane in the period c.1100–1400 has been typified by a thin scatter of charred cereals thought to be from food preparation of whole grain foods such as pottage, together with a range of foods available from remains of fruits and fish found in cesspits. Abundant animal bones provide evidence of the meat consumed.

Areas with both domestic activity and commercial activity including cereal cleaning and brewing have been found at Vine Street and Vaughan Way suggesting these areas supplied the residential areas of the town c.1100–1250. Brewers at Freeschool Lane supplied ale to the townspeople in the period c.1250–1400 on a commercial scale. In addition other crops may have been cleaned and legumes processed at this site. Crop cleaning and possible brewing were also seen at Vaughan Way and St Nicholas Place, the latter perhaps brewing for a large household.

Late medieval domestic occupation evidenced by cesspits with abundant food remains has been found at Freeschool Lane and St Nicholas Place with less intense occupation in the north east quarter. Later occupation in the north east quarter consisted of at least one high status property and an area of trees and possibly gardens. In the southern suburbs from c.1100–1250 onwards and into the post-medieval period's domestic and trade activity concerned with cereal supply was associated with other trades such as tanning.

Evidence from the excavated samples shows the increasing variety of foods available over time, particularly fruit and fish found only in the urban deposits and monastic sites. Further work is planned at University of Leicester Archaeological Services to examine changes in the foods available over time and to investigate agriculture and the supply of plant-based foods to the town using the new evidence from the Highcross excavations.

Acknowledgements

I am grateful to Patrick Clay and Richard Buckley for the opportunity to work on projects at the University of Leicester Archaeological Services, as well as to John Lucas formerly at Leicestershire Archaeological Unit. I would like to thank the many people who have assisted with sample processing and reports particularly Peter Boyer, Stefan Gula, Lucy Wheeler, Martin Shore, Ian Baxter, Wayne Jarvis, John Tate, Alex Beacock and Anita Radini, also the site directors and staff of the excavations who have contributed to this work.

I am particularly grateful to James Greig and Lisa Moffett formerly at Birmingham University for help and advice over the years. Thanks to Wendy Smith for information about germinated medieval oats. Thanks to Richard Buckley for helpful advice and discussion and for allowing time to write this paper at ULAS, also to Allan Hall of the University of York for helpful editorial comments on a draft of this paper. Pictures of seeds and fish remains by Anita Radini.

	Leicestershire and Rutland	Leicester	Leicester Suburbs
SAXON (c.450–850)	12. Eye Kettleby (40.3) 23. Castle Donington (4.9) 24. Willow Farm (1.4) 13. South St. Oakham (4.9)	2. Causeway Lane (12.5)	4. Bonners Lane (1.0)
SAXO-NORMAN (c.850–1100)	28. Whissendine (32.6)*A 20. Wyfordby (566)*A	3b. St. Nicholas Place (8.0) 8. Vaughan Way (344) C 9. Freeschool Lane (146)*M 9. Freeschool Lane (129) P 10. Vine Street (12.2) 3. Undercroft (12.5)	
EARLIER MED (c.1100–1250)	13. South St. Oakham (6.7)* 14. Anstey Ditch (91.4)*A 21. Anstey Houses (9.6) 15. Freeby (37) 16. Saxby (45.4)*# A 17. Garthorpe (0.1) 18. Barrowden (1.9) 19. Claybrook Hall (21)* 22. Long Clawson (9.2) 32. Cottesmore (c.5)	1. Shires (50)*# 2. Causeway Lane (27)* # 2. Causeway Lane (9.8) P 10.Vine St. (526) oats/seeds C 8. Vaughan Way (3100) maslin 8. Vaughan Way (3000)*C 8. Vaughan Way (43) kiln M? 9. Freeschool Lane (7.0)	4. Bonners Lane (16) 5. Oxford St. (255) M 35.Grange Lane(574)# M 35.Grange Lane (190) P
MED (c.1250–1400)	26. Stapleton (1.8)* 27. Seaton, Rutland (9.2) 28. Whissendine (34.0)*A 29. Dunton Bassett (1.8) 30. Sheepy Magna (1.8) 20. Wyfordby (17)* 11. Coleorton (++) ?maslin	1. Shires (10.6) 2. Causeway Lane (4.0) 3b. St Nicholas Place (8.0) 8. Vaughan W. (5000)* oats.M 9. Freeschool Ln. (466)* L. 9. Freeschool Ln.(601) oats M 10. Vine St. (69)*# C 3. Undercroft (703) oats M? 3. Undercroft (190)*# C	4. Bonners Lane (13.5) 34. Abbey Park (13.5)
LATE MED (1400–1500)	33. Gt. Bowden (50) grains 25. Melton, S. St. (446)*	1. Shires (25.8) # 2. Causeway Lane (4.4) 3b. St Nicholas Place (379) P 9. Freeschool Lane (775)* L. 9. Freeschool Lane (16) P 3. Undercroft (138) grains	4. Bonners Lane (8.3) L 5. Oxford St. (36) 6. York Road (8.7)
POST-MED	31. Old Dalby (385)*#A 28. Whissendine (600)*#A Barley 25. Melton S. St.(195)*#	1. Shires (5) more garden plants 2. Causeway Lane (15) few cereals 3b. St Nicholas Place (15.1)	4. Bonners Lane (292) P abundant fruit 4. Bonners Lane (1178) *# C, Barley and seeds 7. Bowling Green Yard (693)*# C

Table 4: Comparison of maximum density of charred plant remains (items per litre of soil) from Saxon, medieval to post-medieval phases of sites by area. Sites numbered in order of analysis in area groups.

*Key: Figure in brackets = maximum density (items per litre of soil) of the best samples of the phase. * = Bread wheat chaff, # = Rivet wheat chaff, A = agricultural waste, C = cereal crop waste, M = malted grains, L = legumes, P = cesspit including mineralised remains . These samples used in table 3 except 32–35.*

Source of information for Table 4:

Sites: 1 (Moffett 1993), 2 (Monckton 1999), 3 (Boyer 1992), 3b (Monckton in Kipling 2009), 4 (Monckton 2004a), 5–7 (Monckton 1999c), 11–18 (Monckton 2004b), 19, 20 (Jarvis 2001, 2002), 21–31 (Monckton unpublished), 32 (Fryer 2008), 33 (Deighton 2005), 34 (Monckton in Buckley 2005), 35 (Monckton and Radini in Thomas in progress). Highcross Excavations: 8 (Monckton 2009), 9 (Radini 2009), 10 (Monckton and Radini 2009).

Bibliography

Amsterdam Museum, 1994. *Beer! The story of Holland's Favourite Drink.* Amsterdam Historical Museum, Kistemarker K. E. and van Vilsteren V. T. (Eds. Dutch edition) Translation Shaffer's English, Amsterdam: Batavian Lion, 1994.

Baxter, I. L., 1992. *The Animal Bone from an Undercroft at Guildhall Lane,* Archive report Leicester Museums.

Baxter, I. L., 2004. 'The Animal Bone from Bonners Lane, Leicester.' In: N. Finn, 2004. *The Origins of a Leicester Suburb: Roman, Anglo-Saxon, Medieval and Post-medieval occupation at Bonners Lane.* BAR British series 372, 2004.

Behre, K-E., 1999. 'The History of beer additives in Europe.' *Vegetation History and Archaeobotany,* 8, 35–38.

Boyer, P., 1999. 'Eggshell from Causeway Lane'. In: A. Connor, and R. Buckley, 1999. *Roman and Medieval occupation at Causeway Lane, Leicester.* Leicester Archaeology Monograph No. 5 University of Leicester 1999. 344–346.

Boyer, P., 1992. *The plant remains from an Undercroft at Guildhall Lane.* Archive report for Leicester Archaeological Unit.

Billson, C. J., 1920. *Medieval Leicester.* Edgar Backus, 46 Cank Street, Leicester.

Browning, J., 2009. 'The animal bones from Freeschool Lane, Leicester.' In: J. Coward and G. Speed, 2009. *Excavations at Freeschool Lane, Highcross Leicester.* ULAS archive report.

Browning, J., forthcoming. 'The evidence from the animal bones from Highcross, Leicester.' In: R. J. Buckley, forthcoming. *Living in Leicester's Past: Archaeological Excavations under the Highcross and related sites 1988–2006.* Leicester: University of Leicester Archaeological Services.

Browning, J., unpublished. *The animal bones from Oxford Street,* Leicester. ULAS Archive Report.

Buckley, R. J., 2006. 'The Archaeology of Leicester Abbey' 1–67. In: J. Storey, J. Bourne and R. J. Buckley, (eds) *Leicester Abbey, medieval history, archaeology and manuscript studies.* Leicester: Leicestershire Archaeological and Historical Society.

Buckley, R. J., forthcoming. *Living in Leicester's Past: Archaeological Excavations under the Highcross and related sites 1988–2006.* Leicester: University of Leicester Archaeological Services.

Cooper, L., 2000. 'Castle Donington, Hemington Quarry.' *Transactions Leicestershire Archaeological and Historical Society,* 74, 233–235.

Courtney, P., 2000. 'Lord's Place, Leicester: an urban aristocratic house of the 16th Century.' *Transactions Leicestershire Archaeological and Historical Society* 74, 37–58.

Coward, J. and Speed, G., 2009. *Excavations at Freeschool Lane, Highcross Leicester.* ULAS archive report.

Deighton, K., 2005. 'The Environmental Evidence.' In: J. Brown, *Excavations at 24–26 Langton Road, Great Bowden Leicestershire.* Northampton, Northamptonshire Archaeology, Report 2007.

Dyer, C., 1989. *Standards of Living in the Later Middle Ages.* Cambridge: Cambridge University Press.

Dyer, C., 2002. *Making a living in the Middle Ages.* Yale: Yale University Press.

Dyer, C., 2006. 'Gardens and Garden Produce in the Later Middle Ages.' In: C. M. Woolgar, D. Seargeantson and T. Woolgar, (eds) *Food in Medieval England, Diet and Nutrition.* Oxford: Oxford University Press, 2006, 27–40.

Finn, N., 2004. *The Origins of a Leicester Suburb: Roman, Anglo-Saxon, Medieval and Post-medieval occupation at Bonners Lane.* BAR British series 372, 2004.

Fox, L., 1935. 'Minister Accounts of the Manor of Leicester.' *Transactions Leicestershire Archaeological and Historical Society* 19, 207.

Fryer, V., 2008. *An assessment of charred plant macrofossils from Mill Lane Cottesmore, Rutland.* Archive report for Rutland County Council.

Greig, J., 1991. 'The British Isles' . In: W. van Zeist, K. Wasylikowa and K. Behre (eds). *Progress in Old World Palaeoethnobotany.* Balkema: Rotterdam.

Greig, J., 1994. *Pollen from The Shires Excavation.* Unpublished archive report for Leicester Archaeological Unit.

Greig, J., 1999. 'Pollen from Causeway Lane' In: A. Connor, and R. Buckley, 1999. *Roman and Medieval occupation at Causeway Lane, Leicester.* Leicester Archaeology Monograph No. 5 University of Leicester 1999, 362–364.

Gidney, L., 1991–93. Leicester, The Shires 1988 Excavations: Animal Bones. Ancient Monuments Laboratory Reports: Roman from Little Lane 56/91, Medieval from Little Lane 57/91, Medieval from St Peters Lane 116/91, Post medieval 24/92, Small mammal and bird bones 92/93. English Heritage; London.

Gidney, L., 1999. 'Animal Bone from Causeway Lane.' In: A. Connor, and R. Buckley, 1999. *Roman and Medieval occupation at Causeway Lane, Leicester.* Leicester Archaeology Monograph No. 5 University of Leicester 1999,.

Hill, A., 2009. *Oysters from Vine Street, Leicester.* ULAS Archive Report.

Jarvis, W., 2001. 'Claybrook Hall, Claybrook Parva: the charred plant remains.' In: Jarvis, W., *ULAS Report 2001*, 102.

Jarvis, W., 2002. 'Wyfordby: the charred plant remains'. In: W. Jarvis, *Melton flood alleviation scheme*, ULAS Report 2002, 76.

Jones, M., 1988. 'The arable field: a botanical battleground.' In: M. Jones, (ed) *The Archaeology of the Flora of the British Isles*. Oxford University Committee for Archaeology Monograph No 14, 1988, 86–92.

Kipling, R., 2009. *Excavations at St Nicholas Place, Leicester.* Including the Animal Bones by J. Browning, Plant Remains by A. Monckton and P. Boyer. ULAS Report 2009–110.

Mellor, J. E. and Pearce T., 1981. *The Austin Friars, Leicester.* CBA Research Report 35, Leicestershire County Council and CBA, 1981.

Moffett L. C., 1991. ' The archaeobotanical evidence for free threshing tetraploid wheat in Britain' . In: *Palaeoethnobotany and archaeology, International Workgroup for Palaeoethnobotany, 8th symposium at Nitra-Nove Vozokany 1989,* Acta Interdisciplinaria Archaeologica, 7. Nitra: Slovac Academy of Sciences.

Moffett, L. C., 1993. *Macrofossil Plant Remains from The Shires Excavation, Leicester.* Ancient Monuments Laboratory Report 31/93, English Heritage.

Moffett, L. C., 1994. 'Charred cereals from some ovens/kilns in late Saxon Stafford.' In: Rackham, J., *Environment and economy in Anglo Saxon England.* CBA Research Report 89, 1994, 55–64.

Moffett, L. C., 2006. 'The Archaeology of Medieval Plant Foods'. In: C. M. Woolgar, D. Seargeantson and T. Woolgar, (eds) *Food in Medieval England, Diet and Nutrition.* Oxford: Oxford University Press, 2006, 41–55.

Monckton, A., 1994. *Oysters from the Shires excavations.* Archive report for Leicester Museums.

Monckton, A., 1995. 'Environmental Archaeology in Leicestershire.' *Transactions of the Leicestershire Archaeological and Historical Society,* 69, 1995, 32–41.

Monckton, A., 1999a. 'The Plant Remains from Causeway Lane'. In: A. Connor, and R. Buckley, 1999. *Roman and Medieval occupation at Causeway Lane, Leicester.* Leicester Archaeology Monograph No. 5 University of Leicester 1999, 346–362.

Monckton, A., 1999b. 'Oysters from Causeway Lane' In: A. Connor, and R. Buckley, 1999. *Roman and Medieval occupation at Causeway Lane, Leicester.* Leicester Archaeology Monograph No. 5 University of Leicester 1999,, 337–341.

Monckton, A., 1999c. *Plant remains from the Southern Suburbs of Leicester.* ULAS archive reports.

Monckton, A. 2004a. 'The charred plant remains from Bonners Lane Leicester.' In: N. Finn, 2004. *The Origins of a Leicester Suburb: Roman, Anglo-Saxon, Medieval and Post-medieval occupation at Bonners Lane.* BAR British series, 372, 2004, 156–166.

Monckton, A., 2004b. Investigating past environments, farming and food in Leicester, Leicestershire and Rutland: the evidence from plant and animal remains. In: P. Bowman and P. Liddle eds, *Leicestershire Landscapes.* Leicestershire County Council 2004, 154–171.

Monckton, A., 2004c. 'Stapleton: Charred plant remains.' In: A. Hyam, *ULAS Report 2004–104.*

Monckton, A., 2007. 'Whissendine: Charred plant remains.' In: J. Browning, *ULAS Report 2007–66.*

Monckton, A., unpublished. *Charred plant remains from excavations in Leicestershire and Rutland 2002–7.*

Monckton, A., 2009. 'The Plant Remains from St Margarets Baths site, Vaughan Way, Leicester, Highcross Project.' In: A. Gnanaratnam and R. Buckley, *The excavation of St Peter's Church and graveyard at Vaughan Way, Leicester, 2004–2006.* ULAS Report 2009, 158.

Monckton, A. and Radini, A., 2009. 'The Plant Remains from Vine Street, Leicester.' In M. Morris and T. Higgins, *Excavations at Vine Street, Leicester, Highcross Project.* ULAS Report 2009–134.

Nicholson, R. A., 1992. 'Fish Remains from Excavations at the Shires Leicester' *Ancient Monuments Laboratory Report 56/92*, English Heritage.

Nicholson, R. A., 1999. 'Fish Remains from Causeway Lane' In: A. Connor, and R. Buckley, 1999. *Roman and Medieval occupation at Causeway Lane, Leicester.* Leicester Archaeology Monograph No. 5 University of Leicester 1999, 333–337.

Radini, A., 2009. 'The Plant Remains from Freeschool Lane, Leicester.' In J. Coward and G. Speed, *Excavations at Freeschool Lane, Leicester, Highcross Project.* ULAS Report 2009, 140.

Radini, A., in progress. *People, diet and living conditions in Leicester and the surrounding area from early to late medieval times: an integrated archaeobotanical approach.* PhD research project, University of York.

Sawday, D. and Davis, S., 1999. The Medieval Pottery. In: A. Connor, and R. Buckley, 1999. *Roman and Medieval occupation at Causeway Lane, Leicester.* Leicester Archaeology Monograph No. 5 University of Leicester 1999,, 165–213.

Stace, C., 1991. *New Flora of the British Isles. Cambridge:* Cambridge University Press.

Skidmore, P., 1999. 'Mineralised flies from Causeway Lane'. In: A. Connor, and R. Buckley, 1999. *Roman and Medieval occupation at Causeway Lane, Leicester.* Leicester Archaeology Monograph No. 5 University of Leicester 1999,, 341–343.

Veen, van der, M., 1992. *Crop husbandry Regimes.* Sheffield Archaeological Monograph 3. Sheffield University.

St Peter's church and cemetery: an insight into mortality, health and disease in medieval Leicester

Harriet Anne Jacklin,
Project Osteologist, University of Leicester Archaeological Services

Introduction

The excavation of St Peter's Church and Cemetery was carried out between April and December 2005 by ULAS on behalf of Shires GP Ltd. The site was located in the north-east quarter of the historic town of Leicester, between Vaughan Way and St Peter's Lane and was one of a series of sites investigated by ULAS as part of the Highcross Leicester redevelopment.

Prior to the commencement of the excavation, the site had been subject to phased archaeological investigations. An initial desk-based assessment (Meek 2000) indicated the archaeological potential of the site, particularly the likelihood of the survival of human remains, which related to the medieval church of St Peter's. An archaeological watching brief which recovered a small quantity of disturbed human bone followed (Buckley 2001, 131–2), yet the precise location of the church and the graveyard remained undiscovered until 2003, when a programme of phased archaeological evaluations and mitigations took place (Gnanaratnam 2003 and 2004).

The skeletal analysis of the human remains recovered from St Peter's church and cemetery took place between 2006 and 2009 and was based on recommendations in Jacklin (2006) and Jacklin (2007). In total 1271 skeletons dating from *c.*1200–1600 were fully analysed. A further 43 skeletons were assessed for age at death and pathological conditions. Twelve skeletons were radiocarbon dated in order to answer specific questions including the start and end date of the cemetery, the date of specific grave types and the date of the communal grave. A number of skeletons with possible tuberculosis were also sampled and tested for the pathogen *Mycobacterium tuberculosis* as part of a collaborative project 'Bimolecular Archaeology of Tuberculosis in Britain and Europe' (Professor Charlotte Roberts and Professor Terry Brown).

Background

The church of St Peter is one of the four 'lost' churches of Leicester. Borough records show that it was dismantled in 1573 to provide building materials for the nearby Free Grammar School. During excavation, the bulk of the ground plan was revealed. The church is thought to have started as a simple two-celled building. The nave was then extended and by the late 12th century a western bell tower had been added, within which was found a large bell-casting pit. Aisles were later added, the chancel extended, and a sunken-floored charnel house built. In its final phase, the church was 32m in length. Very little moulded stone was recovered from the site, however fragments were recovered from the debris from the Free Grammar School. This, together with fragments of 14th century and later floor tile, indicates that the church was still expanding and being embellished into the later medieval period. Following the demolition of the church and disuse of the churchyard, the area was given over to cultivation, (Jacklin 2006).

Burial practices

A number of different types of burial were represented within the cemetery. These included wooden coffins, shrouded burials with anthropomorphic grave cuts, charcoal and ash burials, stone-lined and pillow-stone burials. A substantial amount of disarticulated human bone was recovered from a number of bedding trenches, charnel pits and from the surrounding burial soils.

The corner of a communal grave was found to the north-west of the church. The grave consisted of a large pit containing the remains of twenty-two individuals; infants (aged between birth and three years), children (aged between four and twelve years), adolescents (aged between thirteen and twenty years) and adults (males and females over 21 years). They were buried in 'layers' with a thin scattering of soil and sand in-between and all were placed in the pit at the same time (or within a very short period of time). This was indicated by a complete lack of truncation and the stacking of the bodies to 'best fit' the grave.

The charnel house, located on the south side of the chancel contained a significant quantity of skeletal material, consisting mainly of adult skulls and long bones which had been placed with considerable care. The long bones were stacked length ways along the outer limits of the house whilst the skulls were positioned near the centre. The charnel house may have been originally built to accommodate the growing amount of disturbed human remains following building of church extensions. Examples of charnel houses still in existence (although reconstructed) include Rothwell in Northamptonshire and Hythe in Kent. The St Peter's charnel house differs from the above examples in that the material was found in situ, showing the house immediately before disuse.

The burial population

Osteological and archaeological evidence indicates that the cemetery probably contained upwards of 3000 graves (Jacklin 2009a), hence the skeletons analysed represent just over 40% of the potential burial population. The cemetery is believed to have been in use over a 300-year period which indicates an approximate burial rate of less than eleven people per year. This is unlikely to be a true reflection of the working life of the cemetery as there may have been periods when it was not in use and periods of epidemics when it was used much more frequently. St Peter's was not the only working cemetery in the area; St Michael's was located in close proximity and was in operation at the same time, until its parish was absorbed into St Peter's (Jacklin (2009a) The results of the skeletal analysis of St Michael's burial population can be found in Jacklin (2009b).

The analysis of the St Peter's skeletons has created a large amount of valuable osteological data regarding the health and lifestyle of those who lived in medieval Leicester, the like of which has not been generated before. It must however be remembered that although the osteological evidence gives a direct insight into the period, many diseases from which the people of medieval Leicester may have suffered were either short-lived illnesses which did not affect the skeleton, or life-threatening diseases which caused death before bone

changes could take place. Likewise, we can only surmise how the affected individuals coped with the health problems they encountered from a modern-day perspective. After all, it may have been that such diseases, ill-health and traumas, as discussed below, were simply seen as a consequence of everyday life and were dealt with as such (Jacklin 2009a).

In order to fully appreciate the results of the skeletal analysis of the St Peter's assemblage we should place the burial population in context utilising the historical, documentary and archaeological evidence. As discussed in Jacklin (2006), there is little documentary evidence regarding the people of medieval Leicester, yet recent excavations by ULAS within the heart of the medieval town have revealed a wealth of archaeological, environmental and osteological data which will be combined within a forthcoming publication on the Shires Project.

When looking at the backdrop to life in medieval Leicester consideration must be made of the various factors that could have influenced the life of the urban medieval person. These include society (economic status, population density, social control and social/political instability), urbanisation and living conditions (housing, water supply, hygiene and the disposal of waste), environmental factors (climate and air pollution) and periods of unrest (famines and epidemics). Population density within towns and cities in the medieval period was high and there was no welfare system. Therefore it was important to be in good health, to be economically self-sufficient and to be able to provide for your family into old age. Being ill for many was simply not an option, (Jacklin 2009a).

During the medieval period there was an influx of people into towns and cities in search of work or a better life. With this came the problems of overcrowding, lack of adequate water supply, sewerage issues and refuse problems (in the streets and alleys, a variety of domestic and commercial refuse accumulated due to ineffective waste disposal). Talbot (1967) explains that despite the efforts of most town authorities to prevent them, butchers dumped blood and offal in the streets whilst manure was stacked in heaps along thorough-fares which in turn encouraged a variety of scavengers. To compound this problem, wells were dug near cess pits and sewage was dumped into rivers and streams that were also used to provide drinking water. In addition to this, atmospheric pollutants caused by the burning of wood, coal and lime (due to the increase in manufacture in urban centres) will have affected the health of the medieval population (Brimblecombe 1975). However, Roberts and Cox (2003) suggest that the exposure to an unclean living environment may have actually resulted in a better immune status and lower allergy levels than those evident in relatively sterile western countries today.

Roberts and Cox (2003) suggest that climate can also directly influence health through the interaction of pathogens with both the local and specific environment. The period within which the population of St Peter's lived witnessed an environmental shift that impacted severely on short-term food production and the spread of infection and health. Lamb (1995) explains that in the 13th century the climate gradually became colder compared to the 12th century, maintaining its stability, but which was then followed by a rapid downturn of temperature and climate instability during the early 14th century. The beginning of the 15th century saw extraordinarily hard winters combined with wet and cool summers, a pattern which is thought to have continued into the early 16th century.

During the time in which the medieval population of St Peter's lived, a number of periods of unrest occurred which may have had a detrimental impact on the health of the population. A number of famines occurred, notably between AD 1294–5, 1315–18 and 1437–40. Although these first and foremost affected rural communities, the impact is likely to have been felt, albeit to a lesser extent, in urban centres such as Leicester. Epidemics such as the 'Black Death' (1348–49 AD) had a dramatic effect on the population of Leicester, leaving very few individuals unscathed, by means of their own demise or that of their families. Billison (1920, 143) references a contemporary account of the first visitation of Black Death in Leicester by Henry of Knighton, a canon of Leicester Abbey. In the account Henry records that over 380 people died in the parish of St Leonards, 400 at St Martin's parish and over 700 from St Margaret's parish. St Margaret's church and cemetery is in close proximity to the St Peter's and as such it is

reasonable to assume that the parish of St Peters was equally affected. After 1348–9, subsequent epidemics occurred. Billson (1920, 147) states that later visitations of the plague in Leicester were met by better sanitary measures for coping with the epidemic, such as a policy of isolating infected areas. But contemporary accounts suggest that the visitations continued throughout the 16th century. In 1594 it was recorded that the south side of Leicester was affected by the plague and shortly after the register from All Saints church records that a further 600 people died between 1610–11.

Mortality, health and disease in medieval Leicester

In the text that follows the reader should be aware that 'non-adult' refers to males or females under the age of 21 years and 'male' and 'female' refers to individuals 21+ years, unless otherwise specified.

The results suggest that the majority of males and females from St Peter's passed away during middle age (36 to 50 years), many between 42 and 50 years. The results imply that more females than males survived into old age and that slightly more females than males passed away within the young age category (21 to 35 years), which may reflect problems during childbearing.

The age at which death occurred most frequently within the non-adult assemblage was between four and twelve years, closely followed by birth to three years. The results also reveal that the highest mortality rate within the infant age category was between two and three years and the highest mortality rate for those in the child age category was between four and eight years of age. No specific causes of death have been established within the non-adult assemblage, but it is clear that the majority of non-adults, especially the infants and children, showed evidence of ill-health indicated by non-specific periostitis (bone membrane inflammation), cranial lesions, and metabolic disorders.

Stature
The results of the skeletal analysis reveal that the average stature for adult males was between 1.67 to 1.74m, whilst the average stature for adult females was between 1.55 to 1.63m.

Diet

The diet of those living in the medieval period comprised mainly grain products such as bread, porridge and ale (Hammond 1993). The quantity, range and quality of other foods such as meat and fish were related to an individual's income. In towns and industrialised areas, food had the potential to be varied if one could afford it; fresh meat, poultry, fish, dairy produce and vegetables were brought in from surrounding areas, due to an increase of trade between towns during the period.

Stable isotope (carbon and nitrogen) analysis upon twelve skeletons from the St Peter's assemblage (spanning the life of the cemetery) has provided first hand evidence with regard to the possible diet of those living in medieval Leicester. The ratio of carbon isotopes is used to distinguish between a marine protein diet and a plant protein diet (mostly vegetables, fruit and wheat). Nitrogen isotopes are primarily used to determine the input of plant versus animal protein. Although only a small sample, the results have shown that the diet of those buried at St Peter's was predominantly terrestrial, with a very small marine component. The St Peter's results also suggest there is very little difference between the isotope values of any of the samples. They indicate that that there was no significant difference in diet between those buried within the church and those outside of it (the former thought to be of higher status) and between those interred within the communal grave and those from other areas of the cemetery.

Osteological expressions of metabolic disorders, partly related to diet and malnutrition, include rickets (fig 1), cribra orbitalia (fig 2) and porotic hyperostosis (indicative of iron-deficiency anaemia), and dental enamel hypoplasia (indicative of biological stress). These are discussed below.

Rickets is caused by a deficiency in vitamin D (through a lack of UV light) and if the deficiency occurs during the growing period of an individual, it can then lead to bowing of weight-bearing bones, which bend when crawling and walking commences. Within the St Peter's assemblage, the prevalence rate for rickets was higher within the non-adult and the male assemblage than in the female assemblage.

Cribra orbitalia is a term used for pathological changes which can indicate the presence of iron deficiency anaemia, but also of general ill-health, blood loss through traumatic injury, chronic disease and biological stress. The condition is diagnosed by the presence of 'pinhole like' lesions affecting the eye sockets. Cribra orbitalia was far more frequent within the non-adult assemblage than in the adult assemblage, of which the females showed a higher prevalence rate than the males. The high prevalence rate of active cribra orbitalia lesions amongst the non-adults, compared to the adults of the assemblage, is partly due the condition being primarily a childhood disorder.

Enamel hypoplasia lines are horizontal lines which affect the permanent dentition and are a result of a disruption of the development of the enamel due to biological stress during childhood caused by malnutrition, prolonged ill-health or disease. The male assemblage showed the highest frequency of hypoplasia lines, followed by females and then the non-adults.

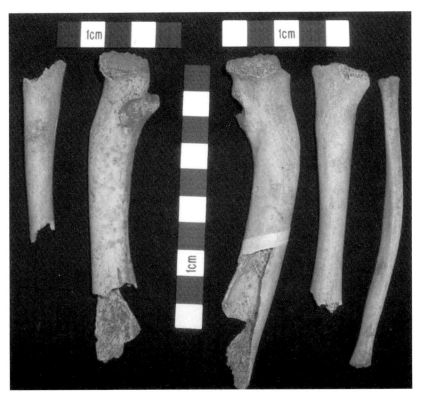

Figure 1: Rickets affecting the left and right legs of a child. St Peter's Church and Cemetery © ULAS 2008

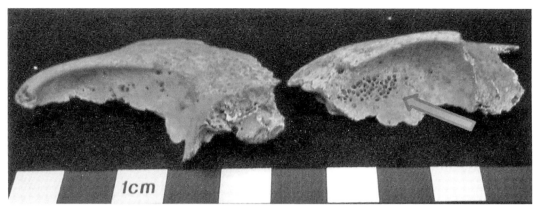

Figure 2: Cribra orbitalia . St Peter's church and cemetery © ULAS 2008

Figure 3: DISH. St Peter's church and cemetery © ULAS 2008

Diffuse Idiopathic Skeletal Hyperostosis (DISH) is a bone forming disease which primarily affects the spine (fig 3). The condition is characterised by the appearance of 'candle wax like' new bone growth affecting the right-hand side of the thoracic vertebrae (mid spine). The precise cause of DISH is still unknown, although it has been suggested to be possibly related to an excess of high-cholesterol foods, due to its association with diabetes and obesity. The usual age of onset of DISH is after 40 years of age. Within the St Peter's assemblage, more males than females suffered from DISH, but this may be partially related to the disorder being primarily linked to males.

Dental health

During the medieval period, dental health and dental hygiene were little understood. This is highlighted by the belief held by some within the medieval period that dental caries (cavities) were actually caused by 'tooth-worms'. Ring (1985) describes a number of popular methods for ridding the teeth of the worm; these included herbal remedies, surrounding the infected tooth to protect the other teeth from further burrowing, applying acid to the infected tooth, and most unpleasant of all, drawing out the worm with the use of a hot iron.

The dental health within the St Peter's assemblage was indeed poor, reflected by a high rate of caries and periodontal disease (a loss of bone surrounding the dentition, caused by soft tissue inflammation via gingivitis/ metabolic disorders) when compared to skeletal assemblages of a similar date. The males, females and non-adults all experienced a high frequency of dental caries. Often cases of multiple caries affecting adjacent teeth were recorded. Abscesses affected the males and females within the assemblage almost equally, whilst non-adults were unaffected. A dental abscess can occur through dental caries and/

or periodontal disease, due to the exposure of the pulp cavity and subsequent infection via bacteria. The abscesses were often found in association with a severe carie, which may have eventually led to *ante-mortem* tooth loss (before death). A high proportion of the males and females also exhibited a build up of dental calculus (plaque) whilst the non-adults were less affected by the condition. The poor dental health of those buried at St Peter's may be partly due to a lack of dental hygiene, but may also be partly associated with the consumption of sugar and carbohydrate-rich foodstuffs.

Joint disease

The commonest joint disease affecting the St Peters population was osteoarthritis (fig 4). This is primarily an age-related disorder and is diagnosed through the presence of new bone growth, porosity and 'polishing' of the joint surface. In some cases osteoarthritis was found in association with severely misaligned fractures, indicating that the individual continued to use the joint and did not give the injury time to re-unite affectively.

Osteoarthritis was relatively common within the middle to older adult age groups and the frequency of osteoarthritis increased with age, especially within the female assemblage. The commonest skeletal location for osteoarthritis within the male and the female assemblage was the scapulae's acromion (shoulder blade) process and the lateral end of the clavicle, with the male population being more frequently affected. These two joint surfaces combine to create part of the shoulder girdle. This perhaps indicates that both the males and the females engaged in similar activities which utilised the shoulders/upper arms although we can speculate that the males engaged in activities of a more frequent or physically demanding nature. With regard to the spine, the male assemblage showed a higher frequency of osteoarthritis affecting the lower back than within the female assemblage.

Trauma

Within the St Peter's burial population more males than females suffered from fractures (an incomplete or a complete break in the continuity to the bone) and only a small percentage of the non-adults were affected. The most commonly affected bones within the non-adult and male assemblage were the ribs, whilst for the female assemblage, the ribs and the bones of the lower arm were most frequently damaged. Fractures to the lower arm are often thought to be suggestive of interpersonal violence.

Schmorl's nodes (protusions of disc material into the seurface of vertebra) are often seen to represent severe wear and tear on the spine, primarily through lifting, bending and carrying heavy loads incorrectly. Within the St Peter's burial population, schmorls nodes seemed to affect males and females equally and a number of severe cases of schmorls nodes were found in association with compression fractures of the spine.

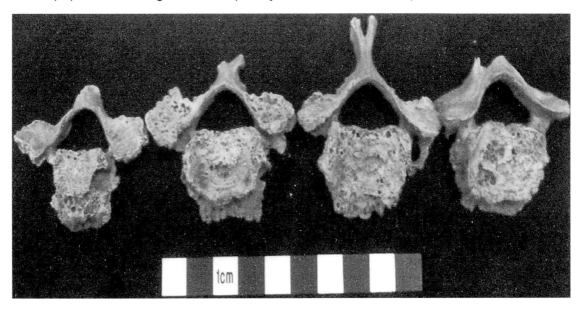

Figure 4: Osteoarthritis of the upper spine. St Peter's church and cemetery © ULAS 2008

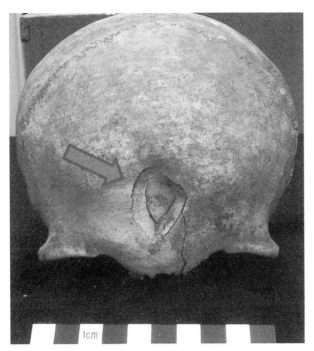

Figure 5: Blunt force trauma to the forehead of a female. St Peter's church and cemetery © ULAS 2008

Infectious disease

Within the St Peter's burial population both males and females were equally affected by possible tuberculosis (fig 6). Tuberculosis is a chronic infectious disease caused by *mycobacterium tuberculosis* which is spread through coughing and sneezing. Within the assemblage evidence of possible pulmonary tuberculosis and gastro-intestinal tuberculosis were found.

Two females infected with possible treponemal disease (syphilis) were also found. Syphilis is a severe bacterial infection transmitted through sexual contact and caused by *treponema pallidum spirochete*. The individuals were radiocarbon dated and the results indicate that they were both pre-Columbian in date (AD1493). The dates add further support for a pre-Columbian origin for treponemal disease in Europe, (Roberts, 1994 and Mays, Crane-Kramer and Bayliss, 2003).

Four males from St Peter's showed evidence of sharp force trauma affecting the head, the arm and the spine, whilst no females were affected. Sharp force trauma is caused by bladed or pointed instruments. A number of males also showed evidence of blunt force trauma affecting the head. Blunt force trauma is caused by blunt objects/ instruments. Many of the injuries are thought to be due to deliberate interpersonal violence and not merely accidental injuries. Only one female was affected by blunt force trauma. The female's forehead was affected and it is likely that the woman either died due to the injury or shortly thereafter (fig 5).

Also in the St Peter's burial population a higher proportion of males than females suffered from periostitis. Periostitis is an inflammation of the bone membrane (periosteum). Some of the periosteal reactions were associated with infectious diseases such as tuberculosis and other more virulent disorders. Whilst in some cases, the presence of periostitis was associated with localised infections and in others with non-specific infections. Where infants were affected by periostitis, the reaction was always active and often very severe (affecting almost the entire skeleton at the time of death). Periostitis in the non-adult and female St Peter's assemblage was often found in association with metabolic disorders such as cribra orbitalia and porotic hyperostosis and in non-adults with rickets.

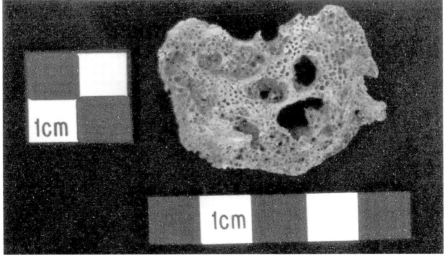

Figure 6: Tuberculosis affecting the spine. St Peter's church and cemetery © ULAS 2008

The analysis of the skeletons of those buried within the communal grave (fig 7) has provided the opportunity to look at a sub-set of the St Peter's burial population who all died within a short space of time, presumably of some type of infectious disease or epidemic. First thoughts immediately turned to the possibility that *yersina pestis* (the 'Black Death') was responsible, but radiocarbon dating of the skeletons indicates a date between the 11th and 12th century, which pre-dates the first wave of the Black Death (AD 1347) in Britain. Of course, although the grave does not date to the Black Death, it does not mean that the people from the St Peter's parish were not affected by the disease between 1347 and the early 16th century. It is likely that those infected were buried elsewhere. Pathological analysis of the skeletons from within the grave has revealed no discernable cause of death, yet all the skeletons show signs of ill health or malnutrition characterised by metabolic diseases such as cribra orbitalia, rickets, and arrested growth. Severe active periostitis was found to affect a number of the infants which, given the location and the extent, indicate an infectious disease active at the time of death. Two females within the grave were also found

with possible early tuberculosis. Statistical analysis of the data on age suggests that over 50% were aged below thirteen years, with 15% dying before reaching three months old. All these indicators point to some type of communicable infectious disease and as Roberts and Cox (2003) explain, there is evidence to suggest that a number of different diseases reached epidemic proportions during the medieval period.

Conclusion

The osteological analysis of the St Peter's assemblage has created a wealth of data regarding the people of medieval Leicester and has highlighted some of the health problems from which they suffered. These ranged from minor ailments to potential life-threatening diseases which may have lead to a premature death. The results paint an overall picture of a working class population where injury (accidental and deliberate) and illness were common place. It is envisaged that further work will take place on the assemblage, comparing the results with the skeletal analysis of the people interred at St Michael's parish cemetery (Jacklin 2009b) and Austin Friars (Mellor and Pearce 1981).

Figure 7: The communal grave. St Peter's church and cemetery © ULAS 2005

Acknowledgements

The author would like to thank all those involved in the excavation and post excavation of the project and extends thanks to ULAS and Shires GP Ltd for providing the opportunity to work on such a large and important assemblage. Special thanks go to Nick Cooper (Post Excavation Manager), Tony Gnanaratnam (Site Director) and Professor Charlotte Roberts (Academic Adviser), for their invaluable help and advice throughout the project. Full details of the results of the skeletal analysis can be found in Jacklin (2009a).

References

Billson, C. J., 1920. *Mediaeval Leicester.* Leicester: Edgar Backus.

Buckley, R., 2001. 'Archaeology in Leicestershire and Rutland 2000'. *Leicestershire Archaeological and Historical Society*, 75.

Brimblecombe, P., 1975. 'Industrial air pollution in thirteenth-century Britain'. *Weather,* 30, 388.

Gnanaratnam, T., 2003. *An Archaeological Mitigation (Phase I) of the Site of the Former St Margaret's Baths, Leicester.* ULAS Report 2003–069.

Gnanaratnam, T., 2004. *An Archaeological Evaluation on the Site of the Former St Margaret's Baths, Leicester.* ULAS Report 2004–152.

Hammond, P. W., 1993. *Food and Feast in Medieval England.* Stroud: Sutton Publishing.

Jacklin, H. A., 2006. *Site 12, Shires West, Leicester. The Human Skeletal Material. Assessment Report and Up-dated Project Design.* ULAS Report No. 2006.

Jacklin, H. A., 2007. *Site 12, Shires West, Leicester. Updated Project Design for Phase 2: Scientific Potential and Analysis of the Human Skeletal Material, St Peters Church and Cemetery, Leicester.* ULAS Report No. 2007.

Jacklin, H. A., 2009a. *Skeletal Report on the Medieval Human Remains, St Peters Church and Cemetery, Vaughan Way, Leicester. Phase 3: Post Skeletal Analysis Research.* ULAS Report No. 2009–047.

Jacklin, H. A., 2009b. *Skeletal Report on the Medieval and Roman Human Remains*, St Michaels Cemetery, Vine Street, Leicester. Phase 3: Post Skeletal Analysis Research. ULAS Report No. 2009–048.

Lamb, H. H., 1995 *Climate History and the Modern World*, London: Routledge.

Mays, S., Crane-Kramer, G. and Bayliss, A., 2003. 'Two probable cases of treponemal disease of medieval date from England'. *American Journal of Physical Anthropology*, 120, 133–43.

Meek, J., 2000. *An Archaeological Desk-based Assessment of the Proposed Redevelopment of Highcross Street/St Peter's Lane, Abbey Ward, Leicester.* ULAS Report 2000–145.

Mellor, J. E. and Pearce, T., 1981. *The Austin Friars, Leicester*, LAU. Council for British Archaeology Research Report, 35.

Ring, M. E., 1985. *Dentistry: An Illustrated History.* New York: Abradale Press.

Roberts, C. A., 1994. 'Treponematosis in Gloucester, England: a theoretical and practical approach to the pre-Columbian theory'. In: O. Dutour, G. Pálfi, J. Berato and J.-P. Brun (eds.), *The Origins of Syphilis in Europe, Before or After 1493?* Toulon: Centre Archéologique du Var, Paris, Errance, 101–8.

Roberts, C. A. & Cox, M., (2003). *Health & disease in Britain: from prehistory to the present day.* Gloucester: Sutton Publishing.

Talbot, C. H., 1967. *Medicine in Medieval England*, London: Oldbourne.